THE WOMEN'S MOVEMENT

References and Resources

Reference Publications on American Social Movements

Irwin T. Sanders
Editor

Other titles available in this series

THE ANTI-ABORTION MOVEMENT

THE CIVIL RIGHTS MOVEMENT

THE SENIOR MOVEMENT

THE U.S. LABOR MOVEMENT

THE WOMEN'S MOVEMENT

References and Resources

Barbara Ryan

G.K. HALL & CO.
An Imprint of Simon & Schuster Macmillan
New York

PRENTICE HALL INTERNATIONAL
London • Mexico City • New Delhi • Singapore • Sydney • Toronto

G.K. Hall & Co.
An Imprint of Simon & Schuster Macmillan
1633 Broadway
New York, NY 10019

Library of Congress Catalog Card Number: 95-46137

Printed in the United States of America

Printing number
1 2 3 4 5 6 7 8 9 10

Library of Congress Cataloging-in-Publication Data

Ryan, Barbara, 1942-
      The women's movement : reference and resources / Barbara Ryan.
          p. cm. — (Reference publications on American social
  movements)
      ISBN 0-8161-7254-4 (alk. papaer)
      1. Women's rights—United States—History—Bibliography. 2. Women in poli-
tics—United States—History—Bibliography. 3. Feminism—UNited States—History—
Bibliography 4. Women social reformers—United States—History—Bibliography. I.
Title. II. Series.
      Z7963.S9R93 1996
      [HQ1236.5.U6]   95-46137
      016.30542'0973—dc20   CIP

This paper meets the requirements of ANSI/NISO Z39.48—1992 (Permanence of Paper).

Contents

Preface   *vii*

Acronyms   *ix*

Chapter 1—First Wave Feminism   *1*

General Philanthropy and Reform   2
Early Woman's Rights Movement   7
Suffrage   10
Women's History: Activism and Everyday Life   14

Chapter 2—Second Wave Feminism   *23*

Contemporary Women's Movement   24
Equal Rights Amendment   43
Reproductive Freedom   48
Violence Against Women and the Women's Health Movement   54
Peace, Ecofeminism and Non-Violent Activism   58
Lesbian Feminism, the Women's Culture, and the Gay/Lesbian
    Movement   63
Academia and Women's Studies   72

Chapter 3—Women Activists: Their Lives, Their Work   *79*

Autobiography   80
Biography   87

Chapter 4—Feminist Discourse   *107*

Feminist Thought   108
Feminist Theory   129
Methodology   141
Sociology, Social Movement Theory, and Social Movement
    Comparisons   146
Identity Politics   158

Multiculturalism   163
Black Feminism and Black Women's Activism   173

Chapter 5—Issues   182

Race, Class, and Gender: Research and Reflections   183
Work, Welfare, and Trade Unions   190
Sex and Pornography   199
Feminist Critique and Contributions   205
Politics, the Law, and Policy   213
Sexism, Discrimination, and Anti-Feminism   220
Religion and Spirituality   223

Chapter 6—Guide to the Sources   228

Bibliographies   229
Funding Sources   236
Library Collections, Archives, Catalogs, and Museums   240
Primary Documents   251
Reference Materials   257
Anthologies and Texts   269

Subject Index   287

Author Index   301

Title Index   313

Preface

When Irwin Sanders first asked me if I would be interested in doing an annotated bibliography on the women's movement in the United States, I was finishing a book on the women's movement and thought this would be a relatively easy task. Now, I can report that I was wrong in that assessment. This bibliography has been a formidable and deeply involved undertaking. When I began, I was concerned about how I was going to get enough entries and where I would get them from. In the middle, I worried that I would not be able to manage what I was finding. And in the end, I have had to weed out and eliminate material I gathered earlier.

However, this work has also, much to my surprise, been interesting and highly engaging. I learned a great deal that I did not know before and, having finished, I can honestly say I am glad I took this project on. I am particularly pleased to know that my efforts will be included in an important reference series G. K. Hall is publishing on social movements in the United States.

The entries included in this bibliography are on the U. S. women's movement and all that is attached to it. Thus, particular issues that the movement has fought for, ideological positions, theories, the generalized spread of a feminist consciousness, schisms, divisions, and hotly debated issues within the movement and in the general society are all part of the changing dynamics of two centuries of feminist thought and activism in American society.

There are many people who assisted me in this project that I would like to thank. For plying me with references of works to consider for this collection, I thank Fred Seymour. Library assistance came from many sources and from many libraries and historical societies. At Widener University, Trish Lenkowski, Social Science Reference Librarian, and Marie Creedon, Inter-Library Loan, were most helpful.

For graciously giving me a place to stay while I was visiting libraries and archival collections, I thank Jan Whitaker, Barton Byg, Prudy Widlak, Edith Ryan, and Lynne Layton. For one highly productive year I had the good fortune to have an energetic and very bright research assistant. Valerie Perry went

beyond assisting me as she waded through the manual of a complex bibliographic software program and instructed me on some of the more difficult
applications. She was also a pleasant companion, and energetic worker, when
visiting libraries in the Philadelphia area.

Funding for travel was essential and much appreciated. I thank Provost
Buck, Dean Skinner, and the Faculty Committee for Research Grants at
Widener University for generously funding my trips to the University of
Wisconsin-Madison, Missouri Historical Society, Library of Congress,
Schlesinger Library at Radcliffe College, and The Sophia Smith Collection at
Smith College. Many of the resources I needed—reference and collection
materials—were not available through interlibrary loan, but were able to be uti-
lized on my research travels. President Bruce, Provost Buck, and the members
of the Faculty Awards Committee have my utmost thanks for the Fall 1994 sab-
batical which allowed me to finish this work.

My editor Catherine Carter has been encouraging and patient. I appreciate the two extensions she allowed me on my contract, and her support for
allowing me to include the Guide to the Sources chapter. I am appreciative of
Irwin Sanders helpful comments throughout this project. His suggestion that
I include women's activism that is often not thought of as feminist or as part
of the women's movement, such as welfare reform, philanthropy, and neighborhood organizing was well received. Also, his reminder that I not forget
social movement theory, sociological theory, and comparative analysis led to
one section covering those works.

Finally, I thank my family, Edith Ryan, Mary Ann Randell, John Ryan, David
Harris, Paul Harris, and Jeanne Harris; and my friends, Janet Rosenberg, Bill
Phillips, Joseph DeMarco, Donna Theis, Geneie Williams-Dowling, Jan
Whitaker, and Krystyna Warchol for being my family and friends.

Acronyms

AAUW	American Association of University Women
ACLU	American Civil Liberties Union
ACP	American Communist Party
AFL-CIO	American Federation of Labor/Congress of Industrial Organizations
AFSC	American Friends Service Committee
ASA	American Sociological Association
AWSA	American Woman Suffrage Association
BPW	Business and Professional Women
CARASA	Committee for Abortion Rights and Against Sterilization Abuse
CD	Civil Disobedience
CDF	Children's Defense Fund
CORE	Congress of Racial Equality
COYOTE	Call Off Your Old Tired Ethics
CR	Consciousness Raising
CU	Congressional Union
CWLU	Chicago Women's Liberation Union
DOB	Daughters of Bilitis
ERA	Equal Rights Amendment
FACT	Feminist Anti-Censorship Taskforce
HOTDOG	Humanitarians Opposed to Degrading Our Girls
ILO	International Labor Organization
LWV	League of Women Voters
LDEF	Legal Defense and Education Fund
MERA	Mormons for ERA
MFDP	Mississippi Freedom Democratic Party
NAACP	National Association for the Advancement of Colored People
NARAL	National Abortion and Reproductive Rights League

NAWSA	National American Woman Suffrage Association
NBFO	National Black Feminist Organization
NOW	National Organization for Women
NWP	National Woman's Party
NWPC	National Women's Political Caucus
NWSA	National Woman Suffrage Association
NWSA	National Women's Studies Association
SCLC	Southern Christian Leadership Conference
SDS	Students for a Democratic Society
SNCC	Student Non-Violent Coordinating Committee
SWP	Society of Women Philosophers
SWS	Sociologists for Women in Society
UAW	United Auto Workers
WAC	Women's Action Coalition
WAP	Women Against Pornography
WCTU	Women's Christian Temperance Union
WEB	Women's Emergency Brigade
WILPF	Women's International League for Peace and Freedom
WITCH	Women's International Terrorist Conspiracy from Hell
WPC	Women's Political Council
WSP	Women Strike for Peace
WTUL	Women's Trade Union League

THE WOMEN'S MOVEMENT

References and Resources

1

First Wave Feminism

Introduction

The first organized movement for women's rights began in 1848 at Seneca Falls, New York. Before that, middle-class white women had been confined to the home as their "proper" role in the family required. Working-class and slave women were allowed into the work world to do the low level jobs that needed to be done and that were not desired by others. Those jobs included working in the homes of middle-class women as servants, cooks, nannies, seamstresses, and personal maids.

The development of cities created social ills and opportunities for involvements outside the private realm. These, then, were the conditions—economic security, opportunity, and leisure—that led to women of privilege first embarking en-masse on social reform activities. Many, appropriately for the times, began in sewing circles as a church-sponsored activity. Indeed, a favorite tee-shirt of the 1970s women's movement read: Member, Women's International Terrorist Sewing Circle.

In this opening chapter of a bibliography on the women's movement in the United States, the entries cover **First Wave Feminism**, a period that runs roughly between the early 1800s and the late 1960s. There are four topical subcategories in this chapter. The first, **General Philanthropy and Reform**, covers a wide array of social causes including activism for women's education, prostitution and prison reform, charity for the poor, the Kindergarten Movement, family planning, birth control, the Settlement House Movement, the Club Movement, temperance, and abolition.

Many of these activities preceded the first woman's rights movement, and others followed its emergence. In the case of abolition and temperance, most of the woman's movement leaders were first initiated into social activism through these movements.

The second category in this chapter is **The Early Woman's Rights Movement**. Selections in this section are specific to works documenting and analyzing the emergence and transformation of an organized women's

1

movement from 1848 until the late nineteenth century when it became centered almost solely on the attainment of woman suffrage. Critiques of religion
and of marriage emerge here, and there are works on the social conditions and
thoughts of the times when women first began organizing in their own behalf.

Suffrage became the focus of the early woman's movement after the Civil
War and the granting of the vote to black men. There are a number of entries
which analyze the change over time in the movement as expediency desires
sometimes overran principled objectives. The annotations in this section cover
the suffrage movement in both England and the United States because of the
close connection these two movements had with each other. There was much
sharing of information, trans-Atlantic travel and interaction among activist leaders. The pageantry displays, parades, and militant tactics used in the suffrage
struggle in the U.S. were first learned by American women who involved themselves in the British campaign.

In the last section, **Women's History: Activism and Everyday Life**, a wide
array of women's involvements are examined. Also included are general histories of women's lives in specific time periods, some offering accounts of major
figures and organizations, while others offer a glimpse of everyday life. This is
also the place where research on the period between suffrage and the emergence of the contemporary women's movement can be found. A time when
most people thought feminism and women's activism was dead was, in fact, a
time of conflict within the women's movement and of perseverance in spite of
strong anti-feminist sentiment in the social/political environment.

This chapter establishes a framework for seeing the social conditions that
existed when women stepped out of their prescribed roles to challenge their
own condition, that of other women, and of society in general. The resistance
to their challenge is part of this history and the reason for their persistence.
The lives of less privileged women, sometimes found in abolition and union
organizing, typically revealed neither the means nor the time to participate in
efforts to change their social condition. These women are silent messages to
the effects of stratification going beyond gender that permeate American society and, in part, determine who participates in social change efforts.

General Philanthropy and Reform

1   BACK, KURT W. 1989. *Family Planning and Population Control: The
     Challenges of a Successful Movement*. Boston: Twayne.
This book outlines the history of the family planning movement in the United
States. The social context, values, and beliefs which constrained the movement
in its origins are presented, along with the struggles and hardships experienced by the early figures in this movement. Discusses the ties that developed
between birth control and population control and the reasons for that occurrence. The activism of leading figures, including Annie Besant, Emma
Goldman, Margaret Sanger, and Mary Ware Denett are included.

2   BORDIN, RUTH. 1990. *Woman and Temperance: The Quest for Power and Liberty, 1873-1900*. New Brunswick, NJ: Rutgers University Press.
A good documentation of the work of the Women's Christian Temperance Union (WCTU) in the temperance movement and the suffrage struggle. The WCTU became a massive world wide organization which spread beyond the confines of temperance activity, entering into much of the reform issues found in the Progressive Era.

3   CAMPBELL, KARLYN KOHRS. 1989. *Man Cannot Speak For Her: A Critical Study of Early Feminist Rhetoric*. Westport, CT: Greenwood Press.
This book provides a glimpse into the formation of feminist thought by women abolitionists active in the U.S. anti-slavery movement and other reform groups.

4   CROCKER, RUTH HUTCHINSON. 1992. *Social Work and Social Order: The Settlement Movement in Two Industrial Cities, 1889–1930*. Urbana: University of Illinois Press.
Seven settlement houses in Indianapolis and Gary, Indiana, operating during the Progressive Era are the focus of this work. Because of the limited reforms and conservative ideology these programs emphasized, Hutchinson finds differences in these settlements from more progressive ones such as Hull House. Backed by evangelical religious commitment, the Indiana settlements instituted Americanization programs, opposed labor unions, and promoted traditional gender values. In spite of the limited view of women's place, poor women often benefited from the services and goods offered by the social reformers involved in this movement.

5   FREEDMAN, ESTELLE B. 1988. *Their Sisters Keepers: Women's Prison Reform in America, 1830–1930*. Ann Arbor: University of Michigan Press.
An often overlooked area of activism for women, particularly in the early 1900s, was prison reform. Middle-class reform-oriented women made significant contributions by calling attention to some of the worst abuses in the early prison system. This work contributes to the history of women's activism and prison reform in the United States.

6   GINZBERG, LORI D. 1990. *Women and Work of Benevolence: Morality, Politics, and Class in the Nineteenth Century United States*. New Haven, CT: Yale University Press.
Philanthropy was seen as an appropriate undertaking for middle and upper class white women in the nineteenth century. And, because it was one of the few ways they could involve themselves in meaningful activity outside the home, many immersed themselves in reform efforts. Ginzberg covers the 1820s to 1885 period of shifting political and social alliances. This book reveals some of the underlying meaning for "good works" found in the tradition of women's benevolent activities.

7   GORDON, LINDA. 1977. *Woman's Body, Woman's Right: A Social History of Birth Control in America*. New York: Penguin Books.
Gordon provides a history of birth control extending over 1,000 years including the many widely practiced methods of ancient civilizations. In the United States, abortion and some forms of contraception were outlawed by 1850. The emergence of an active birth control movement in the late nineteenth century which eventually led to legalization of birth control methods, is well documented here. This history includes Margaret Sanger's pioneering work, the efforts of the general woman's movement, resistance of religious groups, and the influence of patriarchal values.

8   GORDON, LYNN D. 1990. *Gender and Higher Education in the Progressive Era*. New Haven, CT: Yale University Press.
The major thesis of this book is that women's entrance to universities, after being closed out of higher education for most of history, became apparent by the Progressive Years (1890–1920). The impact of women's attendance began to be felt during these years as the university system, including educational offerings, began to change.

9   GUSFIELD, JOSEPH R. 1970. *Symbolic Crusade: Status Politics and the American Temperance Movement*. Urbana: University of Illinois Press.
Gusfield discusses the way a political conflict over drinking behavior actually symbolized changing relations in status politics. Following his doctoral dissertation on the Women's Christian Temperance Union (WCTU), the author expands his analysis to include all components of the Temperance Movement. Gusfield examines the structural, social, political, and cultural roots of the Temperance Movement, an analysis which led to this work becoming a classic study in historical sociology and the sociological study of social movements. The author shows how even if a law (such as Prohibition) is unenforceable, the symbolic importance of passage is important to those involved with reform activities. The status politics Gusfield talks about is the fear of decline by rural protestant "native" Americans in the nineteenth century who feared the effects of new immigrant groups not sharing established cultural norms of self-control and industriousness. Gusfield does not differentiate by gender in his status politics analysis; but since the publication of this book, other motivations for women's temperance organizing have been argued.

10   INGRAHAM, SARAH R., ed. 1988. *Walks of Usefulness: Reminiscences of Mrs. Margaret Prior*, New York: Garland Publishers.
The American Female Reform Society was an early source of activism among white middle-class women. Margaret Prior was hired to be the Reform Society's first city missionary, and her reports show that this work also provided an arena for the development of nineteenth century feminist thought. Ingraham has gathered material for this book from Prior's remembrances of individual activists and organizations involved in reform work at that time.

11 JEFFREYS, SHEILA, ed. 1987. *The Sexuality Debates*. New York: Metheum.

A history of the feminist campaigns against male sexual abuse. The major issues these activists addressed were prostitution, sexual abuse of children, rape in marriage, and the spread of venereal disease. These articles cover the period from 1870 to the 1920s.

12 MARTIN, THEODORA PENNY. 1987. *The Sound of Our Own Voices, Women's Study Clubs, 1869–1910*. Boston: The Beacon Press.

Early organizing for the women's club movement consisted of small local groups of women who regularly met to study history, art, philosophy, literature, geography, and a variety of other subjects in which members were interested. Because of the interest in expanding their horizons and through learning, these clubs were sometimes called seekers or light seekers. Their early organizing was an important precursor to the entry of women into colleges by the turn of the century.

13 PASCOE, PEGGY. 1990. *Relations of Rescue: The Search for Female Moral Authority in the American West, 1874–1939*. New York: Oxford University Press.

This book represents a study of moral reform movements which took place in the western part of the United States in the latter part of the nineteenth and early part of the twentieth centuries. Four cases are highlighted: a home for Chinese prostitutes in San Francisco; a home for Mormon women rejecting polygyny by leaving their marriages in Salt Lake City; a home for unmarried pregnant women in Denver; and a program of assistance for Native Americans on a reservation in Omaha, Nebraska. These missionary rescue homes, the women who established them, the social feminism that underlie their activism, the women they sought to shelter, and the men who opposed them are the focus of this book.

14 ROSENBERG, ROSALIND. 1982. *Beyond Separate Spheres: Intellectual Roots of Modern Feminism*. New Haven, CT: Yale University Press.

Early academic women, particularly in the social sciences, are presented here with an analysis of their work. As Rosenberg shows, these foremothers contributed not only to our intellectual heritage as a nation, they also paved the way for developing modern feminist thought. In pioneering women's entry into university life and serving as role models of successful women in research and teaching positions, they left an important legacy.

15 ROSENTHAL, NAOMI, MERYL FINGRUD, MICHELE ETHIER, ROBERTA KARANT, and DAVID MCDONALD. 1985. "Social Movements and Network Analysis: A Case Study of Nineteenth Century Women's Reform in New York State." *American Journal of Sociology* 90:1022–1054.

Network analysis is tested in this paper by looking at organizational affiliations of women reform leaders between 1840–1914. Researchers looked at the interconnections among organizations, measured the intensity of those relationships, identified clusters of interacting organizations, and specified those women who were central to those clusters. The findings show key clusters organized around the Women's Trade Union League and abolitionists.

16   ROTHMAN, DAVID and SHEILA ROTHMAN, eds. 1987. *The Dangers of Education: Sexism and Origins of Women's Colleges, An Anthology of Nineteenth Century Sources*, New York: Garland Publishing.
A look at the first women's colleges and the resistance they had to overcome to provide higher education for women. The arguments against women's education—women were too physically frail, it would overtax their brains, they were incapable—would be almost laughable today if they had not been taken so seriously (and been used so effectively) to keep women out of colleges and universities. Contributors to this anthology bring in many examples of misogyny at work during the nineteenth century.

17   ———, eds. 1988. *National Congress of Mothers: The First Convention*, New York: Garland Publishers.
Women organized the National Congress of Mothers to meet and discuss ways of providing a sound environment and good future for the next generation. Eventually the Parent Teachers Association evolved from these types of groups, as well as the kindergarten movement which was another example of mothers organizing to promote the well being of their children.

18   SCOTT, ANNE FIROR. 1991. *Natural Allies: Women's Association in American History*. Urbana: University of Illinois Press.
This book provides documentation of the range of activities women's clubs and associations involved themselves in from the eighteenth to the early twentieth centuries. Voluntary associations offered women the opportunity to do good works, advance their own cause, and become professionals at a time when career paths for women were prohibited in both the public and private sectors. Scott shows how women's organizations were more cooperative and wide-ranging than comparable men's groups, and that the often unheralded work they did constituted considerable social and cultural change in American society. The types of organizational work Ladies Aid Societies and Women's Clubs engaged in included war support, anti-war efforts, temperance, abolition, woman's rights, moral reform, municipal housekeeping, prison reform, libraries, schools, playgrounds, health clinics, tree planting, parks, sanitation, welfare, charity, widow's relief, orphanages, and data gathering on factory labor and slum life.

19   SKOCPOL, THEDA. 1992. *Protecting Soldiers and Mothers*. Cambridge, MA: Harvard University Press.
Skocpol brings together studies on gender and welfare policy to analyze the emergence of the early welfare state. She integrates the history of women reformers into the history of welfare, and details the ways women's voluntary groups used essentialist ideology of the early 1900s to argue that women had special needs. Reformers called for state regulation of working

conditions for women and for governmental provisions of aid for poor women and children. These activists were responsible for the development of the Children's Bureau and the institution of subsidized health care clinics. Feminist scholars have critiqued the book for not challenging maternalist programs, ignoring male/female power relations, and failing to analyze the impact of white middle-class women influencing political decisions affecting poor women.

20 SMITH-ROSENBERG, CARROLL. 1979. "Beauty, the Beast and the Militant Woman: A Case Study in Sex Roles and Social Stress in Jacksonian America." Pp. 197–221 in *A Heritage of Her Own*, edited by Nancy Cott and Elizabeth Pleck. New York: Simon and Schuster.

The philanthropy of middle-class women in the first half of the nineteenth century often centered on efforts to eradicate the practice of prostitution and to reform the women involved. In this article, Smith-Rosenberg examines the evangelical women who became activist in this reform effort in New York City in the 1830s. Women reformers focused their efforts on psychologically understanding prostitutes and trying to provide an explanation of their behavior.

21 TUCHMAN, GAYE. 1981. "Contradictions in an Ideology: The Nineteenth Century Doctrine of Separate Spheres." *Quarterly Journal of Ideology* 5 (Sept):5–10.

An examination of the different reactions to the cult of domesticity which led some women to embrace it and others to rebel against it. Both the feminist reaction for autonomy and that of those women who accepted the moral calling of "true womanhood" led to women becoming involved in social reform and social movement activism.

Early Woman's Rights Movement

22 COTT, NANCY F., ed. 1986. *Root of Bitterness: Documents of the Social History of American Women*. Boston: Northeastern University Press.

Cott has gathered journals, autobiographies, fictions, and narratives of women's history from Colonial times to the present. Both unknown women and men, and well-known leaders are included in this anthology. Some examples of selections are: The Church Trial of Mistress Ann Hibbens; Letter from an Indentured Servant; "Proper Conduct of the Wife Towards Her Husband" by Samuel Jennings; "On American Women and American Lives" by Alexis de Tocqueville; "Letters on the Equality of the Sexes" by Sarah Grimké; narratives from escaped slaves; "Free Enquiry" by Frances Wright; "Vindication of the Beecher-Tilton Scandal" by Victoria Woodhull; "Sexual Passion of Men and Women" by Elizabeth Blackwell; "The Snare of Preparation" by Jane Addams; and "Women's Evolution from Economic Dependence" by Charlotte Perkins Gilman.

23   FLEXNER, ELEANOR. 1975. *Century of Struggle: The Woman's Rights Movement in the United States, Revised Edition*. Cambridge, MA: The Belknap Press of Harvard University.

A revision of the 1959 edition of the history of the early woman's movement in the United States. The struggles that existed in both the early organizing and the later suffrage campaign are documented. A thorough and well-researched account of deep seated conflicts that emerged, many of which are still found in various forms in the contemporary movement.

24   GAGE, MATILDA JOSLYN. 1980. *Woman, Church, and State: The Original Expose of Male Collaboration Against The Female Sex*. Watertown, MA: Persephone Press.

This is a reprint of the 1893 edition published by C. H. Kerr. Matilda Joslyn Gage (1826–1898) was a compiler and author with Elizabeth Cady Stanton and Susan B. Anthony of the first three volumes of the six-volume work "History of Woman Suffrage." In this book, Gage discusses her views on women's position in society with particular reference to religion and politics. This edition has a new introduction and includes bibliographical references and an index.

25   GURKO, MIRIAM. 1974. *The Ladies of Seneca Falls: The Birth of the Woman's Rights Movement*. New York: Macmillan Publishing Co.

Gurko writes about the women who initiated the 1848 Seneca Falls Woman's Right's Convention, the influence of those who preceded them, and the story of the campaign for women's rights that followed. The leaders of this movement, Elizabeth Cady Stanton, Lucretia Mott, Susan B. Anthony, the Grimké sisters, and Lucy Stone are well covered. The issues they raised, many still relevant for the women's movement of today, were diverse and complex. The full text of the 1848 Declaration of Sentiments and Resolutions is included.

26   HENSLEY, FRANCES. 1981. *Change and Continuity in the American Women's Movement, 1848–1930: A National and State Perspective*. Dissertation Abstracts: Ohio State University, Ph.D. Thesis.

A view of the women's movement from its origins until 1930 with a focus on the ways it changed, yet continued to exist, in spite of opposition and periods of decline.

27   KLEIN, VIOLA. 1984. "The Historical Background." Pp. 519–532 in *Women: A Feminist Perspective, Third Edition, edited by Jo Freeman*. Palo Alto, CA : Mayfield Publishing Co.

The intent of this article is to provide an understanding of the social conditions and thoughts of the times, both preceding and during women's organizing for betterment of their position in society. Klein documents the social views of 'women's place' and how these changed as social transformation occurred throughout the nineteenth century. The early woman's movement consisted of a small, "much-despised, and even more ridiculed minority." According to Klein, their efforts for change were finally successful due to their tenacity and, perhaps more than anything else, because "their claims were in accordance with the general trend of social development."

28   O'NEILL, WILLIAM L. 1969. *Everyone Was Brave: The Rise and Fall of Feminism in America*. Chicago: Quadrangle Books.

An account by an historian of the early woman's movement and subsequent demise of activism after suffrage was won in 1920. This is an informative and well written monograph of the change within the movement as well as the social/political environment impacting upon it.

29   ———. 1989. *Feminism in America: A History*. New Brunswick, NJ: Transaction Publishers.

This is a revised edition of the original 1969 book on Feminism in America. As with the earlier version, O'Neill interprets the history of feminism through a prism of what has not been achieved. Beginning with the 1830s and going through the 1980s, the author analyzes the lack of progress since the movement's inception. He gives serious attention to the movement and leaders of the various time periods and organizations. Ten movement leaders are highlighted in short vignettes: Josephine Shaw Lowell (philanthropist); M. Carey Thomas (education); Margaret Dreier Robins (trade unionism, WTUL); Jane Addams (settlement work, Hull House); Anna Howard Shaw (suffrage NAWSA); Carrie Chapman Catt (suffrage NAWSA); Alice Paul (suffrage NWP, ERA); Charlotte Perkins Gilman (socialist writer); and Florence Kelley (socialist, settlement house work, The National Consumer's League, protective labor legislation). His thesis is that feminism has failed because the chief obstacle of marriage and the family continues to block the full possibility of women's emancipation.

30   PAPACHRISTOU, JUDITH, ed. 1976. *Women Together*. New York: Alfred A. Knopf.

A valuable collection of historical documents on the early woman's movement and the suffrage movement. Papachristou has gathered essential material to reveal an important and often daring history.

31   RENDELL, JANE. 1985. *The Origins of Modern Feminism: Women in Britain, France and the United States 1780-1860*. London: Macmillan.

The intellectual foundations of feminism are traced by Rendell to the ideals of the Enlightenment and to evangelical religious fervor of the early 1800s. Even with a belief in separate spheres for women and men, and the religious foundation of many activists' lives, feminist ideals are found in this history of early activist women.

32   RUSSO, ANN and CHERIS KRAMARAE, eds. 1991. *The Radical Women's Press of the 1850s*. New York: Routledge.

The editors of this volume use excerpts from six journals from the mid-nineteenth century. Some of the issues covered are battered women, education,

poverty, health, suffrage, and the movement for dress reform. Reading the writing of activist women from this era gives a good feel for the range of feminist
thinking that was in existence at that time.

33   WELLMAN, JUDITH. 1991. "The Seneca Falls Women's Rights Convention:
      A Study of Social Networks." *Journal of Women's History* 3:9–37.
In this article, Wellman examines the different forces that were operating in
1848 to allow Elizabeth Cady Stanton and Lucretia Mott to call for the Seneca
Falls Women's Rights Convention. The author shows that they were able to
organize and assure attendance because people were concerned about divisions within the Quaker community, ongoing agitation over the lack of married
women's property rights, and general political turmoil that was occurring
among Free-Soilers.

34   YOUNG, LOUISE M. 1976. "Women's Place in American Politics: The
      Historical Perspective." *Journal of Politics* 38 (August):295–335.
This article reviews people, documents, and social movements in which
women of the nineteenth century were involved. Religion is found to have
played an important role in women's growing political and social reform
involvements. The Quaker religion, with its emphasis on egalitarianism, was
one of the first to develop a tradition of leadership and civic responsibility for
women.

Suffrage

35   BANKS, OLIVE. 1986. *Becoming a Feminist: The Social Origins of 'First
      Wave' Feminism.* Brighton, England: Wheatsheaf Books.
Although this book is about the early woman's movement in England, the connections between that movement and the woman's movement in the United
States were very close. Some of the militant tactics English suffragists used
were brought back to the U.S. by American women like Alice Paul, Lucy Burns,
and Harriot Stanton Blatch who participated in the English movement while
living there. A study of the process, philosophy, and activism of English feminists such as Harriet Martineau and Christabel Pankhurst adds to an understanding of the development of the movement in the U.S. as well as the
process of becoming a feminist activist in general.

36   BILLINGTON, ROSAMUND. 1982. "Ideology and Feminism: Why the
      Suffragettes Were Wild Women." *Women's Studies International Forum*
      5:663,–674.
This article talks about the English suffragette movement, but the concepts discussed also apply to the militant suffragists in the United States during this
same period. Billington finds the opposition to woman suffrage from 1860 to
1913 was mainly premised on an ideological position of the dictates of "natural womanhood." Because feminists challenged this ideology, they were considered unwomanly deviant women.

37 BJORKMAN, FRANCES and ANNIE G. PORRITT, eds. *1917. The Blue Book, Woman Suffrage: History, Arguments, and Results*. New York: National Woman Suffrage Publishing.
A collection of writings in support of woman's suffrage. Many of the contributors were active in the suffrage movement or at least were strong supporters. One of the selections is by Jane Addams, who discusses "Why Women Should Vote" and offers a social feminist argument for the good women could do for society if they had a say in political decisions.

38 BUECHLER, STEVEN M. 1986. "Social Change, Movement Transformation, and Continuities in Feminist Movements: Some Implications of the Illinois Woman Suffrage Movement." *Research in Politics and Society* 2:35–52.
Buechler notes a process of deradicalization in the Illinois woman suffrage movement from 1870 to 1900. He proposes that the explanations for this change were the major social changes that took place in the social environment of this era.

39 CATT, CARRIE CHAPMAN and NELLIE ROGERS SHULER. 1923. *Woman Suffrage and Politics: The Inner Story of the Suffrage Movement*. New York: Charles Scribner's.
An account of the organizational work of the National American Woman Suffrage Association by the woman who was president during the last years of the suffrage campaign. Catt fails to give credit to other suffrage organizations, like the National Woman's Party, in her account of the activism and victory of the vote for women.

40 DUBOIS, ELLEN CAROL. 1978. *Feminism and Suffrage: The Emergence of an Independent Women's Movement in America, 1848–1869*. Ithaca, NY: Cornell University Press.
A study of the origins of the woman's movement in the United States which established the demand for woman's suffrage at its first conference in 1848. Women activists believed the vote would give them the power to transform society and their relationship to it. Thus, DuBois sees suffrage as a social movement, not just a particular reform within a larger movement. The author argues that suffrage was the first independent movement for women's liberation.

41 ————. 1975. "The Radicalism of the Women's Suffrage Movement: Notes Toward the Reconstruction of Nineteenth Century Feminism." *Feminist Studies* 3 (Sept):63–71.
Suffrage is often thought of as a modest proposal and the campaigns for its achievement as actions of a genteel and conservative social movement. DuBois carefully shows that when placed within its social context, the vote was a radical demand that was perceived as changing women's place in the family and social structure.

42   GARNER, LES. 1984. *Stepping Stones to Women's Liberty: Feminist Ideas in the Women's Suffrage Movement, 1900–1918*. Rutherford, NJ: Fairleigh Dickinson University Press.

An examination of the ideologies, tactics, and strategies found in the suffrage movement after the turn of the century.

43   GERTZOG, IRWIN N. 1990. "Female Suffrage in New Jersey, 1790–1807." *Women & Politics* 10:47–58.

A historical documentation of the efforts on the part of New Jersey women to win suffrage long before it became a national issue. The achievement and then loss of the vote in an 1807 Essex County referendum are explained as a defeat representing shifts in the balance of power on the state level.

44   IRWIN, INEZ HAYNES. 1977. *The Story of Alice Paul and the National Women's Party*. Fairfax, VA: Denlinger's Publishers.

Originally published as *The Story of the Woman's Party* (1921), and reissued in 1964 under the title *Uphill with Banners Flying*, this book is a documentation of the activism of Alice Paul and the suffragist activists in the National Woman's Party who defied the political and cultural system to achieve the vote for women. These women were called militant suffragists because of the tactics they used in the years before passage of the Nineteenth Amendment—picketing in front of the White House, arrest and imprisonment, hunger strikes and forced feeding. This book documents in minute detail the efforts of these women from 1912 to 1920.

45   KRADITOR, AILEEN S. 1981. *The Ideas of the Woman Suffrage Movement, 1890–1920*. New York: W. W. Norton.

Originally published in 1965, Kraditor's book is a well researched documentation of the efforts that finally brought victory in the woman's suffrage campaign. Leaders for which brief vignettes are given include Elizabeth Cady Stanton, Lucy Stone, Susan B. Anthony, Alice Paul, Anna Howard Shaw, Alva Belmont, Harriot Stanton Blatch, Alice Stone Blackwell, Florence Kelley, Carrie Chapman Catt, Charlotte Perkins Gilman, Jane Addams, and Lucy Burns.

46   LEWENSON, SANDRA BETH. 1993. *Taking Charge: Nursing, Suffrage, and Feminism in America, 1873–1920*. Hamden, CT: Garland Publishers.

In documenting the emergence of nursing as a profession, the author demonstrates how feminist activism was intertwined with their struggles for professional status, political power, and personal freedom. The first Nightingale-influenced nursing school was opened in America in 1873 and by 1893, when the medical establishment resisted their move to professionalization, nurses formed regional organizations and a national association. It was through these professional associations that nurses became social movement activists when they engaged in coalition work with women's suffrage groups.

47 LIDDINGTON, J. and J. Norris. 1978. *One Hand Tied Behind Us: The Rise of the Women's Suffrage Movement*. London: Virago Press.
This book on the British women's suffrage movement is useful to researchers in the United States because of the parallels and disjunctions between the two movements. American women gained training in militant and dramatic forms of activism when they were living in London and participating in the suffrage movement there.

48 MACKENZIE, MIDGE. 1975. *Shoulder to Shoulder: A Documentary*. New York: Alfred A. Knopf.
A very thorough book on the British women's suffrage movement. This work is illustrative of the American movement because some of the major figures in the U.S movement were participants in the British campaigns. Alice Paul and Lucy Burns, activists in the National Woman's Party, are shown in this book learning the militant tactics they brought back with them to the United States. Both women were arrested, imprisoned, and forced fed in London, experiences they were destined to repeat in their home country. This book stood as the basis for a filmed documentary that was shown on television in the mid-1970s. The similarities between the two struggles are striking; the differences are interesting and informative.

49 MCDONAGH, EILEEN LORENZI. 1990. "The Significance of the Nineteenth Amendment: A New Look at Civil Rights, Social Welfare and Women Suffrage Alignments in the Progressive Era." *Women & Politics* 10:59–94.
This article compares the vote count in the House of Representatives for women's suffrage with those for civil rights, civil liberties, and social welfare. The findings show that the Nineteenth Amendment was considered to be a part of civil rights concerns throughout its legislative history. McDonagh concludes that this finding challenges earlier interpretations of the vote as an expediency measure to be gained for instrumental purposes. However, the author's conclusion must be questioned on the basis of her understanding the expediency argument. This argument was not relevant to legislator's decisions, but was put forward by scholars of the suffrage movement to explain why some sectors of the movement, particularly those belonging to social feminist groups, wanted women's suffrage.

50 NICHOLS, CAROLE. 1983. "Votes and More for Women: Suffrage and After in Connecticut." *Women and History* 5 (March): 1–92.
A look at the contrast between prevailing notions of the suffrage movement and the views of women in Connecticut on leadership, goals, tactics, ideology and the aftermath of victory. The local experience is found to be different in a number of areas than that of those activists on the national level.

51 TICKNER, LISA. 1980. *The Spectacle of Women: Imagery of the Suffrage Campaign, 1907–1914*. Chicago: University of Chicago Press.
Pictures, captions, and stories of the suffrage campaign from 1907 to 1914, just before the movement became militant in the United States.

52   WIDGERY, DAVID. 1979. "Sylvia Pankhurst: Pioneer of Working-Class
     Feminism." *Radical America* 13 (May):23–39.
A look at Sylvia Pankhurst and the socialist feminist causes she was involved
with in England during the twentieth century. Initially beginning her involvement in the Women's Social and Political Union with her mother and sister,
she eventually began work on her own to organize an independent working-
class women's movement. Much of her work focused on combining socialist
and feminist social change efforts. Sylvia and her mother and sister had
important influential effects on militant suffragists in the United States suffrage movement.

53   YELLIN, JEAN FAGAN. 1973. "Documentation: DuBois' Crisis and
     Woman's Suffrage." *Massachusetts Review* 14 (March): 365–375.
W. E. B. DuBois was the editor of *Crisis*, the NAACP magazine, from 1910 to
1934. During those years, he championed women's rights in his writing. He
endorsed the goals of feminism, particularly suffrage, even as he exposed the
racism that sometimes surfaced in the women's movement. DuBois always ele-
vated the discourse of women's suffrage by placing it within an international
and historical context. When the Nineteenth Amendment passed, he exposed
the states that refused to ratify the Amendment as the same ones that opposed
child labor legislation, failed to support universal education, and had a history
of lynching.

Women's History: Activism and Everyday Life

54   APPLEWHITE, HARRIET B. and DARLINE G. LEVY, eds. 1990. *Women and
     Politics in the Age of the Democratic Revolution.* Ann Arbor: University
     of Michigan Press.
Looking at a variety of eighteenth century revolutions, this work presents a
comparative historical view of gender and political culture in revolutionary
movements. Contributors shed new light on women's activism in a variety of
causes not usually covered in the literature of women's involvements. The
efforts of women were often heroic and the authors of these articles provide
important information on women's historical contributions to social progress.

55   APTHEKER, BETTINA. 1989. *Tapestries of Life: Women's Work, Women's
     Consciousness and the Meaning of Daily Life.* Amherst: University of
     Massachusetts Press.
This book looks at women's everyday lives in the process of social change.
Aptheker explores women's battles for improving the quality of their private
lives and she finds these efforts representative of an invisible form of political
resistance. The author argues against the categorization of women's activities
into feminist and non-feminist labels which serve to block our view of women's
purposeful efforts to support themselves and other women whether it be in
settlement houses, women's colleges, or any activity meant to improve
women's lives.

56 BANNER, LOIS. 1974. *Women in Modern America: A Brief History*. New
    York: Harcourt Brace Javanovich.
This history begins with the position of women in society toward the end of
the nineteenth century and ends with the development of the contemporary
women's movement in the late 1960s and early 1970s. Major areas of interest
are on changes in women's status after World War I, the new attitudes of the
1920s, the hardships of the Depression years, and the galvanization of women
into the work force during World War II. The gains women have made during
the twentieth century are noted.

57 BAXANDALL, ROSALYN, LINDA GORDON, and SUSAN REVERBY, eds. 1976.
    *America's Working Women: A Documentary History, 1600 to the
    Present*. New York: Vintage Books.
The editors of this volume are intent on bringing working-class women's history to the forefront of historical analysis. Included in this volume are essays,
diaries, union records, letters, songs, social workers' reports, statistics, and
photographs that reveal the laboring lives of poor and working-class women of
all races, ethnic backgrounds, and occupational areas.

58 BERG, BARBARA J. 1978. *The Remembered Gate: Origins of American
    Feminism*. New York: Oxford University Press.
Berg centers this work on the origins of American feminism in the 1800–1860
period. The author argues that the growing development of cities led to a crisis in women's roles by narrowing them to the home. A response to this
restricted life led to middle-class women's involvements in benevolent societies. In working with prostitutes and criminals, middle-class women were able
to see the social implications of a dependent gender position and the consequences of not being attached to a man. The author argues that this was the
beginning of a gender consciousness which predated the organizing of the first
woman's rights movement.

59 BOARD, JOHN C. 1967. "The Lady from Montana." *Montana: Magazine
    of Western History* 17:2–17.
Jeannette Rankin's experiences in the suffrage movement led to her decision to
run for Congress in 1916. In winning, Rankin became the first woman to sit in the
U.S. House of Representatives and the only Congressional representative to vote
against both World War I and World War II. This article is an interview in which
Rankin talks about many incidents and anecdotes of her Washington years.

60 BOULDING, ELISE. 1992. *The Underside of History, Volume 2: A View of
    Women Through Time*. Newbury Park, CA: Sage Publications, Inc.
In the first volume of this series, the author set the stage for the development
of male dominance beginning with the pre-Paleolithic Age and ending with the
year 1000. In this volume, Boulding begins at that point and takes the reader
to the present. In the closing chapters she covers twentieth century women's
movements, social transformations, and how these challenges are creating
futures for the twenty-first century.

61   CANTAROW, ELLEN (with SUSAN GUSHEE O'MALLEY and SHARON
     HARTMAN STROM). 1980. *Moving the Mountain: Women Working for
     Social Change*. Old Westbury, NY: The Feminist Press.
Oral history interviews with Florence Luscomb, suffragist, activist in the labor
movement, peace movement, and contemporary women's movement; Ella
Baker, organizer for the civil rights movement; and Jessie Lopez De La Cruz, a
farmworker who worked to organize the United Farmworker's Union.

62   CARLSON, AVIS. 1959. *The League of Women Voters in St. Louis: The First
     Forty Years, 1919–1959*. St. Louis, MO: League of Women Voters.
A record of the activities of the League of Women Voters from the time of its
formation until the time of this publication in 1959. Prior to 1919 this organization was the National American Woman Suffrage Association (NAWSA); after
the Nineteenth Amendment passed in 1920, the group was ready to take a new
name and a new role—preparing women for the responsibilities of citizenship.

63   CHAFE, WILLIAM H. 1972. *The American Woman: Her Changing Social,
     Economic, and Political Roles, 1920–1970*. New York: Oxford University
     Press.
Historical research on the forces that have made women second-class citizens
in the United States. Published in the early days of the contemporary women's
movement, Chafe's book contributed to the store of knowledge being developed on inequities between the sexes.

64   COTT, NANCY F. 1977. *The Bonds of Womanhood: 'Woman's Sphere' in
     New England, 1780–1835*. New Haven, CT: Yale University Press.
In this book Cott is interested in showing the activities that middle-class white
women involved themselves in that led to a sense of power and connectedness. Viewed through the historical period they were living in and the ways
they subverted restrictive expectations, the types of causes in which middle-
class women engaged are seen as precursors to their demands for developing
independent lives. These activities and the internal transformations they
wrought are identified as laying the groundwork for the woman's movement
that arose in 1848.

65   ———. 1987. *The Grounding of Modern Feminism*. New Haven, CT:
     Yale University Press.
The focus of this work is the transition from the achievement of suffrage to the
rise of a new women's movement in the 1960s. The 1920s were years when
issues central to 'modern feminism' were first addressed. Contemporary feminism is broader in content, yet has still been faced with the problem of incorporating sameness and difference into a coherent program for women's
advance. As Cott shows, the failure to argue for both equality and equity meant
women's groups often worked against each other. Failure to consolidate these
issues resulted in the loss of a set of common principles and sense of solidarity. This thoroughly documented work is important for understanding past and
ongoing problem of incorporating diverse views into the women's movement.

There are sections on the National Woman's Party (NWP) as well as a variety of groups working on child labor, peace, socialism, and community causes. Many useful quotes are included as well as a thoughtful interpretation of this period.

66   CRAIG, ROBERT H. 1992. *Religion and Radical Politics: An Alternative Christian Tradition in the United States*. Philadelphia: Temple University Press.

During the 1980s, Christian activism has been fueled by right wing conservative thought. In this book, Robert Craig reveals a history of left wing American Christian politics. Individual life histories, particular organizations, and a variety of movements covering the last 100 years are examined in this work. Included are The Knights of Labor, Women's Christian Temperance Union, the National Association for the Advancement of Colored People, The Catholic Worker, and activists Frances Willard, Mother Jones, W.E.B. DuBois, and Dorothy Day.

67   DINER, HASIA R. 1983. *Erin's Daughters in America: Irish Immigrant Women in the Nineteenth Century*. Baltimore, MD: John Hopkins University Press.

This is women's history which looks at a particular group of women in the nineteenth century. Irish immigrant women tell a story of exclusion, discrimination, and oppression going beyond their gender category. They also tell of strength, aspirations, and their own efforts to change this condition. An interesting social history of American society and this ethnic group's experience.

68   EVANS, SARA. 1989. *Born For Liberty: A History of Women in America*. New York: The Free Press.

This work is a synthesis and comprehensive summary of cultural, historical, and social research on American women over the past twenty years. Included are studies about African-American, Native American, and white European women. Evans develops the concept of "republican motherhood" to explain the nineteenth century rationale for the exclusion of women from public life. Women were expected to be mothers who educated sons to be virtuous citizens. While confining women to the home, this expectation also led to the development of a female culture which challenged separate spheres and promoted the necessity of women's values into public policy arenas. Republican motherhood is applied to her analysis of the post World War II emphases on motherhood and family life which constrained women's opportunities. Continuing emphasis on women's family roles are also examined in the anti-feminist arguments of the 1970s and 1980s, including the opposition to the Equal Rights Amendment.

69   GLUCK, SHERNA BERGER. 1987. *Rosie the Riveter Revisited: Women, the War, and Social Change*. Boston: G.K. Hall.

Gluck has gathered together a collection of oral histories of women workers in the aircraft industry during World War II. The ten stories told in this work come from multicultural backgrounds in which the common experience the women had was related to gender discrimination both during and after their war work.

70   HYMOWITZ, CAROL and MICHAEL WEISSMAN. 1978. *A History of Women in America*. New York: Bantam Books.

A history of women in the United States chronicling everyday women and extraordinary women. Social movement activism in abolition, suffrage, labor, and feminist issues in general constitute the bulk of this book. The authors include the daily lives and progressive reform efforts of colonial women, revolutionary women, black women, early feminists, factory women, immigrant women, and modern women.

71   JENSON, JOAN M. 1986. *Loosening the Bonds: Mid-Atlantic Farm Women*. New Haven, CT: Yale University Press.

Not a book about feminist activists per se, this social history of farm women does show women acting with strength and resolve to create a better condition for themselves and those around them. The narrative is enriching and enlightening about what these women's lives were like. The author also provides an important contribution to the history of the Colonies and the early Republic.

72   KAHN, KATHY. 1973. *Hillbilly Women*. New York: Doubleday.

Oral histories and autobiographical writing from women who live in the Appalachian Mountains. Found in these personal stories are the types of activism these women engaged in, particularly with unions and community organizing.

73   LEMONS, STANLEY J. 1990. *The Woman Citizen: Social Feminism in the 1920s*. Charlottesville: University Press of Virginia.

Social feminism was a name given to those women activists who fought for suffrage on the basis of their belief that women had a stronger moral code which could be used in government for the creation of a more humane society. After women got the vote they attempted to pressure legislators to pass bills for protective labor legislation and child labor laws. Lemon's work documents their efforts and fills in an important, often ignored, history of the forces of progressive reform in the early part of this century.

74   LERNER, GERDA. 1979. "The Lady and the Mill Girl: Changes in the Status of Women in the Age of Jackson." Pp. 182–196 in *A Heritage of Her Own: Toward a New Social History of American Women*, edited by Nancy Cott and Elizabeth Pleck. New York: Simon & Schuster.

Gerda Lerner examines the ways that women's work opportunities changed following the Colonial period in American history. She finds that as movements for professionalization increased, policies were instituted to explicitly exclude women. Beginning in the 1830s class distinctions among women widened, particularly between women who were employed and those who were not. Lerner argues that it was the loss of status and opportunities for recognition available in work opportunities that led middle-class women to organize the first woman's rights convention in 1848 at Seneca Falls, New York.

75 LYNN, SUSAN. 1992. *Progressive Women in Conservative Times: Racial Justice, Peace, and Feminism, 1945 to the 1960s*. New Brunswick, NJ: Rutgers University Press.

Susan Lynn fills in the missing history of a period in which, until recently, little was known about feminist activism. The author discusses activism centered on the advancement of women, the elimination of racism, and the promotion of peace from the end of WWII until the rise of groups specifically oriented to each of these issues in the 1960s. Her work focuses on the social reform efforts of women in the American Friends Service Committee and the Young Women's Christian Association.

76 MATTHEWS, GLENNA. 1992. *The Rise of Public Woman: Woman's Power and Woman's Place in the United States, 1630–1970*. New York: Oxford University Press.

Presenting a different view of American history than most texts allow, Matthews discusses the empowerment of women through consciousness of their own personhood. Beginning in Puritan New England, such actions are displayed by Anne Bradstreet and Anne Hutchinson who were elected to act in public arenas. By the eighteenth century, self-identity becomes tied to group identity as women joined together to work against slavery, engage in working-class struggles, and promote woman's rights. The transformation from personal selfhood to public involvement led to women challenging their containment to the private sphere through writing, employment, and participation in social reform.

77 MILES, ROSALIND. 1989. *The Women's History of the World*. London: Paladin.

Women and their roles throughout history provide the wide scope of this book. Miles brings to light obscure women who led their lives with courage and determination. Women of ability in diverse fields are also discovered and documented. The writing style includes puns and startling images which convey the message that there has been a conspiracy of silence about women's lives throughout time.

78 MURRIN, MARY R., ed. 1985. *Women in New Jersey History*. Trenton: New Jersey Historical Commission, Dept. of State.

A collection of papers presented at the Thirteenth Annual New Jersey History Symposium, December 5, 1981, in Trenton, NJ. Papers covered a broad range of women activists, including those concerned with women's rights.

79 RIDD, ROSEMARY and HELEN CALLAWAY, EDS. 1987. *Women and Political Conflict: Portraits of Struggle in Times of Crisis*. New York: New York University Press.

A mixture of stories and research revealing examples of women's strength in a variety of times and circumstances. Interesting and informative for social change advocates.

80   RUPP, LEILA J. 1992. "Eleanor Flexner's Century of Struggle: Women's History and the Women's Movement." *NWSA Journal* 4 (June):157–169.
A review and reflective account of Eleanor Flexner's classic research on the early woman's movement in the United States. Rupp discusses the importance of this work, particularly since it was published when most people thought the movement was dead (1959). Flexner claimed that history can be a tool for social change and Rupp finds that *Century of Struggle* did just that.

81   RUPP, LEILA J. and VERTA TAYLOR. 1990. *Survival in the Doldrums: The American Women's Rights Movement, 1945 to the 1960s*. Columbus: Ohio State University Press.
A well-documented history and analysis of feminist activism in the period following World War II until the emergence of the contemporary women's movement in the latter part of the 1960s. Combining archival research and interview material, the authors show how the movement maintained itself in a period of political apathy, internal conflict, and anti-feminism. Focusing on the 1950s, a period when feminism was supposedly dead, Rupp and Taylor detail continuing activism within the context of opposing views of the National Woman's Party and most other feminist groups over protective labor legislation and the Equal Rights Amendment. An important contribution to the history of the women's movement, this work also shows the ebbs and flows of movement cycles and survival strategies in conservative times.

82   RYAN, MARY P. 1983. *Womanhood in America: From Colonial Times to the Present*. New York: Franklin Watts.
A history of American women divided into seven chapters: Adam's Rib: The First Century of American Womanhood; Patriarchy in Disarray: Women and Commercial Capitalism, 1750–1820; Creating Woman's Sphere: Gender in the Making of American Industrial Capitalism, 1820–1865; The Breadgivers: Immigrants and Reformers, 1865–1920; The Erosion of Women's Sphere: Heterosexuality and the Streamlined Home, 1910-1940; A Domestic Interlude in a Kaleidoscope of Roles, 1940–1960; Toward Gender Symmetry: Feminism and Family Change, 1960–1980.

83   SCHARF, LOIS and JOAN M. JENSON, eds. 1986. *Decades of Discontent: The Women's Movement, 1920–1946.* Boston: Northeastern University Press.
A collection of articles from historians on the women's movement after suffrage until the end of World War II. This volume fills in information on a time when little was known about women's activism.

84   SCOTT, ANNE FIROR. 1970. *The Southern Lady: From Pedestal to Politics, 1830–1930*. Chicago: University of Chicago Press.
A historical tracing of changes brought about in white Southern women's lives after the Civil War. Discussed are increased opportunities for education, involvement in suffrage campaigns, and changing images that emerged during the 1920s. Included in this book is a bibliography of additional sources.

85   SOCHEN, JUNE. 1973. *Movers and Shakers: American Women Thinkers and Activists 1900–1970.* New York: Quandrangle Books.

By looking at feminist activists and writers for the first 70 years of the twentieth century, Sochen is able to capture the transformation in thought that occurred during those years.

86   SOLOMON, BARBARA MILLER. 1985. *In the Company of Educated Women: A History of Women in Higher Education in America.* New Haven, CT: Yale University Press.

Examining the background and struggles of the movement for higher education for women offers important insights into one of the often overlooked areas of feminist struggle. Even more unacknowledged is what educated women have given back to American society. This book helps to fill this void by offering a look at some of the contributions educated women have provided.

87   TAYLOR, VERTA. 1989. "Social Movement Continuity: The Women's Movement in Abeyance." *American Sociological Review* 54 (Oct):761–775.

A look at the women's movement in a low period of activism and support. After suffrage and until the emergence of the Women's Liberation Movement, there were few groups that called themselves feminist or that worked consistently for the goal of women's equality. Taylor looks at women's groups from 1945–1960, particularly the National Woman's Party, and identifies five characteristics that allow a movement to survive in adverse circumstances: temporality (long term group membership), purposive commitment, exclusiveness, centralization, and culture.

88   WEST, GUIDA AND RHODA LOIS BLUMBERG, eds. 1990. *Women and Social Protest.* New York, NY: Oxford University Press.

Articles from a variety of disciplines on women and social protest which cover different historical periods and cultures. There are four types of social protest that this book covers: economical issues; racial, ethnic and nationalistic reform; nurturing/humanistic protests, and women's rights. Women's activism in tenant and welfare rights are covered in the first category, the civil rights movement in the second, peace and ecology in the third, and the women's movement (with specific articles on movement stages, countermovements, women's educational reform, and lesbian organizing) covered in the last section.

2

Second Wave Feminism

Introduction

The years between suffrage and the re-emergence of the women's movement were years of struggle to keep the issue of women's equality alive. Most notably, in this effort, was the National Woman's Party's continuing endeavor to have the Equal Rights Amendment introduced into Congress each year. For some time, Alice Paul, author of the ERA in 1923, and NWP members were the only activists who supported the Amendment and who called themselves feminist. This small group was an important bridge connecting the earlier movement to the newly formulated one that arose in the late 1960s.

Other groups were also, in different ways, working for women's interest during these years. Peace groups, unions, activists for protective labor legislation, and black liberation were all active in the years preceding the rise of the contemporary women's movement. Indeed, much like a century earlier, it was involvement in the New Left, student movement, anti-war, and civil rights movement that led many women to think about organizing in their own behalf.

The first category listed in this chapter on **Second Wave Feminism is the Contemporary Women's Movement**. Entries include writings on the mass movement and small group sectors, the origins of the contemporary movement, consciousness-raising, the International Women's Year, National Organization for Women, trashing, civil disobedience, direct action tactics, disability rights, the prostitutes' rights movement, political groups, and service organizations.

The Equal Rights Amendment constitutes a separate category because of the amount of activism and research that has gone into efforts to achieve this goal. **Reproductive Freedom** is similar to ERA in this regard, and follows it as a separate listing. Birth control, abortion, and the politics involved in reproductive issues are found here.

The next category is **Violence Against Women** which includes anti-rape activism and the battered women's movement. **The Women's Health Movement** is also found here because much of this movement's efforts have

23

been connected to ways of improving women's health, including recovery from neglect and abuse.

Peace, Ecofeminism, and Non-Violent Activism make up the next group of entries. Peace work has been an important area of activism for feminist women since the early part of this century; ecofeminism is a part of the contemporary movement and the environmental movement of the 1970s. The emergence of peace camps, first in Greenham Commons, England, and then in Romulus, New York in the early 1980s is a new innovation in this type of activism. Direct action non-violent tactics arose in the late 60s, died down as movement activism split between separatism and political involvement, then became prevalent again during the early 1980s. These tactics continue sporadically whenever some group decides to draw attention to an issue in a media focused way. Direct action tactics have a common link to some of the earlier tactics used by militant suffragists in the years before passage of the Nineteenth Amendment.

Lesbianism, the Women's Culture, and the Gay/Lesbian Movement is a section which contains references to a vital sector of the contemporary women's movement. Both involved with the movement and challenging it, lesbianism has created gender awareness that literally did not exist before.

Academia and Women's Studies close out this chapter. Here are writings related to academic feminism, scholarship, women's place in the academy, their contributions to knowledge development, and the politics of Women's Studies within academia, as well as the divisions within Women's Studies itself.

Contemporary Women's Movement

89   ALLEN, PAMELA. 1970. *Freespace: A Presentation on the Small Group in Women's Liberation*. Albion, CA: Times Change Press.

Allen uses her own experience in a consciousness-raising group (Sudsofloppen) in San Francisco to talk about feminist small group dynamics. The author presents this information as a handbook and guide for future groups to form; but for those interested in understanding the importance of these groups, this is an informative view of the meaning these groups had for the participants involved in them in the late 1960s and early 1970s.

90   ATKINSON, TI-GRACE. 1974. *Amazon Odyssey*. New York: Links.

A collection of essays, many of which were speeches Atkinson wrote between 1967 and 1972. Her developing radical feminist thought is seen as this work progresses. A number of the selections became famous because of the issues she raised or the commotion she caused when she spoke to particular groups. Her resignation as New York NOW president when she attacked the organization for operating with a hierarchical power base and her "anti-religious" speech at Catholic University are included.

91   BADER, ELEANOR J. 1990. "NOW Confronts Racism." *New Directions for Women* 19 (Nov.):3,11.

This article looks at perceptions of racism in the National Organization for Women, and NOW's efforts to make the organization more open to women of color. Black women report that the issues which dissuade them from becoming activists in NOW are: an anti-religious atmosphere, tokenism, the use of acquiescent women of color to validate policies and programs, vicious internal infighting, poor race consciousness in local chapters, and the overarching priority of ERA and choice issues. An April 1990 survey of 51 state NOW chapters revealed only four states have affirmative action policies to place more women of color on the national board, only eight states have committees to address minority outreach, and only one chapter—Dallas NOW—has transformed itself into a multicultural organization. Dallas NOW accomplished this by holding meetings in an African-American/Latino neighborhood, advertising in race/ethnic newspapers, providing child care, sponsoring a discrimination clinic, volunteering at a homeless shelter, and working in coalition with the local Southern Christian Leadership Conference (SCLC) to improve wages of low income workers. The chapter is 45 percent white, 45 percent African-American, and 10 percent Latina.

92   BIRD, CAROLINE, ed. 1979. *What Women Want: The Official Report to the President, the Congress, and the People of the United States.* New York: Simon and Schuster.

This is a report from the National Commission on the Observance of International Women's Year (IWY) on the National Women's Conference held in November 1977 in Houston, Texas. Bird compiled the materials which include the resolutions proposed, whether they passed or failed, and the arguments for and against them. Includes pictures and an introductory statement by Gloria Steinem.

93   BOURNE, JENNY. 1983. "Towards an Anti-Racist Feminism." *Race and Class* 25 (June):1–22.

Bourne argues that the U.S. women's movement has concentrated on expanding sexual freedom rather than changing the structure of society. The author claims that the interconnections and debt to the black civil rights movement have never been fully acknowledged, and white feminists have generally failed to place their efforts on challenging the state. In contrast, Bourne says that women of color, Third World women, and working-class women have worked for a restructuring of society and social relations. In spite of the fact that there is some validity to this thesis, the tone of this article is overarching and it fails to acknowledge those areas where the women's movement has been anti-racist and revolutionary.

94   BOYLAN, ESTHER. 1991. *Women and Disability.* London: Zed Books.

The movement for disability rights is part of the general social movement struggle that began in the 1960s to recognize people from various walks of life and to accord them equitable treatment in society. This book contains both social analysis and personal stories of discrimination. The struggle for disability rights has been successful on a number of levels and has now become an international issue. Boylan looks particularly at the needs of disabled women and their contributions to this ongoing social movement.

95   BUCK, MACKY, CINDY DEITCH, DALE MELCHER, LYDIA NETTIER, ANN WASSELL, and EDIE SPIELMAN. 1978. "Socialist-Feminist Unions: Past and Present." *Socialist Review* 8 (March):37–57.
Between 1972 and 1975 over fifty socialist feminist unions formed across the United States. But by the end of the 1970s, they were all gone. The authors of this article report on the rise and fall of these groups and the internal contradictions over theory, practice, leadership, organizational structure, and conflict resolution that existed within them.

96   BUNCH, CHARLOTTE. 1980. "Woman Power: The Courage to Lead, the Strength to Follow, and the Sense to Know the Difference." *Ms.* 9 (July):45–48,95–97.
Bunch discusses the ambivalence over leadership in the women's movement. In spite of the desire for a non-hierarchical group, Bunch shows the critical role feminist leaders play. Various leadership styles are outlined.

97   CARABILLO, TONI, JUDITH MEULI, and JUNE BUNDY CSIDA. 1993. *Feminist Chronicles, 1953–1993*. Los Angeles: Women's Graphics.
This is an important reference book on the activities of the contemporary women's movement, particularly the National Organization for Women. Intended as the first installment of a larger work on the women's movement in the twentieth century, this book alone took thirteen years to compile. The authors are all long time activists in NOW and the Feminist Majority. Landmark events, life stories, issue discussions, NOW reports and position papers, and photographs provide a year by year account of the gains and losses for feminist goals over the last 40 years.

98   CARDEN, MAREN LOCKWOOD. 1974. *The New Feminist Movement*. New York: Russell Sage.
Based on empirical research and sociological analysis, this book examines the different feminist groups that arose in the late 1960s and early 1970s, and the women who joined them. In reading periodicals and newsletters, and from interviews of group members, Carden finds differences in structure and orientation which produced two types of feminist groups, defined as women's rights and women's liberation. Using relative deprivation theory, the author explains how a focus on gender results in a 90 percent white middle-class membership in both types of groups since there are no class/race/ethnic barriers to participant's achievement expectations. The establishment of coalitions, conflict within and between feminist groups, and positions on issues are discussed.

99   ———. 1978. "The Proliferation of a Social Movement: Ideology and Individual Incentives in the Feminist Movement." *Research in Social Movements, Conflicts and Change* 1:179–196.

Carden uses a resource mobilization framework to explain the proliferation of feminist groups during the 1970s. The data for this study includes interviews with group members, participant observation, and printed sources. The causes for the increase in groups are diverse ideological positions, differing incentives based on participants' skills and interests, and contrasting emphases on unity through sisterhood or personal autonomy goals. Carden takes the position that an increase in diversity among feminist groups is a positive outcome of social movement growth allowing for innovation in strategies and tactics.

100   CASSELL, JOAN. 1977. *A Group Called Women: Sisterhood and Symbolism in the Feminist Movement*. New York: David McKay.
A participant observation study of feminist group formation in the small group sector of the women's movement from 1971 to 1973 in New York City. Explored are the processes of becoming a feminist, of defining oneself as a member of a group, and the organizational components of the women's movement.

101   CASTRO, GINETTE. 1990. *American Feminism: A Contemporary History*. Irvington, NY: New York University Press.
Castro outlines the various feminist perspectives found within the contemporary movement and places particular feminists within one of the categories she has identified. For instance, she places Betty Friedan and NOW into liberal feminism; Kate Millet, Ti-Grace Atkinson, and New York Radical Women are categorized as radical feminists. There are two problems with this categorization scheme: Castro fails to adequately cover all the currents that are involved in the feminist movement over the last quarter century, and she does not acknowledge the overlap that exists among these perspectives.

102   CHAFE, WILLIAM H. 1977. *Women and Equality: Changing Patterns in American Culture*. New York: Oxford University Books.
An analysis of social and economic change in the twentieth century. Chafe carefully examines the ways that sexual and racial inequality are similar and the ways that they differ. The contemporary women's movement is placed within the context of ongoing challenges and transformations in American society.

103   COHEN, MARCIA. 1988. *The Sisterhood: The True Story of the Women Who Changed the World*. New York: Simon and Schuster.
Cohen writes in a journalistic narrative style on the well-known events and leaders of the contemporary women's movement, particularly those leaders involved in the early formation of the movement during the late 1960s. Events, actions, personality characteristics, and antidotal accounts of feminists' lives are included. Defined as an intimate history, the author presents her material as an "inside story" of the birth of NOW, the defeat of ERA, the push for abortion, and lesbianism within the movement. Activist leaders featured are Betty Friedan, Gloria Steinem, Kate Millett, and Germaine Greer.

104   COOTE, ANNE AND BEATRIX CAMPBELL. 1988. *Sweet Freedom: The
        Struggle for Women's Liberation*. New York: Basil Blackwell.
A general view of the fight for women's equality with a focus on the economic
foundation of the social and political differences between the sexes.

105   COSTAIN, ANNE N. 1992. *Inviting Women's Rebellion: A Political Process
        Interpretation of the Women's Movement*. Baltimore, MD: Johns
        Hopkins University Press.
Costain examines the interaction between political opportunity structures,
movement organizing power, and levels of participant empowerment during
times of movement emergence, success, and decline. Her contribution in looking at the changing relations between the movement and the government is
useful; however, she leaves out the influence of other forces such as the New
Right, the loss of an activating issue (the ERA), and changing economic conditions in the 1980s.

106   DAVIS, FLORA. 1991. *Moving the Mountain: The Women's Movement in
        America Since 1960*. New York: Simon & Schuster.
This book details aspects of the contemporary women's movement by showing
how some issues were won and others lost. Davis uses examples of actions and
strategy implementation, anecdotal material, and quotations from interviews in
a "war story" format. The ins and outs of lobbying, establishing a battered
women's center, and getting a bill through Congress are shown by specific
example. Discussions of issues include: why the New Right is opposed to gains
won by women; where women stand in politics; how new divorce laws have left
women and children more impoverished than in the past; and why Americans
still do not have government sponsored affordable child care. This is not a work
that utilizes a theoretical framework, nor does it address major divisive issues
among feminist orientations or identity politics.

107   DECKARD, BARBARA SINCLAIR. 1983. *The Women's Movement: Political,
        Socioeconomic, and Psychological Issues, Third Edition*. New York:
        Harper and Row.
Originally published in 1975, each edition of Deckard's book provides a synthesis and update of the women's movement and feminist issues. Using secondary
sources, her work provides a quick reference source on women's history and
social change goals. The first half of the book examines patterns of discrimination, including sexual stereotypes, psychological theory, socialization, the family,
working women, and the law. The second section covers women in different
types of societies, women's activism during different stages of the women's
movement, feminist theory, and contemporary issues such as abortion, ERA,
employment, child care, and violence against women.

108   DOELY, SARAH BENTLEY, ed. 1970. *Women's Liberation and the Church:
        The New Demand for Freedom in the Life of the Christian Church*. New
        York: Association Press.
An early look at the question of feminism and religion. Various articles discuss

religious education for women, the role of nuns in women's liberation, the potential for Christian thought to influence and be influenced by feminist conceptions, and how women in the ministry can contribute to the women's movement.

109   DOUGLAS, CAROL ANNE. 1990. "Looking Back on the Last 20 Years . . . " *off our backs* 20 (Feb.):15–18.
This article discusses the founding of *off our backs: a women's newsjournal*, and the purpose this publication serves. The changes over time in staff, from heterosexual women in the early 1970s to an all lesbian collective by 1988, and the focus of the journal are detailed. The type of coverage found in the years 1985–1989 is listed, including the special issue on activism in the women's movement (February 1986). This publication provides articles on current issues, reports on feminist conferences, international women's movement activities, book reviews, and lively discussions on controversial topics. The women's movement—activism, thought, and conflicts—from 1970 to the present are chronicled each issue.

110   DREIFUS, CLAUDIA. 1973. *Woman's Fate: Raps from a Feminist Consciousness-Raising Group*. New York. Bantam.
This is a personal account of a feminist consciousness-raising group that represents the experiences of many women involved in the small group sector of the women's movement. The author discusses the inner workings of her group of eight women and the dynamics involved in understanding the meaning of "the personal is political." The CR method comes from the 'speak bitterness' campaign instituted in China after the communist revolution and Mao's attempt to bring women into the twentieth century labor force. In discussing their own situations in CR sessions, women are led to see that what they thought were personal problems are really social problems brought about through sexist thoughts and practices.

111   ECHOLS, ALICE. 1988. *Daring to Be Bad: Radical Feminism in America, 1967–1975*. Minneapolis: University of Minnesota Press.
This work applies a critical stance to an analysis of the rise and fall of the radical segment of the contemporary women's movement. Radical feminism is distinguished from socialist feminism and liberal feminism by its goal of restructuring private and public life and because of its claim that it was men who were responsible for women's oppression. Other topics in this book include the emergence of the contemporary women's movement within the context of other social movements of the 1960s, the chauvinism of otherwise progressive men of that era, the Black Power Movement's crucial contributions to the development of radical feminism, and feminist conflicts over structure and leadership. Echols discusses the impacts of radical feminism, such as the establishment of consciousness-raising, legitimation of confrontational politics, identifying power differentials between women and men, and promoting the fight for legal abortion. Its largest failure was the claim for a united sisterhood which denied race and class differences among women. Echols considers the cultural

feminism that supplanted radical feminism to be focused on developing a counterculture rather than an attempt at structural transformation. As such, she considers it to be non-threatening to the powers that be.

112   EISENSTEIN, HESTER. 1991. *Gender Shock: Practicing Feminism on Two Continents.* Boston: Beacon Press.
Eisenstein is a respected author of books on feminism and the women's movement in the United States. In this work, she relates her experience of living for eight years in Australia and working in a "femocracy" administering state policy for women. Both empirically and theoretically, Eisenstein shows how the diversity that exists in the United States and Australia within state agencies and within the women's movement make it difficult to talk in general about either "the state" or "women." She also provides a practical guide for working in policy arenas and demonstrates why pragmatic approaches that make use of available resources are tactics that work in advancing the cause of women.

113   EVANS, SARA. 1979. *Personal Politics: The Roots of Women's Liberation in the Civil Rights Movement and the New Left.* New York: Vintage Books.
A well-researched book by a woman who was also an activist in the 1960s movements. Evans traces the roots of women's liberation to the treatment women received in the New Left, anti-war, and civil rights movements. The lack of women leaders and dismissal of their concerns for their own equality led women to organize the small group sector of the women's movement by the end of the 60s decade. In addition to learning about the origins of one sector of the women's movement, readers will also learn about the Student Nonviolent Coordinating Committee (SNCC) and Students for a Democratic Society (SDS).

114   FARGANIS, SONDRA. 1986. *Social Reconstruction of the Feminine Character.* Totowa, NJ: Rowman & Littlefield.
Farganis has written this book as a way to interpret feminist theory through the sociological framework outlined in Karl Mannheim's work on the sociology of knowledge. Chapters focus on the writings of Viola Klein, the women's movement as a social movement, family, motherhood, morality, reason, and science. The section on the women's movement provides historical background and the context out of which the early movement arose. The contemporary movement is also covered along with the societal level changes that contributed to the re-emergence of the movement in the 1960s.

115   FERREE, MYRA MARX and BETH B. HESS. 1985. *Controversy and Coalition: The New Feminist Movement.* Boston: Twayne.
The authors are interested in showing the diversity of feminism found in the contemporary women's movement. The roots of feminist activism are defined as coming from three strands: moral reform, classical liberal thought, and socialist principles. Ferree and Hess argue that both revolutionary and institutional change, as sought by the various sectors of the movement, have con-

tributed to changes in women's status. Included are sections on the reemergence of a feminist movement, 1963–83; feminist organizations in transition; interest-group politics; triumphs and tensions, 1976–83; aims, accomplishments, and emergent issues.

116 FINE, MICHELLE and ADRIENNE ASCH, eds. 1988. *Women with Disabilities: Essays in Psychology, Culture, and Politics*. Philadelphia: Temple University Press.

Contributors to this collection make gender the focus of their examination of disability. By analyzing disabilities from a gendered perspective they contribute to our understanding of the personal and political realities of the disability rights movement and this movement's connection to feminism and the women's movement.

117 FISHER, BERENICE. 1984. "Guilt and Shame in the Women's Movement." *Feminist Studies* 10, 2 (Summer).

A look at the actions and feelings of women activists in the contemporary women's movement.

118 FREEMAN, BONNIE COOK. 1983. "Anti-Feminists and Women's Liberation: A Case Study of a Paradox." *Women and Politics* 3 (March): 21–38.

A report of a study examining the strategies employed by feminists and antifeminists as each attempts to have a say on the textbook selection process.

119 FREEMAN, JO. 1975. "Political Organization in the Feminist Movement." *Acta Sociologica* 18:222–224.

Published prior to Freeman's book on the women's movement (see entry 120), this article discusses a major finding found in that work. Freeman divides the movement into the older and younger branch in which the older is seen as more moderate and the younger as more radical. The National Organization for Women represents the older branch and the small consciousness-raising groups represent the younger branch. The author discusses the capability of creating change found within each branch. Freeman finds that changes have occurred since the founding of these groups with NOW beginning to draw in younger women by adopting a more informal style and more radical positions. The small CR groups, which arose out of the New Left, have emphasized community organizing and a non-hierarchical structure. Ironically this type of organizing has led to informal power structures which have no responsibility checks. Freeman finds this sector actually tends to be conservative in political effects because of the lack of the institutional foundation needed to carry through on political change efforts.

120 ———. 1975. *The Politics of Women's Liberation: A Case Study of an Emerging Social Movement and Its Relation to the Policy Process*. New York: David McKay.

This is an important book on the origins of the contemporary women's movement. Freeman was both a researcher and an activist during the late 1960s when the movement began. Through interviews of key activists and drawing on her own social movement experiences and skills as a political scientist, she analyzes the multi-faced theoretical and activist impulse of these early years. She provides a structural analysis of organizational and leadership differences in the mass movement and small group sectors, as well as a cogent explanation of how and why things happened as they did. This work served as Freeman's doctoral dissertation and later won a prize for the best work in political science. Her work has stood the test of time and is still one of the best accounts of the formation period of second wave feminism.

121   ———. 1973. "The Tyranny of Structurelessness." *Ms.* 2 (July):76–78, 86–89.

In this article Freeman shows how the leaderless group actually becomes one where power is concentrated in informal elites. She calls for more democratic group structures.

122   ———. 1984. "The Women's Liberation Movement: Its Origins, Structure, Activities, and Ideas." Pp. 543–556 in *Women: A Feminist Perspective, Third Edition*, edited by Jo Freeman. Palo Alto, CA: Mayfield Publishing Co.

Freeman presents a condensed account of the first 15 years of the contemporary women's movement. She covers the beginning of the National Organization for Women, the emergence of small consciousness-raising groups, the campaign for the Equal Rights Amendment, the gay/straight split, Socialist feminist views, and the challenge to the sex/gender role system permeating society.

123   FRITZ, LEAH. 1979. *Dreamers and Dealers: An Intimate Appraisal of the Women's Movement.* Boston: Beacon Press.

Although she calls for diversity, Fritz presents a critical view of liberal feminism which she feels offers no possibility of an alliance with the political Left. Often slipping into a polemic style, this is a subjective and personal account of the author's experiences in the women's movement and the way she interprets conflicts over lesbianism, class, race, and socialist philosophy.

124   GATLIN, ROCHELLE. 1988. *American Women Since 1945.* Jackson: University Press of Mississippi.

Gatlin has put together a history of feminist thought and activism since World War II, both before and after the re- emergence of the women's movement. Moderate and radical strands of the contemporary women's movement are included in this work.

125   GELB, JOYCE and MARION PALLEY. 1982. *Women and Public Policies.* Princeton: Princeton University Press.

Gelb and Palley examine the women's movement and find a segment which focuses on interest group politics. The authors reveal how these groups work in the political arena and show why they are responsible for important policy gains for women in the United States.

126 HANCOCK, BRENDA ROBINSON. 1972. "Affirmation by Negation in the Women's Liberation Movement." *Quarterly Journal of Speech* 58:264–271.

The tendency to develop a "man is the enemy" strategy within radical feminism in the early stage of the contemporary movement was probably beneficial according to Brenda Robinson Hancock. She argues that "man-hating" allowed women to release frustration and to identify female characteristics as valuable. The pro- woman line that emerged was important in providing women with a new identity and sense of efficacy.

127 HANSEN, KAREN. 1986. "The Women's Unions and the Search for a Political Identity." *Socialist Review* 16:67–95.

Hansen examines the socialist feminist women's liberation unions that emerged towards the end of the 1960s decade. Women who formed unions had previously been involved in the New Left and brought much of what they learned in that movement with them into the new women's groups, including Marxist rhetoric and socialist ideas. Hansen discusses the ways this carryover from a male defined movement into a woman defined movement often led to problems.

128 HERSON, LIZ. 1986. *Changes of Heart: Reflections of Women's Independence*. Winchester, MA: Pandora Press.

An investigation into the ways male-female relationships have been effected by the women's movement. Data consists of interviews selected among Herson's contemporaries and her own personal reflections. Her conclusion is that the struggle for equality has not been won yet, although advance has been made. Not a scientific study, but there are some original and thought provoking components to this book.

129 HILLYER, BARBARA. 1994. *Feminism and Disability*. Norman: University of Oklahoma Press.

This book is the 1994 winner of the Emily Toth Award for best single-authored feminist study of American culture by the Women's Caucus for Popular Culture of the Popular Culture Association/American Culture Association. Hillyer examines the frameworks for the feminist and disability-rights movements looking for similarities, differences, and conflicts.

130 HOLE, JUDITH and ELLEN LEVINE. 1984. "The First Feminists." Pp. 533–542 in *Women: A Feminist Perspective, Third Edition*, edited by Jo Freeman. Palo Alto, CA: Mayfield Publishing Co.

This article, which also appeared in the two previous editions of Freeman's anthology, constitutes the first chapter in Hole and Levine's book *Rebirth of Feminism*. The authors point out that the "radical" notions in contemporary feminism parallel the early critique of women's position in social and family arrangements raised by nineteenth century feminists. In both cases, activists have examined the role of women and their relationships with men in all spheres of life. Each movement has defined women as an oppressed group in a male-dominated value system.

131 ———. 1971. *Rebirth of Feminism*. New York: Quadrangle.
Through interviews and document research, Hole and Levine put together a descriptive account of the founding of the contemporary women's movement. They discuss ideological orientations, feminist issues that were raised such as abortion and ERA, and the institutional changes that were required to accomplish the movement's goals. They begin their account of the origins of the Women's Liberation Movement earlier than most writers, dating the activating event as 1960 when The Commission on the Status of Women was instituted by President John Kennedy, the first official recognition of the need to address women's issues since the achievement of women's suffrage in 1920. The authors also tie feminist activism to other social movement involvement, particularly the civil rights movement. Because the book was published in 1971, only the early years are covered but the account is comprehensive and still stands as one of the best works on this phase of feminist activism.

132 HOOKS, BELL. 1990. "Future Feminist Movements." *off our backs* 20:9.
A reflection of the author's experiences in the women's movement and in teaching Women's Studies. hooks feels that too much of the feminist theory that is produced in academia is useless for application to women's lives, particularly poor women's lives. She is critical of the women's movement because it has not put the struggle to end racism at the top of its priority agenda. Similarly, she criticizes black organizations for not addressing women's issues. The women's movement is examined on positions it has taken on issues such as sexuality, housing, welfare, and family. Academic feminists are called upon to look at the inter-connectedness of systems of oppression when talking about any one of them.

133 HOPE, CAROL AND NANCY YOUNG. 1979. *Out of the Frying Pan: A Decade of Change in Women's Lives*. Garden City, NY: Anchor Press.
Based on an empirical study, the authors discuss the ways women have been affected by the contemporary women's movement. The women who were interviewed for this study talk about their life experiences and how they have changed their lives because of their new feminist awareness.

134 JANEWAY, ELIZABETH. 1974. *Between Myth and Morning: Women Awakening*. New York: William Morrow.
Janeway discusses the women's movement and some of the changes brought about because of it. The author contends that issues arising from feminist consciousness and legal/policy changes lead to new issues which will have to be addressed in the future.

135 JAQUITH, CINDY. 1972. "Where is the Women's Political Caucus Going?" *International Socialist Revolution* 33:4–7.

A brief discussion on the strategy of the National Women's Political Caucus in the early 1970s. The emphasis in this paper is on the views of caucus founders Betty Friedan, Shirley Chisholm, and Bella Abzug.

136 JENNESS, VALERIE. 1993. *Making It Work: The Prostitutes' Rights Movement in Perspective*. Hawthorne, NY: Aldine de Gruyter.

This book chronicles the origin and development of COYOTE (Call Off Your Old Tired Ethics), the leading organization of the prostitutes' rights movement. Founded in the early 1970s, COYOTE challenged law enforcement and government officials over discriminatory enforcement of criminal law. Members attended women's movement conferences and contributed to the discourse on violence against women and the right of women to control their own bodies. Through their efforts, COYOTE members were able to link the question of prostitution to the larger issue of women's rights. The author frames prostitution within a work analysis in which prostitution is a service industry that employs professional sex workers. Prostitution, pornography, and sexuality are given a new and different voice in the feminist debate on these issues.

137 JONES, BEVERLY and JUDITH BROWN. 1968. *Toward a Female Liberation Movement*. Cambridge, MA: New England Free Press.

Early activists in the contemporary women's movement, Jones and Brown lay out a plan for the development of Women's Studies and the achievement of women's liberation. The programs they suggest are sensible and written in a down-to-earth style. This tract also appeared in Leslie Tanner's edited volume *Voices from Women's Liberation* (1970) (see entry 129?).

138 Joreen. 1976. "Trashing: The Dark Side of Sisterhood." *Ms.* 9:49–98.

This is a classic article on the trashing (attacking) feminist women did to each other within the movement. Joreen was a pseudonym for Jo Freeman, activist and scholar of the movement. In this article Freeman tells of trashing in general and in more personal tones of the effect it has on the person trashed.

139 JUSTICE, BETTY and RENATE PORE, eds. 1981. *Toward the Second Decade: The Impact of the Women's Movement on American Institutions*. Westport, CT: Greenwood Press.

It is encouraging to see the ways the women's movement challenged and affected changes in American society during the 1970s. Because this book ends before the Reagan/Bush years, it leaves a brighter picture than what was to follow.

140 KAHN, KAREN. 1989. "Challenging Authority: Civil Disobedience in the Feminist Anti-Militarist Movement." *Women's Studies International Forum* 12:75–80.

This article focuses on women's activism in the antinuclear movement and the transformation in consciousness participants experience from doing civil disobedience. The process of overcoming fears of being arrested—which is tied to the fear of challenging male authority—is closely examined, particularly the role it plays in white middle-class women's lives.

141　KAMEN, PAULA. 1991. *Feminist Fatale: Voices From the Twentysomething Generation Explore the Future of the Women's Movement.* New York: Donald I. Fine, Inc.

A member of the 'twentysomething' generation, Paula Kamen travels the country exploring what people in her age group feel about feminism and the women's movement. She reports on young women's aversion to the word feminist which carries connotations in their minds of man-haters, radical lesbians, and angry women. In terms of support for feminist issues, they are highly in favor of equality, career opportunities, shared family responsibilities, reproductive freedom, and an end to violence against women. Kamen lectures 'older' feminists on their failure to address the issues of importance to this age group and for the lack of opportunities in established groups for sharing power with younger women. Recent topics from the latter part of the 1980s and early 1990s are well covered but an understanding of the history of the women's movement, including concerted campaigns on the aforementioned issues, calls for members of the author's generation to do more reading on the ideology and organizing efforts of the feminist activists who came before them.

142　KOMISAR, LUCY. 1971. *The New Feminism.* New York: Franklin Watts.

This is a straight-forward book which presents a quick overview of some of the major issues raised by the contemporary women's movement in the early organizing years. Komisar covers sexism, socialization, work, abortion, women's history, and legal issues. The re-emergence of women's activism in the Women's Liberation Movement is discussed, as well as the potential for international struggles by women in the future.

143　LANGER, HOWARD J. 1983. "The Women's Movement: What N.O.W.?" *Social Education* 47:112–121.

An interview with Eleanor Smeal, former president of the National Organization for Women. Smeal discusses the history of the women's movement, and the hopes for the future. Topical issues addressed include the ERA, abortion, sexual harassment, and the gender gap.

144　LEVINE, SUZANNE AND HARRIET LYONS, eds. 1980. *The Decade of Women: A Ms. History of the Seventies in Words and Pictures.* New York: Paragon Books.

This collection is just what the title says it is. Short captions provide a documentary and pictorial account of the women's movement and feminist achievements during the 1970s.

145　LEX, LOUISE M. 1978. "The Feminist Movement: Its Impact on Women in the State Legislatures." *Dissertation Abstracts International* 38 (May):65–94.

Although dated, this is an empirical research project which looked at the effects of the women's movement on the political process in individual state legislatures.

146   LIEBERMAN, MORTON A. and GARY R. BOND. 1976. "The Problem of Being a Woman: A Survey of 1,700 Women in Consciousness-Raising Groups." *Journal of Applied Behavioral Science* 12 (July):363–379.
The authors propose that CR groups served as an alternative mental health resource. Consciousness-raising was mostly engaged in by white middle-class women who were liberal, college educated, urban, mildly depressed, and ranging in age between 20 and 50. Participants reported the greatest group advantage they received in the CR sessions was the sharing of common experiences.

147   LINDEN-WARD, BLANCHE and CAROL HURD GREEN. 1993. *Changing the Future: American Women in the 1960s.* New York: Twayne.
A look at the diversity of involvement American women were engaged in during the activist decade of the 1960s. Many different arenas of activism are covered such as the civil rights movement, the women's movement, educational reform, and input into popular culture.

148   MANDLE, JOAN D. 1971. "Women's Liberation: Humanizing Rather than Polarizing." *Annual of American Academy of Political and Social Sciences* 1:118–128.
The Women's Liberation Movement consists of many groups working in different ways for women's equality. Mandle finds that their various demands, and differences in the way they organize reflect the many areas of change needed and the broad based support that represents women from all sectors of society.

149   MARTIN, PATRICIA YANCEY. 1990. "Rethinking Feminist Organizations." *Gender & Society* 4 (June):182–206.
Martin is interested in learning what is different about feminist organizations from other organizations. Comparisons were done on ten factors: feminist ideology, values, goals, outcomes for members, founding circumstances, structure, practice, members, scope, and external relations. She calls for examining the outcome effects for women and society by the different ideologies, forms, and strategies found in feminist organizations.

150   NELSON, BARBARA J. and NANCY J. JOHNSON. 1991. "Political Structures and Social Movement Tactics: Feminist Policy Agendas in the United States in the 1990s." *NWSA Journal* 3 (March):199–212.
This article discusses why the goals and tactics of the women's movement changed during the Reagan/Bush years. The State, by the 1980s, was seen as a necessary area of contention to both achieve goals of the women's movement and to prevent the erosion of those gains that had been made. A shift in radical/reform differences in views of working in the policy arena occurred in three periods of the women's movement: the formative years (1966–1972); the rou-

tinized period (1972–1977); and the institutionalizing stage (1978–1987). In the first period feminists were in conflict over utilizing the system, in the second gains were made with ERA and abortion, and in the third there was a shift toward more political involvement as opposition increased. Change was necessary in the last period because of new party alignments, backlash against social liberalism, and the lack of concerted action on the part of Congress. The authors call for 1990s tactics of working in coalitions, using intergovernmental networks, and becoming active in state and local politics.

151   REINHARZ, SHULAMIT. 1986. "Friends or Foes: Gerontological and Feminist Theory." *Women's Studies International Forum* 9:503–414.
This article compares feminist and gerontological theory. Reinharz examines sexism on older and younger women, feminist definitions of the body, and interactions between women of different ages. She concludes that the women's movement is a major player in the anti-ageism movement.

152   ROSENFELD, RACHEL A. and KATHRYN B. WARD. 1991. "The Contemporary U.S. Women's Movement: An Empirical Example of Competition Theory." *Sociological Forum* 6 (Sept.):471–500.
Resource mobilization and competition perspectives are contrasted to explain the rise of the contemporary feminist movement. The authors find that economic and sociodemographic changes led to competition between women and men which led to the rise of the women's movement.

153   ROSSI, ALICE. 1970. "Women—Terms of Liberation." *Dissent* 17: 531–541.
Rossi provides the background, emergence, and future possibilities for the Women's Liberation Movement. She includes autobiographical data on her own experience with sexism in academia and advises women to begin concerted efforts to overcome work discrimination.

154   ROWBOTHAM, SHEILA. 1971. *Women, Resistance and Revolution: A History of Women and Revolution in the Modern World*. New York: Vintage Books.
Rowbotham explores the relationship between feminism and social revolution. She looks at the various forms protest has taken in a number of countries in the West, China, Russia, Cuba, Algeria, and Vietnam.

155   ROWLAND, ROBYN, ed. 1984. *Women Who Do and Women Who Don't Join the Women's Movement*. London: Routledge & Kegan Paul.
Rowland interviewed women who align themselves with the women's movement and those who do not to tell her why they made the choice they did. She lets them speak in their own words, filling in with an introduction and conclusion. There are 24 women from five countries who talk about their beliefs and practices. Issues they cover are the women's movement, men, families, motherhood, and their perceptions of the differences between feminists and antifeminists. Contributors include Gloria Bowles, Ann Curthoys, Margrit Eichler, Juliet Mitchell, Dale Spender, and Lynn Spender.

156 ROWLAND, ROBYN. 1986. "Women Who Do and Women Who Don't Join the Women's Movement: Issues for Conflict and Collaboration." *Sex Roles* 14 (June):679–692.

This article is based on the book *Women Who Do and Women Who Don't Join the Women's Movement* (See entry 155) edited by Rowland. In this piece the author draws on the writings from 24 women, both feminists and anti-feminists, from five countries who discussed their relationship to the women's movement. Rowland was interested in finding the issues that separate women as well as those that unite them. She did not find clear-cut answers since hotly-debated issues such as ERA, abortion, family, sex, race, age, and background were interpreted to serve both pro and anti feminist positions. Rowland concludes with a discussion of the complex interweaving of issues, experiences, and difficulties of being a woman.

157 RUETHER, ROSEMARY RADFORD. 1975. *New Woman, New Earth: Sexist Ideologies and Human Liberation.* New York: Seabury Press.

Ruether takes a socialist feminist perspective in discussing possibilities of success for the women's movement. The sexism of most religions is a main theme in her analysis. In addition to addressing issues related to women's liberation, the author also examines prejudice and discrimination against African-Americans and Jews.

158 RUTH, SHEILA. 1973. "A Serious Look at Consciousness-Raising." *Social Theory and Practice* 2:289–300.

Sheila Ruth makes a persuasive argument for the importance of activities to produce consciousness-raising to envision alternative life-styles and raised self-images for women. The author addresses this issue within the context of a discussion on the current attitudes in society toward feminism and the women's movement.

159 RYAN, BARBARA. 1992. *Feminism and the Women's Movement: Dynamics of Change in Social Movement Ideology and Activism.* New York: Routledge.

This book examines feminist thought and action from 1848 to the present. A historical view of the contemporary women's movement begins with chapters on the early woman's rights and suffrage movement. Social movement transformation is analyzed through changes in inter-movement group relations, strategies, goals, conflicts, the social/political environment, and ideological development. Conflict within the movement is examined through identity politics, ideological purity, race, class, and ethnic divisions. Using an analytical framework based on social movement theory, Ryan draws on empirical evidence representing different sectors of the movement. Her data comes from participant observation, interviews of long term activists, and primary documents. The end result is a thoroughly documented portrayal of the successes and difficulties women have experienced in their efforts to join together to effect social change.

160   ———. 1989. "Ideological Purity and Feminism: The U.S. Women's
       Movement from 1966 to 1975." *Gender & Society* 3 (June):239–257.
Ryan addresses the question of why feminism failed to create unity among
activist women in the organizing stage of the contemporary women's movement; indeed, why it increasingly developed schisms instead. Using movement
literature and interviews with long-term activists, the author argues that it was
not competing ideologies that drove feminists apart. Rather, ideology and theory were used to promote radical identities and to maintain social divisions
that existed prior to the rise of the women's movement.

161   SANDAGE, DIANE and POLLY F. RADOSH. 1992. "The Women's Movement
       and the Rebirth of Feminism: Conflicts and Contradictions." *Humanity
       & Society* 16:277–296.
A review of the history of the contemporary women's movement—the origins,
ties to the Left and civil rights movement, the sectors, conflicts and contradictions.

162   SCHNEIDER, BETH E. 1988. "Political Generations and the Contemporary
       Women's Movement." *Sociological Inquiry* 58:4–21.
An examination of the different ways of relating to the women's movement in
changing political/social climates by young, middle-aged, and older women.
Employing a generational model of analysis, Schneider explains how and when
women come to experience similar perceptions and understandings of reality
which lend themselves to a feminist awareness. The "post-feminist" generation
of college aged women who deny the need for a social movement to achieve
their goals led to this exploration of why the women's movement must transform itself to meet the needs of women over the life course.

163   SCHRAMM, SARAH. 1979. *Plow Women Rather Than Reapers: An
       Intellectual History of Feminism in the United States*. Metuchen, NJ:
       Scarecrow Press.
A historical account of feminism in the United States. This book places a
greater interest on tactical strategies than on ideological differences within the
movement.

164   SEALANDER, JUDITH and DOROTHY SMITH. 1986. "The Rise and Fall of
       Feminist Organizations in the 1970s." *Feminist Studies* 12, 2 (Summer).
The 1970s represent the most volatile period of the contemporary women's
movement. In this article Sealander and Smith look at the rise and fall of a wide
variety of groups during this decade.

165   SHULMAN, ALIX KATE. 1980. "Sex and Power: The Sexual Bases of Radical
       Feminism." *Signs: Journal of Women in Culture and Society* 5
       (June):590–604.
Alix Kate Shulman was a member of a consciousness-raising (CR) group in the
early years of the Women's Liberation Movement. In this article, she discusses
how CR provides an information sharing basis for women to talk about their

lives and learn about patterns of sexism in personal relations. Using actual CR experiences, she shows how sexuality and sex relations can be a meaningful topic for a CR session.

166   SOCHEN, JUNE, ed. 1971. *The New Feminism in Twentieth Century America*. Lexington, MA: D.C. Heath.

A collection of articles on the contemporary women's movement. Includes articles by Aileen Hernandez (second national president of the National Organization for Women) "Editorial from NOW's president," and Martha Weimman Lear "The Second Feminist Wave."

167   SPENDER, DALE. 1983. *There's Always Been a Women's Movement this Century*. New York: Pandora Press.

Spender mainly talks about the British women's movement but her ideas are relevant beyond those borders. She shows, through interviews and other forms of data, the continuity between early and late twentieth century feminist thought.

168   STACEY, MARGARET and MARION PRICE. 1980. "Women and Power." *Feminist Review* 5:33–52.

This article argues that women's gains in political power are a result of the spread of a feminist ideology brought about by the women's movement and that these gains have come about because women are now being treated as individuals. While the authors argue for individualism being applied to women in the same way that it has applied to men, they fail to appreciate the potential for individualism to benefit particular women—most likely more privileged women—rather than women as a group.

169   STAGGENBORG, SUZANNE. 1991. *The Pro-Choice Movement: Organization and Activism in the Abortion Conflict*. New York: Oxford.

A well-researched study on the organizational and activist components of the abortion rights movement. Ideology is subsumed in this work since Staggenborg finds the single issue agenda of pro-choice organizations to be a countermovement reaction to a concerted attack on legalized abortion by anti-abortion forces. The history of activism related to reproductive freedom and the linkages between national and grassroots group are included, as well as a focus on activism in Chicago and the state of Illinois.

170   ———. 1989. "Stability and Innovation in the Women's Movement: A Comparison of Two Movement Organizations." *Social Problems* 36:75–92.

Using archival data and interviews of activists, the author discusses the effects of organizational structure and ideology on the Chicago Women's Liberation Union (CWLU) and the Chicago chapter of the National Organization for Women (NOW). Staggenborg finds the radical feminist ideology and decentralized structure of the Union led to innovative tactics, but failed to provide the necessary ingredients for organizational maintenance. The formalized structure of Chicago NOW led to continuity of the organization, but often meant a narrower range of tactics.

171   STOLOFF, CAROLYN. 1973. "Who Joins Women's Liberation?" *Psychiatry* 36:325–340.
Looking at female graduate students at the University of Michigan, Stoloff compares those who are involved with the women's movement and those who are not. She finds feminist activists are more likely to come from middle or upper middle-class urban families with a low emphasis on religion. Parents were more likely to be college educated and professionals, and to have participated in previous social movements, particularly the civil rights movement and/or peace movement.

172   TAX, MEREDITH. 1988. "The Sound of One Hand Clapping: Women's Liberation and the Left." *Dissent* 35:457–462.
Tax talks about her introduction twenty years ago to the Women's Liberation Movement, first through Cell 16, a radical feminist cadre group led by Roxanne Dunbar, and later in Bread & Roses, a socialist oriented group she helped organize. The ideology, structure, accomplishments, failures, joys, problems, and heartaches of feminist activism in the small group sector of the contemporary women's movement are well documented here. Also the sexism in male dominated leftist groups is thoroughly covered. This is a personal reflection that resonates with an honest presentation of the experience of being a feminist activist in those early heady years.

173   WANDERSEE, WINIFRED D. 1988. *American Women in the 1970s: On the Move*. Boston: Twayne Publishers.
A chronological history of the changing status of women in America. All of the 1970s major developments within the women's movement are covered, including the ERA campaign, the emergence of NOW as a major political force, the growth of the women's culture, the IWY, and the spread of a feminist consciousness. Wandersee also provides an analysis of the impact of the women's movement on American life during this decade.

174   WILLIS, ELLEN. 1981. *Beginning to See the Light: Pieces of a Decade*. New York: Wideview Books.
Willis is a journalist who publishes widely on issues related to feminism. In this collection, she has chosen pieces first published in the *Village Voice* and *The New York Times*. Two topics are discussed more than others: abortion rights and pornography. Willis takes the position that the women's movement makes a mistake by placing too much emphasis on pornography because it positions feminists too closely to the fundamentalism of family politics propagated by the New Religious Right.

175   ZAMITI-HORCHANI, MALIKA. 1983. "Review Symposium: Feminist in Politics." *Social Science Quarterly* 64:880–894.

This is a report on a symposium that was held on the topic of Alice Rossi's book *Feminist in Politics: A Panel Analysis of the First National Women's Conference* (1982). This conference, part of the International Women's Year (IWY), was held in November 1977 in Houston, Texas. Although there were confrontations between right wing and feminist women, both in the delegate selection process and the introduction of resolutions at the conference, a feminist agenda was adopted. Rossi used survey research to identify attributes of the participants, and much of her book is a report on those findings.

Equal Rights Amendment

176   ARRINGTON, THEODORE S. AND PATRICIA A. Kyle. 1978. "Equal Rights Amendment Activists in North Carolina." *Signs: Journal of Women in Culture and Society* 3:666–680.
In a survey of women and men activists for and against the Equal Rights Amendment, these researchers found that anti-ERA activists were much more likely to be religious fundamentalists. The results of this survey also showed that anti-ERA women were more strongly connected to fundamentalism in their religious beliefs than were the anti-ERA men activists.

177   BECKER, SUSAN D. 1981. *The Origins of the Equal Rights Movement: American Feminism Between the Wars*. Westport, CT: Greenwood Press.
This book documents the origins of the Equal Rights Movement and the women's movement between the two world wars. Most books on the ERA only discuss the contemporary period, leaving out the 50-year period preceding congressional passage. The ERA was written by Alice Paul and introduced into Congress in 1923 and every year after that. For most of the time after its introduction until the rise of the contemporary movement, the National Woman's Party was the only group supporting it. Becker brings back an important history of the women's movement, including the protective labor arguments against ERA.

178   BERRY, MARY FRANCES. 1986. *Why ERA Failed: Politics, Women's Rights, and the Amending Process of the Constitution*. Bloomington: Indiana University Press.
Berry, a former member of the U.S. Commission on Civil Rights, analyses the failure of the Equal Rights Amendment within an ideological, political, and constitutional framework. Much can be learned about the U.S. political process by reading this book. Berry does a good job of tracing the relationship between the amending process and the women's rights movement.

179   BOLES, JANET K. 1980. "Feminists as Agents of Social Change: Lobbying for the Equal Rights Amendment." *Peace and Change* 6:1–19.
An article that looks at how efforts to achieve the Equal Rights Amendment go beyond that particular issue. Boles shows how the campaign itself drew in

more activists and created a feminist consciousness about unquestioned gender issues throughout the social structure.

180   ———. 1979. *The Politics of the Equal Rights Amendment*. New York: Longman.
A thorough study of the progress of the ERA campaign for state ratification. Boles explains how the political climate in 1972 worked well in getting ERA off to a good start but then, as social and economic changes took hold, it stalled by the mid-1970s in the state legislatures. The author provides an interesting analysis of feminist organizing in the form of a case study approach to states that ratified early, late, or not at all.

181   BROWN, BARBARA A. and ANN E. FREEDMAN. 1977. *Women's Rights and Law: The Impact of the ERA on State Laws*. New York: Praeger Books.
A report of a study on the ways the Equal Rights Amendment can be expected to effect state law.

182   BUTLER, MATILDA and WILLIAM PAISLEY. 1978. "Equal Rights Coverage in Magazines, Summer 1976." *Journalism Quarterly* 55 (March):157–160.
Twenty-eight magazines for women were analyzed to reveal the level of ERA coverage they contained. Both pro and anti articles were counted and compared.

183   COTT, NANCY F. 1990. "Historical Perspectives: The Equal Rights Amendment Conflict in the 1920s." Pp. 44–59 in *Conflicts in Feminism*, edited by Marianne Hirsch and Evelyn Fox Keller. New York: Routledge.
In this article Cott outlines the difference between the NWP's single issue women's rights approach to the ERA and opposing women's organizations which took a multi-alliance women's protection approach. The underlying conflict was the sameness/difference view of women vis-à-vis men. The author points out the legacy of this controversy which continues to create divisions among women into the present. Cott discusses the historical development of the relations between opposing women's groups, including those of the National Woman's Party, the National American Woman Suffrage Association, League of Women Voters, National Women's Trade Union League, Women's Christian Temperance Union, and the General Federation of Women's Clubs.

184   DEUTCHMAN, IVA E. and SANDRA PRINCE-EMBURY. 1982. "Political Ideology of Pro and Anti-ERA Women." *Women and Politics* 2 (March):39–55.
Using survey material on a small sample, Deutchman and Prince-Embury draw out differences on political orientation, ideology, religion, and attitudes among pro and anti-ERA women.

185   EISENSTEIN, ZILLAH. 1982. "Some Thoughts on the Patriarchal State and the Defeat of the ERA." *Journal of Sociology and Social Welfare* 9 (Sept.):388–390.
Eisenstein argues that the defeat of ERA was an attempt to destroy the

women's movement. The author feels the state has a fear of a strong well organized women's movement and the ERA campaigns revealed the radical potential for a mass movement.

186   FREEMAN, JO. 1986. "The Quest for Equality: The ERA vs. Other Means."
      Pp. 46–78 in *Ethnicity and Women*, edited by Winston A. Van Horne.
      Milwaukee: University of Wisconsin System.
A review of the history of the ERA looking at who the participants in this struggle have been and why they took such divergent positions. Possible alternative
routes for improving the position of women in the social structure are discussed with an emphasis on examining how each strategy could differentially
affect particular racial or ethnic groups. Freeman sees the ERA as symbolically
important in ways other options lack because raising the status of women via
governmental approval creates expectations going beyond the victory of pass-
ing a constitutional amendment.

187   FRY, AMELIA R. 1983. "Alice Paul and the ERA." *OAH Newsletter* 11:13–16.
Looks at Alice Paul's work in attempting to achieve passage of the Equal Rights
Amendment and her other efforts on behalf of women's equality.

188   GEIDEL, PETER. 1980. "The National Woman's Party and the Origins of
      the Equal Rights Amendment, 1920–1923." *History* 42:557–582.
An examination of the efforts by the National Woman's Party to gain support
for the ERA. The conflict between NWP members and social feminist groups
concerned about protective labor legislation is highlighted.

189   GILL, SANDRA K. 1985, October. "Attitudes toward the Equal Rights
      Amendment: Influence of Class and Status." *Sociological Perspectives*
      28:441–462.
Support for the Equal Rights Amendment is explained through a variety of theoretical perspectives including functionalism, Marxism, and feminism.

190   GINSBURG, RUTH BADER. 1973. "The Need for the Equal Rights
      Amendment." *American Bar Association Journal* 59:1013–1019.
Long before she was appointed to the Supreme Court and shortly after
Congress passed the Equal Rights Amendment, Ruth Bader Ginsburg argued
for ratification. She took the position that without the Amendment, it was
unlikely that there would be an overhaul of laws that differentiate on the basis
of sex.

191   HANDBERG, ROGER and WANDA LOWERY. 1980. "Women State
      Legislators and Support for the Equal Rights Amendment." *The Social
      Science Journal* 17 (Jan.):65–71.
Report of a survey done in 1977 of 418 U.S. women legislators on their position on the Equal Rights Amendment. Highest support was found by party affiliation with Democrats scoring higher than Republicans; significance was also
found by education level with higher education showing higher ERA support.
No correlation with support for ERA was found by age, region, or occupation.

192   HARRISON, CYNTHIA E. 1980. "A New Frontier for Women: The Public
        Policy of the Kennedy Administration." *The Journal of American
        History* 67 (Dec.):630–646.
An examination of the debate over the Equal Rights Amendment within the
Commission on the Status of Women that John F. Kennedy established early in
his term. Harrison finds that the ERA was rejected because the majority of
members were concerned about maintaining protective labor laws.

193   HOFF-WILSON, JOAN, ed. 1986. *Rights of Passage: The Past and Future of
        the ERA*. Bloomington: Indiana University Press.
Hoff-Wilson dedicates this book to Alice Paul, author of the Equal Rights
Amendment. Contributors' essays fall into three sections of the book: 1)
Origins and Early Disagreements over the ERA, with articles, "Alice Paul and the
ERA" by Amelia Fry, and "Why Were Most Politically Active Women Opposed to
the ERA in the 1920s?" by Kathryn Kish Sklar; 2) Reasons for the Defeat of the
ERA, with articles on cultural politics, direct action, communication; and 3)
Significance of the Defeat of ERA, with articles on the legal impacts and
renewed hope.

194   LANGER, ELINOR. 1976. "Why Big Business is Trying to Defeat the ERA."
        Ms. Magazine 4 (May):11.
An explanation of why business would be opposed to the Equal Rights
Amendment. Langer shows how the business community perceives the idea of
equality in the work place and the costs it would entail to pay and promote
women on the same basis as men.

195   LANGLOIS, KAREN. 1982. "An Interview with Sonia Johnson." *Feminist
        Studies* 8, 1 (Spring).
An interview with the leader of the fast in Springfield, Illinois for the ERA in the
spring of 1982. Johnson was also a founder of Mormons for ERA, a Group of
Women, and a primary initiator of direct action civil disobedience in the early
1980s women's movement.

196   MANSBRIDGE, JANE J. 1986. *Why We Lost the ERA*. Chicago: University of
        Chicago Press.
An empirical study on gender politics and social movements focused on the
failure of the women's movement to get the Equal Rights Amendment ratified before the end of the 1982 deadline. Although she only concentrates on
the efforts to pass ERA from the 1970s on, Mansbridge argues that the issues
involved in passage changed over time. But, the major focus of her study are
the mistakes feminist activists made. In presenting her explanation for the
failure of passage in this way, she downplays the forces of the opposition,
the entrenched gender structure of the country, and the rise of conservative
politics that dramatically increased during the latter part of the ERA campaign.

197 MARSHALL, SUSAN E. 1990. "Equity Issues and Black-White Differences in Women's ERA Support." *Social Science Quarterly* 71:299–314.

In looking at attitudes toward women's equality, racial equality, and financial well-being, this research investigates why black women support ERA to a greater extent than white women. Marshall finds that although ERA support is similar for women of both races, the disadvantage of being both black and female results in stronger support for equality issues for black women in general and black feminists in particular.

198 MATHEWS, G. DONALD and JANE SHERRON DE HART. 1990. *Sex, Gender, and the Politics of ERA: A State and the Nation*. New York: Oxford University Press.

Using interview material, participant observation, and written sources, Mathews and De Hart chart the course of the ERA ratification campaign in North Carolina. The intense debate and ideological positions that defined the pro-ERA and anti-ERA forces are illuminated in this interesting narrative. In addition to the case study approach, the authors analyze gender politics in general through their discussion of the New Right's incorporation of "cultural fundamentalism" and the National Organization for Women's priority strategy of electoral politics. This work provides primary source materials on the history of the women's movement as well as a model of integrating the structural and ideological contributions to mobilization efforts.

199 MCGLEN, NANCY E. and KAREN O'CONNOR. 1988. "Toward a Theoretical Model of Counter Movements and Constitutional Change: A Case Study of the ERA." *Women & Politics* 8:45–71.

An examination of the growth of anti-ERA groups. The authors use a resource mobilization framework to analyze motivations to oppose passage of the Equal Rights Amendment to the U.S. Constitution.

200 MILLER, MARGARET I. and HELENE LINKER. 1974. "Equal Rights Amendment Campaigns in California and Utah." *Sociology* 11:40–53.

A comparison between the ERA drives in the states of California and Utah. The ERA passed in California, but in Utah proponents were unprepared for the onslaught of HOTDOG (Humanitarians Opposed to the Degradation of Our Girls) which was successful in defeating the amendment. The political climates of the two states also contributed to the outcomes of these campaigns.

201 MLOTT, SYLVESTER, RITA T. BOSTICK, and FRANK T. LIRA. 1977. "Dogmatism and Locus of Control in Young Women Who Support, Oppose or Voice no Opinion on the Equal Rights Amendment." *Journal of Clinical Psychology* 33 (July):746–748.

The results of this study show that young women who do not support the Equal Rights Amendment scored higher on indicators for behavior characteristics which were more conforming, fearful, inflexible, and authoritarian than their counterparts who support ERA.

202 MUELLER, CAROL and THOMAS DIMIERI. 1982. "The Structure of Belief Systems Among Contending ERA Activists." *Social Forces* 60 (March):657–675.
A comparative study on the structure of belief systems on feminist issues between those who are activists in support of the Equal Rights Amendment and those who are activist against it. ERA proponents revealed greater constraint, consensus, and position extremity.

203 PRINCE-EMBURY, SANDRA and IVA E. DEUTCHMAN. 1981. "Identity Status in Politically Active Pro and Anti ERA." *The Journal of Mind and Behavior* 2:309–321.
Based on interviews with supporters and opponents of ERA, the authors examine identity status as a factor in subjects' stance. Prince-Embury and Deutchman define identity status based on level of adherence to parental attitudes and to degree of absoluteness in thinking.

204 SLAVIN, SARAH. 1982. "The Equal Rights Amendment: The Politics and Process of Ratification of the Twenty-Seventh Amendment to the U.S. Constitution." *Women & Politics* 2, 1–2 (Spring/Summer).
A two-volume special symposium issue of this journal with all articles featuring some aspect of the Equal Rights Amendment. When this issue came out, the ERA had failed (deadline June 30, 1982). After ten years of an intense struggle for ratification, there was much to be said about that campaign.

205 WHITE, KENDALL O. 1985. "A Feminist Challenge: Mormons for ERA as an Internal Social Movement." *Journal of Ethnic Studies* 13 (March):29–50.
Mormons for ERA (MERA) is examined using a resource mobilization framework. Considerations this study investigated were the relationship of MERA to the Mormon Church; the organizational structure of MERA; MERA's relationship with other feminist groups; strategies and tactics; and the reaction to the formation of this group by the Mormon Church.

Reproductive Freedom

206 ALAN GUTTMACHER INSTITUTE. (quarterly). *Family* Planning Perspectives. *New York: The Alan Guttmacher Institute.*
This is the most widely referenced source for analysis, data collection, policy, and legal aspects of contraception and abortion. *Family Planning Perspectives* details information on the United States and other countries related to reproductive issues. Most of the articles are based on empirical research.

207 DAVIS, SUSAN E. 1988. *Women Under Attack: Victories, Backlash, and the Fight for Reproductive Freedom*. Boston: South End Press.
Sponsored by The Committee for Abortion Rights and Against Sterilization Abuse, this edited volume covers the range of issues raised by reproductive

rights activists who have been involved with this movement over the last two decades.

208 DILORIO, JUDITH and MICHAEL R. NUSBAUMER. 1993. "Securing Our Sanity: Anger Management Among Abortion Escorts." *Journal of Contemporary Ethnography* 21:411–438.

The experiences of abortion clinic escorts are described and the process of managing their anger is analyzed in this paper. Feminist organizations practice emotional monitoring, debriefing, and collective joking in order to manage emotionally negative feelings. These strategies establish normative boundaries for anger expression and reveal how feeling and cognition relate to ideology and social action. The authors find that this emotional work forges social bonds, cohesion, and a sense of community among activists.

209 FAUX, MARIAN. 1988. *Roe v. Wade: The Untold Story of the Landmark Supreme Court Decision that Made Abortion Legal*. New York: Macmillan.

This is a good source book for those who are interested in knowing the nitty gritty details of the historic abortion legality case of 1973. Included are minute accounts of client meetings, organizational planning by pro choice groups, legal strategies, litigation discussions, courtroom drama, and insider views of the shaping of this case. Reading the book gives a feeling of being a participant in the deliberation process, as well as the negotiations that went on among the Justices that eventually led to a pro-choice outcome. Interview material and much additional source material results in a thoroughly documented account of a landmark victory for the women's movement.

210 FERRARO, BARBARA and PATRICIA HUSSEY with JANE O'REILLY. 1990. *No Turning Back: Two Nuns' Battle with the Vatican over Women's Right to Choose*. New York: Poseidon Press.

During the 1984 presidential race when vice-presidential candidate Geraldine Ferraro was attacked for being a pro-choice Catholic, a group letter signed by twenty-four nuns, six priests, and sixty-nine lay people was printed in the New York Times. The letter stated that a diversity of opinions regarding abortion exists among committed Catholics. Of those who signed, nuns Barbara Ferraro and Patricia Hussey were the last to refuse the retraction the Catholic Church demanded. Eventually this standoff led to their decision to leave their religious community. This book chronicles those events, but more than anything it shows the growing tensions feminist ideas have raised within the Catholic Church since the rise of the contemporary women's movement.

211 FREID, MARILYN GERBER, ed. 1990. *From Abortion to Reproductive Freedom: Transforming a Movement*. Boston: South End Press.

An anthology containing essays by activists and researchers involved in birth control, abortion, and reproductive freedom. A focus of the papers is the process of broadening the definition of reproductive health. This collection includes essays on defining and redefining issues, discussions of various perspectives, social change effects, and the activities of the people involved at various stages of social activism for women's control over their reproductive lives.

212   GINSBURG, FAYE D. 1989. *Contested Lives: The Abortion Debate in an American Community*. Berkeley: University of California Press.

Ethnographic study of an abortion clinic in Fargo, North Dakota since its opening in 1987. The pro-choice and anti-abortion activists' positions reveal the tension between two different views of women, also found in lifestyle, race, class, ethnic, and generational differences. In an unusual methodological application, Ginsburg uses "procreational stories" as a way of explaining differences between these two groups of women activists. A theme of pro-choice supporters was the feeling of confinement after having children; whereas, antiabortion activists spoke of the release of leaving the workplace to have children. Both interpretations are shown to be representative of the anxieties experienced by women's family/work roles today.

213   HARRISON, BEVERLY WILDUNG. 1983. *Our Right to Choose: Toward a New Ethic of Abortion*. Boston: Beacon Press.

Religious objections and historical Christian teachings about abortion are critically examined in this book. The author then develops a set of conditions that would be necessary to allow an ethic of choice. In her conclusion, she finds that allowing fetal life to be the determining factor in this moral debate is in actuality a sexist position. Rather, Harrison argues for non-coercive childbearing as the foundation for social good in reproductive decision making.

214   JOFFE, CAROLE. 1986. *The Regulation of Sexuality: Experiences of Family Planning Workers*. Philadelphia, PA: Temple University Press.

Joffe reports on her field work at a family planning clinic. She focuses on the workers and the effects of feeling under siege from abortion opponents. Continuing to be involved in reproductive choice, given the attacks upon them and their work, results in these workers being more than employees. They are also involved in feminist activism, whether they call themselves feminist or not. Not all family planning clinics are feminist, but because the anti-abortion movement is opposed to the clinics—both contraception and abortion—the "pro-family" movement has placed clinic workers in a defensive position and caused them to be allied with the pro-choice forces. Joffe provides a history and analysis to the complexity of reproductive politics and the workplace experience surrounding the provision of services embedded in controversy and conflict.

215   JONES, ELISE F. 1989. *Pregnancy, Contraception, and Family Planning Services in Industrialized Countries: A Study of the Alan Guttmacher Institute*. New Haven, CT: Yale University Press.

The Alan Guttmacher Institute is the premier research organization in the United States for gathering data on reproductive technology and family planning decisions. This book is based on a study which sought to discover why U.S. rates of abortion and unplanned pregnancies are higher than they are in other Western industrialized countries. The results focus on the way services are provided (or not provided). Other explanations, such as the anti-abortion movement, the higher gap between the haves and have nots, the suppression of sex education, and the lack of advertising for birth control methods are not well developed in this work.

216   KOLBERT, KATHRYN. 1989. "Webster v. Reproductive Health Services: Reproductive Freedom Hanging by a Thread." *Women's Rights Law Reporter* 11:153–162.

In this article Kathryn Kolbert, who later argued the pro-choice position in Casey v. Planned Parenthood of Southeastern Pennsylvania, discusses the 1979 Supreme Court case of Webster v. Reproductive Health Services. In Webster, the state of Missouri attempted to restrict abortion availability through the use of state regulation. Webster was also an attempt to reverse Roe v. Wade, the 1973 Supreme Court case which established the legality of abortion. Thirty-two pro-choice briefs submitted in the Webster case are printed in this issue of the Women's Rights Law Reporter.

217   LADER, LAWRENCE. 1973. *Abortion II: Making the Revolution*. Boston: Beacon Press.

Lader describes how he became involved in the abortion movement after the publication of his book *Abortion* in 1966. He wrote that book in response to learning about the hardships of bearing unwanted children through his readings of the life of Margaret Sanger. After his book was published, women began contacting him for referrals. Eventually, assisting women in locating services led to a full time commitment which lasted until the women's movement's efforts to legalize abortion were successful in the Supreme Court's 1973 Roe v. Wade decision.

218   LUKER, KRISTIN. 1984. *Abortion and the Politics of Motherhood*. Berkeley: University of California Press.

This book is based on research Luker did in California on pro and anti-abortion rights activists. Using literature and interviews of more than 200 people on both sides of the issue, Luker found that the base of the opposing views were found in the different social circumstances of the activists. The social worlds of these activists fit with their position and views of abortion. Pro-life activists (anti-abortion) were more likely to be full-time homemakers, be highly religious, have more children, less family income, and less education than abortion rights activists. Pro-choice activists were more likely to be never married or divorced, and to have fewer or no children.

219   MILLER, PATRICIA G. 1993. *The Worst of Times: Illegal Abortion—Survivors, Practitioners, Coroners, Cops, and Children of Women Who Died Talk About Its Horrors*. New York: HarperCollins.

Reading this book helps explain why the contemporary women's movement took up the issue of legal abortion as one of its primary early goals. Miller interviewed people who had received or performed illegal abortions before 1973 and offers an oral history of the horrors of the pre-Roe era. The collection of voices is inclusive in representation of race, religion, class, and age. The stories go back as far as the 1920s through the 1960s. Two appendices include a history of abortion law and a review of the incidence and methods of illegal abortion.

220 O'BRIEN, MARY. 1981. *The Politics of Reproduction*. Boston: Routledge and Kegan Paul.

This is a thorough review on the development of feminist thought on reproduction. Well versed in political theory, O'Brien also knows about gender differentiated roles in reproduction from her years of being a midwife. She argues that women and men have a different consciousness toward reproduction based on their dissimilar experiences in the reproductive process. Yet, most of philosophy and law has come from men and, thus, reflects male consciousness. She outlines the need for a centrality of reproductive thought from a feminist materialist perspective. Providing an analytical base for her views she draws on the "male-stream thought" of Plato, Hegel, Marx, and Freud. Then she brings in the work of Millett, Firestone, and Rowbotham to demonstrate gender differences in women's reproductive thinking. Her thesis builds on feminist insights even as she acknowledges the failings of some feminist writing too.

221 OVERALL, CHRISTINE. 1987. *Ethics and Human Reproduction: A Feminist Analysis*. Winchester, MA: Pandora Press.

A comparison survey of three views on reproductive issues concerned with such topics as abortion, surrogate mothers, and birth control. The three views are feminist, non-feminist, and anti-feminist.

222 PETCHESKY, ROSALIND POLLACK. 1984. *Abortion and Woman's Choice: The State, Sexuality and Reproductive Freedom*. Boston: Northeastern University Press.

Abortion and reproductive freedom are often the subject of feminist discourse, usually in terms of a human rights or privacy issue. In this book, Petchesky's takes a different direction by developing a feminist materialist analysis of abortion. She begins by tracing the history of state regulation of abortion to show the political components of this debate. She then examines abortion practice since the 1970s focusing on differences by race and class. Sexual politics of the 1980s constitutes the subject matter for the third section. Here she shows the ways the Religious Right has exploited the issues of abortion, sex, and the family in order to gain political power.

223 PLUTZER, ERIC and BARBARA RYAN. 1987. "Notifying Husbands About an Abortion: An Empirical Look at Constitutional and Policy Dilemmas." *Sociology and Social Research* 71:183–189.

A report on a research study of married women and abortion. The data gathered for this research came from counselor administered surveys at an abortion clinic. Results showed over 90 percent of married women consult with their husbands about the abortion and the other 10 percent have compelling reasons for not telling. This information is placed within the context of the spousal consent laws that were struck down by the Supreme Court in 1976 and the spousal notification legislation frequently proposed by state legislators (although struck down for the Pennsylvania Abortion Control Act in the early 1990s). Constitutional issues with these policies are examined.

224 ROTHMAN, BARBARA KATZ. 1991. *In Labor: Women and Power in the Birthplace*. New York: W. W. Norton & Co.
Rothman presents a feminist analysis of how women came to lose control of pregnancy and childbirth to a male dominated medical profession. Instead of a "natural" condition, pregnancy became a medical condition requiring technology and experts. Rothman questions what this change has meant for women's identity and autonomy. Topics covered include infertility, pregnancy, childbirth, child care, midwives, and new technologies.

225 ———. 1989. *Recreating Motherhood: Ideology and Technology in a Patriarchal Society*. New York: W. W. Norton & Co.
In this book Rothman provides a feminist analysis of motherhood. The author addresses the social trends of the 1980s which she sees as leading to a recreation of the concept of motherhood and the commodification of children. She looks at new procreative technology, the history of abortion, the reconstruction of abortion, the case of Baby M, and the possibilities for future feminist social policy. Her work represents the application of feminist theory to a particular social issue of relevance for contemporary women's lives.

226 RYAN, BARBARA and ERIC PLUTZER. 1989. "When Married Women Have Abortions: Spousal Notification and Marital Interaction." *Journal of Marriage and the Family* 51:41–50.
Based on research at an abortion clinic, Ryan and Plutzer document the types of marital interaction that take place in making the abortion decision. Although the data show that in almost all cases married women and men come to a mutual agreement, very little discussion or support was offered by husbands beyond agreeing with the decision. Less than 10 percent of the time married women made the decision on their own without telling their husband. When not telling, women gave reasons such as: fear of being forced to go through with the pregnancy; they were separated or the marriage was in trouble; the co-conceiver was not the husband; he would beat her up if he knew; or she was afraid he would be upset and could not handle the strain.

227 TRIBE, LAURENCE H. 1993. *Abortion: The Clash of Absolutes*. New York: W. W. Norton & Co.
This is a revised edition with a new forward and afterword that provides up-to-date analyses on controversial Supreme Court decisions on abortion, including the 1992 case of Planned Parenthood of Southeastern Pennsylvania v. Casey. Tribe is an authority on constitutional law and an expert on the Equal Rights Amendment and the abortion controversy. In this book he examines the history of the abortion debate and offers new approaches to the discourse that

reflect the convictions of activists on both sides of this issue. This work provides a solid background on the controversies surrounding abortion.

Violence Against Women and the Women's Health Movement

228 ACT UP/NY WOMEN and AIDS BOOK GROUP. 1990. *Women, AIDS and Activism*. Boston: South End Press.
Over 40 essays discuss why there is a lack of knowledge and awareness about women and HIV/AIDS. Beyond this overarching theme, articles examine how the social construction of gender promotes a silence surrounding women affected with AIDS, and the social and psychological impact of being HIV positive for socially marginal people such as lesbians, sex workers, and women of color. Also included are the experiences of women AIDS activists and the strategies for change they advocate.

229 ADAMS, DAVID, JAN JACKSON, and MARY LAUBY. 1988. "Family Violence Research: Aid or Obstacle to the Battered Women's Movement." *Response to the Victimization of Women and Children* 11 (Sept.):14–16.
A review of ninety-three papers presented during conferences at the University of New Hampshire which show that abuse of women, although clearly found to be a common occurrence, is still often spoken of in terms of individual or family pathology. The social structural roots of violence against women is typically avoided.

230 BROWNMILLER, SUSAN. 1975. *Against Our Will: Men, Women and Rape*. New York: Simon & Schuster.
This was a groundbreaking book when it was published as it brought the discussion of rape into the open. Brownmiller changed the terms of rape when she defined it as an act of power and dominance of men over women, rather than a sexual act. In one chapter of the book she also opened the debate among feminists on the issue of pornography. The author called on feminists to develop a new approach to this issue as she argued against the defense of censorship, citing the propaganda effects pornography perpetuates in overall violence against women in society. This work places radical feminism in opposition to socialism's primacy of class analysis and black activists' views of the centrality of race.

231 BUSH, DIANE MITSCH. 1992. "Women's Movements and State Policy Reform Aimed at Domestic Violence Against Women: A Comparison of the Consequences of Movement Mobilization in the United States and India." *Gender & Society* 6:587–608.
This article compares the Battered Women's Movement in the United States with the Anti-Dowry-Violence Movement in India. In both movements violence against women is redefined from a private family concern to a public issue call-

ing for judiciary policy reform. However, Bush argues that the result of this demand has been a focus on protection rather than empowerment because it fails to challenge the overall sex/gender system of the state which perpetuates women's vulnerability to dependency and abuse.

232   DAVIS, NANETTE J. 1988. "Battered Women: Implications for Social Control." *Contemporary Crisis* 12 (Dec.):345–372.
The author of this article examines three periods of policy/program initiatives related to woman battering. In different ways, each period is connected to issues of social control related to changes in ideology and practice over time. The first phase is defined as a period when women were seen as dependent on men; the second stage, after the rise of the contemporary women's movement, led to the emergence of a battered women's movement and the focus on shelters and protective legislation; and phase three represents the involvement of the state through funding and professionalization of shelter services. The question of how well battered women are being served under state supervision, which at times is anti-feminist, is discussed.

233   DONEGAN, JANE B. 1978. *Women and Men Midwives: Medicine, Morality and Misogyny in Early America*. Westport, CT: Greenwood Press.
An interesting analysis of the connection between the rise of feminism and the woman's movement in the nineteenth century with the usurpation of women's midwifery role by men.

234   EHRENREICH, BARBARA and DEIDRE ENGLISH. 1973. *Witches, Midwives and Nurses: A History of Women Healers*. Old Westbury, NY: Feminist Press.
Ehrenreich and English present a positive view of women as witches and healers across time and cultures. Midwifery and nursing have long been done by women, and historically were seen as work that was necessary, valued, and highly respected. The authors point out that witches were often viewed with the same level of esteem (before the witch hunts), as well as being viewed as powerful women who could control their own destiny.

235   HAMMER, JALNA and MARY MAYNARD, eds. 1987. *Women, Violence and Social Control: Essays in Social Theory*. Atlantic Highlands, NJ: Humanities Press.
A good review of the literature which includes detailed accounts of past feminist research on violence against women. New questions and theoretical implications are raised and discussed.

236   KHOSLA, PUNAM, ed. 1992. *Safety in Numbers: Resisting Men's Violence Against Women and Girls*. Ann Arbor: The University of Michigan Press.
An anthology of writings from workers in the field who are organizing against male violence towards women. Insights from their experiences provide challenging thoughts on how to address male violence in the home, at work, and

on the streets. Documentation of the work being done in shelters and other service providers is insightful. Individual articles discuss ways of working with the state, what the meaning of the men's movement is, and the importance of coalition work with other feminist groups.

237　KLEIN, DORIE. 1981. "Violence Against Women: Some Considerations Regarding Its Causes and Its Elimination." *Crime and Delinquency* 27 (Jan.):64–80.

The connection between gender domination and violence against women is strongly made in this article. Crimes against women that are considered in this work are restrictions on birth control and abortion, rape, wife battering, and witch hunting.

238　MATTHEWS, NANCY A. 1994. *Confronting Rape: The Feminist Anti-Rape Movement and the State*. New York: Routledge.

Matthews documents twenty years of anti-rape activism, from the grass roots beginnings to the professionalization of rape crisis centers. In studying six rape crisis centers, Matthews looks at how state funding has changed rape crisis work. She finds the therapeutic component of the anti-rape movement has been emphasized and the feminist challenge to gender relations has declined.

239　MORGEN, SANDRA. 1986. "The Dynamics of Cooptation in a Feminist Health Clinic." *Social Science and Medicine* 23:201–210.

The focus of this article is the ways the state shapes the direction of grassroots organizing. Morgen's data consists of over two years of participant observation at a feminist health clinic. Her interest is on the changes that occurred after State funding became part of the clinic's operation. Findings show state funding resulted in less collective decision making, almost a sole emphasis on service delivery, elimination of other activities, and a decrease in political autonomy. Morgen uses Gramsci's theory of the influence of dominant ideology from powerful forces (like the state) on dependent peoples to explain these results.

240　MURRAY, SUSAN B. 1988. "The Unhappy Marriage of Theory and Practice: An Analysis of a Battered Women's Shelter." *NWSA Journal: A Publication of The National Women's Studies Association* 1:75–92.

This article provides a brief review of the history of the battered women's movement and then examines one shelter organization in detail. The author discusses the contradictions that have emerged between feminist ideology and practice. Specific problems include the transformation from a feminist self-help focus to professional service, the movement from efforts to eliminate male violence through structural change to fixing women, the call for women's empowerment through self-sufficiency without providing a means to alleviate financial need, a professed symmetry in power relations within an organizational structure of expert and client, and the class/racial differences that exist between residents and staff.

241 SCHECHTER, SUSAN. 1982. *Women and Male Violence: The Visions and Struggles of the Battered Women's Movement*. Boston: South End Press. This is a history and documentation of the battered women's movement. Schechter does a good job of showing the successes (growth of women's shelters) and the troubles (internal struggles, lack of funding), and some of the difficulties of working with the government and criminal justice system. The transformation of shelters from voluntary efforts on the part of radical feminists to salaried positions by career professionals has a mixed message in it. Schechter makes the case for placing violence against women within a socialist feminist perspective in which the dictates of capitalism are seen as the underlying cause of male to female violence. She argues for the battered women's movement to be more than a service agency and to become a political actor in the movement for fundamental change in American society.

242 SWITZER, M'LISS and KATHERINE HALE. 1987. *Called to Account: The Story of One Family's Struggle to Say No to Abuse*. Seattle, WA: Seal Press.
This is an account of one woman's life with the man who repeatedly beat her. In telling her story she hopes to show the importance and necessity of domestic abuse programs such as the one she turned to in Minnesota. This is an emotional book, but it is one that eventually tells the story of a successful escape from a battering relationship.

243 THE BOSTON WOMEN'S HEALTH BOOK COLLECTIVE. 1992. *The New Our Bodies Ourselves: A Book By and For Women, Third Edition*. New York: Simon and Schuster.
Since the first edition of this book in 1973, *Our Bodies, Our Selves* has become a resource for the women's health movement. The first edition was less than 300 pages and the current edition is over 700 pages long. This version is called an updated edition for the 1990s and provides expanded references to new products, problems, and choices women face, such as RU-486, breast implants, Norplant, AIDS, chronic fatigue syndrome, and mastectomies. Issues are covered from a feminist perspective and there are many voices presented, including strong and vulnerable women. From the first printing, an aim of this book has been to contribute to the women's movement by providing information on how women can gain control of their bodies.

244 WHARTON, CAROL S. 1987. "Establishing Shelters for Battered Women: Local Manifestations of a Social Movement." *Qualitative Sociology* 10 (June):146–163.
Wharton interviewed activists in the battered women's movement who were involved in shelters at various stages of development. She was interested in uncovering the ways a decentralized movement operated at the local level. She found that groups which organized on the basis of local resources accepted differences, took into consideration regional conditions, and allowed for new innovations to be explored.

Peace, Ecofeminism, and Non-Violent Activism

245 ADDAMS, JANE. 1983. *Peace and Bread in Time of War*. Silver Spring, MD: National Association of Social Workers.
Writing about peace efforts during World War I (1914–1918) and after, Addams provides insider information on the forming of the Woman's Peace Party and, later, the Women's International League for Peace and Freedom. This edition is a reprint of an original Macmillan publication in 1922.

246 ADDAMS, JANE with EMILY G. BALCH and ALICE HAMILTON. 1915. *Women at the Hague: The International Congress of Women and Its Results by Three Delegates to the Congress from the United States*. New York: Macmillan Co.
The title tells the reader that this book is about the remembrances of what took place at the first meeting of the International Congress of Women by three American peace activists. These entries serve as primary data for those interested in peace studies, particularly women's early efforts, as well as the founding of the Women's International League for Peace and Freedom.

247 ALONSO, HARRIET HYMAN. 1993. *Peace as a Women's Issue: A History of the U.S. Movement for World Peace and Women's Rights*. Syracuse, NY: Syracuse University Press.
Syracuse University Press has put out a series on peace and conflict resolution and this book constitutes an important part of that series. It is well researched and provides a comprehensive view of the contributions American women have made to peace efforts. The gender connections to war and peace and the implications for women's rights are included in this work.

248 ———. 1989. *The Women's Peace Union and the Outlawry of War, 1921–1942*. Nashville: University of Tennessee.
After the attainment of suffrage, many suffragists turned their attention to world peace. The Women's Peace Union formed immediately after World War I and worked for the next twenty years for a constitutional amendment to outlaw war. Alonso documents the activities, feminist and pacifist ideologies, and organizational structure of this group. In the last part of the book she connects the Women's Peace Union with contemporary women's peace groups such as the Seneca Women's Peace Encampment.

249 BROCK-UTNE, BIRGIT. 1985. *Educating for Peace: A Feminist Perspective*. New York: Pergamon Press.
A history and documentation of women's peace activities. The role women have played in peace education is emphasized. The author is strongly opposed to women serving in the military and does not see such service as an equal rights issue. The connections between war, the military, and patriarchy are made, but theory is given slight attention in this work.

250   CALDECOTT, LEONIE and STEPHANIE LELAND, eds. 1983. *Reclaim the Earth: Women Speak Out for Life on Earth*. London: The Women's Press.

An anthology from the ecofeminist branch of the women's movement. Included are poems, interviews, and essays representing activists and writers from many countries who are involved in peace and environmental issues. Topics they cover are wide ranging, such as, anti-nuclear weapons, population, childbirth, the environment, health, food, sanitation, and urban problems. Primarily the foundation of their concerns are the need to recognize the inter-relationship between human society and the earth's environment. Examples of selections are: "Feminism and Ecology: Theoretical Connections," by Stephanie Leland; "Alternative Technology: A Feminist Technology?," by Chris Thomas; and "Saving Trees, Saving Lives: Third World Women and the Issue of Survival" by Anita Anand.

251   CATALDO, MIMA, RUTH PUTTER, BRYNA FIRESIDE, and ELAINE LYTEL. 1987. *The Women's Encampment for a Future of Peace and Justice: Images and Writings*. Philadelphia: Temple University Press.

The Peace Encampment in Romulus, New York, the subject of this book, was a replication of the Greenham Commons encampment in England. In this case, women organized the camp to provide a base for protesting the deployment of missiles from the nearby Seneca Army Depot. The book contains over 100 photographs, poems, and diaries of the encampment, the origin of the idea and planning for the camp, and the experiences of many of the women who took part in direct action protest during the summer of 1983.

252   COLLARD, ANDREE and JOYCE CONTRUCCI. 1989. *Rape of the Wild: Man's Violence Against Animals and the Earth*. Bloomington: Indiana University Press.

Utilizing an ecofeminist position, the authors present documentation of the misuse of the environment and the need for a feminist ecological revolution. The use of the term man in the title is not a "generic he" mistake.

253   COONEY, ROBERT and HELEN MICHALOWSKI. 1977. *The Power of the People: Active Nonviolence in the United States*. Culver City, CA: The Peace Press.

A visual history on the practice of nonviolence in the United States. The role nonviolent struggles played in connecting the major social movements of the twentieth century is documented in this excellent historical and pictorial record. Included are: woman's suffrage, the labor movement, the anti-war movement, the civil rights movement, United Farm Workers Union, the peace movement, ecological struggles, and a history of the roots of American non-violence from 1650 to 1915.

254   DEMING, BARBARA. 1974. *We Cannot Live Without Our Lives*. New York: Grossman Publishers.

Moving prose and down-to-earth talking from Barbara Deming on her philosophy of life and love of peace. Deming, who died of cancer, was a much loved member of the pacifist feminist community. Her writing is emotional and strong.

255   FOSTER, CATHERINE. 1989. *Women for All Seasons: The Story of the Women's International League for Peace and Freedom*. Athens: University of Georgia Press.
This work provides a history of the founding of the Women's International League for Peace and Freedom (WILPF) in 1915 to its current activities. Through the use of interviews of members such as Mildred Scott Olmsted, a Quaker in Philadelphia where the headquarters of WILPF are housed, and Angela Gethi, a member who formed a chapter in her own country of Kenya during the 1980s, the author provides a view of the goals and membership base of this important women's organization.

256   HARFORD, BARBARA and SARAH HOPKINS, eds. 1984. *Greenham Common: Women at the Wire*. London: The Women's Press.
In 1981 women in Greenham Common, England set up a peace camp to protest the U.S. missile base there. Their actions galvanized feminist women from distant parts of England and other countries to become activists for disarmament. An important outcome of this camp for the U.S. was the inspiration it provided for the establishment of the 1983 Seneca Peace Encampment in upstate New York. In this book Harford and Hopkins bring the voices of women who participated in the encampment from 1981 to 1984 to the printed page as they explain their feminist philosophy, their commitment to peace activism, and their experiences at the camp.

257   HARRIS, ADRIENNE and YNESTRA KING, eds. 1989. *Rocking the Ship of State: Toward a Feminist Peace Politics*. Boulder, CO: Westview Press.
The contributors to this volume are interested in revealing the complex components of a feminist peace politics that does not rely on traditional assumptions about women's more passive, nurturing nature. A balance of theory, practice, and history are included in the selections, which include: What does feminism mean? by Dorothy Dinnerstein; A Gender Diary by Ann Snitow; Mothers and Men's Wars by Sara Ruddick; Masculinity, Heroism, and the Making of War by Nancy Hartsock; Women and the Economics of Military Spending by Lourdes Beneria and Rebecca Blank; Feminine Behavior and Radical Action: Franciscans, Quakers, and the Followers of Gandhi by Phyllis Mack; Pure Milk, Not Poison: Women Strike for Peace and the Test Ban Treaty of 1963 by Amy Swerdlow; Seneca Women's Peace Camp: Shapes of Things to Come by Rhoda Linton.

258   KOEN, SUSAN and NINA SWAIN. 1982. *Ain't Nowhere We Can Run: A Handbook for Women on the Nuclear Mentality*. Trumansburg, NY: Crossing Press.
Koen and Swain begin this book by stating their ecofeminist position. They see the actions of nuclear proponents to be directly related to the treatment of women in society, including violence against women, and the disregard for

weaker people with the disregard of the environment. One way they promote their position is to highlight the work of women activists for a nuclear-free world. Some of the women covered are Holly Near, Karen Silkwood, Helen Caldicott, and Grace Paley. In the conclusion the authors offer suggestions for becoming involved in social change.

259 KRASNIEWICZ, LOUISE. 1992. *Nuclear Summer: The Clash of Communities and the Seneca Women's Peace Encampment*. Ithaca, NY: Cornell University Press.
Based on fieldwork from 1983 to 1987 anthropologist Louise Krasniewicz analyzes the collective identity conflicts that arose from the peace encampment near the Seneca Army Depot in upstate New York. Two contrasting identities of the women taking part in the encampment from two different population groups emerge from this research: local residents' perception of a deviant and threatening identity, and the women's own perception of a female centered identity. Conflicts among encampment participants over spirituality, food, decision making, and sexual orientation are also discussed.

260 MCALLISTER, PAM, ed. 1982. *Reweaving the Web of Life: Feminism and Nonviolence*. Philadelphia: New Society Publishers.
Over fifty contributors provide many voices on the joy of women's pacifism. The reader is treated to a mixture of poems, plays, songs, interviews, stories, essays, photographs, and artwork that express the feelings of feminist women involved in non-violent activism. McAllister has done an excellent job of putting these voices together and of explaining the resistance to patriarchy's violence that led to the commitment of pacifist women to finding ways to work for change that do not use the patriarchy's methods. Topics covered include: racism, class, sexism and militarism, civil disobedience, male sexuality, draft resistance, reproductive freedom, and women's self defense.

261 ———. 1991. *This River of Courage: Generations of Women's Resistance and Action*. Philadelphia: New Society Publishers.
A historical overview of centuries of non-violent struggle by women to obtain equality, justice, and control over their lives. Stories come from mythology, ancient times, diverse cultures, and present times. There are over 200 tales of women's non-violent actions, such as the 1600 Iroquois women who protested the control of war time decisions by men; the daring actions of American women in the mid-1800s for dress reform when they experimented (and were ridiculed for doing so) with the bloomer style dress; the efforts of women in India in the early 1700s to prevent the destruction of trees; and the many acts of heroism exhibited against colonial powers, apartheid, and fascist regimes.

262 ———. 1988. *You Can't Kill the Spirit*. Santa Cruz, CA: New Society Publishers.
This book consists of stories of women from as far back as 13th century B.C. Egypt using non-violent protest to fight for freedom and justice. In spite of anger, frustration, and deeply held convictions of the need for change, the

courage of these women activists is most vivid in the restraint they use in work-ing to achieve their goals. Their commitment to non-violent activism is a model that, if followed, would eliminate untold numbers of death and destruction throughout the world.

263   MCDANIEL, JUDITH. 1987. *Sanctuary: A Journey*. Ithaca, NY: Firebrand
        Books.
Through the use of poetry and personal essays, McDaniel explores the rela-tionships between feminism and pacifism. In journal fashion, the author dis-cusses connections between the politics of war and sexuality, and notes the impact of lesbian feminism in the Women's Peace Encampment at the Seneca Army Depot. The more generalized sanctuary movement which is supported by mainstream churches poses a problem because of sexism and homophobia often found in these institutional settings. One of the issues that is identified as troublesome is the paradox of women defining their place in coalition poli-tics, even within the peace movement.

264   MERCHANT, CAROLYN. 1980. *The Death of Nature: Women, Ecology, and
        the Scientific Revolution*. San Francisco: Harper and Row.
This book chronicles changing social orientations towards women and nature over the last 500 years. Merchant argues that the emergence of capitalism and science transformed earlier views of respect for nature with ones of exploita-tion. According to the author, this domination of nature is replicated in the domination of women. The witch hunts of the sixteenth and seventeenth cen-turies are used as an example of this occurrence. The connection between the women's movement and the ecology movement are drawn out in Merchant's account of social change processes since they share similar interests. Critical interpretations are included of Bacon, Descartes, Hobbes, and Newton.

265   MEYERDING, JANE, ed. 1984. *Barbara Deming: We Are All Part of One
        Another*. Philadelphia: New Society Publishers.
Jane Meyerding has put together a wonderful collection of Barbara Deming's essays, poems, speeches, letters, and narratives over a forty year period. Deming's work on peace and feminism are fully felt in these writings. Included are excerpts from *Prison Notes* (1966) (see entry 345), *Running Away From Myself* (1969), *Revolution and Equilibrium* (1971), *We Cannot Live Without Our Lives* (1974) (see entry 254), and *Remembering Who We Are* (1981).

266   PLANT, JUDITH, ed. 1990. *Healing the Wounds: The Promise of
        Ecofeminism*. Philadelphia, PA: New Society Publishers.
The perspective of ecological feminism is heard in this collection through the voices of twenty-five authors. The image is one of interconnections between body, mind, and spirit in joining together to create a world of harmony and respect. The transformation of the world into a global community for healing the earth and all its inhabitants is found in feminist and ecological visions through theory, practice, and reflection. Among the contributors are Susan Griffin, Ursula LeGuin, Dorothy Dinnerstein, and Margaret Adler. Sections include "Healing All

Our Relations: Ecofeminist Politics," "She is Alive in You: Ecofeminist Spirituality," and "The Circle is Gathering: Ecofeminist Community."

267 SCHWARTZ-SHEA, PERAGRINE and DEBRA D. BURRINGTON. 1990. "Free Riding, Alternative Organization and Cultural Feminism: The Case of Seneca Women's Peace Camp." *Women & Politics* 10:1–37.

Using documents, surveys, and participant observation, the authors describe the Seneca Women's Encampment for a Future of Peace and Justice. The authors' analysis shows that open leadership and self-chosen levels of participation led to a free-rider problem. Maintenance work and organizational tasks were not equally shared and those who took on the bulk of these assignments (called suckers) experienced burn-out and felt resentment. The authors argue that the cultural feminist assumptions of women's nature, e.g., cooperative and caring, led organizers to ignore the reality and caused some participants to take on the sucker role.

268 SWERDLOW, AMY. 1993. *Women Strike for Peace: Traditional Motherhood and Radical Politics in the 1960s*. Chicago: University of Chicago Press.

The author details the activities and events surrounding the founding of Women Strike for Peace (WSP) in 1961. As one of the original members, Swerdlow brings insider information to this work as she tells of the successes and problems these activists experienced. WSP consisted mainly of white middle-class women, many involved in the traditional homemaker role, who protested against the nuclear arms race. The organization was investigated by the House Un-American Activities Committee, but eventually WSP succeeded in sending one of its members to Congress to serve as a peace candidate. The legacy this group left for the emergence of the women's movement later in the 1960's decade is an important part of the contemporary movement's history.

Lesbian Feminism, the Women's Culture, and the Gay/Lesbian Movement

269 ABBOTT, SIDNEY and BARBARA LOVE. 1972. *Sappho Was a Right-On Woman: A Liberated View of Lesbianism*. New York: Stein and Day.

This book opened a new area of discussion for lesbianism. The authors present a positive view of lesbians with an emphasis on self-worth and the possibilities of cultural change. Most important are the discussions on the relationship between lesbians and gay liberation, the National Organization for Women, and the women's movement in general. Abbott and Love argue for a lesbian lifestyle as the ideal of feminism and the liberated woman.

270 ABELOVE, HENRY, MICHELE AINA BARALE, and DAVID M. HALPERIN, eds. 1993. *The Lesbian and Gay Studies Reader*. New York: Routledge.

A comprehensive multi-disciplinary collection on the history of sexuality, sexual politics, lesbian and gay studies, and gender issues.

271   ADAM, BARRY D. 1987. *The Rise of a Gay and Lesbian Movement.*
       Boston: Twayne.
Early in this book Adams points out that of all the movements of the 1960s, the
women's movement and the gay and lesbian movement are the only ones to
still be flourishing and that, in spite of this fact, there has been little research
done on the gay movement. He traces the origins of the gay rights movement
to Germany where the Scientific Humanitarian Committee was founded in the
late nineteenth century. He then provides a thorough survey of the contemporary movement covering a wide range of topics. Adams compares the gay
movement and the feminist and lesbian movements, including an analysis of
the effects of the feminist pornography debate on gays and lesbians. A closing
chapter looks at the focus of the New Right on women's roles, the family, and
homosexuality.

272   ALLEN, JEFFNER, ed. 1990. *Lesbian Philosophies and Cultures.* Albany:
       State University of New York Press.
Because lesbians are usually lumped together as constituting one social group,
this book challenges the reader to think beyond identifying anyone by a single
classification. The lesbian writers who contributed to this book are theorists
and activists in a number of social movements. They have written articles
which provide insights into the diversity of lesbian cultures that exist in present day society. Each author reflects on her own cultural identity as well as
ethnicity, race, social class, physical abilities, age, and nationality and how these
group characteristics affect lesbian existence.

273   BAKER, ANDREA J. 1982. "The Problem of Authority in Radical Movement
       Groups: A Case Study of a Lesbian-Feminist Organization." *The Journal
       of Applied Behavioral Science* 18:323–341.
Through interviews and participant observation, Baker analyzes leadership formation in a lesbian feminist organization over a two-year period. The group
had an egalitarian ethos connected to New Left and radical feminist leanings
which prevented leaders from formalizing their positions in the group. The
issues of authority, hierarchy, elitism, and informal leadership are discussed.

274   BRODY, MICHAL, ed. 1985. *Are We There Yet? A Continuing Story of
       Lavender Woman, A Chicago Lesbian Newspaper, 1971–1976.* Iowa
       City, IA: Aunt Lute Book Company.
The most controversial and still current debates surrounding lesbian feminism
emerged in the early 1970s. The passion of these years can be found in the
writings of a lesbian feminist collective in Chicago which published *The
Lavender Woman.* Fifty selections from the twenty-six issues that came out
between 1971 and 1976 are found in this edited volume. Brody also includes
recent interviews with former members of the collective. In reading these articles, you learn about the history of lesbian feminism in the women's movement of that period. Well-covered are debates on separatism, racism, classism,
prejudice and discrimination, exploitation, and the gay lifestyle.

275 BROWN, RITA MAE. 1976. *A Plain Brown Rapper*. Oakland, CA: Diana
     Press.
A collection of essays written by Brown between 1969 and 1975 which explore
issues of the Left, lesbianism, race, and class. In the introduction, the author
discusses the ups and downs of her political career. These essays were originally published in one of three periodicals: *The Furies*, *Quest*, and *Rat*.

276 *Building Feminist Theory: Essays from Quest, A Feminist Quarterly*.
     1981. New York: Longman.
Quest was a journal put out by lesbian and socialist feminists in the early 1970s
that addressed issues of class, race, gender, and sexual orientation. One of the
themes of this collection, originally published in *Quest*, is the crucial role lesbians play in challenging heterosexual expectations which maintain patriarchal
society.

277 CAVIN, SUSAN. 1985. *Lesbian Origins*. San Francisco: Ism Press.
Originally her dissertation, Cavin's book uses data from many countries to support her theory of women's oppression and the solution to it through lesbian
feminist strategies of achieving female power.

278 CRUIKSHANK, MARGARET. 1992. *The Gay and Lesbian Liberation
     Movement*. New York: Routledge.
This book is not about the gay and lesbian liberation movement as the title
indicates, although some coverage of the movement is included. It concerns
everything connected to gay and lesbian life: culture, lifestyle, spirituality,
berdache, novels, poetry, and issues. It is in the area of issues that the book is
strongest as it covers current topics such as censorship, outing, gays in the military, and the reactionary policies of the Religious Right. The review of the literature on lesbian cultural life is a strong asset of this work.

279 DALY, MARY. 1978. *Gyn/Ecology: The Metaethics of Radical Feminism*.
     Boston: Beacon Press.
In this book, Daly discusses how her thoughts have gone beyond her earlier
work—what she calls continuing her journey in be-ing. She refutes some of her
earlier writing, including the use of the terms God, androgyny, and homosexuality. The book is not just about replacing these terms with Goddess and woman-
identified, it is also about gynocentric being, lesbianism, and separatism. It is, as
Daly describes it, about women who choose to be present to each other, as an
invitation to our Selves, and for the lesbian imagination in all women.

280 ———. 1984. *Pure Lust: Elemental Feminist Philosophy*. Boston:
     Beacon Press.
Mary Daly has become an icon in radical and cultural feminist circles for the
language and ideas she develops in her books. In *Pure Lust*, Daly analyzes
patriarchal abuse of lust while simultaneously using the term to describe feminist life-lust and vision. A philosophical, spiritual, and intellectual reading in
lesbian feminist thought.

281 ESTERBERG, KRISTIN G. 1994. "From Accommodation to Liberation: A Social Movement Analysis of Lesbians in the Homophile Movement." *Gender & Society* 8 (Sept.):424–443.

Using competition theory as a framework for analysis, Esterberg examines the origins (1956) and decline (end of 1960s) of the Daughters of Bilitis (DOB). In the last issues of *The Ladder*, the official publication of DOB, lesbians were encouraged to join the Women's Liberation Movement because their goals were increasingly similar. DOB which had a conservative image because of its early assimilationist views, was suffering declining interest because of the draw of the women's movement and of the gay liberation movement. In urging women to join the women's movement, DOB was highlighting the similarities between women, also being done in the woman-identified sector of the women's movement. One problem this transfer causes, though, is the downplaying of multiple identities. Competition theory is unable to deal with conflicts in oppressions, thus, Esterberg brings in New Social Movement Theory which defines identities as multiple, overlapping, and non-hierarchical.

282 FADERMAN, LILLIAN. 1991. *Odd Girls and Twilight Lovers: A History of Lesbian Life in Twentieth Century America*. New York: Columbia University Press.

Using historical and contemporary sources, Faderman shows how lesbian identity has changed over the last century. The author traces the development of lesbian identity from the early part of this century to the present. The diversity of lifestyles within the contemporary lesbian community is a particularly interesting development which is well covered in this work. This book won the 1992 Non-Fiction Book Award of the American Library Association's Gay & Lesbian Task Force.

283 FRANZEN, TRISHA. 1993. "Differences and Identities: Feminism and the Albuquerque Lesbian Community." *Signs: Journal of Women in Culture and Society* 18:891–906.

This article is about race, class, sexuality, and difference in a lesbian community and how three communities of lesbians defined themselves and each other during the years contemporary feminism developed. The three groups were the lesbian bar community, closeted lesbians, and feminist lesbians who were mostly students from a nearby university. The first two groups contained diverse class and racial members and had a history of solidarity among themselves and with gay men. Feminist lesbians espoused a separatist lifestyle and were disdainful of the butch/femme roles practiced by some of the older lesbians. Many of the feminist lesbians were newly out and had previous sexual relationships with men, a life experience that was rare among the bar and closeted lesbian groups. Antagonisms developed as these groups confronted each other over what defined "real" lesbians. However, as feminist lesbians began to interact with a less strident dialogue, a more multicultural feminist lesbian community developed.

284   FREEDMAN, E. B. and B. C. GELPI, eds. 1985. *The Lesbian Issue*. Chicago: University of Chicago Press.

A collection of writings on lesbian identity, lesbian literature, and a history of prejudice and discrimination against lesbians in the United States. Included are scholarly articles about lesbianism that are historical, anthropological, literary, and political. These articles originally appeared in the Summer 1984 issue of *Signs: Journal of Women in Culture and Society*, Vol. 9, No. 4.

285   FUSS, DIANA, ed. 1991. *Inside/Out: Lesbian Theories, Gay Theories*. New York: Routledge.

A collection of original papers which address issues of sexuality, gender identity, and gay and lesbian life. Conventional thought is challenged and diverse points of view are expressed. This book contributes to the development of nontraditional perspectives of social life and sexual behavior.

286   HOAGLAND, SARAH LUCIA. 1989. *Lesbian Ethics*. Palo Alto, CA: Institute of Lesbian Studies.

Hoagland is interested in developing ideals which can be put into practice to create a lesbian community centered on connection. This work reveals her concept of complex lesbian interaction that can lead to that outcome for the women's culture.

287   JENNESS, VALERIE and KENDAL BROAD. 1994. "Anti-Violence Activism and the (In)Visibility of Gender in the Gay/Lesbian and Women's Movement." *Gender & Society* 8 (Sept.):402–423.

Jenness and Broad discuss how the focus of gay and lesbian groups has been on homophobia and hate-motivated violence. The preoccupation of anti-violence organizing and provision of services is similar to the violence-against-women sector of the women's movement. Both of these organizational efforts differ from the general women's movement (including the lesbian separatist women's culture), by their low level of concern over the effects of the patriarchy and the gender relations that sustain it. One theory to explain this omission is that the gay/lesbian movement, with its overwhelming proportion of gay men, has a desire to protect male superiority over women.

288   JOHNSTON, JILL. 1973. *Lesbian Nation: The Feminist Solution*. New York: Simon and Schuster.

Johnston writes autobiographically about her experiences growing up in the 1950s as a lesbian and her confrontations in the women's movement over lesbianism and feminism. She argues that lesbianism is a political commitment requiring activism and resistance. Mythology, scholarship, and sociosexual analysis for the development of political consciousness are incorporated in this work. The author takes the position that lesbians have integrated the personal and political, whereas straight women are legitimizing their own oppression.

289   KATZ, JONATHAN NED. 1992. *Gay American History: Lesbians & Gay*
      Men in the U.S.A., Revised Edition. New York: Penguin Books.
A primary sourcebook for a historical account of American lesbians and gay
men. Included are reprints of documents that reveal 400 years of oppression,
conflict, and struggle over the issue of homosexuality.

290   KENNEDY, ELIZABETH LAPOVSKY and MADELINE D. DAVIS. 1993. *Boots of*
      Leather, Slippers of Gold: The History of a Lesbian Community. New
      York: Routledge.
The central issue this book addresses is the development of identity and how
the meaning of that identity is connected to historical agency. Chapters cover
the early history of working-class lesbian bar life, desegregation of the bars after
World War II, the sociology of lesbian relationships in the 1950s, and the gay liberation movement of the 1960s. Rather than seeing the butch/femme roles of
the lesbian bar scenes of the 1940s and 1950s as heterosexually complicit behavior, Kennedy and Davis argue that these roles challenged heterosexuality
because they were open expressions of participants' sexuality. Butches, especially, were clearly not accommodating to expectations of feminine demeanor.
Thus, the authors maintain that tough bar lesbians were exhibiting a pre-politi-
cal consciousness that insisted on female sexual autonomy.

291   KRIEGER, SUSAN. 1982. "Lesbian Identity and Community: Recent Social
      Science Literature." *Signs: Journal of Women and Culture* 8:91–108.
Krieger provides reference material on articles and books published in the last
thirty years on lesbian identity and community. Much of this writing is related
to nine sociological studies on this topic. Questions arise about whether this
type of community is healthy, and what some of the problems are and how
they might be resolved.

292   ———. 1983. *The Mirror Dance: Identity in a Women's Community*.
      Philadelphia: Temple University Press.
This book is based on research consisting of a year long participant observation
study and interviews of a lesbian feminist women's community. Krieger, who is a
sociologist, found problems of merger and separation, and of conflicts over identity among members of the community. The conflict she found was a promise to
members that they would be accepted and affirmed for who they were, but at the
same time the mores of the group required them to be alike among themselves
(a mirror image). The community, then, was nurturing but also non-accepting of
difference, and thus, there was a threat to individuals' sense of selfhood. In
describing the process of feeling subordinated to the group and or abandoned
when they failed to shape up, images of the way marriage and family are sometimes described often come to mind. This is an interesting and valuable analysis
of identity, connectedness, autonomy, and sense of self.

293   MARCUS, ERIC. 1992. *Making History: An Oral History of the Struggle*
      for Gay and Lesbian Civil Rights, 1945–1990. New York: HarperCollins.
The author presents a portrait of forty-five politically active women and men,

both gay and straight, involved in the gay liberation movement. Coming out stories as the impetus for involvement in the movement forms an important part of these stories, as does the struggle they have engaged in to gain respect and equal protection under the law. This work covers the history of the gay rights movement from the end of World War II to the early 1990s.

294 MYRON, NANCY AND CHARLOTTE BUNCH, eds. 1975. *Lesbianism and the Women's Movement.* Baltimore, MD: Diana Press.
An early collection on lesbian feminism. Selections include: "The Furies" by G. Berson; "Such a Nice Girl" by S. Deeney; "Lesbians in Revolt" by C. Bunch; "Taking the Bullshit by the Horns" by B. Solomon; "Lesbians and the Class Position of Women" by M. Small; "Living with Other Women" by R. M. Brown; "The Shape of Things to Come" by R. M. Brown; "The Normative Status of Heterosexuality" by Purple September staff; "Bisexuality" by L. Ulmschneider; and "Coming Out in the Women's Movement" by C. Reid.

295 POLLACK, SANDRA and JEANNE VAUGHN, eds. 1987. *Politics of the Heart: A Lesbian Parenting Anthology.* New York: Firebrand Books.
An anthology of writings from lesbians who are parents in a variety of different structural arrangements. Discussed are the law, court decisions, lesbians who lose their children, lesbians choosing to have children, same-sex coparenting, and the radical potential of lesbian mothering of daughters.

296 RICH, ADRIENNE. 1980. "Compulsory Heterosexuality and Lesbian Existence." *Signs: Journal of Women in Culture and Society* 5 (June):631–660.
This much reprinted and now classic article argues that idealization of heterosexuality has led to compulsory heterosexuality in order to perpetuate male domination over women. Lesbian existence has been suppressed because it so directly challenges the compulsory view of heterosexual normality. Rich maintains that there are many ranges of sexual behavior and diverse ways for women to support women, and that this range constitutes a lesbian continuum rather than discreet categories. The lesbian continuum includes women loving women, women who refuse to marry, friendship, co-workers, and comrades.

297 SCHULMAN, SARAH. 1994. *My American Story: Lesbian and Gay Life During the Reagan/Bush Years.* New York: Routledge.
Schulman has been an activist in the feminist, lesbian and gay movements over the last twelve years. In this book she tells a personal, yet political, story of why she left the women's movement and became involved in the gay/lesbian movement instead. The author describes the women's movement as having once been a radical and creative movement which has become outdated, mired in old non-effective tactics, and stuck in rigid identity politics. She writes of how, in the mid-1980s, she and other lesbians were forced out of CARASA (Committee for Abortion Rights and Against Sterilization Abuse) over conflicts of tactics and accusations of being separatist. In turning to the gay/lesbian

movement, she found new and effective tactics in ACT UP which attempts to raise consciousness through the use of direct action tactics. Unlike past years, Schulman finds the gay movement (at least this segment of it) to be seriously concerned about sexism.

298   SIMONS, MARGARET A. 1992. "Lesbian Connections: Simone de Beauvoir and Feminism." *Signs: Journal of Women in Culture and Society* 18:136–161.

In *The Second Sex*, Simone de Beauvoir defined a theoretical framework for understanding sex/gender relations that formed an ideological core for both activism and theory in the women's movement for over twenty years. More recently, her writing has been criticized as being heterosexist, masculinist, and "Sartrean." In this article, Simons argues that de Beauvoir had lesbian connections which call for a re-reading of her work. Simons suggests that de Beauvoir's life and philosophy challenge boundaries of heterosexual and lesbian identity, and thus, provide a need to explore lesbian connections as a source of inspiration in the feminist movement.

299   Special Gay and Lesbian Issue. 1990. *Radical America* 24 (Sept.).

Articles in this issue include "Multi/Queer/Culture" by Phillip Harper et al.; "Discourses of Discrimination and Lesbians as (Out)Laws" by Ruthann Robson; "The Color of My Narrative" by Mariana Romo-Carmona; "Clearing a Space for Us: A Tribute to Audre Lorde" by Kate Rushin; and "Community Organizing and the Religious Right: Lessons from the Measure 9 Campaign" interview with Suzanne Pharr.

300   STEIN, ARLENE, ed. 1993. *Sisters, Sexperts, Queers: Beyond the Lesbian Nation*. New York: Plume, Division of Penguin Books.

A collection of essays about lesbian culture and politics in the 1990s. Included is a look at the complex sense of community, variations in lesbian identities, and the impact of race, class, and sexual practices among lesbians, including re-emerged butch/femme roles. The ideas of this new generation of lesbian activists and writers is contrasted with the 1970s movement which focused on revelations of oppression, encouragement for coming out, and attempts to create a common culture. Today's lesbian discourse is more likely to center on sadomasochism, donor insemination, parenting, and diversity among lesbians.

301   TAYLOR, VERTA and NANCY E. WHITTIER. 1992. "Collective Identity in Social Movement Communities." In *Frontiers in Social Movement Theory*, edited by Aldon D. Morris and Carol McClurg Mueller. New Haven, CT: Yale University Press.

Taylor and Whittier trace the evolution of lesbian feminism from the radical feminists of the early 1970s to the women's culture of the 1980s-1990s. Their interest is in the ways this branch of the women's movement organized around the concept of collective identity. This work is based on an empirical study utilizing published primary materials, interviews, and the authors' own experiences.

302 TAYLOR, VERTA. 1991. "Women's Culture and Lesbian Feminist Activism: A Reconsideration of Cultural Feminism." *Signs: Journal of Women in Culture and Society* 19:32–61.

Taylor is interested in enlarging the view of cultural feminism beyond an essentialist view of differences between women and men, and the separatism that seems to follow that position. She argues that this way of seeing cultural feminism is only one tendency within dynamic and diverse lesbian feminist communities.

303 THOMPSON, MARK, ed. 1994. *Long Road to Freedom: 'The Advocate' History of the Gay and Lesbian Movement*. New York: St. Martin's Press.

This work provides a view of the complex dynamic that exists between lesbians and gay men, including the love and hate, the distance and interconnections, the different periods of struggle they have gone through, and the lessons they have learned about their relationships to each other. The Gay/Lesbian Movement is traced in this book through the pages of *The Advocate*, a gay magazine that began publishing in 1967. Each chapter covers a year. Selections include lesbians' positions on joining the gay movement or the women's movement as both positive and negative experiences. The changing relationships of lesbian women with gay men are clearly documented in this collection.

304 TREBILCOT, JOYCE. 1994. *Dyke Ideas: Process, Politics, Daily Life*. Albany, NY: State University of New York Press.

Trebilcot has long been involved in the development of lesbian thought and in this book has put together a fine collection of essays of her thoughts, feminist theory, and philosophical explorations on everyday life.

305 WESTON, KATH. 1991. *Families We Choose: Lesbians, Gays, Kinship*. New York: Columbia University Press.

Taking place in individual lives and new family constellations is an undeclared social movement of change in how families are defined and organized. Most particularly this is occurring in the gay and lesbian communities. Challenging conceptions and legal restraints on who can be considered family members, lesbian and gay activists are going to court, experimenting with alternative insemination methods, having children and raising them.

306 YOUNG, ALISON. 1991. *Femininity in Dissent*. New York: Routledge.

Using the example of media representations of separatist feminist activism, this work broadly examines the construction of sex difference through cultural beliefs and mythologies of womanhood. In this case study of women's antinuclear protests in Greenham Common, England, participants used a women-only peace encampment to visually demonstrate a connection between patriarchal values and nuclear weapons. Incorporating feminist and poststructuralist theory, the author illustrates how the meaning of deviance is created when the media was able to convey an image of Greenham Common women as lesbians and as members of a witches' coven which threatened the family and community.

Academia and Women's Studies

307 AIKEN, SUSAN HARDY, KAREN ANDERSON, MYRA DINNERSTEIN, JUDY
NOLTE LENSINK, and PATRICIA MACCORQUODALE, eds. 1988. *Changing
Our Minds: Feminist Transformations of Knowledge*. New York: State
University of New York Press.
In identifying gender studies as part of the women's movement, these writers
articulate the need for institutions of higher education to acknowledge gender
as an organizing principle in society and culture. The articles were written by
academics, most of whom are outside of Women's Studies, who met in discussion groups at the University of Arizona to consider the question of integrating
gender studies into their teaching. The result of this effort led participants to
change their minds about the foundations of their disciplines. The authors
describe this process and advocate ongoing explorations of the cultural construction of gender and gendered constructions of culture, including the ways
efforts to transform traditional ways of knowledge are affected by the politics
of gender within academia.

308 AISENBERG, NADYA and MONA HARRINGTON. 1988. *Women of Academe:
Outsiders in the Sacred Grove*. Amherst: University of Massachusetts
Press.
An empirical study based on interviews with over sixty academic women in a
variety of disciplines. The authors discuss the struggles women have experienced in their efforts to gain a place in academia. Also covered are the ways
academic women have been able to use their authority to change practices that
failed to reflect diversity in their professions.

309 AL-HIBRI, AZIZAH Y. and MARGARET A. SIMONS, eds. 1990. *Hypatia
Reborn: Essays in Feminist Philosophy*. Bloomington: Indiana
University Press.
Feminist women philosophers have formed an organization, Society of Women
Philosophers (SWP), and a journal, *Hypatia*, to discuss the complex meanings
of gender and women's lives within patriarchal culture. The essays in this collection are from the first three issues of *Hypatia*, which were originally published in *Women's Studies International Forum* as special issues (1983 to
1985). The collection documents the path women philosophers have taken,
going from silence to speaking out. This transition has led to the development
of a feminist philosophy as well as new sources of empowerment for women
engaged in intellectual enterprises.

310 APTHEKER, BETTINA. 1981. "Strong Is What We Make Each Other:
Unlearning Racism Within Women's Studies." *Women's Studies
Quarterly* 9 (Dec.):13–16.
A discussion of the subjective and institutional barriers to interracial solidarity
within the women's movement. Aptheker's remarks are particularly aimed at
race and class divisions in Women's Studies.

311 BUNCH, CHARLOTTE and SANDRA POLLACK, eds. 1983. *Learning Our Way: Essays in Feminist Education*. Trumansburg, NY: The Crossing Press.

A collection of over thirty articles consisting of analysis, personal stories, philosophical discussions, examples of success and of mistakes, meant to contribute to the development of feminist ways of teaching. Selections include: Radical Feminism in Academia, The Politics of Black Women's Studies, Teaching Writing in Prison, College for Neighborhood Women, All-Women Classes and the Struggle for Women's Liberation, The New Right Challenge, Teaching the Feminist Minority, Alternative Structures for Feminist Education, and many more by a diverse assortment of academics and activists.

312 BUTLER, JOHNELLA E. 1982. "Black Studies and Women's Studies: Search for a Long Overdue Partnership." *Women's Studies Quarterly* 10 (June):10–16.

Arguing that black women have been ignored by both Black Studies and Women's Studies, the author of this article calls for the two to work together and establish a cooperative relationship in which black women are included in both programs

313 CHAMBERLAIN, MARIAM K., ed. 1988. *Women in Academe: Progress and Prospects*. Ithaca, NY: Russell Sage Foundation.

This collection of essays covers the progress women have made in the various branches of academia, how victories were won, and the ongoing barriers that still exist.

314 DuBOIS, ELLEN CAROL, KELLY PARADISE, ELIZABETH LAPOVSKY KENNEDY, CAROLYN W. KORSMEYER, and LILLIAN S. ROBINSON. 1987. *Feminist Scholarship: Kindling in the Groves of Academe*. Urbana: University of Illinois Press.

A synthesis across disciplines (history, philosophy, literature, anthropology, and education) which examines feminist scholarship arising from concerns raised by the contemporary women's movement. The authors describe the process of identifying male bias and the ways new conceptual frameworks utilizing feminist awareness are developed. In the mid-section of the book there is a chapter outlining research on women's oppression, followed by a chapter on remedies to oppression. In the final section, a survey of scholarly journals shows that there has been an increase in papers focusing on gender, including critiques of dominant scholarship which has either ignored or distorted views of women and 'women's issues.' The last chapter reveals an ideological framework, premised on women's position in stratification systems, providing the common theme for both the women's movement and feminist scholarship.

315 EVANS, MARY. 1990. "The Problem of Gender for Women's Studies." *Women's Studies International Forum* 13:457–462.

The focus of this article is the meaning of the shift in terminology from Women's Studies to Gender Studies. The author argues that this transformation indicates a shift from feminist centered work with the radical implication of challenging the sex/gender system of patriarchal domination to socialization and the differences between women and men.

316   FARNHAM, CHRISTIE, ed. 1987. *The Impact of Feminist Research in the Academy*. Bloomington: Indiana University Press.
This anthology contains eleven essays which reflect upon the ways feminist scholarship has affected academic disciplines. Includes articles by Louise Lamphere (anthropology), Joan Wallach Scott (history), Carol P. Christ (religious studies), Carol Gilligan (moral development), Carol Nagy Jacklin (psychology), Ruth Bleier (science), Barbara Bergmann (economics), Virginia Sapiro (political science), Nellie McKay (black women), Jessie Bernard (sociology), and Carolyn Heilbrun (literature).

317   FREEMAN, JO. 1971. "Women's Liberation and Its Impact on the Campus." *Liberal Education* 57:468–478.
Freeman acknowledges the benefits of Women's Studies classes for raising consciousness among women. At the same time she voices her concerns about segregating these classes into what could become the new "home economics" ghetto.

318   GLAZER, NONA Y. 1987. "Questioning Eclectic Practice in Curriculum Changes: A Marxist Perspective." *Signs: Journal of Women in Culture and Society* 12 (Dec.):293–304.
In considering the integration of Women's Studies' course material throughout the curriculum, Glazer asks what is actually getting transmitted. First, she worries that this integration might displace Women's Studies, and secondly she worries that the message will be one of eclectic gender appreciation rather than a radical and Marxist challenge to capitalism. Glazer argues that women's "problems" cannot be divorced from capitalism's effects on women and the ways the economy is run for the profit of the few.

319   HUNTER COLLEGE WOMEN'S STUDIES COLLECTIVE. 1983. *Women's Realities, Women's Choices: An Introduction to Women's Studies*. New York: Oxford University Press.
An interdisciplinary approach to studying women put together through the collaboration of eight scholars. The book is divided into three parts beginning with the individual which examines images of women, women's bodies, their nature, personalities, and social roles. The second part focuses on statuses women occupy such as being daughters, wives, and mothers. One chapter in this section is on alternative relationships. The final section looks at public life and women's interactions with social institutions such as religion, education, health, work, and politics. The conclusion presents a chronology of feminist accomplishments and comments on the possibilities for the future.

320 KENNEDY, MARY, CATHY LUBELSKA, and VAL WALSH. 1993. *Making Connections: Women's Studies, Women's Movements, Women's Lives.* Bristol, PA: Taylor & Francis.

Feminist knowledge and politics are revealed in the diversity of perspectives and identities found in this volume. A major theme of this collection is how to make connections across diversities without privileging some women over others. Many of the essays are addressed to political developments in Women's Studies in the 1990s.

321 KESSLER-HARRIS, ALICE. 1992. "The View from Women's Studies." *Signs: Journal of Women in Culture and Society* 17:794–805.

As the director of a Women's Studies Program, Kessler-Harris gives her views on problems that have emerged within Women's Studies and academia in general. She addresses the backlash against multiculturalism that has been expressed as political correctness, and the divisions within Women's Studies programs that have resulted in factional politics. The author calls for discussions of differences and a critical look at an identity politics that resists uniting for freedom and dignity. The author calls for working out internal problems in ways that encourage thinking about commonalities as well as difference. Other issues she addresses center on the tensions between pedagogy and content, and between feminist philosophy and institutional requirements.

322 KRAMARAE, CHERIS and DALE SPENDER, eds. 1992. *The Knowledge Explosion: Generations of Feminist Scholarship.* New York: Teachers College Press.

In this anthology forty-four activists and scholars discuss the last two decade's of Women's Studies scholarship. In addition to the diversity of scholarly work that is covered, writers document some of the problems feminist academics have experienced in their disciplines and the general resistance to women's initiatives they have encountered. Among the contributors are Mary Ellen Capek on Women's Studies funding, Susan Searing on the expanse of feminist publications, and Marilyn Frye on theoretical developments.

323 LEIDNER, ROBIN. 1991. "Stretching the Boundaries of Liberalism: Democratic Innovation in a Feminist Organization." *Signs: Journal of Women in Culture and Society* 16:263–289.

The early 1990s saw the breakdown of the National Women's Studies Association (NWSA) beginning with the walk out of the Women-of-Color and Lesbian caucuses at a national conference. Later the officers of the organization all resigned and a new head was appointed who was a woman-of-color, although another Women's Studies organization for women-of-color only, was also organizing. Leidner analyzes the events and organizational structure of NWSA that led to this breakdown. She finds the extra delegates allowed double oppressed groups resulted in what many white heterosexual women felt was an over-use of the caucuses' power which led to shutting non-caucus members out.

324 MCDERMOTT, PATRICE. 1994. *Politics and Scholarship: Feminist Academic Journals and the Production of Knowledge.* Champaign: University of Illinois Press.

A description of the scholarly enterprise, including conceptions of rigor and political relevance. Feminist scholarship is shown to be a product of alternative institutional structures and cultural practices. The author maintains that the effect of this different orientation and practice is a tension that divides feminist scholarship from much of traditional scholarship.

325 MINNICH, ELIZABETH, JEAN O'BARR, and RACHEL ROSENFELD, eds. 1988. *Reconstructing the Academy: Women's Education and Women's Studies.* Chicago: The University of Chicago Press.

The essays in this book originally appeared between 1978 and 1988 in *Signs: Journal of Women in Culture and Society.* In a variety of ways various contributors are exploring the possibilities of transforming the curricula to serve women's education better than has been done in the past. Many of the problems and tensions in academic feminism are addressed here such as attempts to change the curriculum, curriculum integration or separatism, exclusionary practices in Women's Studies, internalized oppression, external resistance to change, women's colleges vs. co-education, the paradox of women as role models, and the identity crisis in feminist theory.

326 O'BARR, JEAN FOX. 1994. *Feminism in Action: Building Institutions and Community Through Women's Studies.* Chapel Hill: University of North Carolina Press.

Using Women's Studies curriculum and classroom activities as frameworks, O'Barr demonstrates the ways gender, race, and class can become inclusive models of education.

327 SCHRAMM, SARAH SLAVIN. 1977. "Women's Studies: Its Focus, Idea Power, and Promise." *The Social Science Journal* (April):5–13.

Women's Studies is seen by Schramm as a parallel development with the contemporary women's movement. It is not clear whether she sees it as part of the movement or something set apart. In this article she traces the origins and development of Women's Studies over the past 5-6 years. Schramm finds inconsistencies between the ideology and theories being developed in Women's Studies and the practices being employed by the women's movement. Although many feminists would not agree with her, she takes the position that the movement needs to listen to the theorists, rather than the other way around.

328 SIMEONE, ANGELA. 1987. *Academic Women, Working Towards Equality.* South Hadley, MA: Bergin & Garvey.

Simeone argues in this book that despite the efforts of the women's movement, academic women are still not equal in status with men. She basis her comparison on appointments, promotions, tenure, and salaries. Basically, Simeone is replicating Jessie Bernard's study published in *Academic Women* in the late

1960s. Problematically, almost no attention is paid to the efforts on the part of academic women to improve their position, particularly the complaints, research, published articles, and lawsuits. She does provide a useful review of research which has shown the ways sexism operates to keep women in a lowered place, from sexual harassment to lack of support for the work they do.

329   SPENDER, DALE, ed. 1981. *Men's Studies Modified: The Impact of Feminism on the Academic Disciplines*. New York: Pergamon Press.
The articles in this book argue that the academic curriculum is, in actuality, 'men's studies' passed off as human knowledge. The essays constitute a challenge to male authority by documenting how women have been left out of codified thought. Academics from diverse disciplines examine their own fields to show how and why the world has been explained in terms of men's experiences, but not women's. Included are essays on literary criticism (Annette Kolodny), philosophy (Sheila Ruth), history (Jane Lewis), sociology (Helen Roberts), and anthropology (Carol P. MacCormack).

330   THIBAULT, GISELE MARIE. 1987. *The Dissenting Feminist Academy: A History of the Barriers to Feminist Scholarship*. New York: Peter Lang.
The author is interested in chronicling three periods of feminist dissent within academia and the connection of that dissent to women's activism for change in the general society. The first period, the late nineteenth and early twentieth century was focused on disproving women's inferiority to men. The second period, the late 1960s and early 1970s, represents the push for equal opportunity in universities, especially in the hiring and promotion of women faculty. The third period, the 1980s to the present, centers on the mainstreaming of feminist research into academic disciplines and the full development of Women's Studies as an important source of knowledge for intellectual thought.

331   WATSON, BARBARA BELLOW, ed. 1976. *Women's Studies: The Social Realities*. New York: Harper's College Press.
An early text in Women's Studies, this collection has classic articles that came out of the contemporary movement and feminist writers that preceded it. Sections are divided into: Part One, Arguments for Equality, The Classic Texts; Part Two, The Social Roles of Women and Men, A Sociological Approach; Part Three, Sex Role Stereotypes, A Psychological Approach; Part Four, Peaceable Primates and Primitive People, An Anthropological Approach; Part Five, The Feminist Movement, 1820-1920; Part Six, The Women's Liberation Movement.

3

Women Activists: Their Lives, Their Work

Introduction

There is no social movement except for the people who define it, engage in it, do the work of it, and accomplish social change through it. Activists are the movement, once they organize themselves into a group with goals and strategies for achieving them.

Involvement in a social movement is a reciprocal relationship. One's identity and associates become connected to the movement they help form. In reading about the lives of women activists, we learn about their beliefs, joys, sorrows, and life choices. We also learn about the social world they interact in, and the reasons they commit themselves to particular causes, the ways they contribute to change processes, and the ways they are changed by those involvements.

There are two categories in this sector. The first is **Autobiography**, and here we find a wide array of women activists who have written about their lives and their work in social movements, some overtly feminist and others more focused on other issues. Autobiography offers the advantage of self-reflection. If they choose to, and they often do, authors tell us their thoughts and feelings as well as their actions.

The second category, **Biography**, provides biographers with a different task. They are engaged in the business of learning, analyzing, and interpreting someone else's life. Perhaps the subject is deceased and everything must be learned from written records and those survivors, if any, who knew the person well. Even when writing the life of a living person who cooperates with the biographer, there can be problems. For instance, Carolyn Heilbrun talks about having a running argument with Gloria Steinem on how to interpret Steinem's life.[1]

The emerging emphasis on women's biography has opened up possibilities for learning about feminist women's lives and the forces that move them to create a better world for themselves and other women. This is a history that has often been hidden. I am reminded of the importance of this work in myriad ways as when my computer spell check suggests I use "forefathers" since "foremothers" is not found in the dictionary listing.

Women's biography has lagged far behind that of men's. For many reasons, then, women's lives—and in this case, activist women's lives—are important for historical and present knowledge bases. What can these women activists tell us? They can tell us about ourselves, our past and the society we live in, the same as men's biography—only more so—since what has been left out is brought to the fore.

Note

1. While Heilbrun was writing a biography of Steinem, they met once a week in Steinem's New York apartment to discuss her life. Heilbrun spoke of this and of writing about women's lives in general at Rosemont College, Philadelphia, Spring 1994.

Autobiography

332   ADDAMS, JANE. 1960. *Twenty Years at Hull House*. New York: New American Library.
This is Jane Addams story of Hull House, the settlement house she founded in Chicago, and directed from 1889 to 1909. It gives an autobiographical account of Addams life and work among poor immigrant families, sweatshop workers, unwed mothers, the sick, and aged.

333   ANGELOU, MAYA. 1981. *The Heart of a Woman*. New York: Random House.
Maya Angelou has written a number of autobiographical books detailing various phases of her life. *The Heart of a Woman* is the fourth in this series. In this book she talks about moving to New York and joining the Harlem Writers Guild. While intent upon building a career as a writer, she also becomes involved in the civil rights movement through her activism in the Southern Christian Leadership Conference. Encounters with Malcom X and Martin Luther King are discussed.

334   BERNARD, HOLLINGER F., ed. 1985. *Outside the Magic Circle: The Autobiography of Virginia Foster Durr*, Tuscaloosa: The University of Alabama Press.
Writing about her own life, we learn that Virginia Foster Durr dedicated herself to the work of achieving civil rights. Taking this road left her alienated from her class position and she experienced many difficulties adjusting to these two pulls. In the end, she placed her strongest allegiance with the work for social justice.   An unusual story which falls outside the typical pattern of social activism.

335   BLACKWELL, ELIZABETH. 1977. *Pioneer Work in Opening the Medical Profession to Women: Autobiographical Sketches*. New York: Schocken Books.
Elizabeth Blackwell writes of her and her sister Emily's struggles to gain admittance to medical schools in the United States. Until the 1870s only women's medical schools were available but there were few of them, and after graduation the possibilities of finding an internship were slim. Their eventually successful efforts led to more opportunities for women in spite of continued resistance on the part of the all male keepers-of-the-gate. Blackwell tells readers of the sisters' early years in England, their efforts to be admitted to medical schools, their difficulties in earning enough money to pay for their education, their work and study in both England and the United States, and their many efforts to improve the health of women.

336   BLATCH, HARRIOT STANTON and ALMA LUTZ. 1940. *Challenging Years: The Memoirs of Harriot Stanton Blatch*. New York: G. P. Putman.
An autobiography of Harriot Stanton Blatch, daughter of Elizabeth Cady Stanton. Blatch spent time in England and learned tactics from the suffrage movement there that she brought back to the United States. Most of her activism took place in New York City where she introduced street speaking and parades. She provides analysis of why suffrage was failing to pass, such as new immigrant men being paid with liquor by manufacturing interests to vote against it (often the question would be placed on a pink ballot so non-English speakers would know which one it was). She also theorized that the South was opposed because they were afraid women voting would raise the issue of blacks voting and they had instituted grandfather clauses and literacy tests to prevent that—policies they did not want challenged. After the Nineteenth Amendment became law, she traveled to Europe to write and work for peace.

337   CHICAGO, JUDY. 1975. *Through the Flower: My Struggle as a Woman Artist*. Garden City, NY: Doubleday.
Autobiography of Judy Chicago's commitment to creating a distinctive female art and of participating in the efforts to change traditional cultural values.

338   CHISHOLM, SHIRLEY. 1973. *The Good Fight*. New York: Harper and Row.
Shirley Chisholm was the first black woman to run for president of the United States in a primary campaign. In this autobiographical work, she talks about her 1972 campaign and the events surrounding this political experience, including George Wallace being shot as he campaigned for the same upcoming election. Speeches she gave during this time are included in an appendix.

339   ———. 1970. *Unbought and Unbossed*. Boston: Houghton Mifflin.
In this segment of her autobiographical writing, Chisholm had not yet made the decision to run for president of the United States. Here she talks about her early years in Barbados, living in Brooklyn, teaching, marriage, political life, her campaign for Congress, the subject of abortion, and women's liberation.

340   CLARK, SEPTIMA POINSETTE. 1962. *Echo In My Soul*. New York: E.P.
       Dutton.
Septima Clark is well known in the civil rights movement for the work she did
to educate blacks about their rights and the need to fight for them. She was an
activist in the NAACP and spent many years at the Highlander School in
Tennessee training future leaders of the black liberation movement. She also
became involved in the Southern Christian Leadership Conference in order to
continue her efforts to teach literacy to poor blacks so they would be able have
a voice in the policies that kept them in an oppressed condition.

341   CONWAY, JILL K., ed. 1992. *Written by Herself: Autobiographies of
       American Women, An Anthology*. New York: Vintage Books.
Beginning with Harriet Jacobs' autobiographical account of the trials of
resisting slavery, to the writings of contemporary feminist Gloria Steinem,
this collection reveals insights into women's lives. We learn about doctors,
artists, scientists, writers, reformers, athletes, singers, and others. Well-
known contributors include: Maxine Hong Kingston, Margaret Sanger, Babe
Didrikson Zaharias, and Marian Anderson.

342   DALY, MARY. 1992. *Outercourse: The Be-Dazzling Voyage, Containing
       Recollections from My Logbook of a Radical Feminist Philosopher
       (Being an Account of My Time/Space Travels and Ideas—Then, Again,
       Now, and How)*. San Francisco: Harper/San Francisco.
Daly takes readers into the process of developing radical feminist philosophy
through the telling of her life. She discusses the concepts presented in her previous books and offers insights into the development of that work. The author
provides autobiographical material to reflect her own participation in Be-ing,
her term for the heart of women's revolution. Readers will learn about her
insatiable appetite for acquiring academic degrees, being denied tenure at
Boston College, her discovery of being a lesbian, her understanding of an
ecofeminist consciousness, and her ongoing philosophical reflections on a
Women's Liberation Movement in which women participate in their own
becoming.

343   DAVIS, ANGELA. 1988. *Angela Davis, An Autobiography*. New York:
       International Publishers.
Angela Davis has led many lives and has seen many myths grow up around her.
In this autobiography she has the opportunity to set the record straight. This
is a powerful life story that Davis tells with openness, wit, and sincerity.

344   DE BEAUVOIR, SIMONE. 1975. *All Said and Done*. New York: Warner
       Books.
The fifth in a series of autobiographical writing, in this volume de Beauvoir covers her political activities and travels from 1962 to 1971. She includes interactions with people who are close to her, personal reflections and experiences,
and such world shaping events as her and Sartre's part in the International
Tribunal which condemned American intervention in Vietnam. She discusses

her philosophy on life and her brand of feminism. De Beauvoir's life and the people and thoughts in it make for interesting reading.

345 DEMING, BARBARA. 1985. *Prisons That Could Not Hold, Prison Notes 1964-Seneca 1984*. San Francisco: Spinsters Ink.

The bulk of this book is a description of a two month incarceration and protest fast by peace activists in a prison in Albany, Georgia in 1964. Deming and a small group of peace activists were arrested in the course of a peace walk from Quebec to Cuba for marching through the town against the wishes and without permission of the police chief. Prison notes provides readers with a portrait of events which have helped transform consciousness and social practice. In this case, the protesters' arrests called attention to the denial of dissidents' Constitutional rights to free speech and assembly. In a short section at the end of the book, Deming discusses a 1984 Seneca peace march by women honoring women's unwritten history which provoked hostility, imprisonment, and near violence to participants.

346 DENNIS, PEGGY. 1977. *The Autobiography of an American Communist: A Personal View of a Political Life, 1925–1975*. Westport, CT: L. Hill.

This autobiography provides the reader with an inside look into what it was like to be a member of the American Communist Party in its heyday and when people were being sent to prison. Dennis was born into a communist family through her Russian immigrant parents and then was married for thirty-three years to the man who headed the American Communist Party (ACP). Feminists can learn a lot from reading Dennis' account of her life and fifty year association with the ACP, particularly her assessments of both the socialist and feminist movements. Her life was a full one and her political involvements were rewarding, but there was also pain and sacrifice. An important part of her story is her marriage to Eugene Dennis. Because of his political involvements and later imprisonment during the McCarthy years, she was left with almost full responsibility for childrearing and other family work. The level of honesty that Dennis reveals in her autobiography, including her ambivalence about her deeply intimate marriage, makes this book hard to put down.

347 FLYNN, ELIZABETH GURLEY. 1972. *The Alderson Story: My Life as a Political Prisoner*. New York: International Publishers.

Elizabeth Gurley Flynn was a labor organizer and agitator. The Alderson Story is an autobiographical telling of the two years and four months she spent in Alderson Federal Women's Reformatory. She called herself a political prisoner because of her arrest for political, not legal, reasons.

348 GARROW, DAVID J., ed. 1987. *The Montgomery Bus Boycott and the Women Who Started It: The Memoir of Jo Ann Gibson Robinson*. Knoxville: University of Tennessee Press.

In her memoir, Jo Ann Gibson Robinson shows how black women began the modern civil rights movement. Having been humiliated through eviction from a bus in 1949, Robinson joined the newly organized Women's Political Council

(WPC) where she helped launch the 1955–56 Montgomery bus boycott after Rosa Parks was arrested for not going to the back of a bus. When the WPC disseminated over 50,000 leaflets calling for a one day boycott, other black leaders joined the movement. Subsequently, with multi-organizational support, the boycott lasted thirteen months and succeeded in ending segregation of transportation facilities. Because historical accounts have tended to miss black women's contributions to the civil rights movement, this memoir calls attention to the need for black women to write about their history themselves.

349   GILMAN, CHARLOTTE PERKINS. 1935. *The Living of Charlotte Perkins Gilman: An Autobiography*. New York: Harper Colophon Books.
Charlotte Perkins Gilman (1860–1935) was a feminist theorist, economist, sociologist, and activist for women's autonomy and equality. In this autobiography she tells of her theories, travels, commitments, and difficulties throughout her life.

350   GLUCK, SHERNA, ed. 1976. *From Parlor to Prison: Five American Suffragists Talk About Their Lives*. New York: Vintage Books.
The stories of five suffragists told in their own words. These are enlightening stories about the life of activists in the early part of this century, the forces that led them to take the steps they did, and the experiences they had in the movement. Included are Jessie Haver Butler "On the Platform" and Ernestine Hara Kettler "In Prison."

351   JONES, HETTIE. 1990. *How I Became Hettie Jones*. New York: E.P. Dutton.
Hettie Jones writes about her life with LeRoi Jones and beyond. When her husband went through the changes which led to his becoming a spokesperson for a Marxist revolution among blacks, she kept her faith and in the process became her own person. Leaving behind the chaos of her earlier life, Jones went on to write children's books containing black and Native American stories.

352   LARCOM, LUCY. 1985. *New England Girlhood: Outlined from Memory*. Boston: Northeastern University Press.
A fascinating memoir of the life of a 'mill girl' which provides an important social history of the immigrant working-class experience during the early years of the industrial revolution. The development of a capitalist society in the United States is described in illuminating detail. This autobiography provides insights on personal life as well as the early years of the factory system.

353   LENSINK, JUDY NOLTE. 1989. *A Secret to Be Buried: The Diary and Life of Emily Hawley Gillespie, 1858–1888*. Iowa City: University Press of Iowa.
Diaries and personal letters provide some of the best sources of primary data for uncovering what life was like for everyday people in particular historical times and places. In this published diary of a thirty year period in the life of a

woman living in the United States during the nineteenth century, there is the added advantage of interpretation and analysis. Lensink is skilled at utilizing concepts from Women's Studies and feminist theory to enliven our understanding of the meaning of Gillespie's written words.

354   LORDE, AUDRE. 1982. *Zami: A New Spelling of My Name*. Watertown,
      MA: Persephone Press.
Audre Lorde, well-known poet and essayist, writes about her life as a black lesbian feminist. She tells of growing up in Harlem as the daughter of immigrant Grenadians, and of the racism she experienced in attending a white high school. Her autobiographical account includes her feelings when she first became aware of her attraction for women, including her first affair, and the isolation she felt in the black community where lesbianism was not discussed.

355   MILLETT, KATE. 1974. *Flying*. New York: Knopf.
This book is an autobiographical account of Millett's experiences after publication of her book *Sexual Politics*. It is a way for her to explain to herself, and others, what happened to her when she became a celebrity because of her feminist work. She was attacked from within because of the attention she received which was against the radical feminist principle of a leaderless movement, and from without when she announced that she was bisexual. It is a painful accounting of what happened to a number of women who received media attention and were then 'trashed' by their former friends and colleagues in the women's movement.

356   MOODY, ANNE. 1968. *Coming of Age in Mississippi*. New York: Dial Press.
In this autobiographical work, we learn what it was like to grow up in the Deep South in the 1950s. Unwilling to follow the pattern of older generations, Anne Moody resented being a domestic in a white family's home. Nor did she find solace in religion as her elders did. Her hatred of the system went beyond resentment of whites to also include blacks who accepted their position. When Moody won a scholarship to college she was introduced to other like-thinking people and found her way into the civil rights movement. This is an important record of the experiences she had in the Woolworth lunchcounter sit-ins and voter registration drives for SNCC and CORE.

357   MURRAY, PAULI. 1987. *Song in a Weary Throat: An American
      Pilgrimage*. New York: Harper and Row.
Pauli Murray's life is filled with interesting and diverse activities, including becoming an Episcopal priest (an event that occurs after the close of this autobiography). Murray tells of her college years at Hunter College, her involvement in civil rights causes, and her growing awareness of sexism when she was the only woman in law school at Howard University. Murray was one of the principal players in getting sex included in Title VII of the Civil Rights Legislation and later became one of the founders of the National Organization for Women in 1966.

358   SHOWALTER, ELAINE, ed. 1978. *These Modern Women: Autobiographical Essays from the Twenties*. Old Westbury, NY: The Feminist Press.

Showalter compares the women's movement in the 1920s with the movement in the 1970s. She finds interesting similarities in which there is a general belief among women that they are now liberated and there is not much more to be done. The press in the 1920s and the 1970s regularly announced the women's movement was dead. We know that the movement was not dead, nor were women liberated in the 1920s or the 1970s; which makes reading the reflections of a group of 1920s feminists so revealing and informative for the present struggle. The seventeen stories gathered for this anthology were originally published anonymously in *The Nation* between 1926 and 1927. Showalter has identified the writers and provided a cogent analysis about what they had to say. Authors include: Inez Haynes Irwin "The Making of a Militant;" Crystal Eastman "Mother-Worship;" Elizabeth Stuyvesant "Staying Free;" Phyllis Blanchard "The Long Journey;" Victoria McAlmon "Free—For What?" and Garland Smith "The Unpardonable Sin." Psychologists' responses were provided by Beatrice Hinkle "Why Feminism?" and John B. Watson "The Weakness of Women."

359   TRIMBERGER, ELLEN KAY, ed. 1991. *Intimate Warriors: Portraits of a Modern Marriage, 1899–1944: Selected Works by Neith Boyce and Hutchins Hapgood*. New York: The Feminist Press at the City University of New York.

A personal view of the lives of a politically and culturally radical couple of the early twentieth century. Using letters, fiction, poetry, and dramatic dialogues about their life together, Trimberger shows how Boyce and Hapgood continually struggled to create and maintain an egalitarian marriage. In the process, we learn about gender relationships in the Progressive Era; the leftist, feminist, anarchist, bohemian lifestyle of Greenwich Village; and Mabel Dodge's 5th Avenue Salon. Along with their intellectual and activist friends, such as Emma Goldman, John Reed, and Bill Haywood, they attempted to link political radicalism with personal liberation. Seeing themselves as feminists, Boyce and Hapgood worked against the odds to enact a relationship committed to autonomy and independence for women within marriage.

360   WADE-GAYLES, GLORIA. 1993. *Pushed Back to Strength: A Black Woman's Journey Home*. Boston: Beacon Press.

This is an autobiographical recollection of a civil rights activist. Wade-Gayles talks about her early years and the importance of the strength of the people around her when she was growing up in racially segregated Memphis, Tennessee. The black church and the role modeling she observed of strength, dignity, and faith provided her with the desire to become involved in social change efforts, including going to prison.

361   WELLS-BARNETT, IDA B. 1972. *Crusade for Justice: The Autobiography of Ida B. Wells*. Chicago: University of Chicago Press.

Edited by her daughter, Alfreda M. Duster, this autobiography by Ida B. Wells-Barnett tells of her public commitments to end racial injustice and of her private family life. Born a slave in Mississippi during the Civil War, Wells-Barnett became a crusader against all forms of racism, particularly against lynching. She was a founder of the NAACP, a leader in the Black Women's Club Movement, and an activist involved in efforts to end discrimination and segregation. She was also a devoted parent, and an important part of her story is how she was able to maintain her involvement in both of these realms. Because of her concern that African-Americans have been allowed so little knowledge of their past, she wrote this book on her life to contribute to the development of a history of her race.

Biography

362 ABELOVE, HENRY, BETSY BLACKMAR, PETER DIMOCK, and JONATHAN
   SCHNEER, eds. 1984. *Visions of History*. New York: Pantheon Books.
Under the auspices of the Radical Historians Organization, this edited volume brings the reader thirteen interviews with historians who are credited with pioneering the fields of black history, women's history, and the history of the working-class. Interviewees talk about their political commitments, life experiences, and their work. Those interviewed include E. P. Thompson, Eric Hobsbawn, Sheila Rowbotham, Linda Gordon, Natalie Zemon Davis, David Montgomery, Herbert Gutman, and C.L.R. James.

363 ADLER, KAREN S. 1992. "Always Leading Our Men in Service and
   Sacrifice: Amy Jacques Garvey, Feminist Black Nationalist." *Gender &
   Society* 6 (Sept.):346–375.
A biographical account of Amy Jacques Garvey's involvements in Garveyism and the Black Nationalist Movement. As the second wife to Marcus Garvey, she has never been acknowledged for her accomplishments in the Garvey movement. Adler argues that she was a committed and effective activist who's lack of recognition was tied to race, class, and gender attitudes which interacted to shape a "helpmate" image instead of an important social movement contributor.

364 ALLEN, POLLY WYNN. 1988. *Building Domestic Liberty: Charlotte
   Perkins Gilman's Architectural Feminism*. Amherst: The University of
   Massachusetts Press.
Charlotte Perkins Gilman is usually considered a socialist feminist, utopian feminist, or economic theorist with a feminist perspective. The focus of her work was women's oppression through familial role expectations and, most particularly, women's confinement to the home. The author of this book considers Gilman to be an architectural feminist interested in developing communal environments which liberate women from the authoritarian design of the single family home. This book adds to the understanding of an important early feminist theorist.

365   ANTICOGLIA, ELIZABETH. 1975. *Twelve American Women*. Chicago: Nelson-Hall.
A book of biographical sketches which includes women who were active in a variety of social activist groups, the promotion of feminist thought, the woman's suffrage movement, and the birth control movement. Included are Emma Willard, Margaret Fuller, Susan B. Anthony, Dorothea Dix, Jane Addams, Margaret Sanger, Eleanor Roosevelt, and Margaret Mead. A bibliography provides further reference sources.

366   ARLING, EMANIE NAHM. 1972. *The Terrible Siren: Victoria Woodhull*. New York: Arno Press.
Written in the 1920s, this biography illuminates an early feminist and socialist who was considered quite radical in her politics and personal life. Woodhull was an activist for woman's rights and suffrage and an advocate of free love. With her sister, Tennessee Claflin, she published the *Woodhull and Claflin Weekly* in the 1870s editorializing about the need for freedom and independence for women; she also contributed articles to *The Revolution*, a publication of the National Woman Suffrage Association. She was the first woman to run for president of the United States, doing so in 1872. Woodhull was associated with the Stanton/Anthony branch of the suffrage movement until she precipitated a scandal by revealing an affair between the president of the American Woman Suffrage Association (Henry Ward Beecher) with one of his married parishioners (Elizabeth Tilton).

367   ASHBAUGH, CAROLYN. 1976. *Lucy Parsons: American Revolutionary*. Chicago: C.H. Kerr.
Lucy Parsons was an African-American woman and socialist feminist. Throughout her adult life Parsons organized for social change and the rights of oppressed people, particularly for workers, women, and minority rights. She experienced personal tragedy as the widow of the martyred Albert Parsons, one of the four radical leaders hung in the aftermath of the 1886 Chicago Haymarket Riot. After her husband's death, Parsons continued her activity in the socialist labor movement into the 1930s.

368   BACON, MARGARET HOPE. 1993. *One Woman's Passion for Peace and Freedom: The Life of Mildred Scott Olmsted*. Syracuse, NY: Syracuse University Press.
This is a biography of one of the leading figures in the peace movement of the twentieth century. Olmsted's contribution to the Women's International League for Peace and Freedom was immense, and in turn the WILPF has been an effective organization for confronting issues of peace and equality. Since the first world war WILPF has focused on peaceful means of conflict resolution, but in conjunction with the contemporary women's movement members have also taken part in women's encampments to protest weapon deployments. WILPF has also provided strong support for struggles to gain greater levels of freedom for oppressed groups. Activism for the Equal Rights Amendment was engaged

in during the late 1970s and early 1980s. This biography shows some of the motivations, trials, and rewards such commitment to activism entails.

369 ———. 1980. *Valiant Friend: The Life of Lucretia Mott*. New York: Walker and Company.

One of the organizers of the 1848 Seneca Falls Woman's Rights Convention, Lucretia Mott was an activist in a variety of causes all her life. She was a Quaker minister in the Hicksite faction of the Society of Friends. Her religious belief in an 'inner light' guided her in the many causes she took on, particularly abolition and women's rights. In this biography her public and private life of wife and mother of six children are documented. She was the founder of the Philadelphia Anti-Slavery Society, helped to found the first women's medical college, and served as a model of activism for Susan B. Anthony and other women's rights leaders. When Alice Paul wrote and had the Equal Rights Amendment introduced into Congress in 1923, she called it the Lucretia Mott Amendment. Sources of archival research are included in the bibliography.

370 BANNISTER, ROBERT C. 1991. *Jessie Bernard: The Making of a Feminist*. New Brunswick, NJ: Rutgers University Press.

Jessie Bernard is a noted sociologist, now in her 80s, who continues to publish work on women and gender. Bernard wrote the classic study on "Marriage: His and Hers," and was involved in the formation of the contemporary women's movement in the late 1960s. In the 1980s she led the way for the need to create a global feminist solidarity movement. This biography covers both her personal and professional life.

371 BARRY, KATHLEEN. 1988. *Susan B. Anthony: A Biography of a Singular Feminist*. Irvington: New York University Press.

A thorough presentation of Susan B. Anthony's life and work. The author traces the evolution of Anthony's growing political activism from her childhood experiences to her status as the premier feminist organizer of the early woman's movement. Anthony was first an activist in abolition and temperance work, but when she learned of the 1848 Seneca Falls Convention, she soon became involved in the woman's rights movement too. Before long, women's rights became her life's work. Barry is a skilled researcher and provides interpretive analysis in addition to factual information to make this an interesting and valuable biography of an early and dedicated feminist activist. In a postscript Barry provides a description of her research methodology for writing biography.

372 BERNARD, JAQUELINE. 1990. *Journey Toward Freedom: The Story of Sojourner Truth*. New York: The Feminist Press.

This is a reprinted edition of a biography originally published in 1967. Bernard utilizes a feminist vision in presenting Sojourner Truth's life within a context of social events and the history of slavery. After gaining her freedom, Truth participated in the first national Woman's Rights Convention, the Akron convention where Frances Gage was asked to prevent Truth from speaking, a request she denied. Truth went on to give her famous "Ain't I A Woman" speech. During 1851–53 she became a traveling spokesperson against slavery and the Fugitive Slave Act. Through Bernard's careful writing style, we see the woman's movement through Sojourner's eyes and we learn of the power relations within the abolitionist movement, the brutality of slavery, racism by some white women in the suffrage movement, the sale of her son who later refused to acknowledge her, and even her ostracism by other slaves when she became an outsider to her own people.

373   BLACKWELL, ALICE STONE. 1971. *Lucy Stone: Pioneer of Woman's rights*. Detroit, MI: Gale Research.

Lucy Stone was a founder of the early woman's movement. She worked tirelessly for the cause of women's rights—traveling, speaking, and serving as a role model when, for instance, she kept her birth name upon marriage. She was also an activist in the abolition movement and it was the clash of these two movements' goals over suffrage that led to the split in the woman's movement after the Civil War. Stone was a leader of one side of this split, founding the American Woman Suffrage Association and publishing the *Woman's Journal*. This biography is written by her daughter, and the caring relationship they shared shows in the writing. It is also a well-documented source of American history and an inspiring look at an important activist in the great social movements of the nineteenth century.

374   BOYD, MELBA JOYCE. 1994. *Discarded Legacy: Politics and Poetics in the Life of Frances E. W. Harper, 1825–1911*. Detroit, MI: Wayne State University Press.

Frances E. W. Harper was a black woman activist, poet, orator, and essayist. She was involved with abolition, and demands for suffrage for both women and black men. She was a social reformer in general, a feminist, and a creative writer. Boyd brings out her story and her contributions in this biography.

375   BRADY, KATHLEEN. 1989. *Ida Tarbell: Portrait of a Muckraker*. Ithaca, NY: University of Pittsburgh Press.

Not all activist women who champion the rights of people and fight for justice are also feminist. This is the case of Ida Tarbell, whose ideology and involvements in social issues are admired by feminist activists even though she never took up the cause of women. Reading about her life offers a window on understanding more about high achieving dedicated women who are not everything you expect them to be, but who are admirable anyway.

376   BROWN, ELAINE. 1992. *A Taste of Power: A Black Woman's Story*. New York: Pantheon.

Elaine Brown was an activist in the Black Panther Party and the Party chair when her lover and Panther founder, Huey Newton, fled to Cuba. She tells about the founding of the Panthers, its transformation, demise, and misogynist attitudes and sexist treatment of women. Her own involvement and leadership led to a change in tactics from confrontational politics to electoral politics to bring power to African-American people. In this work, the author gives us a glimpse of women's involvement in the Black Power Movement of the 1960s.

377   CHESLER, ELLEN. 1992. *Woman of Valor: Margaret Sanger and the Birth Control Movement in America*. New York: Simon & Schuster.
A definitive biography of birth control crusader Margaret Sanger and the social movement she spawned. Sanger's work and life are combined to show her own sexual radicalism and the theoretical link she drew between the control of fertility and women's social/economic progress and freedom from domination by men. Her family background, socialist leanings, connections to anarchist Emma Goldman, imprisonment, exile, alliances with wealthy philanthropists and racial purity proponents are presented in an analytical portrayal of the politics of the movement. Details of strategic decisions show how the ideological and experiential influences of Sanger's life confronted a conservative social environment which eventually led to the transformation of a woman-focused birth control movement to a movement that was often involved in the development of restrictive family planning policies.

378   CONRAD, EARL. 1969. *Harriet Tubman*. New York: P.S. Eriksson.
A biography of Harriet Tubman and the work she did in the underground railroad to free slaves before the Civil War. Conrad originally published this book in 1943 and was the first researcher to do a full biography of Tubman's life (1820–1913). This is a well researched work and goes beyond the earlier limited biography by Sarah Bradford which only covered Tubman's life until 1869.

379   COOK, BLANCHE WIESEN. 1992. *Eleanor Roosevelt: Volume One 1884–1933*. New York: Viking Press.
This biography shows Eleanor Roosevelt to be a sincere and tireless worker for world peace, women's rights, children's rights, worker's protections, and justice for racial/ethnic groups. Included is an account of the reasons Roosevelt favored protective labor legislation over passage of the Equal Rights Amendment. The author provides a feminist portrait of Roosevelt which stresses the influence of women friends and role models, particularly Nancy Cook and Marion Dickerman, a lesbian couple who shared a cottage with her at her private retreat and worked with her in running a progressive girls' school. Defusing the widely believed perception of Roosevelt as the lonely spurned wife of her husband's extra-marital affair, Cook examines evidence of her probable love affair with her bodyguard and with journalist Lorena Hickok. Cook credits the women's movement with giving her the ability to see beyond previous stereotypes, and in so doing to bring Roosevelt to life as a woman with an independent character who made a life for herself through commitment to social causes.

380   COTE, CHARLOTTE. 1988. *Olympia Brown: The Battle for Equality*. Racine, WI: Mother Courage Press.
This is a biography of the first ordained woman minister in the United States and of her activism in the woman's movement. A friend of Susan B. Anthony

and Elizabeth Cady Stanton in the early days of the suffrage movement, Brown also joined with Alice Paul and Lucy Burns to do militant activism in the Congressional Union/National Woman's Party in the final years of the suffrage campaign when she was in her eighties. Her life story covers more than seventy years of activism for women's rights, including experimenting with the Bloomer costume for dress reform.

381   CROMWELL, OTELIA. 1971. *Lucretia Mott*. New York: Russell and Russell. Biography of an early abolitionist, adherent of Quakerism (including being a Quaker minister), and woman's rights activist. Mott (1793–1880) was a co-founder with Elizabeth Cady Stanton of the first Woman's Rights Convention in Seneca Falls, New York in 1848. Her frustration with the Quaker community in Philadelphia and the narrowness of many followers' beliefs led her to become an activist in many other social movements. The sexism she experienced in the abolition movement moved her to organize for women's rights. Wherever she found injustice, she sought to make it right. This is a thorough and well-researched biography of an important social reformer of the nineteenth century.

382   CROWDER, RALPH L. 1979. "Black Women: A Neglected Dimension in History." *Black Collegian* 9 (May):103–109.
This is a short article that gives a brief description of six activist black women who have contributed in a variety of ways to American society. Except for Ida B. Wells, a leader of the anti-lynching crusade, these African-American women are seldom included in history books. The unknown activists Crowder discusses are Esland Goode Robeson, author and activist for social justice; Mattie Proctor Thompson, a leader in the black community; Lucy Gathering Parsons, one of the founders of the Industrial Workers of the World; and Sarah Evans Lewis, a founder of a farming settlement.

383   DANIELS, DORIS GROSHEN. 1989. *Always a Sister: The Feminism of Lillian D. Wald*. New York: The Feminist Press.
A biography of Lillian Wald and a detailed history of the social world she lived and worked in. The influence Wald had on that world is substantial, particularly on issues related to social welfare. Her work in the Settlement House movement, women's unions, suffrage, and peace are well documented.

384   DAVIS, ALLEN FREEMAN. 1975. *American Heroine: The Life and Legend of Jane Addams*. New York: Oxford University Press.
A biography of Jane Addams (1860–1935), Settlement House founder, peace activist, feminist, reformer, suffragist, and Nobel Prize winner. In this biography Davis tells us of her life and motivations as well as the important work she did in the public setting. Her years at Hull House take up a good deal of this book, but also fully covered are her efforts on behalf of women's suffrage, the Progressive movement, women's unions, and peace activism including the founding of the Women's International League for Peace and Freedom. The author provides a critical appraisal of Addams life and work, calling attention to her accomplishments and her limitations.

385   DEEGAN, MARY JO. 1988. *Jane Addams and the Men of the Chicago School, 1892–1918*. New Brunswick, NJ: Transaction Books.
Deegan's intent in this work is to recognize Jane Addams as a sociologist and to acknowledge the importance of her contributions to sociological thought. Using historian's techniques and archival records, Deegan documents the sex segregated nature of sociology that developed at the University of Chicago. Beliefs of men as abstract thinkers and women as practical thinkers (applying their knowledge to social work) led to a denial of the contributions Addams and other women sociologists made to the founding of the discipline. The interaction that took place between Hull House, the social settlement Addams founded, and academics from the University of Chicago is well established. What Deegan does is to go beyond this point to reveal the intellectual foundation of Addams contributions that are embedded in the founding of American sociology.

386   DEEGAN, MARY JO, ed. 1991. *Women in Sociology: A Bio-Bibliographical Sourcebook*. New York: Greenwood Press.
This edited volume reveals the work of women sociologists from 1840 to 1990. Because women sociologists have had to fight to get into and be taken seriously in their profession, these biographical essays show the lack of response (including critiques) to the work women sociologists have done. Each contributor was asked to write about who their subject was networked with, what their most important writings were, who their mentors were, their major accomplishments, and the honors they received. Included are essays on Harriet Martineau, Florence Kelly, Jane Addams, Charlotte Perkins Gilman, Ida B. Wells-Barnett, Edith Abbott, Jessie Taft, Alva Myrdal, Jessie Bernard, Mirra Komarovsky, Hannah Arendt, Simone de Beauvoir, Matilda White Riley, Rosalie Wax, Rose Laub Coser, Alice Rossi, Joan Huber, Helena Znaniecka Lopata, and others.

387   DOUGLAS, EMILY TAFT. 1975. *Margaret Sanger: Pioneer of the Future*. Garrett Park, MD: Garrett Park Press.
A biography of Margaret Sanger's life (1879–1966) and her work in the birth control movement. Her achievements and failures, early background, arrests, divorces, and political involvement in sexuality research, socialism, feminism, eugenics, and birth control technology are all covered.

388   DREIER, MARY E. 1975. *Margaret Dreier Robins: Her Life, Letters, and Work*. Washington, D.C.: Zenger Publishing.
Margaret Dreier Robins (1868–1945) was an activist of great repute during the early part of the twentieth century. This biography shows her involvement in the Women's Trade Union League including her term as editor of the organization's publication *Life and Labor*, her close connection with Jane Addams and Hull House, and her role in the garment worker's strikes of 1909–1911 in Chicago, New York, and Philadelphia.

389   DRINNON, RICHARD. 1976. *Rebel in Paradise: A Biography of Emma Goldman*. New York: Harper and Row.
Biography of Emma Goldman (1869–1940), an anarchist theorist and impor-

tant contributor to the women's movement in the early part of the twentieth century. Goldman was a Russian immigrant and inspiring speaker who became involved in labor organizing and the birth control movement. Often involved in controversy for her views, Emma Goldman always spoke them and she lived her life in accordance with the values she espoused. She was supportive of women's equality but opposed the vote because of her anarchism.

390   EDELMAN, MARIAN WRIGHT. 1992. *The Measure of Our Success: A Letter to My Children and Yours*. Boston: Beacon Press.
Marian Wright Edelman, best known as the founder and director of the Children's Defense Fund, has been an activist for African-Americans and poor women and children for most of her life. In this book she has written a combination memoir and policy position that represents her learned experiences. Edelman began fighting for civil rights while she was a student at Yale Law School. In the 1960s, she was the first black woman to be admitted to the Mississippi Bar, she opened an NAACP Legal Defense Office in Jackson, Mississippi, and founded the Children's Defense Fund (CDF) which in the 1990s has a staff of more than 100 people and a budget over $10 million. The CDF advocates compassionate welfare reform and lobbies for universal health care, child-care, and family sustaining wages to help welfare recipients adopt independent lives.

391   EVANS, MARY. 1985. *Simone de Beauvoir: A Feminist Mandarin*. New York: Tavistock.
The Second Sex is widely regarded as a major feminist text and its author, de Beauvoir, as an exemplary example of a self-defining autonomous feminist life. In this biography, Evans instead argues that de Beauvoir exaggerated the dichotomy between women and men, and that she led a life which accepted many male patterns of thought and action. Both the positive and negative aspects of de Beauvoir's work are discussed.

392   FAUSET, ARTHUR HUFF. 1971. *Sojourner Truth: God's Faithful Pilgrim*. New York: Russell and Russell.
Biography of a former slave who became an activist in both the abolitionist and early woman's movement during the 1800s. Within the woman's movement, Truth is probably best known for her speech "Ain't I A Woman" at the 1852 Woman's Rights Convention in Akron, Ohio. Born in New York in 1797 and named Isabella Van Wagener, Truth experienced herself as being reborn around the age of forty. She took a new name to signify what her life would consist of and created a new identity by devoting herself to the abolitionist cause. This book was originally published in 1938; the style of writing falls more on the popular than scholarly side.

393   FITZPATRICK, ELLEN. 1990. *Endless Crusade: Women Social Scientists and Progressive Reform*. New York: Oxford University Press.
Biographical accounts of four women reformers in the early part of this century: Sophonisba Breckinridge, Edith Abbott, Katharine Bement Davis, and

Frances Kellor. All attended graduate school at the University of Chicago before becoming reform crusaders. Their activism spanned many arenas including prison reform, suffrage, labor legislation, settlement work, and Progressive Party politics.

394   FORSTER, MARGARET. 1984. *Significant Sisters: The Grassroots of Active Feminism, 1839–1939*. New York: Oxford University Press.
A portrait of eight women's rights advocates during the nineteenth and twentieth centuries: Caroline Norton, Elizabeth Blackwell, Florence Nightingale, Emily Davies, Josephine Butler, Elizabeth Cady Stanton, Margaret Sanger, and Emma Goldman. In the lives of these determined leaders, Forster draws out the roots of modern feminism. The areas in which they sought change included the law, professions, employment, education, sexual morality, politics, birth control, abolition, temperance, women's equality, and cultural ideology.

395   FOWLER, ROBERT BOOTH. 1986. *Carrie Catt: Feminist Politician*. Boston: Northeastern University Press.
A biography of the leader of the National American Woman Suffrage Association (NAWSA) during the final years of the suffrage campaign. Catt was a gifted organizer and her skills were well utilized when she took over the presidency of NAWSA for the second time. Those last years were crucial to achieve the victory of the Nineteenth Amendment. Later Catt continued her activism on the international scene.

396   GARLAND, ANNE WITTE. 1989. *Women Activists: Challenging the Abuse of Power*. New York: The Feminist Press.
In this book, Anne Witte Garland provides profiles of fourteen women who became activists against unfair and dangerous corporate and government practices. The protests they raised involved the environment, peace issues, and community needs. The writing is smooth, the narratives compelling.

397   GARRISON, DEE. 1989. *Mary Heaton Vorse: The Life of an American Insurgent*. Philadelphia: Temple University Press.
Mary Heaton Vorse (1874–1966) lived the life of a radical in early twentieth century America. Active in the suffrage movement and a labor journalist, Vorse committed herself to the attainment of socialism, feminism, and world peace.

398   GOERTZEL, TED G. 1992. *Turncoats and True Believers: The Dynamics of Political Belief and Disillusionment*. Buffalo, NY: Prometheus Books.
This work consists of biographical profiles of political and social movement leaders. The ideological scripts, irrational beliefs, and self-defeating actions of the subjects are highlighted. The feminist leaders examined are Kate Millett and Germaine Greer. Anti-feminist leader Phyllis Schlafly is also included.

399   GRIFFITH, ELISABETH. 1984. *In Her Own Right: The Life of Elizabeth Cady Stanton*. New York: Oxford University Press.
A biography on the life of Elizabeth Cady Stanton (1815–1902). Stanton was considered the philosopher and theorist of the early woman's rights move-

ment. She was one of the co-founders (with Lucretia Mott) of the first woman's rights conference which was held in the town she lived in (Seneca Falls, NY). Stanton and Susan B. Anthony teamed up in the early 1850s to form a life long partnership organizing and agitating for women's rights in general and, after the Civil War, for suffrage in particular. Stanton was one of the first feminists to criticize marriage and religion for their effects on women. She wrote a non-sexist religious tract called *The Woman's Bible*.

400 HALL, JACQUELINE DOWD. *Revolt Against Chivalry: Jessie Daniel Ames and the Women's Campaign Against Lynching*. Irvington, NY: Columbia University Press.
A biography of a highly dramatic and energetic woman who undertook a difficult political cause. In reading about Jessie Daniel Ames life, the reader also learns about racial attitudes and human relations in the early part of twentieth century America.

401 HERTHA, PAULI. 1962. *Her Name was Sojourner Truth*. New York: Appleton Century Crofts.
This biography was taken from an earlier 1850 version written for Truth by Olive Gilbert so that she could sell copies on her speaking tours. It tells the story of Truth's life and work for abolition and later for the early woman's movement.

402 HOLT, RACKHAM. 1964. *Mary McLeod Bethune: A Biography*. Garden City, NY: Doubleday.
An important activist for African-Americans and women's rights, Bethune was a founder of the Bethune-Cookman College in Daytona Beach, Florida and the National Council of Negro Women in 1935. She was also a speaker and supporter of Delta Sigma Theta, a black Sorority founded in 1913. Education, occupational opportunities, and civil rights issues for blacks was her lifelong work. Although this biography is not a scholarly work, it is an interesting account of Bethune's life and social activism.

403 HOROWITZ, HELEN LEFKOWITZ. 1994. *The Power and Passion of M. Carey Thomas*. New York: Alfred A. Knopf.
Biography of M. Carey Thomas, known for her activism for women's higher education. Thomas was born into a Quaker family in Baltimore and later served as president of the Quaker college for women, Bryn Mawr College, from 1894–1922. In her private life she had a woman lover who lived with her for twenty-five years until Thomas fell in love with another woman and tried (successfully for a time) living with both of them by splitting up the weekday and weekend times. She was a fighter for women's rights, but she was also an elitist and racist. She never admitted a black student nor were there any Jewish faculty hired. A very interesting biography of a complex woman.

404 HUCKLE, PATRICIA. 1991. *Tish Sommers, Activist and the Founding of the Older Women's League*. Knoxville: University of Tennessee Press.

A biography of a woman who led an activist life and when she became older was a major contributor to founding an organization for aging women.

405   JOHNSON, SONIA. 1981. *From Housewife to Heretic*. Garden City, NY: Doubleday & Co.

The subtitle of this book is "One Woman's Struggle for Equal Rights and Her Excommunication from the Mormon Church," and that is an accurate summary of the contents of this biographical work. Johnson chronicles her conversion from the Mormon church, wife, and mother to a radical feminist activist who founded Mormons for ERA. After twenty years of marriage and lifelong involvement with Mormonism, her awakening recognition of sex inequality led her to agitate against those conditions and then, subsequently, to lose both of those sources of identity. In this book she tells of her rebirth within the women's movement and her progression from self-denial to activism.

406   ———. 1987. *Going Out of Our Minds: The Metaphysics of Liberation*. Freedom, CA: The Crossing Press.

This is a continuation of Sonia Johnson's biographical accounts of her activism in the women's movement and her developing thoughts on the meaning of feminism. In this book she tells of the thirty-seven day fast she led in 1982 in Springfield, Illinois with seven other women for the ERA. That same year she ran for president of the National Organization for Women and carried 40 percent of the votes. The following year she organized a Women's Gathering for women who were looking for alternatives to the present women's movement and who were interested in using civil disobedience for what they believed. She discusses previous civil disobedience actions she was involved with, including the Seneca Depot protests. She explains why, in 1984, she ran for president of the United States on a third party ticket.

407   JOSEPHSON, HANNAH. 1974. *Jeannette Rankin, First Lady in Congress: A Biography*. Indianapolis, Indiana: Bobbs-Merrill.

A look at the life of Jeannette Rankin, who became the first woman to be elected to the U.S. House of Representatives. In learning about Rankin's life in Montana and Washington, D.C., the author also covers politics, feminism, suffrage, and pacifism in the first half of the twentieth century.

408   KEAN, HILDA. 1989. *Deeds Not Words: The Lives of Suffragette Teachers*. Winchester, MA: Unwin Hyman.

Women teachers, who were also active in the suffrage movement, are highlighted here in collective biography form. These women were often involved in more than one cause and most would be classified as feminists, socialists, and activists in general. The period covered is the turn of the century into the Depression years.

409   KERR, ANDREA MOORE. 1992. *Lucy Stone: Speaking Out for Equality*. New Brunswick, NJ: Rutgers University Press.

In this biography, the author presents a scholarly and empathic view of an early and highly activist feminist. Lucy Stone kept her own name upon marriage in the mid-nineteenth century and continued her activism for the rights of women and blacks. When the woman's movement split into two factions after the Civil War, Stone was a leader of the American Woman Suffrage Association which had supported gaining the vote for black males first and working on woman's suffrage after achieving that goal. This placed her on opposite sides with Susan B. Anthony and Elizabeth Cady Stanton's National Woman Suffrage Association until 1890 when the two organizations joined to form the National American Woman Suffrage Association. Stone became the president of NAWSA shortly before she died.

410   KUHN, MAGGIE WITH CHRISTINA LONG. 1991. *No Stone Unturned: The Life and Times of Maggie Kuhn*. New York: Ballantine Books.
Maggie Kuhn was the founder of The Grey Panthers and an activist on behalf of older people and women for many years. This is a biography of a remarkable woman.

411   LANE, ANN J., ed. 1988. *Mary Ritter Beard: A Sourcebook*. Boston: Northeastern University Press.
Mary Ritter Beard was an activist for social justice, particularly in the campaigns for suffrage and labor reform. In this book, Ann Lane has gathered the theoretical and historical writings of Beard which reveals her thoughts on social change possibilities.

412   LOCKE, MAMIE E. 1990. "Is This America? Fannie Lou Hamer and the Mississippi Freedom Democratic Party." Pp. 27–38 in *Women in the Civil Rights Movement: Trailblazers and Torchbearers, 1941–1965*, edited by Jacqueline Anne Rouse, Barbara Wood, Vicki L. Crawford. Brooklyn, NY: Carlson Publishing.
An essay on the life and work of Fannie Lou Hamer who played an important part in the Mississippi Freedom Democratic Party and who lost her sharecropping job trying to register people to vote.

413   LOGAN, ONNIE LEE. 1989. *Motherwit: An Alabama Midwife's Story*. New York: Dutton.
In the finest tradition of oral history, Onnie Lee Logan tells her story of a black woman's journey in an oppressed culture. Logan's life provides a basis to think about the struggles between race and class that so many people in American society confront.

414   LOWY, BEVERLY. 1993. "Always In Your Face: Flo Kennedy, An Activist Forever." *On The Issues* 26 (March):21–23.
In this article the author talks about the activism of Flo Kennedy and provides portions of an interview Lowy did with her in 1985. Kennedy was one of the first African-American women to graduate from Columbia University School of Law (1951) and went on to found a number of organizations dedicated to fight-

ing for women's rights and civil rights, e.g., Coalition Against Racism and Sexism, and The Feminist Party. She was one of the original founders of NOW and at the 1991 conference spoke forcefully against Clarence Thomas' confirmation to the Supreme Court. She called Thomas an embarrassment to African-Americans and praised Anita Hill, citing her as contributing to a revival of the feminist movement. In discussing white/black feminist relations, Kennedy argues that the question "why aren't black women involved in the women's movement" begs the question "why aren't white women involved in the civil rights movement?"

415   LUMPKIN, KATHARINE DU PRE. 1974. *The Emancipation of Angelina Grimké.* Chapel Hill: University of North Carolina Press.
In this biography of Angelina Grimké (1805–1879) the focus is on the development of her anti-slavery sentiments and her activism in the abolition movement.

416   LUNARDINI, CHRISTINE A. 1988. *From Equal Suffrage to Equal Rights: Alice Paul and the National Woman's Party, 1910–1928.* New York: New York University Press.
Although not a full biography, this work covers an important period in the life of Alice Paul, a woman who dedicated herself to the fight for women's equality. The National Woman's Party was founded by Paul to draw in militant women for the suffrage campaign. NWP members were arrested and jailed for picketing in front of the White House for the vote for women. Many, including Paul, went on hunger strikes and were then forcibly fed while in prison. After the Nineteenth Amendment was passed, Paul and the NWP began the fight for passage of the Equal Rights Amendment.

417   MARCUS, JANE, ed. 1989. *The Young Rebecca: The Writings of Rebecca West, 1911–1917,* Bloomington: Indiana University Press.
Rebecca West is best known for her literary skills but she was also an activist for women's rights. This collection of her work goes back to some of her earliest writing. Most of the selections have never been published before. This work shows the level of passion West felt for the political issues of her day. She writes of the causes she supports, her experiences in the suffrage campaign, and literary events she participated in.

418   MARK, JOAN. 1988. *A Stranger in Her Native Land: Alic Fletcher and the American Indians.* Lincoln: University of Nebraska Press.
The life of anthropologist Alic Fletcher is recreated from her diaries, letters, and records of her work among the Plains Indians. Fletcher was an activist for social justice and change. She worked for reform in the reservation system, land allotments, and attitudes towards Native Americans. She was also concerned about the position of women in American society and, by words and deeds, attempted to change long held views of women that limited their options and opportunities.

419　MATHES, VALERIE SHERER. 1990. *Helen Hunt Jackson and Her Indian Reform Legacy*. Austin: University of Texas Press.

Working with Native Americans became the life work of Helen Hunt Jackson. This is an accounting of that life and what Jackson was able to accomplish by her efforts for reform in government practices and assistance to the Native peoples she came to love. It is also a book that provides informative background on understanding the policies of the U.S. government that led to the plight of many tribes during the 1800s and into the present.

420　MERRIAM, EVE, ed. 1971. *Growing Up Female in America: Ten Lives*. New York: Dell Publishing Co.

The ten lives highlighted in this volume cover the range of unknown to famous activist women before the emergence of the contemporary women's movement. The stories are told in the women's own words as accounts are drawn from autobiographical works, letters, journals, and diaries. Their lives reveal the restrictions they felt in their everyday experiences and their developing feminist consciousness. Included are the stories of Elizabeth Cady Stanton, Mother Jones, Dr. Anna Howard Shaw, and Susie King Taylor.

421　MILLS, KAY. 1993. *This Little Light of Mine: The Life of Fannie Lou Hamer*. New York: Dutton.

This is a biography of a Mississippi sharecropper who became a voice for justice in the civil rights movement. Hamer believed people had a right to a decent life and that the pain of poverty was a socially constructed status which was enforced through race and gender oppressive systems. She was born the youngest of twenty children and had to leave school in the sixth grade to contribute to the support of her family. Involuntarily sterilized at a young age, she later became a civil rights leader and is best remembered for her speech at the 1964 Democratic convention for the Mississippi Freedom Democratic Party, and for her singing of "This Little Light of Mine." Speaking on behalf of unions, feminism, and African-Americans, she was an integral part of a supportive community of committed activists. These networks of involvement do not prepare the reader to learn that in the last years of her life, she died a slow death in which she felt abandoned.

422　MORGAN, ROBIN. 1977. *Going Too Far: The Personal Chronicle of a Feminist*. New York: Random House.

Morgan tells her own story of evolving political/personal thought from the early 1960s to the late 1970s. It is the journey of daughterhood, artist, marriage, motherhood, New Left activist, and radical feminist. The book consists of a collection of papers written over this period. Each section has an introductory piece which places the original work in the context of when and why it was written, and what Morgan was experiencing at that time. This writing details the emergence of the small group sector of the Women's Liberation Movement, the disruption of the Miss America Pageant in 1968, articles from WITCH, Morgan's disillusionment with Leftist men and growing connections to radical feminism, her thoughts on rape, lesbianism, Women's Studies, international feminism, and art.

423 MOSER, CHARLOTTE. 1987. *Clyde Connell: The Art and Life of a Louisiana Woman*. Austin: University of Texas Press.
Life history of a Southern woman who was active in the civil rights movement. Later in her life, Connell took up sculpting and became a locally recognized artist. Participating in the civil rights movement in Louisiana in the 1950s was not something Southern women were supposed to do, nor was becoming a sculptor when one was a senior citizen. These accomplishments are the heart of what makes this book so interesting.

424 MUELLER, CAROL. 1990. "Ella Baker and the Origins of Participatory Democracy." Pp. 51–70 in *Women in the Civil Rights Movement: Trailblazers and Torchbearers, 1941–1965*, edited by Vickie L. Crawford, Jacqueline Anne Rouse, and Barbara Woods. Brooklyn, NY: Carlson Publishing.
Ella Baker was a grassroots organizer in the civil rights movement who influenced and inspired many of the people that worked with her. Mueller discusses Baker's ideology and values of non-hierarchical, egalitarian leadership that were adopted by the Student Nonviolent Coordinating Committee.

425 NIES, JUDITH. 1977. *Seven Women: Portraits From the American Radical Tradition*. New York: Viking Press.
Biographical accounts of seven women radicals representing a wide variety of social causes. The stories of their lives and work are interesting and inspiring. Nies creates a nice mix of personal background information with the causes they took up. By reading about their commitments, the overlap in activism becomes evident as they collectively worked for or supported most of the following: labor reform, union organizing, advancement for women, suffrage, racial justice, birth control, and peace. The women are Sarah Moore Grimké, abolition and women's rights; Harriet Tubman, underground railroad; Elizabeth Cady Stanton, early women's rights and suffrage; Mother Jones, labor organizer; Charlotte Perkins Gilman, theorist, socialist, and visionary; Anna Louise Strong, international journalist; Dorothy Day, co-founder of the Catholic Worker Movement.

426 PALMIERI, PATRICIA ANN. 1995. *In Adamless Eve: The Community of Woman Faculty at Wellesley*. New Haven, CT: Yale University Press.
A collective biography in the form of individual sketches woven into a narrative story of the first generation of women professors at Wellesley. The reader will learn about women's colleges in general and the experiences of women intellectuals in the early twentieth century. This work contributes to the field of women's studies, American culture, and the history of education in the United States.

427   PECK, MARY. 1944. *Carrie Chapman Catt: A Biography*. New York: H. W.
       Wilson.
A biography of a dynamic leader in the final years of the suffrage campaign.
Catt is credited with having strong organizational skills as the president of the
National American Woman Suffrage Association.

428   PEEBLES-WILKINS, WILMA and ARACELIS E. FRANCIS. 1990. "Two
       Outstanding Black Women in Social Welfare History: Mary Church
       Terrell and Ida B. Wells-Barnett." *Affilia* 5:72–100.
Using Terrell and Wells-Barnett's own writing and other secondary sources, the
authors of this article reveal the contributions these two reformers made to
human rights causes of the nineteenth and twentieth centuries.

429   PERRY, ELISABETH ISREALS. 1987. *Belle Moskowitz: Feminine Politics
       and the Exercise of Power in the Age of Alfred E. Smith*. Philadelphia:
       Temple University Press.
A look at women activists of the past, with a particular focus on Belle
Moskowitz, who worked for a more just society in a variety of ways. There are
valuable lessons to be learned for present social movement activists in this
book.

430   RICH, ADRIENNE. 1979. *On Lies, Secrets, and Silence: Selected Prose
       1966–1978*. New York: W. W. Norton.
A personal account of her own life journey and discoveries. Rich is a poet and
feminist theorist who traces her developing lesbian feminist consciousness in
these writings. She examines motherhood, racism, history, poetry, scholarship,
and language. In covering the years 1966–1978, Rich also provides a historical
document of the women's movement during this period.

431   RICHARDSON, DOROTHY. 1990. *The Long Day: The Story of a New York
       Working Girl*. Charlottesville: University Press of Virginia.
Narrative of what it was like for a young woman of eighteen in 1905 to go to
New York City with no money, skills, or friends. In the process of learning how
Richardson managed to seek her livelihood and survive, readers also learn a
social history of working-class life for women in urban areas in the early part of
this century.

432   RICHARDSON, MARILYN, ed. 1987. *Maria W. Stewart: America's First
       Black Woman Political Writer, Essays and Speeches*. Bloomington:
       Indiana University Press.
Even before Frederick Douglass or Sojourner Truth began writing and speaking about women's rights (as well as black rights and the end of slavery), Maria
Steward was defending the rights of women. She was the first black American
to do so and the articles in this collection recall her life and activism.

433   ROUSE, JACQUELINE ANNE. 1989. *Lugenia Burns Hope, Black Southern
       Reformer*. Athens: University of Georgia Press.
A biography of the life of Lugenia Burns Hope and her work for black equality.

Her early activism was in social reform and charity in Chicago, including at Hull House. After her marriage she moved to Atlanta (she had been born in St. Louis) where her husband was president of Atlanta Baptist College (later Moorehouse) and Atlanta University. Hope continued her charitable work in Atlanta where she also became a lecturer for the National Council of Negro Women and a vice president of the Atlanta branch of the NAACP.

434 RUDDICK, SARA and PAMELA DANIELS. 1977. *Working It Out: 23 Women Writers, Artists, Scientists, and Scholars Talk About Their Lives and Work*. New York: Pantheon Books.

This is an interesting and inspiring collection of women writing about their lives and work. Biographical in nature, these writings are validations of women's life experiences. The sketches make for pleasurable reading and, in combination, reveal the gender commonalities and diversities found in modern social life. Twenty-three selections are included from a rich array of women artists, scientists, scholars and writers. In the foreword, Adrienne Rich comments that this work contributes to "the long process of making visible the experience of women."

435 SCOTT, KESHO YVONNE. 1991. *The Habit of Surviving: Black Women's Strategies for Life*. New Brunswick, NJ: Rutgers University Press.

The five chapters that make up this book consist of biographical accounts of five women (including the author) discussing their lives as children, adult family members, workers, and activists. These oral histories were drawn from intensive interviews of what Scott calls "hidden feminists." Some of the topics covered include color prejudice and male priorities within the African-American community, the suppression of black women's intelligence and leadership abilities, and the difficulties of maintaining family and working for social change.

436 SOLOMON, MARTHA. 1987. *Emma Goldman*. Boston: Twayne Publishers.

This biography focuses on Emma Goldman as a writer and rhetorician. Solomon provides a brief chronicle of Goldman's life that highlights her development as an anarchist and agitator for change. The remaining chapters discuss her general theories and her essays on social issues. Most of these essays originated as lectures and many were published in Mother Earth or pamphlets. Goldman's autobiographical writing in *My Disillusionment in Russia* and *Living My Life* are also examined.

437 STANTON, THEODORE and HARRIOT STANTON BLATCH. 1922. *Elizabeth Cady Stanton: As Revealed in Her Letters, Diary and Reminiscences*. New York: Harper & Brothers.

A biographical work of a major leader in the early woman's rights movement and the suffrage movement by her son and daughter. Stanton's personal writing forms a large part of this work.

438   STERLING, DOROTHY. 1991. *Ahead of Her Time: Abby Kelley and the Politics of Antislavery*. New York, NY: W.W. Norton & Company.
A biography of a Quaker abolitionist and woman's rights activist. Like the well-known Grimké sisters, Kelley developed a feminist consciousness out of the negative treatment she received, as a woman, in lecturing against slavery. Her first public speech took place at a Philadelphia Women's Anti-Slavery convention that ended with the meeting hall being set on fire. Traveling on the lecture circuit for two decades, Kelley is credited with having inspired feminist activism in Lucy Stone and Susan B. Anthony, both of whom later went on to become leaders in the woman's rights movement.

439   ———. 1979. *Black Foremothers: Three Lives*. Old Westbury, NY: The Feminist Press.
This book contains biographical sketches of three African-American women who were activists in causes for women and blacks: Ellen Craft, an activist in the abolition movement and a teacher for freed slaves; Mary Church Terrell, involved in advancing efforts for black education and a contributing member of the National Association of Colored People and The National Association of Colored Women; and Ida B. Wells, a well-known journalist and leader in the anti-lynching movement.

440   STEVENSON, BRENDA, ed. 1989. *The Journals of Charlotte Forten Grimké*. New York: Oxford University Press.
Publication of the journal entries of Charlotte Grimké, a reformer, teacher, and writer gives readers insight into her thinking and activism. Grimké was an intelligent observer of people and events, and her writings reveal intimate and informative views of nineteenth century race relations, including the Civil War and Reconstruction periods of American history.

441   STEVENS, DORIS. 1920. *Jailed for Freedom*. New York: Boni & Liveright.
A biographical account of her activities in the militant campaigns of the National Woman's Party for Suffrage. Stevens talks about the actions she and other suffragists took and the consequences they faced when they were arrested and imprisoned. This work, published in 1920, was before Stevens and Alice Paul had a falling out.

442   SUNSTEIN, EMILY W. 1975. *A Different Face: The Life of Mary Wollstonecraft*. Boston: Little, Brown and Co.
Mary Wollstonecraft was the mother of Mary Shelley (author of *Frankenstein*) and author of *A Vindication of the Rights of Woman* (1791). In the 1970s she was heralded as the symbolic founder of the women's movement. In this book, Sunstein provides a biography of this important eighteenth century thinker drawn from Wollstonecraft's essays, novels, and letters.

443   SWARTZ, GERALD, ed. 1989. *A Woman Doctor's Civil War: Esther Hill Hawks' Diary*. Columbia: University of South Carolina Press.
The story of a full life by a Northern woman who went South to doctor black

Union troops and to teach literacy to newly freed slaves. Hawks' diary shows she lived many lives—as a physician, school administrator, suffragist, and abolitionist.

444 WARE, SUSAN. 1987. *Partner and I: Molly Dewson, Feminism, and New Deal Politics*. New Haven, CT: Yale University Press.
This biographical work of Molly Dewson fills in an important part of the history of the New Deal. As director of the Women's Division of the Democratic National Committee, Dewson contributed to an expanded role for women in the government during the 1930s. Prior to this time Dewson had worked with Florence Kelley at the National Consumer's League and fought for a minimum wage for women workers. Representing one direction feminist activism took after suffrage, the life of Molly Dewson also reveals a woman centered existence with her partner Polly Porter and how her private and political world interacted and contributed to each other.

445 WEIKE, DAVID THOREAU. 1991. *A Woman from Spillertown: A Memoir of Agnes Burns Weike*. Carbondale: Southern Illinois University Press.
In this biography of his mother, David Weike documents her career as a labor activist where she rose to become a leading force in the coal mining struggles of southern Illinois. As she gained recognition for her efforts to organize miners, she became known as the "Mother Jones" of Illinois, a compliment to her tenacity and success.

4

Feminist Discourse

Introduction

The women's movement, like all social movements, consists of organized activity for social change. Within this broad definition, there exists a wide variety of organizational forms and interactive patterns. Differences among groups making up a social movement usually represent alternative plans for reaching the same goal, particular emphases, or mirror reflections of the diversity of people involved in a multifaceted movement. Sometimes differences represent opposing views, such as the sharp division within the women's movement over how to view pornography.

Feminist thought is a way of seeing the world through a woman's perspective, and the women's movement is meant to be for all women. Here, in these two ideas, is the challenge of finding a feminism that speaks for women from every social group. But, that goal—popularly known as "universal sisterhood"—has been attacked as a way for privileged women to ignore the disparities among women. Perhaps, then, at least for now, it is better to speak of feminist voices since, beyond gender, there are many dissimilarities in women's lives.

As noted in the last chapter, social movements are made up of people—that is fundamentally what a movement is. Given the reality of an unequal social structure, it is not surprising that the women's movement is a multifarious, and often, conflicted movement, or that there would be divisions over ideology, theory, organization, structure, strategies, and ways of "being." Up to a point, the diversity of people and ideologies are what make the women's movement the exciting and vital movement that it is. Beyond that point, divisiveness can be destructive. But exactly where is that point?

Chapter 4, **Feminist Discourse**, includes selections that address questions of diversity in feminist thought, theory, philosophy, organization, and goals. The first category, **Feminist Thought**, includes a wide ranging look at feminism as a particular view of the world, a consciousness that continues to emerge and to develop in increasingly more complex ways. Gender, as a center of analysis, constitutes much of the contributions in this section. Philosophical, psychological, and sociological perspectives are included, as well as the contributions of feminist men and their relationship to the women's movement.

Feminist Theory includes works discussing the range of feminist theories that have been part of an ongoing exploratory dialogue. The level and extent of these works represents a change from earlier periods of the women's movement when theory was rarely discussed. Here can be found well developed debates on Marxist, socialist, radical, liberal, and separatist feminism.

The section on **Methodology** looks at the ways research has left out women and how to change that practice. Beyond that, the reader will find proposals for the development of a distinctive feminist perspective in numerous academic disciplines.

A broad-based theoretical framework is provided in the section on **Sociology, Social Movement Theory, and Social Movement Comparisons**. Here historic and academic research on social movements, resource mobilization, New Social Movement Theory, and comparative social movement analysis is presented. Comparisons are framed within analytical and theoretical insights between the U.S. women's movement in different time periods, the U.S. movement in contrast to feminist movements in other countries, and the women's movement compared with other social movements.

Identity Politics entails one of the most divisive elements of the contemporary women's movement. Discussions on this topic center on the connections and discord surrounding race, class, ethnicity, age, sexual orientation, and gender. This section is a reflection of the disarray of the movement in the highly charged anti-feminist 1980s and, alternatively by mid-decade, of the flourishing 'womanist' consciousness of women of color.

Rather than focusing on the lack of inclusiveness of the women's movement as identity politics does, the section on **Multiculturalism** focuses on particular social group characteristics beyond gender. Writers, often in personal terms, reveal what their place in the social structure has meant to them as women. Pieces are informational, effective, group enhancing, and consciousness-raising.

Black Feminism and Black Women's Activism, although a part of multicultural feminism and identity politics, is a separate category because of the volume of writing that has been produced specifically on African-American women's lives and social analysis. The distinctions between the last three categories in this chapter are not particularly clear and anyone interested in any one of them should look closely at all three. They are clearly interwoven categories as they engage each other in their mutual efforts to create a women's movement that combines unity with diversity.

Feminist Thought

446   ADAM, BARBARA. 1989. "Feminist Social Theory Needs Time: Reflections on the Relation Between Feminist Thought, Social Theory and Time as

an Important Parameter in Social Analysis." *Sociological Review* 37:458–473.

Much discussion in the family and gender literature is the double burden women carry of family and work obligations. Yet, feminist theory has not actively incorporated "time" as a privileged/oppressed characteristic of gender differentiation. Adam begins such an analysis in this article and calls on feminist theorists to include time in their social theory work. The author argues that understanding the social world through the eyes of women involves critically examining preconceived conceptions that have been developed from male experience. Revisionist analysis is called for in all areas.

447   ALLEN, ANITA L. 1990. *Uneasy Access: Privacy for Women in a Free Society*. Savage, MD: Rowman & Littlefield.

What are often thought of as family or gender issues are presented in this work as privacy issues. The author is particularly concerned about the lack of a conceptual understanding of privacy rights for women. Privacy and the lack of privacy rights is explored in relationship to abortion, birth control, motherhood, courtship rituals, harassment, pornography, prostitution, and rape. The overall societal message related to these issues is one of low social regard for women's privacy.

448   BARUCH, ELAINE HOFFMAN and LUCIENNE J. SERRANO. 1988. *Women Analyze Women in France, England, and the United States*. New York: New York University Press.

Combining feminist theory and psychoanalysis into a therapeutic context, the authors discuss the potential this combination has for transforming European and American cultures and individual women.

449   BELENKY, MARY FIELD, BLYTHE MCVICKER CLINCHY, NANCY RULE GOLDBERGER, and JILL MATTUCK TARULE. 1986. *Women's Ways of Knowing: The Development of Self, Voice, and Mind*. New York: Basic Books.

The authors of this book are interested in understanding why, in spite of the gains of the women's movement, women still feel silenced. According to their analysis of the interviews of the 135 women comprising this study, it is because models of intellectual development have come from the male experience. Taking an essentialist view, this book argues that mothering proscriptions develop different qualities for women which lead them to incorporate intuition, personal meaning, and understanding in their quest for knowledge. This book won an award from the Association of Women in Psychology, but will fail to fully satisfy anthropologists, historians, and sociologists because of its limited data base (mostly U.S. college students), ahistorical presentation, and the lack of discussion of the effects of women and men occupying different and unequal positions in a stratified gender structure.

450   BUNCH, CHARLOTTE. 1981. *Feminism in the '80s: Facing Down the Right*. New York: Inkling Press.

Bunch discusses the growing threat of the Right Wing, particularly the Religious Right, to feminism and gay liberation. Serving as the basis for her keynote address at the Second National Lesbian Conference, this paper argues for a radical new vision of change on the societal, political, structural, and personal levels.

451   ————.1987. *Passionate Politics*. New York: St. Martin's Press.

This book consists of essays on feminist theory in action written by Charlotte Bunch between 1968–1986. Her essays trace the contemporary women's movement and link feminist concerns of today with those of the past. Topics include lesbian feminism, theory, leadership, strategies, separatism, movement organizing, and global feminism. Her practical approach is enlightening and reading her book removes either/or positions from consideration. For instance, she argues that it is a waste of time to talk about whether a goal is revolutionary or reformist, since what is important is whether it is good for women. This is an insightful book from an important lesbian feminist activist.

452   BURNHAM, LINDA. 1985. "Has Poverty Been Feminized in Black America?" *Black Scholar* 16 (March):14–24.

Burnham argues that poverty is not related to gender, but rather it is a consequence of class, race, and sex. The author finds that poverty among all women has increased due to the increase of single parenting, but that there is still a significant difference between white and black women in poverty rates (14.7 percent and 44.9 percent respectively). Burnham calls for a synthesis of class, race, and sex in analyses of poverty in order to illuminate the reality of poverty in the United States today. The author argues that failure on the part of the women's movement to do so will only perpetuate the perception that the movement represents white middle-class feminism.

453   BURTON, GABRIELLE. 1972. *I'm Running Away from Home But I'm Not Allowed to Cross the Street*. Pittsburgh, PA: Know, Inc.

Called a primer to women's liberation, this small book is a delight to read. Written in a non-threatening and witty style, it demonstrates with humor the underlying discontent of women who are looking for a different kind of life than the restrictive roles many have found themselves locked into. It is a feminist book for beginners that relies on personal experience rather than anger, intensity, or theoretical analyses.

454   CHAMBERS-SCHILLER, LEE. 1984. *Liberty, A Better Husband: Single Women in America, The Generations of 1780–1840*. New Haven, CT: Yale University Press.

In the years preceding the rise of the woman's rights movement, by law and custom, a woman lost her autonomy upon marriage. For many women, the only way they could participate in the world on their own terms was to remain single. In this book, Chambers-Schiller explores the social conditions and lives of women who chose this option.

455   CHODOROW, NANCY J. 1989. *Feminism and Psychoanalytic Theory*.
      New Haven, CT: Yale University Press.
Expanding upon her earlier work in *The Reproduction of Mothering*, Chodorow examines the inter-relationships between gender, self, and society. The overall focus of this work is the development of an unconscious gendered self that begins in infancy. The gendered self perceives sex differences as fundamental and innate, and it is this thinking that leads to gender differences permeating social institutions and personal interactions. Thus, according to Chodorow, it is gender thinking that leads to inequalities in social structures and cultural thought.

456   ———.1978. *The Reproduction of Mothering: Psychoanalysis and the Sociology of Gender*. Berkeley: University of California Press.
This book created quite a stir when it was first published because it raised controversial issues over the role of motherhood, fatherhood, and family. Chodorow presents a feminist-Freudian social role theory of mothers dominating their children because they are the primary caretaker. In contrast to women's mothering role, fathers are mainly absent in their children's lives. These gender roles lead children to socially reproduce the same roles as their parents when they become adults and, thus, to perpetuate the gender differences found in society. The solution to this repetitious cycle, according to the author, is for men to take an equal role in child rearing.

457   CLOUGH, PATRICIA TICINETO. 1994. *Feminist Thought: Desire, Power and Academic Discourse*. Cambridge, MA: Blackwell Publishers.
A review of the range of feminist theories since the 1970s. Clough shows how feminist thought has transformed the way we think about social science, sexuality, power, race, class, ethnicity, and nationality.

458   COLLINI, STEFAN, ed. 1989. *John Stuart Mill: On Liberty*. Cambridge: Cambridge University Press.
John Stuart Mill (1806–1879) is credited with laying a philosophical foundation for contemporary liberal thought. In this collection, Collini has put together some of Mill's most important works including *The Subjection of Women* (1861) and his writing on socialism.

459   COTT, NANCY F. 1989. "What's in a Name? The Limits of Social Feminism or Expanding the Vocabulary of Women's History." *Journal of American History* 76 (Dec.):809–829.
A critique of terminology used by historians for women's activism. For instance, William O'Neill contrasted "social feminism" with "hard core feminism" (*Everyone Was Brave: The Rise and Fall of Feminism in America*, 1969). Cott finds this incorrect, especially when applied to women's groups and the

overlap between family, career, and gender socialization. The author finds fault with the polarizing concepts of Gerda Lerner's differentiation between women's rights and women's emancipation; and similarly with Daniel Scott Smiths differentiation between public feminism and domestic feminism. Cott also ciriticizes J. Stanley Lemons's distinction between social feminists, and feminists (*The Women Citizen: Social Feminism in the 1920s*) who, like O'Neill, uses a two-category model to incorrectly assume mutually exclusive categories. The author calls for a conception of feminism that has continuity over time and that is centered on an awareness of gender hierarchy.

460 CURTHOYS, ANN. 1988. *For and Against Feminism: A Personal Journey into Feminist Theory and History*. Winchester, MA: Pandora Press.
After analyzing feminism from pro and con positions, Curthoys concludes that the women's movement has become a valuable, diverse, complex, and dynamic movement.

461 DAVIS, ANGELA. 1989. *Women, Culture and Politics*. New York: Random House.
A collection of essays Davis has written over the years. Topics covered include sexism, racism, poverty, illiteracy, the homeless, joblessness, inequality, and homophobia.

462 DAVIS, ELIZABETH GOULD. 1971. *The First Sex*. Baltimore, MD: Penguin.
Davis argues that before the destructiveness of patriarchy, there were matriarchal social systems premised on peaceful nurturing relations. She calls for a return to women's values as the only hope for the future of humankind. Although this work is polemical and frequently misuses anthropological and historical data, it represents an essentialist view of womanhood which continues to be voiced in various forms by some sectors of the women's movement.

463 DINNERSTEIN, DOROTHY. 1976. *The Mermaid and the Minotaur: Sexual Arrangements and Human Malaise*. New York: Harper and Row.
One of the early books with a psychological focus to explore sources of patriarchy and of women's status within that system. Dinnerstein continued the thought process developed by de Beauvoir that man is the subject and woman is 'other' under male rule. Explored are placement in stratification systems, status positions, role valuation, and psychological effects.

464 ECHOLS, ALICE. 1992. "We Gotta Get Out of This Place: Notes Toward a Remapping of the Sixties." *Socialist Review* 22 (April):9–33.
Two things have been lacking in historical writings on the 1960s: the degree of discord between feminist women and New Left males, and the things they had in common. Echols engages these issues as well as the interconnections with the Black Liberation Movement. Books which are critically analyzed include: Todd Gitlin's *The Sixties*, and Tom Hayden's *Reunion*. The author finds that women's demands were ignored as race and class became the "exalted" categories for radical activism to focus on.

465 EHRENREICH, BARBARA. 1983. *The Hearts of Men: American Dreams and the Flight from Commitment*. Garden City, NY: Anchor Press/Doubleday.

Ehrenreich, a noted socialist feminist, explains in this book that it was men who walked away from women in search of their freedom before the women's movement began to demand changes in social and personal life. The role men wanted to leave was the oppressive breadwinner role under capitalist society. In sympathy with that response, Ehrenreich, nevertheless, takes men to task for walking away from responsibilities for women and children before working for women's equality. Anti-feminist women are, according to Ehrenreich, reacting to their fears of men's abandonment. Their family values platform is an attempt to force men back into the fold. Feminist women are making demands on the economic and political institutions because they are left to take care of themselves and their children, even though they still do not have equality.

466 EICHENBAUM, LUISE and SUSIE ORBACH. 1989. *Between Women: Love, Envy, and Competition in Women's Friendships*. New York: Penguin Books.

This is an interesting and appealing book which touches on the experiences of women in relationship to each other. How women relate to other women in dyads or in groups is well analyzed and informative. The topic of women's friendships contributes to an understanding of the gendered nature of social relations, including those among women (and feminists) themselves.

467 EISENSTEIN, HESTER. 1983. *Contemporary Feminist Thought*. Boston: G. K. Hall.

Eisenstein takes a chronological approach to the development of radical feminist thought since the early 1970s. She reviews the works of early theorists Juliet Mitchell, Kate Millet, and Shulamith Firestone and their arguments related to women's oppression and biology/role differences. Their work is followed by a look at the writings of Adrienne Rich and Susan Griffin who, in reaction to these earlier theorists, explored a woman-centered perspective which would focus on a valuing of women's difference. Eisenstein argues that a reactionary return to an essentialism (difference) position emerged in the writing of Mary Daly which asserts the superiority of women. The author argues that assimilating into the patriarchal world as liberal feminism seems apt to do, or retreating from it as radical feminism advocates, will not accomplish the goals either of these forms of feminism hope to achieve. Instead, she concludes by calling on feminist activists to proactively engage the patriarchal structure and work to change it.

468 EISENSTEIN, ZILLA R. 1984. *Feminism and Sexual Equality*. New York: Monthly Review Press.

Eisenstein presents a critique of liberalism, the New Right, and revisionist feminism by examining the crisis of welfare-state policies. The author considers revisionist feminism to be demonstrated in the writings of Jean Elshtain and Betty Friedan (among others) and defines this thinking as taking a position which highlights sexual differences in arguing for gender equality. Eisenstein considers this a retrograde step and calls instead for policies that acknowledge sexual particulars in working toward an equal and free society.

469   ELSHTAIN, JEAN BETHKE. 1981. *Public Man, Private Woman: Women in Social and Political Thought*. Princeton: Princeton University Press.
Elshtain examines classical political theory to find the place of women within it. Given the negative results of this search, she recommends contemporary feminist alternatives. Her main interest in this book is to analyze the changing distinction between the public and private sectors.

470   FELSTINER, MARY LOWENTHAL. 1980. "Seeing the Second Sex through the Second Wave." *Feminist Studies* 6 (June):247–276.
A critical review of the ways Simone de Beauvoir's classic text *The Second Sex* (1952) fails to address current issues in the women's movement such as lesbianism, motherhood, housework, concepts of otherness, determinism, and materialism.

471   FERGUSON, ANN. 1991. *Sexual Democracy: Women, Oppression, and Revolution*. Boulder, CO: Westview Press.
Ferguson writes a critical analysis of contemporary society and of the feminist awareness she has gained. She traces socialist feminist theory from the New Left's post-Marxist postiions. The author discusses the problems with the idea of sisterhood when women are divided by race, class, and sexual orientation.

472   FIGES, EVA. 1970. *Patriarchal Attitudes*. New York: Stein and Day.
An early contribution to the ideas of the contemporary women's movement, Figes looks at patriarchy and the way women have been viewed through the ages. Her critical eye touches on myth, religion, Freud, marriage, capitalism, economic dependence, socialization, blocked opportunities, male chauvinism, traditional gender attitudes, men's refusal to relinquish power, and women's failure to rebel.

473   FLAX, JANE. 1989. *Thinking Fragments: Psychoanalysis, Feminism, and Postmodernism in the Contemporary West*. Berkeley: University of California Press.
A well thought out analysis of the distinctions and connections between psychoanalysis, feminism, and postmodernism. Flax presents both a critical and supportive perspective to the three subject areas and treats all three in a fair and even-handed manner.

474   FOWLER, M. G., R. L. FOWLER, and M. VANDERIE. 1973. "Feminism and Political Radicalism." *Journal of Psychology* 83:237–242.
The authors of this article draw the connections between feminist ideology and political activism that can border on radicalism.

475   FRENCH, MARILYN. 1992. *The War Against Women*. New York: Summit Books.

Using feminist literature and mass media sources, French argues that there is systematic and wide-spread oppression against women worldwide. Individual chapters address economic exploitation, religion, science, ideology, and male violence against women. Her discussion of the rise of fundamentalism is a careful analysis of this phenomenon, however, most of the book presents information in a journalistic rather than academic style. Much of what she writes about is already known by Women's Studies researchers, but her inclusion of other countries adds depth to these areas of study.

476   FRIEDAN, BETTY. 1963. *The Feminine Mystique*. New York: W.W. Norton.
Considered a feminist classic and stimulus for the re-emergence of the women's movement, this book spoke to the personal feeling of discontent white middle-class women were experiencing throughout the 1950s and early 1960s. Friedan talks about her own unfulfilled longings and calls her dissatisfaction "the problem that has no name." All of the messages in the popular media proclaimed women in her situation to be the fortunate recipients of a contented lifestyle organized around family and home. As she researched these messages, she began comparing them with messages about women during World War II which praised independent working women. The identity crisis she was feeling she attributed to the promotion of a happy housewife myth perpetuated by government and business interests to reserve jobs for men after the war, ensure that husbands would be served by wives so they could devote themselves to their work, and create an environment for the raising of children who would be needed in the labor market of the future.

477   ———. 1982. *The Second Stage*. New York: Summit Books.
Friedan defends the organization she helped found, the National Organization for Women, against the radical feminists who she sees as destroying the progress liberal feminism has made. She believes the first stage of the movement demanded career roles based on a male model. She argues that not much changed in the work structure, and moreover, the second stage now requires the additional incorporation of women's desires to have family needs met. She calls for women and men working together to restructure social institutions to meet work and family needs for both sexes.

478   FRITZ, LEAH. 1975. *Thinking Like a Woman*. New York: WIN Books.
This is a collection of essays written by Fritz between 1967 and 1975. The writings constitute a progression in her developing feminist awareness and are often biographical in nature. She discusses her transference from activism in the anti-war and civil rights movement to the women's movement. Later she wrote *Dreamers and Dealers: An Intimate Appraisal of the Women's Movement* (1979) which continued her personal look at feminism but includes an analysis of divisions within the movement, what the future holds, and how to get there.

479 FRUG, MARY JOE. 1992. *Postmodern Legal Feminism*. New York: Routledge.
The author integrates feminist theory into legal studies to demonstrate the difficulties and promise of the postmodern challenge to feminist goals. Examining feminist theory by liberal, radical, and cultural components, Frug shows how current feminist thought offers greater possibilities than earlier liberal traditions which limited the understanding of gender to equal rights under male defined conditions. The author backs up her position with jurisprudential material, legal doctrines and texts.

480 FUSS, DIANA. 1989. *Essentially Speaking: Feminism, Nature and Difference*. New York: Routledge, Chapman and Hall.
The author examines essentialism and nominalism, a frequently debated issue within the women's movement. Fuss is interested in clarifying the issues of "pure essence" and social construction in the development of the gendered nature of women and men. Is there a genetic component to the differences we see and experience, or is there only what is socially constructed within social relations? These are the questions she explores in tackling the sameness/difference arguments that have plagued women's rights activists since the beginnings of the organized movement. In addition, Fuss raises these same questions with regard to race and sexual orientation.

481 GARRY, ANN and MARILYN PEARSALL, eds. 1989. *Women, Knowledge, and Reality: Explorations in Feminist Philosophy*. Winchester, MA: Unwin Hyman.
A collection of essays and articles by feminist philosophers who are interested in the scholarship of revisionist philosophy which incorporates a feminist perspective. Includes, among others, Marilyn Frye, Allison Jagger, and Sandra Harding.

482 GILLIGAN, CAROL. 1982. *In a Different Voice: Psychological Theory and Women's Development*. Cambridge, MA: Harvard University Press.
Critiquing developmental theories that have been based solely on men's lives, Gilligan offers an alternative view of women's moral development. Qualities often thought of as women's weaknesses are shown to be strengths instead.

483 GILLIGAN, CAROL, JANIE VICTORIA WARD, and JILL MCLEAN TAYLOR, eds. 1990. *Mapping the Moral Domain*. Cambridge, MA: Harvard University Press.
Following in the tradition of Gilligan's ground breaking work on moral decision making in *In A Different Voice* (See entry 482), this work continues to enlarge the concept of personhood and meaning.

484 GORDON, LINDA. 1994. *Pitied But Not Entitled: Single Mothers and the History of Welfare*. New York: The Free Press.
Gordon presents an analysis of the origins of welfare which shows elite women social workers who worked for Aid to Dependent Children in the 1930s were

imbued with maternalist sentiment which was largely out of touch with the reality of those families they were seeking to protect. Basically, the plan they worked for was one meant to prop up the male-breadwinner family rather than create a family support system for low income parents. Instead of a guarantee of support for families with children, welfare became a needs based program. The women social workers were more interested in providing guidance and scrutiny (they claimed to have special knowledge and authority in the domestic sphere) than financial assistance. According to Gordon, if social workers had advocated for social insurance for single women, rather than seeing single mothers as different from the rest of us and in need of their guidance (the author sees this as a ploy to protect social worker's "special turf"), we might today see the same kind of entitlement programs for poor mothers that we see for the unemployed, elderly, and disabled.

485 GORNICK, VIVIAN. 1978. *Essays in Feminism*. New York: Harper and Row.
As a writer for the *Village Voice*, Gornick had the opportunity to write about her developing feminist awareness. In this collection of essays from her column, she has put together a diverse assortment which covers many areas including personal experience, Radcliffe women, and particular feminist activists.

486 GREER, GERMAINE. 1972. *The Female Eunuch*. New York: Bantam.
This book is considered a classic of the contemporary women's movement as it drew a great deal of attention when it came out by raising questions of sexuality, marriage, motherhood, and love. Of these four issues, Greer finds women's sexuality has been underrated while marriage, motherhood and love have been overrated. Although she contributes little to feminist theory or activist solutions, her aim is to provide emotional confidence to women's attempts at independence and freedom. The book was well-received for this message and for the witty style the author used in getting her ideas across.

487 GRUBER, JAMES E. and LARS BJORN. 1988. "Routes to Feminist Orientation Among Women Autoworkers." *Gender and Society* 2 (Dec.):496–509.
This article reports on the results of survey research on 150 women autoworkers to determine what factors led them to a feminist orientation. The demographic variables of age, marital status, and education had no affect except when combined with job satisfaction variables such as seniority level, skill level, and job security. Self-esteem, feeling trapped in a job, and feeling competent also had an effect. The interrelationships among variables led the researchers to conclude that there are two paths towards a feminist orientation: high seniority level workers with high skills, job competence, and high self-esteem; and younger, divorced, college-educated workers with low seniority, low job skills, feelings of low competence, and high feelings of job entrapment.

488   HAGAN, KAY LEIGH, ed. 1992. *Women Respond to the Men's Movement: A Feminist Collection*. New York: HarperCollins.
Women want a men's movement, but what kind do they want? This edited volume contains the views of feminist activists to the response by men who have organized around gender concerns. Issues of rape, domestic violence, battered women, reproductive rights, sexism, sexual harassment, child custody, politics and work place equality all portend involvement on men's part. These writings call the question on how men are responding to these issues and how feminist women would like to see them respond. Many of the essays express a view which sees growing, not reduced, resistance to women's advance. Critical analysis of Robert Bly's men's movement finds few of women's concerns related to male violence addressed; nor does there appear to be a strong desire for shared power, equal partnership, or gender justice. Among others, contributors include Z. Budapest, Phyllis Chesler, Nicole Hollander, bell hooks, Barbara Kingsolver, Ursula LeGuin, Margaret Randall, Rosemary Radford Ruether, Charlene Spretnak, and Starhawk.

489   HARE-MUSTIN, RACHEL T. and JEANNE MARACEK, eds. 1990. *Making a Difference: Psychology and the Construction of Gender*. New Haven, CT: Yale University Press.
This edited volume concentrates on the thoughts of five leading feminist psychologists who discuss the question of differences between women and men. For the most part, they take a social constructionist position in which differences are seen as creations of society. Their views fall more on a sociological than a psychological perspective which results in their challenge to the field of psychology to pay more attention to social relations.

490   HEIDE, WILMA SCOTT. 1985. *Feminism for the Health of It*. Buffalo, NY: Margaret Daughters.
Wilma Scott Heide was a nurse, scholar and the third national president of the National Organization for Women (NOW). Heide was a dynamic leader, once participating in a delegation of NOW members to interrupt a congressional meeting to demand they take up the issue of ERA. She was also a thoughtful speaker and writer on feminism and the women's movement. Her views on a wide range of issues are presented in this book. Topics cover: health care, welfare, education, feminist scholarship, communications, the media, language, and international feminism.

491   HOFF-WILSON, JOAN. 1987. "The Unfinished Revolution: Changing Legal Status of U.S. Women." *Signs: Journal of Women in Culture and Society* 13:7–36.
Hoff-Wilson traces the nineteenth and twentieth century efforts of women to be included in the constitution and to gain legal and political rights. She chronicles constitutional challenges, law cases, Supreme Court decisions, and activist campaigns. Activism for suffrage, Married Women's Property Act, protective labor legislation, abortion, ERA, The Equal Pay Act, the 1964 Civil Rights

Acts, and various Executive Orders are all covered. In assessing these legislative and legal attempts for change, the author discusses the conflict that exists within the women's movement over a philosophy of equal rights between the sexes and one premised on justice which recognizes differences between women and men.

492   HURTADO, AIDA. 1989. "Relating to Privilege: Seduction and Rejection in the Subordination of White Women and Women of Color." *Signs: Journal of Women and Culture* 14:833–855.

Moving away from the view that conflicts between white feminists and feminists of color are intrinsic to their interactions, Hurtado turns the lens instead to the relationship each of these groups have to white men. In using this structural framework, she finds that both white women and women of color are oppressed, but the dynamic is different for each of them. White women are seduced into subordination and women of color are reduced in value by rejection.

493   JANEWAY, ELIZABETH. 1987. *Improper Behavior: When and How Misconduct Can Be Healthy for Society*. New York: William Morrow & Co.

This is one of Janeway's most enjoyable books. In a personal and enlightening way, the author tells you why you feel the way you do, who else does too, and what can be done about it. Good insights and well thought out understandings from a feminist perspective which focuses on making gender the center of analysis.

494   JARDINE, ALICE and PAUL SMITH, eds. 1987. *Men in Feminism*. New York: Methuen.

This book represents a discussion by women and men on men's role in feminism. Some of the essays are dialogues on this question, others focus on substantive questions about whether, how much, and in what ways men should be included in the fight for women's liberation.

495   JOHNSON, SONIA. 1991. *The Ship that Sailed into the Living Room: Sex and Intimacy Reconsidered*. Albuquerque, NM: Wildfire Books.

Johnson explores the breakup of her relationship with her lover Susan, and mediates on the meaning of relationships, love, commitment, and coupling. Living her life at the present time in a community of women, she addresses this writing to lesbian couples but heterosexual couples will also find it thought provoking. Johnson feels that most relationships are bonded by emotional dependency rather than love and that women settle for very little in order to maintain relationships. Because of internalized oppression, women have greater levels of emotional dependency, and where emotional dependency reigns, intimacy cannot flower. She considers participation in the women's movement and lesbian coupling to be hazardous for women because they have yet to search "within" to rid themselves of their dependencies and internalized oppression.

496   ———. 1989. *Wildfire: Igniting the She/Volution*. Albuquerque, NM:
       Wildfire Books.
In this episode of her life, Sonia Johnson tells of her radically changed thinking about activism on behalf of women. She explains that she no longer
believes change can be accomplished in a patriarchal system. Rather, women
need to leave that system and create nurturing communities of their own.
Many of her proposals have a utopian ring to them, but many are also inspira-
tional and moving. This book has been criticized for ignoring the class and race
differences among men, and for supporting a separatist position that excludes
heterosexual women and women with strong identities to their ethnic/racial
groups. Johnson has become more controversial over time as her radical and
anarchist feminism has become more clearly defined. But regardless of how
you feel about her ideas, her writing makes for pleasurable reading because of
the passionate spirit she brings to her work.

497   KIMMEL, MICHAEL S. and THOMAS E. MOSMILLER, eds. 1993. *Against the
       Tide: Pro-Feminist Men in the United States, 1776–1990, A
       Documentary History*. Boston: Beacon Press.
This book is part of a series on men and the making of masculinity from
Beacon Press. A social constructionist and feminist analysis provide the framework for this research-based series from the humanities and social sciences.
Kimmel and Mosmiller provide a documentary history of men who have supported women's efforts for equality, suffrage, reproductive freedom, and other
causes addressed by the women's movement. The beliefs and writings of these
men are supplemented by the editors discussion of the extent to which their
expressed feminist values were implemented in their daily lives. Pro-feminist
men examined in this anthology include Alan Alda, Howard Cosell, John
Dewey, Thomas Paine, and Gore Vidal, among others.

498   LANDRY, DONNA and GERALD MACLEAN. 1993. *Materialist Feminisms*.
       Cambridge, MA: Blackwell Publishers.
As the intellectual field of Marxism has declined, the feminist debate on class
analysis has shifted to cultural materialism and post-structuralist literary theory. Included in the new discourse are questions of race, ethnicity, sexuality,
colonialism, and environmental issues which have been merged into a framework focused on gender and class. Arguments over the last thirty years, noted
texts, and currents of cultural theory are covered in this book.

499   LEGHORN, LISA and KATHERINE PARKER. 1981. *Woman's Worth: Sexual
       Economics and the World of Women*. Boston: Routledge and Kegan
       Paul.
The authors of this book are concerned with answering the question of why
women have so few economic resources. They see that in all social systems
women's work sustains the economy, but their efforts provide little in return
in either monetary reward or political power. Leghorn and Parker find
women's status to be connected to how much value is placed on women's fertility, their access to resources, and their involvement in networks of authority.

In most societies women have minimal levels of these three criteria, in some they have token status, and in a few they are in a position of negotiating power. They call for ways to think about developing an alternative economy which would better serve everyone in the society.

500   LERNER, GERDA. 1993. *The Creation of Feminist Consciousness: From the Middle Ages to 1870*. New York: Oxford University Press.
This scholarly book refutes the image of feminism as a recent phenomenon originating in Western European and North American societies. Not only does Lerner trace the history of the emergence of feminist thought over 1300 years, she illuminates the interruptions and suppression of this development by documenting how the desire for emancipation was voiced in women's religious cultures long before they could take action for solutions to their situation. Religious traditions provided women access to creativity, learning, and leadership roles, and it was in their reading of the Bible that they came to the recognition that views of women and men are culturally derived. The writings of over twenty women from the twelfth century up to Elizabeth Cady Stanton's *Woman's Bible* in 1895 are included. The ways women were denied an intellectual tradition, the isolation imposed upon them, and their attempts to understand their situation are reflections of both tragedy and celebration.

501   MACKINNON, CATHARINE A. 1990. *Toward a Feminist Theory of the State*. Cambridge, MA: Harvard University Press.
An analysis of sexuality and the law from a feminist perspective. MacKinnon exposes the political aims of a patriarchal valuing system which underlies concepts of justice and challenges us to rethink our intellectual discourse on males, females, and equality. In addition to an informed critique of a social system built on sex inequality, this work also provides a vision for a new social order.

502   MCCLAIN, EDWIN W. 1978. "Feminists and Non-feminists: Contrasting Profiles in Independence and Affiliation." *Psychological Reports* 43 (Oct.):435–441.
A study to determine if significant differences could be found in independence and affiliation between subjects classified as feminist or non-feminist. The instrument used was a battery of four personality tests. Results confirmed the expectation that feminists would score significantly higher on independence scales and non-feminists would score significantly higher on affiliation scales.

503   MILLER, JEAN BAKER. 1971. "On Women: New Political Directions for Women." *Social Policy* 2 (July):32,40–45.
In this article, Miller argues that political necessity requires activist groups to change the consciousness of the public in order to make gains for women. This level of change is necessary because success will only be possible when the value connected to the acquisition of goods is transformed into a priority for achieving a decent quality of life for all people.

504   ———. 1976. *Toward a New Psychology of Women*. Boston: Beacon
       Press.
A popular feminist psychology book. Miller makes a strong case for the development of female authenticity and how to go about doing it.

505   MILLETT, KATE. 1970. *Sexual Politics*. New York: Doubleday.
This book was typecast as a representative sample of what became known as
strident feminism. Millett analyzed intellectual traditions in literature to develop a thesis of sexual politics as power relations. She defined the social structure in American society as patriarchal domination premised on a sexual caste
system. Numerous examples of misogynist writing are presented from such
authors as Norman Mailer, D. H. Lawrence, and Henry Miller. Millett's early
analyses influenced the direction of feminist literary criticism for later academics and established a framework for broadening the range of feminist
thought.

506   MITCHELL, JULIET and ANNE OAKLEY, eds. 1986. *What is Feminism?* New
       York: Pantheon Books.
The eleven contributors to this volume re-examine the concept of feminism
from a variety of angles revealing new and original meanings to the question
"What is feminism?" Examples of the type of analysis found in this anthology
are: Nancy Cott's comparison of the contemporary women's movement with
the movement of the nineteenth and early twentieth centuries in which she
finds the elimination of gender roles to be a common goal. Juliet Mitchell
shows how feminism can result in social change processes the women's movement never intended. Other essays cover a variety of issues and include writings by Linda Gordon, Judith Stacey, and Anne Oakley, among others.

507   MITCHELL, JULIET. 1984. *Women, The Longest Revolution: Essays on
       Feminism, Literature and Psychoanalysis*. New York: Pantheon Books.
A classic piece of early feminist writing from the contemporary women's movement, first published in *New Left Review* in 1966. This is a creatively original
piece in which Mitchell defines the separate structures of women's condition
to be production, reproduction, sexuality, and socialization. Other pieces in
this collection show the development of Mitchell's thoughts over a twenty year
period. Included are writings on literary criticism, tracts on feminism, and
explorations of psychoanalysis.

508   MORGAN, ROBIN. 1982. *The Anatomy of Freedom: Feminism, Physics,
       and Global Politics*. Garden City, NY: Anchor Press/Doubleday.
In this book, Robin Morgan meditates on the meaning of freedom by using the
analogy of quantum physics (relativity and interconnectedness) to create a
basis for her developing thoughts. Chapter by chapter Morgan dissects social
constructs such as marriage, sex, family, death, art, and politics. Philosophical
and personal writing is interwoven throughout the text. She enters the realm
of controversy when she champions the anti-pornography movement and cas-
tigates those feminists who disagree. Not agreeing with her on some issues

does not take away from the recognition that, as usual, Morgan is passionate in her views and effective in her writing.

509 MUELLER, CAROL MCCLURG. 1987. "Collective Consciousness, Identity Transformation, and the Rise of Women in Public Office in the United States." Pp. 89–108 in *The Women's Movements of the United States and Western Europe*, edited by Mary Fainsod Katzenstein and Carol McClurg Mueller. Philadelphia: Temple University Press.

Mueller looks at an important result of the women's movement—the development of a collective conscience that became more feminist over time. This new consciousness contributes to a change in identity and the way women see themselves. A noticeable indicator of that change is the increase in the number of women running for and winning public office. It is interesting to note that this change in collective conscience was occurring even as the ERA was being defeated, but it was the campaign itself, and the arguments in favor of women's equality, that caused a change in public awareness.

510 NELSON, KRISTINE and ARNOLD S. KAHN. 1982. "Conservative Policies and Women's Power." *Journal of Sociology and Social Welfare* 9 (Sept.):435–449.

This article takes the position that men have control of power sources and it is in this domain that they are able to maintain a superior position to women. According to the authors, women's attempts to gain power have led to the conservative backlash which aims to maintain unequal gender power relations. In turn, the feminist reaction to the New Right has been a greater focus on the attainment of power than before.

511 NODDINGS, NEL. 1989. *Women and Evil*. Berkeley: University of California Press.

This is a noteworthy look at the ways women, and the characteristics historically associated with the essence of being a woman, have been associated with evil. After reading this book, anyone who is still trying to maintain an ideal of femininity will re-consider that attempt.

512 NORRIS, PIPPA. 1987. *Politics and Sexual Equality: The Comparative Position of Women in Western Democracies*. Boulder, CO: Lynne Rienner Publishers, Inc.

A comparative view of advances in women's rights in democratic industrialized societies. Some of the data is important for analyzing past and future strategies as there are wide differences in a number of areas among nations. Good insights are found here for feminist thinking and planning.

513 OAKLEY, ANNE. 1981. *Subject Women*. New York: Pantheon Books.

Oakley explores women's position in contemporary society using data from history, sociology, psychology, biology, anthropology, and other fields to describe six components of women's experience: legal changes in the status of women; the biological and cultural construction of femininity; women's relationships with men, children, and other women; women in the work force; power and politics. Oakley argues that women have made progress in all these areas but are still constrained by the conditioning of society.

514 O'MALLEY, SUSAN GUSHEE, ROBERT C. ROSEN, and LEONARD A. VOGT, eds. 1990. *Politics of Education: Essays from "Radical Teacher."* Albany: State University of New York Press.

Radical Teacher is a journal of feminist and socialist perspectives on teaching. This collection consists of thirty selected articles concerned with ways to democratize classes and to give students tools for self-empowerment.

515 POSTON, CAROL H., ed. 1988. *Mary Wollstonecraft: A Vindication of the Rights of Woman.* New York: W. W. Norton.

This is the second edition of Poston's edited volume of Mary Wollstonecraft's famous treatise "A Vindication of the Rights of Woman." Wollstonecraft (1759–1797) was one of the earliest recorded women to write a feminist tract arguing a rationale for women's equality. Poston presents the text, background, criticism, and particulars of the Wollstonecraft debate.

516 PRATT, MINNIE BRUCE. 1984. "Who Am I If I'm Not My Father's Daughter?" *Ms.* 12:72–73.

Originally given as a speech at the 1983 National Women's Studies Association meeting in Columbus, Ohio, Pratt talks about the efforts to overcome her background, particularly the racism she grew up with in the South. At the same time, she remarks on the need to recognize and be recognized for herself and to respect her own identity.

517 REARDON, BETTY A. 1985. *Sexism and the War System.* New York: Teachers College Press.

The connection between sexism and militarism, both of which lead to violence, is the subject of this book. To change the direction of oppression and violence worldwide, Reardon argues for the adoption of a feminist consciousness in order to affect structural change in the economic, political, and social realms.

518 REDFERING, DAVID L. 1979. "Relationship Between Attitudes Toward Feminism and Levels of Dogmatism." *Journal of Psychology* 101 (March):297–304.

In a survey of more than 1500 women in the United States, comparisons of dogmatism levels were made on subjects who scored above the 75th percentile on a feminism scale and those who scored below the 25th percentile. The results showed that women who strongly support women's equality were less closed-minded and more goal oriented. There was no difference between them and the low level women in anxiety levels or ego strength.

519 REED, EVELYN. 1971. *Problems of Women's Liberation.* New York: Pathfinder.

Reed presents a Marxist analysis of women's condition, often called "the woman problem." Women are seen as victims of capitalism, both as consumers and as sexual products to be sold. Patriarchy is also examined and condemned for exploiting women. Neither of these systems is seen as inevitable as the author theorizes on an earlier historical period when primitive communism and matriarchy permitted peaceful and egalitarian social relations.

520   RICH, ADRIENNE. 1986. *Blood, Bread and Poetry: Select Prose 1979–1985*. New York: W. W. Norton.

A collection of writings from an important contributor to feminist thought within the women's movement. Many of the selections are from lectures given on college campuses to stimulate the thinking of the next generation of women activists. Her often quoted article "Compulsory Heterosexuality and Lesbian Existence" (see entry 296) is included in this anthology.

521   ROTHSCHILD, JOAN. 1990. *Machina Ex Dea: Feminist Perspectives on Technology*. Elmsford, NY: Pergamon Press.

Questions about whether technology has created more or less work for women in the home, resulted in more or less skilled labor, and created a better or more alienating society have been debated for nearly half a century. Joan Rothschild enters this debate by bringing in a feminist perspective that offers new ways of looking at women and technology.

522   ROWLAND, ROBYN. 1989. *Woman Herself: A Women's Studies Interdisciplinary Perspective on Self-Identity*. New York: Oxford University Press.

In this book, Robyn Rowland explores the ways the patriarchy has contributed to creating an identity for women that renders them inferior to men. The political, social, and emotional realms of the relational and social order are examined.

523   RUBIN, GAYLE. 1975. "The Traffic in Women." In *Toward an Anthropology of Women*, edited by Rayna R. Reiter. New York: Monthly Review Press.

An early example of how academic disciplines operated without a gender perspective in developing theoretical explanations for social phenomena. Rubin applies a feminist perspective to the research and theories of anthropologist Claude Levi-Strauss to show that gift-giving between tribes was not just a way to ensure friendly relations. The gift giving entailed exchanges of women, and was thus a way of showing ownership of property, a classic example of patriarchal control of men over women.

524   SACKS, KAREN. 1976. "Class Roots of Feminism." *Monthly Review* 27 (Feb.):28–48.

Sacks claims that the nineteenth century woman's movement was really three movements: industrial working-class women looking for economic gains, black women seeking racial equality, and white middle-class women working for legal equality.

525 SCHAEF, ANNE WILSON. 1985. *Women's Reality: An Emerging Female System in a White Male Society*. New York: Harper & Row.
An examination of the psycho-social differences between women and men. In *Women's Reality*, the focus is on the ways women view themselves, how they see men, and their views on a social system which has benefitted white males to a much greater extent than other groups. The analysis Schaef presents is one based on differences in the male and female experience. First published in 1981, this book has been a popular introduction to looking at gender differences in a male-defined world.

526 SEGAL, LYNNE. 1988. *Is the Future Female? Troubled Thoughts on Contemporary Feminism*. New York: Peter Bedrick Books.
Examines British and North American literature and finds fragmentation and division over sexuality concerns, motherhood, male violence and war. The aim of this book is to respond to the 1980s inclination in radical feminism to emphasize gender differences that stress the higher values found in the female world over the violence and hierarchy of the male world. The author takes the position that such polarized thinking is inadequate and inaccurate. The evidence presented posits male/female characteristics as social constructs rather than biological or psychological artifacts.

527 SIDEL, RUTH. 1990. *On Her Own: Growing Up in the Shadow of the American Dream*. New York: Viking.
Study of the dreams and aspirations of today's young women. Interviews with over 150 young women between the ages of twelve and twenty reveals that they have unrealistic dreams—they all plan to have careers and children. Their belief is that they have to "make it on their own" and they assume they will. There is no demand to change the rules of society even though they report that life looks hard.

528 SNODGRASS, JON, ed. 1977. *For Men Against Sexism: A Book of Readings*. Albion, CA: Times Change Press.
An anthology which reveals a developing consciousness of men who have been affected by the Women's Liberation Movement. The writings in this volume reflect the efforts of men to question their position and to attempt transformation of the self and society. Explored are male sexuality, socialization, masculinity, patriarchy, male power and privilege, and women's oppression. There are separate sections on Third World men, working-class men, and gay men.

529 SOCHEN, JUNE. 1972. *The New Woman: Feminism in Greenwich Village 1910–1920*. New York: Quadrangle Books.
This is an appealing look at a segment of feminist practice that fit into the category of cultural and personal life style more than collective action. As Sochen shows, the social experiments Greenwich women attempted were challenges to social expectations of that time period.

530 SPENDER, DALE. 1985. *For the Record: The Making and Meaning of Feminist Knowledge*. London: The Women's Press.

Dale Spender has probably published more primary pieces on feminisism than any other writer. In this work she illuminates the development of feminist thought by surveying classical texts of the contemporary women's movement. Included are writings by Betty Friedan, Alice Rossi, Germaine Greer, Juliet Mitchell, Robin Morgan, Kate Millett, Shulamith Firestone, Eva Figes, Adrienne Rich, Mary Daly, Anne Oakley, and Phyllis Chesler. She includes comments she has received on her critiques of these writers. Spender presents a careful analysis of the works she includes and also presents a less seriously examined list of other books of interest.

531 ———. 1982. *Women of Ideas (and What Men Have Done To Them) from Aphra Behn to Adrienne Rich*. Boston: Routledge and Kegan Paul.

An essential book for understanding the importance of women's writing and theorizing. Spender includes a wide variety of women, their creative thinking, and their scholarship. She also examines what has happened to their ideas, thereby giving the reader a thorough review of centuries of erasure of women's words. This expansive work (close to 600 pages) provides a highly useful reference source on the history and development of feminist thought.

532 STEINEM, GLORIA. 1994. *Moving Beyond Words*. New York: Simon and Schuster.

A collection of essays pointing out that equality has not yet arrived. There are six sections in this work: Freud, bodybuilding, magazine advertising, rich women, global economics, and aging. The framework Steinem uses is to take a tacit assumption and critique it to reveal the unexamined sexual stereotypes in our thinking. With Freud she uses a tongue-in-cheek gender reversal scheme. The serious work of this critique is found in the footnotes where she employs scholarship and Freud's own writing to reveal a man who was sexually abused as a child and who, as an adult, generalized his own pathologies into theory. Steinem also challenges the belief that women body builders and wealthy women are not feminist; links economics to everyday life; presents an expose on advertising using the experience of Ms. magazine; and describes turning sixty with a recollection of living in India in the 1950s which opened her mind to feminism and activism.

533 ———. 1983. *Outrageous Acts and Everyday Rebellions*. New York: Holt, Rinehart and Winston.

This is an anthology of essays from a feminist media star, noted author and sought-after speaker. Some of the selections are personal and others address feminist topical issues. Much of Steinem's writing is witty and some of the pieces contain inspiring thoughts on life experiences. Included is her classic exposé "I was a Playboy Bunny" and a cynical piece pondering how perceptions would change "If Men Could Menstruate."

534   STIMPSON, CATHARINE R. 1988. *Where the Meanings Are*. New York: Methuen.
A collection of essays written between 1970 and 1987, most of which have been previously published in a variety of sources. Stimpson talks about how she has found in feminism a place "where the meanings are," even though it is also the stuff for which people argue, unite, split, and re-unite. In the first article, Stimpson describes her experience as a young white untenured English professor in the late 1960s teaching a class about black literature, and why she eventually refused to teach this class again. The final essay discusses feminism's disagreements over culture and how some of these issues have been reconciled.

535   SYFERS, JUDY. 1973. "Why I Want a Wife." Pp. 60–62 in *Radical Feminism*, edited by Anne Koedt, Ellen Levine, and Anita Rapone. New York: Quadrangle Books.
This is a classical early feminist article which continues to be reprinted in women's studies texts. Syfers uses a humorous approach to protest women's double burden in the work place and in the home. She describes all the things she would like a wife for, such as taking children for their medical check-ups, cleaning, cooking, entertaining guests, and being sexually available when she wanted sex.

536   TONG, ROSEMARIE. 1989. *Feminist Thought: A Comprehensive Introduction*. Boulder, CO: Westview Press.
An introduction to feminist thought as political thought. This book surveys the important critical analyses of women in society and provides a background to the richness of feminist intellectual traditions. Representing wide ranging views in feminist thought, Tong surveys liberal feminism, Marxist feminism, radical feminism, psychoanalytic feminism, socialist feminism, existentialist feminism, and postmodern feminism. Selected readings represent essential writings in feminist discourse from Wollstonecraft, Engels, de Beauvoir, Dinnerstein, Daly, Mitchell, and Cixous.

537   WALBY, SYLVIA. 1990. *Theorizing Patriarchy*. Oxford: Basil Blackwell Ltd.
In this book Walby writes theoretically about patriarchy. She does this by reviewing various arguments that have been used to establish and maintain women's secondary position in society. This overview is followed by an examination of changes that have occurred in gender relations during the latter half of the twentieth century. Contemporary feminist theories are discussed along with debates on post-structuralism and essentialism. Individual chapters focus on paid labor, unpaid work in the home, culture, sexuality, violence, and state authority. The nature and significance of gender is examined in each sphere through the theoretical debates that have emerged around them.

538   WALSH, MARY ROTH, ed. 1988. *The Psychology of Women: Ongoing Debates*. New Haven, CT: Yale University Press.
The debates that have gone on for sometime on the psychology of women are

well covered in this collection of articles. Not only are the general principles from the various schools of thought included, but the interconnections between positions are examined.

539 WOLFF, JANET. 1991. *Feminine Sentences: Essays on Women and Culture*. Berkeley: University of California Press.
The lack of inclusion in historical and sociological accounts of social process is criticized in this collection of essays. Wolff challenges the separation of sociology from both cultural studies and feminist theory. The author supports the notion that women must define their lives through the medium of writing because of the reflective nature of this work and the meaning of shared experience the printed word allows. A connecting theme of Wolff's essays is her call for a feminist cultural politics.

540 WOOLF, VIRGINIA. 1957. *A Room of One's Own*. New York: Harvest/HBJ Book.
One of Woolf's most famous feminist tracts, *A Room of One's Own* is an argument for women's private space and autonomy. Why have men always had power, influence, fame, wealth, and art, while women have had children? According to Woolf, it is because they have lacked an income and space in which to be creative. Her writing in this book is an inspiration for the liberation of women.

541 YATES, GAYLE GRAHAM. 1975. *What Women Want: The Ideas of the Movement*. Cambridge, MA: Harvard University Press.
In this book the author divides the ideological pull of the women's movement into three categories: male superiority, female superiority, and androgyny. Yates considers mass movement groups like the National Organization for Women, the Women's Equity Action League, and the National Women's Political Caucus to fall into the first (and largest) category because members of these groups believe men are in control of the world and they want equality with them. The second group wants a female-centered universe, best reflected in the writings of Shulamith Firestone and Kate Millett. The androgynous group, which is the one Yates supports, consists of people like Elizabeth Janeway, Carolyn Heilbrun, and Germaine Greer. This group believes women and men are equal to each other but some social change is necessary in order for equality to come about.

Feminist Theory

542 ALTBACH, EDITH HOSHINO, ed. 1971.*From Feminism to Liberation*. Cambridge, MA: Schenkman
This collection of articles, poems, and essays reveals an early socialist feminist perspective. Many of the selections were originally published in a 1970s issue of *Radical America*. The introduction provides a look at recent women's history and the rise of women's activism. Well-known articles include Mari Jo

Buhle on the Socialist Party from 1901 to 1914, Juliet Mitchell's classical piece "The Longest Revolution," Marlene Dixon's "Where Are We Going?" and "Bread and Roses" by Kathy McAfee and Myrna Wood.

543   ASSITER, ALISON. 1990. *Althusser and Feminism*. London: Pluto Press.
This is an analytic look at the work of Althusser and other French structuralists and post-structuralists such as Lacan and Foucault and the effect their work has had on Marxist feminist thought. Although the author finds value in structuralism and post-structuralism, she disputes the claim that they have had a significant impact on Marxism or feminism.

544   BARRETT, MICHELE. 1981. *Women's Oppression Today: Problems in Marxist Feminist Analysis*. New York: Schocken Books.
Using a Marxist feminist analysis, Michele Barrett explores the possibilities for a synthesis of the Marxist and feminist perspectives. Discussed are the conceptual problems in Marxist-feminist theory and the relationship between ideology, education, work, the role of the state, and women's liberation.

545   BUHLE, MARI JO. 1981. *Women and American Socialism, 1870–1920*. Urbana: University of Illinois Press.
An important part of American women's activism is often overlooked because women who were involved in socialist party activities were believed to be only interested in the improvement of working conditions. This view is disputed by the actions of Leftist women who became radical feminists after their involvement with the male dominated Left of the 1960s. But this belief has persisted, and it has left us with a history lacking in awareness of the many socialist feminist women who supported suffrage and other women's issues from the latter part of the nineteenth century to the present. Although for the most part, socialist organizations considered the woman's movement to be bourgeois, there were socialist women who not only contributed to the woman's movement but also attempted to raise gender issues within socialist circles. Buhle's book fills in this missing feminist activism of the past.

546   CARROLL, BERNICE A. 1980. "Political Science, Part II: International Politics, Comparative Politics and Feminist Radicals." *Signs: Journal of Women in Culture and Society* 5 (March):449–458.
Looking for a synthesis between Marxism and feminism, Carroll examines radical writings from different sectors of the women's movement. The selections come from lesbian, socialist, and Marxist perspectives.

547   DALY, MARY. 1973. *Beyond God the Father: Toward a Philosophy of Women's Liberation*. Boston: Beacon Press.
Daly presents a philosophy of a radical feminist, how she would be in the world, what space she would occupy, how her language would change, and what people she will encounter.

548   DE BEAUVOIR, SIMONE. 1952. *The Second Sex*. New York: Alfred A. Knopf.

The Second Sex rates the status of a classical text in feminist theory. Still found in most syllabi of women's studies classes, de Beauvoir's work presents a historical and contemporary look at the nature of sex/gender relations in both the personal and societal realms. The concept of woman as the 'other' is developed in this book which leaves readers deeply aware of the profound impact of gendered systems of thought and social organization.

549 DELPHY, CHRISTINE. 1984. *Close to Home: A Materialist Analysis of Women's Oppression*. Amherst: University of Massachusetts Press.
Delphy employs the view of French feminism in this collection of ten articles written between 1970 and 1981. She argues for feminist materialism superseding Marx's historical materialism because Marxism was inadequate on the woman question, particularly domestic labor. Other topics she covers are class, divorce, family, marriage, and the interconnections between the women's movement and Left politics. She is critical of Marx although she is Leftist and she speaks to Marxist feminists when she tells them it is time to place feminist analysis in the forefront of their work and to stop idolizing a man who left them out of the development of social class theory.

550 DIXON, MARLENE. 1980. *Women in Class Struggle*. San Francisco: Synthesis Publications.
A Marxist feminist analysis of the women's movement and feminist issues from the 1970s to the 1980s. Dixon argues for the centrality of women in class struggle, highlights the super-exploitation of women, discusses the wages for housework issue, and critiques the "bourgeois" contemporary women's movement.

551 DONOVAN, JOSEPHINE. 1985. *Feminist Theory: The Intellectual Traditions of American Feminism*. New York: Frederick Ungar Publishing Co.
This work constitutes a comprehensive guide to the study of the roots of the variations in feminist thought found in the women's movement. Donovan presents thorough discussions of Marxist feminism, Enlightenment ideals found in liberal feminism, the contributions of Freud, existentialist philosophy, cultural and radical feminism, and the conceptions of nineteenth century and current feminist moral visions.

552 DOUGLAS, CAROL ANNE. 1990. *Love and Politics: Radical Feminist and Lesbian Theories*. San Francisco: Ism Press.
A survey of the ideas of radical feminist and lesbian feminist theories covering the period from the late 1960s to the end of the 1980s. A broad range of topics are discussed. There are eighteen photos included in this book.

553 DWORKIN, ANDREA. 1974. *Woman Hating*. New York: Dutton.
Using many examples of misogyny historically and cross culturally, Dworkin presents a radical feminist analysis of men's attitudes and treatment of women. The persecution of old and single women as witches during the Middle Ages,

foot binding in China that lasted over 1,000 years, and the linkage between fairy tales and pornography are well documented. Dworkin uses these examples to argue that males control women, not just for power, but because they hate and fear them. The exploitative nature of race and class are also examined.

554   EHRENREICH, BARBARA, BARBARA DUDLEY, and MICHELLE RUSSEL. 1975. "The National Conference on Socialist Feminism." *Socialist Revolution* 5 (Oct.):85–93.

A collection of papers and summaries of speeches presented at the July 4, 1975 Yellow Springs, Ohio National Conference on Socialist Feminism. Selections include Barbara Ehrenreich (New American Movement) who called for social feminist unity based on theoretical and ideological agreements; the necessity for an overarching theory to combat current sexist ideologies by the Berkeley-Oakland Women's Union; Michelle Russel's call for feminists to reach out to Third World women; and weaknesses and strengths of the women's movement as outlined by Barbara Dudley. In spite of a high level of heated confrontations, the conference did come up with four resolutions: 1) the need for an autonomous women's movement; 2) a recognition of the inter-relationship of all forms of oppression; 3) the legitimacy of a socialist feminist movement; and 4) the need for a spirit of unity within socialist feminism.

555   EISENSTEIN, ZILLAH R., ed. 1979. *Capitalist Patriarchy and the Case for Socialist Feminism*. New York: Monthly Review Press.

The articles in this collection are focused on various aspects of the synthesis of feminism and Marxism. They present a unified understanding of socialist feminist theory explored through various levels of social interaction. Some of the most well-known articles are Nancy Harstock on feminist theory, Linda Gordon on reproductive freedom, Ellen Carol DuBois on the suffrage movement, and Rosalind Petchesky on Marxist feminist groups. Also included are position statements from the Berkeley-Oakland Women's Union and the Combahee River Collective.

556   ———. 1981. *The Radical Future of Liberal Feminism*. New York: Longman.

A documentation of how feminism developed out of liberal theory and the ways it attempts to transcend it. Eisenstein argues that liberal feminism has the potential to subvert patriarchal capitalism. Taking seriously the ideology of liberalism and its commitment to individualism and equality, Eisenstein argues that liberal feminism will be forced to go beyond legal reforms because they are insufficient to overcome a system premised on women's subordination. The author calls for a re-evaluation of the limits and the potential of liberal feminism, particularly because of the conservative social environment since the mid-1970s. Eisenstein provides analyses of early liberal philosophy found in the writings of Locke, Rousseau, Wollstonecraft, Mill, Harriet Taylor, and Elizabeth Cady Stanton. Also examined are contemporary times as demonstrated in the work of Betty Friedan, NOW, and issues such as ERA, reproductive rights, and the 1977 International Women's Year Conference in Houston.

557 FARGANIS, SONDRA. 1994. *Situating Feminism: From Thought to Action*. Thousand Oaks, CA: Sage Publications, Inc.

Three decades of formulating and reformulating feminist theory are reviewed in this work. The interaction between feminist thought, competing philosophies, similarities/differences among women, and social movement activism are explored. The various components of the women's movement are examined through the lens of changing theoretical frameworks. To highlight the ways feminist theory is affected by and affects social/political views, Farganis analyzes four controversial women-centered court cases: the Sears Case, the Baby M Case, the Hedda Nussbaum Case, and the Hill/Thomas Hearings.

558 ———. 1991. "The Women's Movement in the United States: Theory and Practice." *International Journal of Moral and Social Studies* 6:217–232.

Farganis examines the interaction between feminist theory and particular issues that confront the women's movement, such as: how feminist theory explains legal cases; the ways participants in legal cases are affected by feminist theory; and how particular legal cases reshape feminist theory.

559 FARRAR, ANNE. 1970. "The Seattle Liberation Front, Women's Liberation, and a New Socialist Politics." *Socialist Revolution* 1 (Sept.):124–136.

Feminist women in the Seattle Liberation Front (one of the last New Left organizations of the 1960s era) found themselves in a struggle as they were developing ways of working for the full liberation of women in society and inside Leftist groups.

560 FIRESTONE, SHULAMITH. 1970. *The Dialectic of Sex: The Case for Feminist Revolution*. New York: William Morrow.

Firestone presents a radical feminist theory of the elimination of sex/gender differences. Citing the failure of socialist feminism to address the ultimate site of women's oppression—reproductive and sexual relations—she argues that what is needed to achieve equality is the removal of biological differences between the sexes. Firestone calls for artificial reproduction to release women from childbearing, community child rearing, economic independence and sexual freedom for women and children. Using modern technology, the work place would be transformed to eliminate repetitive low level jobs reserved for women and, rather than developing ways to alter the present sexual division of labor in the family, she calls for the abolition of the family itself.

561 FRITZ, LEAH. 1975. "Feminism vs. Socialism: What Are Our Priorities?" *Liberation* 19 (Feb.):6–10.

Fritz believes activists in the Women's Liberation Movement need to achieve socialist goals. She calls for combining socialism and feminism in order to achieve self-help centers, welfare reform, and child care.

562   FRYE, MARILYN. 1983. *The Politics of Reality: Essays in Feminist Theory*.
        Trumansburg, NY: The Crossing Press.
Drawing on the work of feminist writers such as Ti-Grace Atkinson, Mary Daly
and Andrea Dworkin, the author presents a synthesis of feminist political and
philosophical thought that leads to a politics of separatism rather than assimi-
lation. The book consists of essays, many originally prepared for presentations,
in which she blends philosophical thought with the data of women's experience. Her goal is to make the lives of women intelligible and to make sense of
women's feelings, motivations, desires, and actions by taking into account the
forces in society which keep women subordinate to men. Because she is
attempting to make sense of "what did not make sense before," these essays
provide an interpretation of life experiences that otherwise are often felt to be
simply frustrating and baffling. The essays are thought provoking and constitute an important contribution to the development of radical feminist thought.

563   GILMAN, CHARLOTTE PERKINS. 1966. *Women and Economics*. New
        York: Harper and Row.
Gilman, a socialist feminist and critic of capitalism, believed that women's economic dependence kept them in a lowered position in society. She also maintained that the nuclear patriarchal family was probably the strongest area of
male dominance. Gilman was an early movement theorist whose work is still
relevant today, even as women's involvement in the work structure has greatly increased.

564   GRANT, JUDITH. 1994. *Fundamental Feminism: Contesting the Core
        Concepts of Feminist Theory*. New York: Routledge.
Grant explores feminist theory from its origins in the contemporary movement
to the present stage of feminist thought. She finds a need for revision in three
core concepts: woman, experience, and personal politics. Debates within the
women's movement are linked to the flaws in these three concepts, such as
the hegemony of the white feminist perspective, the conflict over pornography, and new challenges brought about by postmodern society.

565   HANISCH, CAROL. 1971. "The Personal is Political." Pp. 152–157 in *The
        Radical Therapist*, edited by J. Agel. New York: Ballantine Books.
This article was originally published in *Notes from the Second Year: Women's
Liberation* (1970), an edited volume published for three years by Shulamith
Firestone and Anne Koedt on radical feminist thought. The personal is politi-
cal became the slogan of the Women's Liberation Movement; it was coined by
Hanisch in this article.

566   HANSON, KAREN V. and ILENE PHILIPSON, eds. 1989. *Women, Class and
        the Feminist Imagination: A Socialist-Feminist Reader*. Philadelphia:
        Temple University Press.
A collection of articles on socialist feminism. Many of the authors are well
known and the articles represent some of the most serious commentaries writ-

ten in the period represented by the contemporary women's movement. Thought provoking, often controversial, these essays continue to be worthwhile readings. The most important contributions these articles provide are the critiques of society. Topics are broad, ranging from women and economics to patriarchy and pornography.

567   JAGGAR, ALISON. 1983. *Feminist Politics and Human Nature*. Sussex: Harvester Press.

A study of the relationship between gender and class and the interrelationship of political philosophy, feminist theory, and theories of human nature. Also included are useful and well thought out descriptions of Marxist, materialist, and socialist feminism.

568   JENNESS, LINDA, ed. 1972. *Feminism and Socialism*. New York: Pathfinder.

Contributors to this anthology offer a socialist feminist view of the women's movement. The need for the end of capitalism and the liberation of all people is voiced through interviews, position statements, and articles. Using a Marxist analysis, Kate Millett's book *Sexual Politics* (1970) is critiqued for taking a radical feminist stance that condemns men rather than the economic system of exploitation that promotes both sexes' degradation. Various writers argue for the need for all people to unite and for the inclusion of African-American and Chicana women in the women's movement. Other issues that are covered are the family, ERA, and abortion.

569   JONES, MARGARET C. 1993. *Heretics and Hellraisers: Women Contributors to the Masses, 1911–1917*. Austin: University of Texas Press.

The Masses was an early twentieth century Left Wing magazine which provided an outlet for writing on radical thought and social movement activities. This was an influential publication that supported feminism and was an important voice in giving shape to women's concerns. Contributors included Inez Haynes Irwin, Louise Bryant, Elsie Clews Parsons, Dorothy Day, and Mary Heaton Vorse. Jones reexamines these writers' analysis of social issues in light of 1990s feminist thought. This revisionist work focuses on early feminist views of birth control, patriarchy, the labor movement, women's suffrage, pacifism, and ethnicity. Biographical sketches of the writers are included.

570   KELLY, JOAN. 1984. *Women, History, and Theory*. Chicago: The University of Chicago Press.

As a founder of Women's Studies, Joan Kelly also was an early contributor to the growing body of scholarship on women. Her approach is a combination of Marxism and feminism within a framework of historical analysis. Essays include "The Social Relation of the Sexes," "The Doubled Vision of Feminist Theory," "Early Feminist Theory," and "Did women have a Renaissance?"

571   KLEIN, RENATE D. and DEBORAH LYNN STEINBERG, eds. 1989. *Radical Voices: A Decade of Feminist Resistance from Women's Studies International Forum*. New York: Pergamon Press.
A selection of written material over the last ten years from the journal *Women's Studies International Forum*. The articles chosen for this anthology are those which illustrate the development of radical feminist thinking and the interaction between ideas and actions in the Women's Liberation Movement. The intent is to address the growing separation of academic writing from the activism of the women's movement. Three fundamental questions are focused on: what is the meaning of woman and how does this cultural meaning contribute to women's subjugation; what constitutes patriarchy and how does patriarchy oppress women; what is feminism and how can it liberate women? Contributing articles by Pauline Bart, Sarah Hoagland, Renate Klein, Catherine MacKinnon, Shulamit Reinharz, and Sheila Ruth, among others.

572   KOEDT, ANNE and SHULAMITH FIRESTONE, eds. 1971. *Notes From the Third Year: Women's Liberation*. New York: Notes.
Koedt and Firestone put together a collection of writings from the Women's Liberation Movement called *Notes for the First, Second, and Third Year* (1969, 1970, 1971). These collections are hard to find because they were published independently and few libraries have copies. Many of the writings from these edited volumes (particularly from the Third Year) were selected for an anthology edited by Koedt with Ellen Levine and Ann Rapone in 1973 called *Radical Feminism* (see entry 573). Essays in *Third Year Notes* cover women's literature, suffrage, black feminism, prostitution, lesbianism, media, religion, ageism, and the law.

573   KOEDT, ANNE, ELLEN LEVINE, and ANITA RAPONE, eds. 1973. *Radical Feminism*. New York: Quadrangle.
This anthology is a must for understanding the thinking of the early radical feminists who formulated the contours of feminist theory and initiated some of the daring actions of the late 1960s and early 1970s. There are forty-five articles, most of which were previously published in the short lived feminist annual *Notes*. Many of these articles have become classics, such as "The Bitch Manifesto" (Joreen), "Why I Want a Wife" (Judy Syfers), "The Building of the Gilded Cage" (Jo Freeman), "Psychology Constructs the Female" (Naomi Weisstein), "The Myth of the Vaginal Orgasm" (Anne Koedt), "The Woman Identified Woman" (Radicalesbians), "The Tyranny of Structurelessness" (Joreen), and "A Political Organization to Annihilate Sex Roles" (The Feminists).

574   KUHN, ANNETTE and ANN MARIE WOLPE, eds. 1978. *Feminism and Materialism: Women and Modes of Production*. Boston: Routledge, Kegan and Paul.
A collection of essays on women's social and historical condition framed by an analysis of women's relationship to modes of production and reproduction. The writings are attempting to deal with issues raised by the women's movement such as patriarchy, paid and unpaid labor, and the state. These articles

make clear how family and labor constitute overarching themes in understanding women's situation.

575 LENIN, V. I. 1966. *The Emancipation of Women*. New York: International Publishers.
A selection of writings by Lenin which cover a wide variety of topics related to women in society. Included are discussions on the origins and persistence of oppressive practices and discriminatory attitudes, and the role of women in social movements. Lenin writes of the need for women to have independent organizations within the socialist movement and the necessity of women's commitment to the class struggle in order for it to succeed. Clara Zetkin's article "Lenin on the Woman Question" is found in an appendix.

576 MACKINNON, CATHERINE A. 1987. *Feminism Unmodified: Discourses on Life and Law*. Cambridge, MA: Harvard University Press.
In this book MacKinnon discusses why male dominance is so powerful and why feminism cannot be moderate in overthrowing this system. She considers anything less than radical feminist analysis and action to be a modified, and therefore ineffectual, form of feminism. MacKinnon calls for women to insist on an uncompromising need for social change.

577 MARTIN, GLORIA. 1986. *Socialist Feminism, The First Decade, 1966–76*. Seattle, WA: Freedom Socialist Publications.
A documentary history of socialist feminism in the contemporary women's movement. Socialist feminism was found in a number of different groups, but was most well known in the women's unions beginning with the Chicago Women's Liberation Union. By the end of the 1970s they had all dissolved.

578 MILES, ANGELA. 1993. *Integrative Feminisms: Building a Global Vision, 1960s to 1990s*. New York: Routledge.
Various forms of radical feminism are examined in Canada and the United States from the 1960s through the early 1990s. Miles argues that radical feminism from women of color, self-defined ideological radicals, lesbian activists, and Third World feminists offers transformative power to the women's movement. The author refutes charges of naiveté, utopianism, and essentialism and argues instead that radical feminism and separatism offer an integrative potential for world wide feminist connection. Data is drawn from interviews with feminist activists and documentary materials.

579 MILLETT, KATE. 1976. *Prostitution Papers: A Quartet for Female Voice*. New York: Ballantine Books.
In this publication Millett has collected four written accounts of prostitution from members of the profession. Millett's own comments offer a view of a radical feminist perspective on this topic.

580 MILLS, SARA. 1989. *Feminists Reading/Feminist Readings*. Charlottesville: University Press of Virginia.
A practical and useful text which explains feminist theories to Women's Studies

students who are being introduced to some of these ideas for the first time. The authors also provide information on how to apply theory to practice.

581   MITCHELL, JULIET. 1971. *Woman's Estate*. New York: Pantheon.
Mitchell was an early writer on the re-emergence of feminist thought and activism. She wrote "Women: The Longest Revolution" which became a classic when it was published in *New Left Review* in 1966. This article was a critique of socialism's failure to incorporate women into its analysis and a call for socialism and feminism to recognize their need to co-exist in the development of social criticism. Using both a socialist feminist framework and psychoanalysis, Mitchell explains why the family and the labor market are intermingled in the repression of radical consciousness and egalitarian social structures.

582   MOON, TERRY. 1986. "Eleanor Marx in Chicago, 1886: Revolutionary Feminism and the Haymarket Centenary." *Quarterly Journal of Ideology* 10:55–59.
The Haymarket riot of 1886 is a marker in labor and anarchist history. It was also the year Eleanor Marx traveled throughout the United States speaking on the socialist ideas of her father. Wherever she spoke she defended the prisoners (even though she did not agree with anarchism) because of their unjust imprisonment. Moon interprets her behavior to also be an appeal to the revolutionary fever of the workers. During her U.S. visit, Marx spoke of the activist potential of women in the labor movement. She argued that there was a much stronger relationship between suffragists and the working-class in the United States than was true in England and other places.

583   MORGAN, ROBIN. 1992. *The Word of a Woman: Feminist Dispatches, 1968–1992*. New York: W. W. Norton.
Robin Morgan began writing about the women's movement as it emerged in 1968. This collection of eighteen articles reveals her thinking on feminist issues for the last twenty-four years. Reading these texts, some of which had a tremendous effect on feminist thought at the time they were published, continues to be consciousness-raising activity. She is a radical feminist who strongly believes in the concept of universal sisterhood where feminist struggle goes beyond history and culture. Her call for recognition of universal connections based on shared gender experiences is a call for a sisterhood that has been attacked for its neglect of power differences between women based on race, class, and ethnicity. Morgan's radical feminist position claims not to ignore these differences, but to incorporate them into the revolutionary force of change she sees the women's movement capable of achieving.

584   REDSTOCKINGS. 1976. *Feminist Revolution*. New York: Random House.
Redstockings was one of the early consciousness-raising groups of the Women's Liberation Movement. Some of the most dynamic feminist activists were members of this group and this anthology reveals much of their thinking. Classical texts are included here in a valuable documentary collection of radical feminist writing during the organizing stage of the contemporary women's movement.

585 ROWBOTHAM, SHEILA. 1983. *Dreams and Dilemmas: Collected Writings*. London: Virago Press.
A collection of Sheila Rowbotham's writings over a twenty year period (1960 to the early 1980s). The selections in this volume represent a clear presentation of socialist feminist theory as it developed in both the United States and Britain. For an interesting comparison with the U.S. women's movement, see her writing on the evolution of the women's movement in England (entries 154 and 586). Rowbotham is one of the best feminist thinkers and writers around.

586 ———. 1973. *Woman's Consciousness, Man's World*. Baltimore, MD: Penguin Books.
This is an early book by Rowbotham, who went on to write many more fine pieces on feminism and the women's movement. Much of her work is on the English movement but most of her writing transcends national boundaries. In this book, she lays out her socialist feminist framework for understanding how and why a feminist impulse would emerge under capitalism. She demonstrates how the condition of women in this system demands a feminist revolution for change. The author argues for the need to engage working-class women into the movement if it is to be successful.

587 RUTHCHILD, ROCHELLE. 1983. "Sisterhood and Socialism: The Soviet Feminist Movement." *Frontiers* 7:4–12.
Although not about the women's movement in the United States, this article is interesting for what it can tell us about socialist feminism in a (former) communist country. Ruthchild provides a descriptive account of the emergence of a feminist movement in the USSR sixty years after the Bolshevik Revolution. Discussed are general policies towards women, official attitudes, dissident attitudes, internal disagreements, sexuality, work, family, and spirituality. Two Soviet feminist groups are compared: Women & Russia and Club Maria.

588 SARGENT, LYDIA, ed. 1981. *Women and Revolution: A Discussion of The Unhappy Marriage of Marxism and Feminism*. Boston: South End Press.
A collection of writing by feminist authors who question the capability of Marxist materialism to provide an adequate explanation of women's secondary position in society. Heidi Hartmann's essay "The Unhappy Marriage of Marxism and Feminism" became a classic feminist text as she argued that the marriage of Marxism and feminism is similar to the traditional conception of marriage between a husband and wife, i.e., Marxism and feminism are one, and that one is Marxism. A more equal union is needed or, Hartmann argues, the situation calls for a divorce. There are 12 other articles, each presenting cogent and critical positions ranging from radical, anarchist, socialist, and Marxist feminist perspectives. Contributors bring in ideologies and views that cover the nature of the relationship between patriarchy and capitalism, and the need for incorporating analyses of race and sexual orientation into feminist theory. Contributors include Gloria Joseph, Sandra Harding, Lise Vogel, Carol Erlich, Azizah Al-Hibri, and Zilla Eisenstein.

589   SOPER, KATE, ed. 1983. *Harriet Taylor Mill: Enfranchisement of Women*. London: Virago.

Harriet Taylor Mill is often credited with influencing John Stuart Mill's liberal philosophy with a feminist component. Her article "Enfranchisement of Women" showed her to be ahead of her time and to have written of the need for women's equality sometime before Mill did. In this collection, Soper has included Harriet Taylor Mill's "Enfranchisement" article and John Stuart Mill's article on "The Subjection of Women" with an introduction to each of these writings.

590   SPENDER, DALE, ed. 1983. *Feminist Theorists: Three Centuries of Key Women Thinkers*. New York: Pantheon Books.

This anthology contains short critical works by a variety of scholars on early feminist activists who have dared to question male power. Feminist activists included in this book are Mary Wollstonecraft, Lucy Stone, Margaret Fuller, Christabel Pankhurst, Simone de Beauvoir, and Emma Goldman. In the Introduction, Ellen DuBois provides a historical perspective and, in the conclusion, Spender includes a brief essay on feminist theorists. This work is part of ongoing projects to bring awareness of women's past, particularly their rebellion over unjust conditions, to the forefront of knowledge.

591   STEINEM, GLORIA. 1983. "Women Grow More Radical with Age." *Women's Political Times* 7:4.

Women's Political Times is the official publication of the National Women's Political Caucus, an organization Steinem helped to found. In this piece, she talks about how women, unlike men who are radical when they are young, become more radical the longer they live in patriarchal societies.

592   VOGEL, LISE. 1983. *Marxism and the Oppression of Women: Toward a Unitary Theory*. New Brunswick, NJ: Rutgers University Press.

This book presents a Marxist perspective on women's liberation. Vogel discusses the emergence of socialist feminism in the United States in the late 1960s and 1970s within a milieu of social activism. However, she argues against the synthesis of socialist and feminist thought in favor of classical Marxist theory which she maintains offers a more complex analysis for combating systems of inequality. The author provides a review of relevant writings by Marx and Engels as well as a chronology of the nineteenth century socialist movement.

593   ———. 1979. "Questions on the Woman Question." *Monthly Review* 31 (June):39–59.

Marxists have used the term "the woman question" to talk about women's inequality and the quest for liberation. Within this broad framework there are different emphases and interpretations of socialist thinking.

594   WARTENBERG, THOMAS E. 1989. *The Forms of Power: From Domination to Transformation*. Philadelphia: Temple University Press.

This is a thoughtful analysis of the ways male domination are implemented in everyday interactions between women and men, including those social situations and relationships that are fully harmonious. Wartenberg is one of the relatively few male social theorists to adopt feminist theory thoroughly into his thinking and then to write about it for a general audience.

595   WATERS, MARY ALICE. 1976. *Women and the Socialist Revolution*. New York: Pathfinder Press.
This is a thirty page pamphlet that provides a background on the early woman's movement and suffrage movement in the United States and in England, and the ways the women's movement and socialist movement have followed a similar path. For instance, Waters points out that 1848 was not only the year the first woman's rights conference was held, it was also the year *The Communist Manifesto* was published which she notes as the beginning of the working-class movement. Waters argues that the struggle for ERA, abortion, and black liberation are parts of the socialist revolution. The author concludes that all of these movements are for human liberation and each is needed for the other to succeed.

596   WEINBAUM, BATYA. 1978. *The Curious Courtship of Women's Liberation and Socialism*. Boston: South End Press.
Weinbaum uses Marx's concepts but restates them around sex and age. This work is a critique of Marxism for its failure to incorporate women fully into its theories. The author raises this critique and a solution in the hope of promoting an eventual collaboration between Marxism and feminism.

Methodology

597   ALPERN, SARA, JOYCE ANTLER, ELISABETH ISRAELS PERRY, and INGRID WINTHER SCOBIE, eds. 1992. *The Challenge of Feminist Biography: Writing the Lives of Modern American Women*. Urbana: University of Illinois Press.
The recent interest in writing women into history has led to a number of books and articles on the methodology of doing feminist biography. This collection of articles centers on writing about contemporary American women and provides insights into the differences in writing about men and writing about women. An important theme in this work is the necessity (and ways) of providing a feminist consciousness to events in each woman's life. This means that life histories of women may be interpreted differently than the way men's biographies have been written. In addressing women's biography, the articles also raise interesting issues for biographical writing in general.

598   ASCHER, CAROL, LOUISE DeSALVO, and SARA RUDDICK, eds. 1984. *Between Women: Biographers, Novelists, Critics, Artists and Teachers Write About Their Work on Women*. Boston: Beacon Press.
In this book a wide variety of writers discuss their work and the perspectives they apply when writing about women. This collection consists of essays, articles, literary works, biographical pieces, and methodological discussions.

599   BARRY, KATHLEEN. 1989. "Biography and the Search for Women's
       Subjectivity." *Women's Studies International Forum* 12:561–577.
Barry develops her ideas on ways of doing biography on women that differ
from traditional conceptions of biographical work.

600   ———. 1990. "The New Historical Synthesis: Women's Biography."
       Journal of Women's History 1:75–105.
Barry, who is a sociologist and author of a biography on Susan B. Anthony
(entry 371), theorizes a new approach to biography from a critical and feminist
perspective. She argues that a person's life cannot be understood as the study
of uniqueness, but must instead be grounded in the social and political history of the subjective experience. In this approach, the "great man" model of biographical analysis is rejected in favor of understanding the interaction between
everyday life and political/social history.

601   EICHLER, MARGRIT. 1987. *Nonsexist Research Methods: A Practical
       Guide*. Winchester, MA: Pandora Press.
A good resource for preventing sexist bias from creeping into social science
research. The author provides a clear and systematic approach to identifying
and eliminating bias from the beginning conceptualization through the data
gathering and analysis. Writing the report is another area Eichler covers on
non-sexist presentation of one's work.

602   FONOW, MARY MARGARET and JUDITH A. COOK, eds. 1991. *Beyond
       Methodology: Feminist Scholarship as Lived Research*. Bloomington:
       Indiana University Press.
An anthology on feminist research, many pieces written for this book. The fifteen articles are diverse but all are interested in methodological issues related
to feminist oriented sociology. Topics range from Verta Taylor and Leila Rupp's
piece on the contradictions between previous assumptions and research findings, and Liz Stanley and Sue Wise's discovery of the ways their activism subjected them to negative reactions from others. An informative and interesting
collection.

603   GEIGER, SUSAN. 1990. "What's so Feminist about Women's Oral
       History?" *Journal of Women's History* 2:169–182.
Because oral history is not a new research methodology and because it can and
has been used by all kinds of researchers, we cannot claim that this is solely a
feminist research method. In this article, Geiger is interested in determining
how oral history can be feminist. She considers the criteria to be what kind of
questions to ask, how evidence is verified, the relationship between the
researcher and the researched, what audience is this research being done for,
who benefits from the findings, and what direction does the interpretation
take.

604   GLUCK, SHERNA. 1977. "What's So Special About Women? Women's Oral
       History." *Frontiers* 2:3–17.

Making a case for the value of oral history, Gluck points out that this research method is particularly relevant for women's history because women are less likely to have left written sources than more educated men would be able to leave.

605 GLUCK, SHERNA BERGER and DEPHNE PATAI. 1991. *Women's Words: The Feminist Practice of Oral History*. New York: Routledge.
The contributors to this volume challenge assumptions about feminist ethnography and oral history interviews which call for equal relations between the scholar and the subject in the research process. The major theme to emerge in these writings is that the relationship between field researchers and informants is more complex and problematic than egalitarian models propose. The sixteen authors come from a variety of academic disciplines including anthropology, history, linguistics, literature, and sociology.

606 HALL, JACQUELYN DOWN. 1987. "On Writing a Feminist Biography." *Feminist Studies* 13 (March).
Feminist biography has increasingly become a part of Women's Studies. Hall presents some methodological discussions on how writing a feminist biography might differ from traditional biography.

607 HEILBRUN, CAROLYN G. 1988. *Writing a Woman's Life*. New York: Ballantine Books.
Heilbrun invites women to write truthfully of women's lives, including their own. She discusses the ways traditional biographies have hidden the reality of women's lives in order to conform to society's expectations. Using examples of celebrated women such as George Sand, Virginia Woolf, Adrienne Rich, and Heilbrun herself, she shows how women authors have taken male identities, names, pseudonyms, and "fallen" reputations in order to free themselves from the restrictions they might otherwise be bound to obey. Heilbrun is interested in examining how women's lives have been contrived and then written about within this limitation. She develops feminist ways of writing from a self-conscious woman's identity.

608 ILES, TERESA, ed. 1990. *All Sides of the Subject*. Elmsford, NY: Pergamon Press.
During the 1980s and 1990s women's biography has taken on an importance within Women's Studies in the United States and many other countries. This collection is international in scope and brings together articles that cover the main issues involved in writing biography.

609 LIEBLICH, AMIA and RUTHELLEN JOSSELSON, eds. 1994. *Exploring Identity and Gender: The Narrative Study of Lives*. Thousand Oaks, CA: Sage Publications, Inc.
This work on qualitative methods focuses on the use of narrative in writing about women's lives. Identity issues are covered, including individual identity in the context of family and how one's sense of individuality impacts on orga-

nizational style. Also examined are other issues such as constructing the lives of women in biographical work, and the ways the women's movement influenced women's lives. Articles include "Feminist Biography: The Pains, The Joys, The Dilemmas" by S. Reinharz; and "Linking Individual Development and Social Events: The Women's Movement and Women's Lives" by A. Stewart.

610 NIELSEN, JOYCE MCCARL, ed. 1990. *Feminist Research Methods: Exemplary Readings in the Social Sciences*. Boulder, CO: Westview Press.

This book is intended as a practical guide to conducting research using feminist methods. It provides both theoretical concepts and examples of actual research. The introduction by Nielsen covers philosophy of science, history of science, and sociology of knowledge issues. The introduction lays a foundation for understanding the ways a feminist perspective acts to transform scientific methodology. Part One of the book consists of commentary on feminist and traditional methods. Part Two reveals particular examples of the use of feminist method such as oral history and linguistic analysis. Seven articles by contributors cover women's suffrage, women as shamans, sex differences in suicide rates, sex differences in cognitive abilities, gender and public policy, gender dominance through conversation, and the dichotomies of public/private spheres.

611 REINHARZ, SHULAMIT. 1992. *Feminist Methods in Social Research*. New York: Oxford University Press.

Reinharz has been involved in the development of experiential and qualitative methods for some time. The methods of research she has written about have been identified by many researchers as feminist, but her emphasis in this book is not what particular method researchers should be using; it is what feminists do when they are involved in research. Each chapter covers a particular data gathering method covering the range of possibilities, and in each case she provides examples of feminist scholarly work. The author makes the point that feminist scholarship can be found in diverse methods. The extensive bibliography she provides reveals the variety and depth of feminist research over the past twenty years. After reading this book, the question for feminist research is no longer about the method itself.

612 ———. 1979. *On Becoming a Social Scientist: From Survey Research and Participant Observation to Experiential Analysis*. San Francisco: Jossey-Bass.

A critique and review of sociological research methods such as survey research and participant observation. Both strengths and weaknesses of each method are discussed from a feminist perspective. Using examples of her own research experiences, Reinharz proposes the use of personal experience for experiential analysis in social scientific research.

613 ROBERTS, HELEN, ed. 1981. *Doing Feminist Research*. Boston: Routledge & Kegan Paul.

A collection of writings by feminist sociologists on doing research within a male defined academic environment. Contributors are concerned with addressing the ways women have been invisible in sociological research in the past, the necessity and ways of including women, developing a feminist perspective into the research agenda, and the theoretical foundation of a feminist sociology. Includes articles on women in stratification studies, occupational mobility, interviewing women, men and the process of sociological inquiry, and academic publishing.

614   ROSSER, SUE V. 1988. *Teaching Science and Health from a Feminist Perspective: A Practical Guide*. New York: Pergamon Press.
A guide that focuses on the content and methodological approaches for teaching science courses from a feminist perspective. Six curricula are discussed which range from beginning to advanced courses. How to integrate perspectives other than that of the dominant racial/ethnic groups are included. Over thirty syllabi are provided. Course topics cover biology, sexuality and human reproduction, health and disease, psychology of women, and changing pedagogical methods.

615   RUPP, LEILA J. 1980. "Imagine My Surprise: Women's Relationships in Historical Perspective." *Frontiers* 5 (Sept.):61–70.
In the past, and often in the present, it is difficult to determine what type of relationship women have with each other because of the hidden messages which are often misinterpreted or purposely suppressed. Women's relationships may be lesbian, love, friendship, feminist, admiring, or friendly. It is not always determinable, but placing their interactions within a historical context particularly looking for subtle verbal descriptions—often gives clues. Simply lumping all of women's relationships together misses key essentials of historical research.

616   SEARING, SUSAN E. 1985. *Introduction to Library Research in Women's Studies*. Boulder, CO: Westview Press.
This book is designed for beginning and upper level library instruction for research projects on women. Faculty and librarians will also find this guide useful for identifying research tools and for guiding student research.

617   STANLEY, LIZ, ed. 1990. *Feminist Praxis: Research, Theory and Epistemology in Feminist Sociology*. London: Routledge.
The papers in this volume discuss the various components of a methodology for feminist sociology. Most of the papers came out of a collective effort for research in methodology by the Manchester Studies in Sexual Politics in England. There is also a useful review of the literature on feminist methodology and a bibliography on methods in the back of the book.

618   ———. 1990. "Movements of Writing: Is there a Feminist Auto/Biography?" *Gender & History* 2:58–67.
Is there a distinct feminist auto/biography? Stanley believes there is and points

to instances of it in recent feminist autobiography even though, for the most part, feminist biography has stayed within conventional form. She predicts that a distinct feminist biographical form will emerge from epistemology concerns within Women's Studies and feminist social science.

619 ————, ed. 1988. *The Writing I, the Seeing Eye: Papers from Two Writing Feminist Biography Conferences.* Manchester, England: University of Manchester.

Selections for this collection came from two conferences on feminist biography held in 1987 and 1988 in Manchester, England. Papers include works on filling silences, the witch craze of the sixteenth and seventeenth centuries, a feminist reconstruction of friendship, understanding relationships when there is a lack of correspondence between subjects, the ways photographs speak to us, and how to construct characters in biography.

620 THE PERSONAL NARRATIVES GROUP, eds. 1989. *Interpreting Women's Lives: Feminist Theory and Personal Narratives.* Bloomington: Indiana University Press.

A collection that talks about the feminist methodology of using and writing personal narratives of women's lives.

Sociology, Social Movement Theory and Social Movement Comparisons

621 ALLEN, SHEILA, FLOYA ANTHIAS, and NIRA YUVAL-DAVIS. 1991. "Diversity and Commonalty: Theory and Politics." *International Review of Sociology* 2:23–27.

This article discusses the interrelationships of race, class, ethnicity, and gender that were presented at the World Congress of Sociology in 1990 in Madrid, Spain. The theoretical grounding of mainstream sociology is seen as marginalizing race, ethnicity, and gender. New work on the civil rights and Black Power Movement in the United States, the use of migrant labor, and the growth of the women's movement offer reconceptualizations along these lines.

622 BANKS, OLIVE. 1981. *Faces of Feminism: A Study of Feminism as a Social Movement.* New York: Basil Blackwell.

Covering the women's movement in England and America from 1840 to the present, Banks reveals the philosophical and political strands that exist within feminism at various periods and the connections between the past and contemporary movements. Banks provides a sociological analysis of the women's movement as a social movement rather than the usual focus on women's issues, gender inequality, or women's place in society. The comparison between the movements in England and the United States is an interesting one that shows many striking similarities, and some differences which reflect particular cultural components from their respective ideological origins.

623   BASSNETT, SUSAN. 1986. *Feminist Experiences: The Women's Movement in Four Cultures*. London: Allen & Unwin.
A view of the women's movement in the United States, Great Britain, Italy, and the German Democratic Republic (formerly East Germany). Having lived in these countries and participated in the movement in each of them, Bassnett presents a comparative analysis that shows a variety of aims, tactics, and priorities. The emphasis in Britain is class, in the GDR it is on state socialism, in Italy activists are involved in intellectualism, and in the United States the focus is on pragmatic solutions.

624   BERNARD, JESSIE. 1982. *The Female World*. New York: Free Press.
Jessie Bernard wrote some of the first tracts in sociology that looked at women's issues and introduced feminist reflections on sociological questions. Bernard's interests were wide, although most of her Women's Studies interest focused on marriage and the family. Her emphasis is on women seeing themselves as autonomous and valuable people deserving of rights in the world.

625   ———. 1973. "My Four Revolutions: An Autobiographical History of the ASA." *American Journal of Sociology* 78:773–791.
Bernard cites four periods of social revolution in the American Sociological Association: the introduction of empirical research papers at the annual meetings in the 1920s; the 1930s declaration of independence from the University of Chicago; the organization of the Society for the Study of Social Problems in the 1950s; and the feminist revolution of the 1970s. Regarding the latter, Bernard proposes that deficiencies caused by sexist bias can be eliminated.

626   BOGGS, CARL. 1986. *Social Movements and Political Power: Emerging Forms of Radicalism in the West*. Philadelphia: Temple University Press.
Boggs was one of the early writers on New Social Movement Theory which considered the women's movement, environmental movement, and gay and lesbian movements to be cultural challengers rather than social/economic challengers. The author is interested in exploring the dynamics of these movements, their origins, history, ideologies, symbols, emotionalism, and social bonding in comparison to earlier types of movement organizing.

627   BOLES, JANET K. 1982. "Systemic Factors Underlying Legislative Responses to Woman Suffrage and the Equal Rights Amendment." *Women & Politics* 2 (March):5–22.
A comparative study of state legislative responses to woman suffrage and the Equal Rights Amendment. The similarities Boles found are: long term political organizing for passage (over fifty years for each); their connection to more generalized women's movements for equality; and the similar civil and equal rights components each claimed. The differences she found were: alliances, political organization, policy precedents, perceived legal impact, opposition forces, and historical timing. This article is in a special issue of *Women & Politics* featuring articles from a symposium on the Equal Rights Amendment.

628   BOUCHIER, DAVID. 1984. *The Feminist Challenge*. New York: Shocken
      Books.
Although the focus of this book is the women's movement in Britain, Bouchier
uses the contemporary women's movement in the United States for comparative purposes. Literature from both countries are utilized in understanding the
various meanings of feminism and the activist forms the two movements
employ.

629   BUECHLER, STEVEN M. 1990. *Women's Movements in the United States:
      Woman Suffrage, Equal Rights, and Beyond*. New Brunswick, NJ:
      Rutgers University Press.
This work compares and contrasts the early U.S. woman's rights and suffrage
movement with the contemporary women's movement. Buechler uses periods
of intense activism to describe women's movements; thus, instead of using a
chronological format, a comparative analysis is presented on the topics of movement origins, organizational forms, ideological visions, classes and races, counter
movement dynamics, and endings and futures. The sociological framework of
resource mobilization is used to illicit the mobilization process of feminist organizing, and women's movements are used to evaluate resource mobilization theory. This book presents a thorough account of the topics covered, although the
form of presentation does lead to repetition.

630   CARDEN, MAREN LOCKWOOD. 1975. "Communes and Protest
      Movements in the United States, 1960–1975: An Analysis of Intellectual
      Roots." *International Review of Modern Sociology* 6 (March):13–22.
Carden examines student protest, civil rights, black power, feminism, and the
hippie movement to develop theories of the origins of communal experiments
and social movements. She finds a radical ideology underlies the communes
and social movements from 1960 to 1975. Radical philosophy is premised on a
view of human rights which includes the right to autonomy, the development
of potential, a sense of belonging, and a self-defined identity.

631   CHAFETZ, JANET SALTZMAN and ANTHONY GARY DWORKIN. 1986.
      *Female Revolt: Women's Movements in World and Historical
      Perspective*. Totowa, NJ: Rowman and Allanheld.
A cross cultural historical approach to understanding how women become
concerned about sex inequality. Women's movements are divided into two
time periods, 1850–1950 and 1960 to the present. Chafetz and Dworkin, both
sociologists, describe forty-eight movements from many countries, compare
them, and then test their theory about the connection between industrializa-
tion and urbanization for the development of a gender consciousness which
leads women (mainly middle-class women) to act in their own behalf. In addition to the traditional forms of women's organizing, they include witchcraft,
spirituality, moral reform movements, and food riots.

632   CHAFETZ, JANET SALTZMAN. 1988. *Feminist Sociology: An Overview of
      Contemporary Theories*. Itasca, IL: F.E. Peacock.

A survey of feminist theory in sociology and related social science/humanity disciplines that have developed since 1970. Beginning with an introduction that defines feminist theory and introduces the reader to classical theorists and general sociological theory, Chafetz reviews the work of contemporary feminist theorists. The theoretical work she analyzes are identified as Marxist-feminist, anthropological, everyday life approaches, neo-Freudian, eclectic structural, exchange theory, micro-interactional, and socialization theories. The book is divided into four sections: causes of gender inequality, maintenance and reproduction of gender systems, social consequences of gender stratification, and changing systems of gender inequality.

633   CHAFETZ, JANET SALTZMAN and ANTHONY GARY DWORKIN. 1983. "Macro and Micro Process in the Emergence of Feminist Movements: Toward a Unified Theory." *Western Sociological Review* 14:27–45.
Arguing that contagion theory (the effects of prior social movement participation) does not adequately explain the rise of the contemporary women's movement, Chafetz and Dworkin find a more plausible explanation in combining macro and micro processes to explain the appeal of feminism. They cite the massive entry of women into the labor force as the primary factor in the development of a feminist consciousness.

634   DAHLERUP, DRUDE, ed. 1986. *The New Women's Movement: Feminism and Political Power in Europe and the USA*. Newbury Park, CA: Sage.
A comparative analysis of the development of the contemporary women's movement in the United States and ten European countries. In each country the abortion debate is compared and contributors analyze the contending strategies for engaging in efforts for political change within the system or attempting change from outside the system. The countries examined are: Italy, Ireland, France, Britain, Iceland, Finland, Turkey, Spain, Denmark, and the Netherlands.

635   EPSTEIN, BARBARA. 1991. *Political Protest and Cultural Revolution: Nonviolent Direct Action in the 1970s and 1980s*. Berkeley: University of California Press.
This book is a compilation of the many types of citizen and social movement actions which challenged the political, economic, and cultural status quo of the 1970s and 1980s. Epstein dispels the notion that the Reagan era was so widely accepted that protest was muted throughout his two presidential terms. The author presents a history of activism and inspiration for future involvement in progressive politics.

636   ———. 1990. "Rethinking Social Movement Theory." *Socialist Review* 90:35–65.
Epstein is interested in looking at the social movements that have arisen during and since the 1960s and the ways social movement theory has addressed these new forms of activism. She defines these movements as cultural movements and shows how, in many cases, they have converging orientations (e.g.,

anarchism, environmentalism, peace, and feminism). The author claims that Marxist analysis and Resource Mobilization frameworks have not adequately addressed issues of cultural transformation, and it was this failure that led to the development of New Social Movement Theory. Epstein reviews the history and theoretical basis for New Social Movement Theory and concludes that it provides a way of understanding new arenas of struggle, particularly identity, community, symbolism, and aesthetics. However, she finds this theory applies specifically to the direct action segment of movements and, thus, fails to explain other sectors, the movement as a whole, the working-class, or how to transplant utopian visions into strategic objectives.

637 EYERMAN, RON and ANDREW JAMISON. 1991. *Social Movements: A Cognitive Approach*. College Park: Pennsylvania State University Press.
In this book the authors propose a social movement theoretical framework based on cognitive praxis. Using concepts from the sociology of knowledge and critical theory, they show how this approach can be applied to new social movements in addition to, or as a replacement of, social psychological (New Social Movement Theory) and structural (Resource Mobilization) approaches. The civil rights movement is used as an example of applying this theoretical model for social movement analysis. Other social movements, such as the women's movement in the United States and Europe, are discussed utilizing this model.

638 FREEMAN, JO, ed. 1983. *Social Movements of the Sixties and Seventies*. New York: Longman.
An anthology on contemporary social movements providing insights into particular movements and theoretical frameworks on social movements in general. Analysis is provided on movement actions, strategies, tactics, and organizational forms. Chapters are organized around the headings of Origins, Mobilizations, Organization, Strategy, and Decline. National, local, radical, reform, social, religious, famous, and unknown movements are discussed in this volume. Also noted are tenants, the disabled, draft resisters, farmers and farm workers, as well as civil rights, anti-nuclear, and women's liberation groups. Many of the articles come from participants in the various movements.

639 GOETTING, ANN and SARAH FENSTERMAKER, eds. 1994. *Individual Voices, Collective Visions: Fifty Years of Women in Sociology*. Philadelphia: Temple University Press.
Autobiographical reflections from women sociologists. The dynamic between personal biography and sociological practice and between individual change and institutional change are discussed, as contributors talk about their lives and careers.

640 KANDAL, TERRY R. 1988. *The Woman Question in Classical Sociological Theory*. Miami: Florida International University Press.
The author of this book discusses views of women by sociological theorists and writers from the nineteenth and twentieth centuries, including John Stuart Mill, Alexis de Tocqueville, Auguste Comte, Herbert Spencer, Emile Durkheim,

Max Weber, Georg Simmel, Ferdinand Tonnies, Alfredo Pareto, Karl Mannheim, Talcott Parsons, and C. Wright Mills. Although this list maintains the patriarchal slant of classical sociological knowledge, it is one way of introducing women and gender issues into the discussion while still covering the classics.

641 KATZENSTEIN, MARY FAINSOD and CAROL MCCLURG MUELLER, eds. 1987. *The Women's Movements of the United States and Western Europe: Consciousness, Political Opportunity, and Public Policy*. Philadelphia: Temple University Press.

The types of feminist activism found in seven Western democratic countries since the 1980s provides the basis of the articles selected for this anthology. Examined are the varied and complex political intersections between movement goals and consciousness with political parties and state institutions. Articles highlighting the women's movement in the United States include "Comparing the Feminist Movements of the United States and Western Europe: An Overview" (Mary Fainsod Katzenstein), "Collective Consciousness, Identity Transformation, and the Rise of Women in Public Office in the United States" (Carol McClurg Mueller), "Equality and Autonomy: Feminist Politics in the United States and West Germany" (Myra Marx Ferree), "Strategy and Tactics of the Women's Movement in the United States: The Role of Political Parties" (Anne N. Costain and W. Douglas Costain), "Whom You Know Versus Whom You Represent: Feminist Influence in the Democratic and Republican Parties" (Jo Freeman), "Social Movement 'Success:' A Comparative Analysis of Feminism in the United States and the United Kingdom" (Joyce Gelb).

642 KOMAROVSKY, MIRRA. 1988. "The New Feminist Scholarship: Some Precursors and Polemics." *Journal of Marriage and the Family* 50:585–593.

From the perspective of a sociology of sociology, Komarovsky examines feminist scholarship which is critical of mainstream (male perspective) sociology. The author finds a number of areas that have been strongly impacted by the theory of gender stratification, such as new areas of social problem definitions, more complete knowledge bases, and challenges to many accepted theories.

643 ———. 1991. "Some Reflections on the Feminist Scholarship in Sociology." *Annual Review of Sociology* 17:1–25.

Komarovsky examines the contribution feminist scholarship has made on sociology. The major area she discusses is the theoretical debates within the sociological discourse between maximalists and minimalists who disagree over the biological and cultural factors contributing to women's status.

644 LARUE, LINDA. 1970. "The Black Movement and Women's Liberation." *Black Scholar* 1:36–42.

In comparing the black movement with the women's liberation movement, LaRue finds that they share some similarities. She also finds there are differences; primarily, the black movement includes men and the women's liberation movement sometimes only includes white middle-class women.

645   MCADAM, DOUG. 1988. *Freedom Summer*. New York: Oxford University
      Press.
Being an activist in Freedom Summer of 1964 was a turning point in the New
Left and the lives of white college students who participated in the civil rights
movement of that era. Other findings McAdam reports on from his survey and
interviews is that the long lasting effects of this involvement kept these educated middle-class whites further to the Left and more politically active than
their counterparts. In general, the people he studied have remained active in
a variety of social causes, but the women are more active than the men, many
having gone from the civil rights movement to the women's movement.

646   MCGLEN, NANCY and KAREN O'CONNOR. 1983. *Women's Rights: The
      Struggle for Equality in the Nineteenth and Twentieth Centuries*. New
      York: Praeger.
A historical view of feminism showing the connections to the activism of the
nineteenth century with that of the present day movement. The focus of this
book is the effort to achieve educational, political, employment, and familial
rights.

647   MEYER, DAVID S. and NANCY WHITTIER. 1994. "Social Movement
      Spillover." *Social Problems* 41 (May):277–298.
Meyer and Whittier make the point that social movements are not distinct iso-
lated phenomena. Instead they interact with diverse intra-movement groups,
other social movements, non-affiliated supporters, and members who overlap
into all kinds of other networking circles. In this article they look at the ways
the feminist movement has affected the peace movement during the 1980s.

648   MORGAN, ROBIN, ed. 1984. "Sisterhood is Global: The International
      Women's Movement Anthology." Garden City, NY: Anchor Press/
      Doubleday.
This book serves as a reference tool for looking at the state of women and feminism in over seventy nations. The contributors are from the country they write
about and represent a mix of social positions, including activists, political leaders, and writers. The short essays do not provide a basis for analysis, only basic
information. The bulk of the entries are from Third World countries which provides information that is difficult to find elsewhere. Statistical data on each
country cover demography, government, economy, marriage, divorce, family,
welfare, contraception, abortion, illegitimacy, homosexuality, incest, sexual
harassment, rape, battery, and prostitution. Short bibliographies are provided.
These sources do not provide in-depth understandings of the countries or
women's position in them, but instead serve as a starting point for further
research.

649   MORRIS, ALDON D. and CAROL MCCLURG MUELLER, eds. 1992. *Frontiers
      in Social Movement Theory*. New Haven, CT: Yale University Press.
A cutting edge collection of articles on social movement theory by noted sociologists. Selections include: "The Social Psychology of Collective Action" by

William A. Gamson; "The Social Construction of Protest and Multi-Organizational Fields" by Bert Klandermans; "Collective Identity in Social Movement Communities: Lesbian Feminist Mobilization" by Verta Taylor and Nancy Whittier; "Communities of Challengers in Social Movement Theory" by Clarence Y. H. Lo; "Looking Backward to Look Forward: Reflections on the Past and Future of the Resource Mobilization Research Program" by Mayer N. Zald; and "Political Consciousness and Collective Action" by Aldon D. Morris.

650　NEBRASKA SOCIOLOGICAL FEMINIST COLLECTIVE, eds. 1988. *A Feminist Ethic for Social Science Research*. Lewiston, NY: The Edwin Mellen Press.

This collective of four sociologists, Beth Hartung, Jane Ollenburger, Helen Moore, and Mary Jo Deegan, were at one time either faculty or graduate students at the University of Nebraska-Lincoln. The articles in this work originated in a special issue for *Humanity and Society* which began with their desire to work on a project that allowed them to articulate their anger at the sexism they found in sociology. Articles cover a range of feminist issues such as prostitution, lesbianism, black women, medicine, language, research, and academia.

651　OBERSCHALL, ANTHONY. 1993. *Social Movements: Ideologies, Interests, and Identities*. New Brunswick, NJ: Transaction.

A collection of journal articles and essays, most of which have been previously published. Some of the author's most well-known pieces are included, such as his work on the 1960s sit-ins, the L.A. riots, and the decline of the 1960s movements. This is a useful book which has gathered together important writings from a social movement theorist.

652　OFFE, CLAUS. 1985. "New Social Movements: Challenging the Boundaries of Institutional Politics." *Social Research* 52 (Dec.):817–868.

From the end of World War II until the 1970s social movement analysis has been concerned with issues of economic growth and distribution. Offe describes how institutional practices implemented these values in the work social activists did. He also describes how new ways of thinking about social movements began to develop in the 1970s. Four types of movements are found in non-institutional politics: ecological/environmental, feminism and human rights, peace, and communal movements. One problem Offe finds is that the roots of these new movements are found in the middle-class where class consciousness is often missing.

653　OPPENHEIMER, MARTIN, MARTIN J. MURRAY, and RHONDA F. LEVINE, eds. 1990. *Radical Sociologists and the Movement: Experiences, Lessons and Legacies*. Philadelphia: Temple University Press.

A collection of autobiographical essays from radical sociologists. One of the themes to emerge from these writings is the impact of the discipline of sociology on their developing consciousness. The contributors also examine personal influences and historical themes that affected their activism. A wide range of activist causes from the 1960s are included in this mix of social movement involvement, including the women's movement.

654   ORLANS, KATHRYN P. MEADOW and RUTH A. WALLACE, eds. 1994. *Gender and the Academic Experience*. Lincoln: University of Nebraska Press.
A collection of stories from women in sociology about their academic experiences from the 1950s to the present.

655   PIVEN, FRANCES FOX and RICHARD A. CLOWARD. 1979. *Poor People's Movements: Why They Succeed, How They Fail*. New York: Vintage Books.
The authors examine four movements of lower-class groups in the twentieth century: The Unemployed Worker's Movement, The Industrial Workers' Movement, The Civil Rights Movement, and The Welfare Rights Movement. In the introduction they lay a theoretical foundation for examining social movements and doing comparative work. Piven and Cloward assess whether poor people are more successful when they engage in the political arena or in mass mobilization in the streets.

656   PLATKE, DAVID. 1990. "What's So New About New Social Movements?" *Socialist Review* 90:81–102.
This article critiques New Social Movement Theory for overstating the novelty of the movements it analyses, selectively depicting aims as cultural, exaggerating their separation from conventional political activism, ignoring other sectors of social movements, derogating efforts to attain legal equality and distributive equity, and for being based on theoretical formulations from Western European societies which differ critically from the United States. Moreover, Plotke argues that cultural concerns are not new. In the late eighteenth and early nineteenth centuries, religion was a major area of contestation; and race, gender, and sexual norms have been contested on political and cultural grounds since at least the mid-eighteenth century. What is new is the emphasis on identity for individuals. He questions this emphasis on identity when people have more than one identity. In particular, the author is concerned about the de-emphasis on class in cultural identity organizing.

657   POPE, JACQUELINE. 1989. *Biting the Hand That Feeds Them: Organizing Women on Welfare at the Grass Roots Level*. New York: Praeger.
This book is a study of the Brooklyn Welfare Action Council, 1967–73. Established by women of color who received public assistance, and associated with the National Welfare Rights Organization, its purpose was to change the system in order to gain economic benefits for its members. In addition to economic improvement in their lives, activists were attempting to achieve dignity and power for themselves and others who make up the poorest segments of society. Personal interviews of activists constitute a major source of data for chronicling the strengths and weaknesses of the Council. The research is framed within a resource mobilization and organizational theory analysis. This work focuses on social change efforts, strategic choices, motivations, and group interests.

658 RAMAZANOGLU, CAROLINE. 1989. "Improving on Sociology: The Problems of Taking a Feminist Standpoint." *Sociology* 23:427–442.
The author discusses the importance of taking a feminist standpoint (the incorporation of women's experiences into analysis). Doing so leads to gendered meanings for commonplace assumptions where a male-centered analysis has been the standard used to develop knowledge of the social world. While this type of research improves on sociology of the past, it too has problems. How to take a feminist standpoint and still make sociological knowledge relevant and convincing is the question the author poses in this article.

659 RICHARDSON, LAUREL. 1988. *The Dynamics of Sex and Gender: A Sociological Perspective, Third Edition* New York: Harper and Row.
An excellent text for gender studies. Topics include culture, language, socialization, education, mass media, religion, law, health care system, gender stratification, inequality, work, home, intimate relationships, social movements, feminism, social change.

660 RYAN, BARBARA. 1982. "Thorstein Veblen: A New Perspective." *Mid-American Review of Sociology* 7:29–47.
Thorstein Veblen is known as a sociologist and economist who presented a cogent, and often tongue-in-cheek, critique of capitalism. In this article, Ryan brings out another component of Veblen's thinking and writing—the division between the sexes, which he considers to be the first and deepest of social divisions. Veblen considers all divisions among people to be status divisions without merit in their own right. He finds status divisions are most clearly seen in the conspicuous consumption patterns of the upper class in the late 1800s. Upper class women were part of this pattern as it was necessary for them to be idle to show that men could afford the luxury of a non-working wife. Many of these thoughts are laid out in his most famous treatise *The Theory of the Leisure Class* (1899). Ryan finds feminist thought in much of his writing and questions why this fact is rarely mentioned in the biographies that have been written about his life.

661 SARAH, ELIZABETH, ed. 1983. *Reassessment of First Wave Feminism*. New York: Pergamon Press.
This is a collection of articles on feminism and the women's movement in Europe and the United States over the last two centuries. The feminist sexuality campaigns of 1880–1914 are an interesting contribution.

662 SCHUR, EDWIN M. 1984. *Labeling Women Deviant: Gender, Stigma, and Social Control*. New York: Random House.
A book focused on the relation between gender and definitions of deviance. Schur, a sociologist, has written extensively on deviance in general and in this work discusses the emergence of women's deviance through gender norms, the production of female deviance, victimization of women, and the implication for social change. He places his analysis within the framework of labeling theory to explain how and why women have been labeled aggressive, bitchy,

hysterical, fat, homely, masculine, and promiscuous—to produce a stigma (devalued and spoiled identity) on the category of female.

663 SIMON, RITA J. and GLORIA DANZIGER. 1991. *Women's Movements in America: Their Successes, Disappointments and Aspirations.* Westport, CT: Praeger.
A review of social change attempts and achievements by women in the nineteenth and twentieth centuries. Covered are campaigns for suffrage, legal status, political participation, property rights, education, employment, and equality in gender and family relations. Also included are public opinion polls on American attitudes, and data illustrating either progress or the lack of progress in women's social, political, and economic position. This work provides no new research findings, is not theoretical, analytical, or ideological; but it does serve as a resource for statistical information and survey data.

664 SMITH, DENNIS. 1991. *The Rise of Historical Sociology.* Philadelphia: Temple University Press.
Historical sociology, sometimes called soft sociology, has gained more legitimacy in recent times. Smith shows how the focus on social history within sociological study was nearly eliminated during the period of fascism and Stalinism and how, since the end of World War II, it has become an important development in contemporary sociology. A guide is provided for the type of work being done by historical sociologists. This book, without explicitly intending, validates the call for a feminist methodology that has often gone unheeded by traditional methodologists.

665 SMITH, DOROTHY E. 1987. *The Everyday World as Problematic: A Feminist Sociology.* Boston: Northeastern University Press.
This book consists of a series of papers developed from the 1970s through the 1980s on sexism in sociology, an academic discipline focused on understanding society and social relations. Smith provides a critique of sociology because it has been derived almost exclusively from the perspective of men. A proposal for a feminist alternative to the false universalizing the discipline has promoted is offered. The papers are defined as originating in the women's movement's efforts for raising consciousness about women's experience of living in an intellectual and cultural world from whose making they have largely been excluded.

666 SOLOMON, IRVIN D. 1989. *Feminism and Black Activism in Contemporary America: An Ideological Assessment.* Westport, CT: Greenwood Press.
Although the intention of this book is to examine the relationship between the civil rights movement and the contemporary women's movement, the result is mainly a history of their separate development. The author fails to find a theoretical intersection between the two and basically claims their mass mobilizations were historical coincidences. Even though the book as a whole is a disappointment, the chapter notes and bibliography are worthwhile reading.

667 STAGGENBORG, SUZANNE. 1988. "The Consequences of Professionalization and Formalization in the Pro-Choice Movement." *American Sociological Review* 53 (August):585–605.

Staggenborg is interested in learning what the effects of professional leadership and formal organizations are for social movements. In analyzing movement/organizational documents and interview material from fifty subjects in the pro-choice movement, she derives five propositions: 1) professional movement entrepreneurs are important players in initiating movements and developing new tactics; 2) professional leaders formalize the movements they are involved in; 3) formalized organizations maintain movements during the declining periods of activism; 4) professional leaders and formalized organizations lead to institutionalization of tactics; 5) professionalization and formalization result in greater levels of coalition work.

668 STEWARD, MARY. 1984. "Feminism and Sociology: An Unfortunate Case of Nonreciprocity." *Humanity and Society* 8 (Nov.):414–422.

A critique of the discipline of sociology for the slow pace it has taken in recognizing the value of gender based research, particularly in relationship to social class and power.

669 TOURAINE, ALAIN. 1988. *Return of the Actor: Social Theory in Postmodern Society*. Minneapolis: University of Minnesota Press.

Touraine is widely known in social movement circles, particularly in Europe, for his theoretical contributions to postmodernist social movement organizing, and for his questioning how "community" is even possible in the wake of urban-industrial change of the late twentieth century. In this book he brings back the concept of the actor—social activists—who become part of the social forces transforming the world they live in. He credits feminism and the women's movement as representing a new form of social/political/cultural challenge that offers hope for a better world.

670 TOURAINE, ALAIN and DAVID ROBERTS. 1984. "Social Movements: Special Area or Central Problem in Sociological Analysis?" *Thesis Eleven* 9 (July):5–15.

The authors of this article are interested in defining sociological analysis by change and conflict rather than social systems (i.e., functionalism). Social movements are examined by whether they are responsive or active and where they focus their efforts—either on power relationships in general or on specific issues. The women's movement is used to explain their ideas and is also cited by Touraine and Roberts as one of today's most important cultural change movements.

671 TRIMBERGER, ELLEN KAY. 1979. "Women in the Old and New Left: The Evolution of a Politics of Personal Life." *Feminist Studies* 5:432–461.

In developing analyses for understanding differences between the Old Left and the New Left in the United States, Trimberger points to the changes in personal relations, particularly family structure. This article makes the point that the effects of larger social forces played themselves out within the American social-ist movement by transporting personal life experiences into changed social movement activism.

672   WOOD, JAMES L. and MAURICE JACKSON. 1982. *Social Movements: Development, Participation, and Dynamics*. Belmont, CA: Wadsworth Publishing.
A discussion of social movement dynamics—how and why movements change and the ways they effect society. A thorough review of social movement theo-ry is included.

Identity Politics

673   BULKIN, ELLY, MINNIE BRUCE PRATT, and BARBARA SMITH. 1984. *Yours in Struggle: Three Feminist Perspectives on Anti-Semitism and Racism*. Brooklyn, NY: Long Haul Press.
The three essays in this book were originally prepared for a racism and anti-Semitism panel at the 1983 National Women's Studies Association conference. In "Identity: Skin Blood Heart," Pratt writes of her struggles against racism and anti-Semitism and of the difficulty she has in these areas because of her cultural upbringing as a white southerner. Smith's essay "Between a Rock and a Hard Place: Relationships Between Black and Jewish Women," discusses the ten-sions between black and Jewish people in the United States and within the women's movement. In spite of the difficulties she identifies, she calls for greater understanding and coalition work to eradicate all oppressions in soci-ety. Bulkin's essay "Hard Ground: Jewish Identity, Racism, and Anti-Semitism," provides personal experience, historical treatment of Jews, analysis of racism among Jewish people and anti-Semitism among people of color, and a pre-scription for overcoming barriers to change. These essays provide a sensitive exploration of difficult issues and an important contribution to work that looks at the interconnections of race, class, gender, and ethnicity.

674   BUTLER, JUDITH. 1990. *Gender Trouble: Feminism and the Subversion of Identity*. New York: Routledge, Chapman and Hall.
Butler is opposed to organizing around gender since it reinforces the very thing feminists are trying to deconstruct. She argues that political activism does not have to be centered around unity and solidarity. Coalitions, including those with inherent contradictions, can work on particular issues. Rather than identity politics, activism should be focused on subverting the categories of gender. A serious lack in this book is the narrowed focus on identity politics. For instance, race identity is not explored in a meaningful way.

675   CARAWAY, NANCIE. 1991. *Segregated Sisterhood: Racism and the Politics of American Feminism*. Knoxville: University of Tennessee Press.
This is a documentation of racism in the early woman's rights movement, abo-lition movement and suffrage movement. An alternative, more inclusive femi-

nism, which would include the work of African-American activists such as Ida B. Wells, is presented. Exclusionary practices in the contemporary women's movement, although reduced from the earlier era, are also shown. Alternatively, essentialist comments by African-American feminists are revealed which show a level of insensitivity similar to Euro-American women's practice of privileging their life experiences over those of others. Two noticeable omissions in this work are the failure to discuss poor white women and the lack of distinguishing differences among women of color.

676   CARBY, HAZEL V. 1990. "The Politics of Difference." *Ms.* 1 (Sept.):84–85.
Carby raises the question of whether the emphasis on diversity in feminist thought and practice is a way to avoid the politics of race even as it appears that racism is being confronted. The politics of difference has become a way for feminists to show their concern that the concept of woman is plural rather than unitary. But in the process, the complexity of difference within racial and ethnic groups is denied. The author believes Women's Studies has created a black female subject for its own consumption—the black woman can be used as an example of either patriarchal oppression or as the nobleness of womanhood. Most importantly, the new black woman subject allows the white woman to berate herself (and others) for racism and, thereby, cleanse her soul. According to the author, white women who speak with political correctness reward themselves with self-satisfaction.

677   CONLON, FAITH, BARBARA WILSON, and RACHEL DA SILVA, eds. 1989. *The Things That Divide Us: Stories by Women*. Seattle, WA: Seal Press.
In raising the issue of multiculturalism, the sixteen essays in this anthology discuss the meaning of race, ethnicity, and class among women. The authors discuss the difficulty of joining together as women on issues of sex/gender without losing the identities and issues of importance for other areas of their lives. Many of the stories are personal, although analytical insights are also found throughout the collection. Some of the contributors are well-known feminist writers and activists. This work provides an experiential knowledge base on how to address racism, anti-Semitism, and classism within the women's movement.

678   DAVIS, ANGELA. 1981. *Women, Race and Class*. New York: Random House.
Davis points out instances of racism in the women's movement of the past and present. She particularly looks at how analyses of rape have contributed to perpetuating the image of the black male rapist and the white female victim.

679   DE LAURETIS, TERESA, ed. 1986. *Feminist Studies/Critical Studies*. Bloomington: Indiana University Press.
When this book came out it was selected by many feminist discussion groups for review. The discourse that emerges from group think and from de Lauretis' writing sets an agenda for accepting differences within feminism rather than creating divisions or spending what is often wasted time trying to resolve them. When you read this book you are bound to do some quiet thinking

about what you have been reading, particularly the way the author describes her views on the changing meaning of gender and identity.

680   DUCILLE, ANN. 1994. "The Occult of True Black Womanhood: Critical Demeanor and Black Feminist Studies." *Signs: Journal of Women in Culture and Society* 19:591–629.

A personal and critical look at the "hot commodity" black women's voices have become. duCille says she has begun to think of herself as "a kind of sacred text" (p.591). In this article she questions the rise of the occult in black womanhood in which black women have been objectified, idealized, and romanticized. She has mixed feelings about the recognition now being expressed for the kind of studies she has been doing for twenty years, and places this new attention within a framework of a multicultural movement that became "politically correct, intellectually popular and commercially precious" (p.594). The essence of this article is duCille's defense of identity politics at the same time she questions how it is socially constructed.

681   HENNESSY, ROSEMARY. 1993. "Queer Theory: A Review of the Differences Special Issue and Wittig's "The Straight Mind." *Signs: Journal of Women in Culture and Society* 18:964–973.

Hennessy contrasts two critiques of heterosexuality and identity politics: queer theory and materialist feminism. The author uses the Summer 1991 special issue of *Differences*, titled "Queer Theory: Lesbian and Gay Sexualities" and the writing of Monique Wittig in *The Straight Mind* to define the similar and contrasting perceptions they offer. Queer theory challenges categories upon which conventional notions of sexuality rely, offers an explicit critique of hetero-normativity, and denies the assumption of monolithic gay and lesbian identities. Wittig's work is compatible with these conceptions, but disagrees with Queer theory's presumption that cultural change is commensurate with social change. She argues that the construction of sexual subjects is more than a cultural event. Her materialist view conceptualizes the social/cultural as an economic, political, ideological order in which difference is enacted as dominance. Both queer theory and materialist feminism challenge the legitimacy of identity politics where identity is reified through one's body and collectivity is assumed through group affiliation premised on authentic embodiment.

682   KAUFFMAN, L. A. 1990. "The Anti-Politics of Identity." *Socialist Review* 90:67–80.

Kauffman examines the implications of identity politics which challenge forms of domination and exclusion based on social group characteristics. The author documents how identity politics emerged in the civil rights movement within the Student Non-Violent Coordinating Committee (SNCC) and the Black Power Movement, the women's liberation segment of the women's movement, and the gay and lesbian liberation movement. Identity politics represents a major shift in political thinking which de-emphasizes the role of institutions and highlights the role of culture in creating and perpetuating discrimination and exploitation. Kauffman finds the results of this orientation to be problematic since "organizing around your own oppression" tends to reduce efforts for coalition building among diverse groups. Also, seeing everything as political makes it difficult to formulate effective political strategies, which she argues has led to the replacement of political change struggles to efforts for self-transformation. Her strongest critique rests on the depoliticization of identity politics into lifestyle politics which promotes individual solutions to social problems.

683   MCCLUSKEY, AUDREY, ed. 1985. *Women of Color: Perspectives on Feminism and Identity*. Bloomington: Women's Studies Program of Indiana University.
A good collection that looks at the issues of identity and the conflicts for women of color between race and gender issues. Fits into the discourse of identity politics and the women's movement.

684   MILES, ANGELA. 1984. "Integrative Feminism." *Fireweed* 19 (June): 55–81.
Integrative feminism is inclusive of feminist concerns along a wide range of issues and philosophic backgrounds. It is the joining together of socialist feminists, radical feminists, liberal feminists, and lesbian feminists to struggle together on issues of peace, the environment, reproductive freedom, and other issues related to women. Another important component in the concept of integrative feminism is the need to pay attention to the diversities among women as well as the commonalities.

685   MOGHADAM, VALENTINE M., ed. 1994. *Identity Politics and Women: Cultural Reassertions and Feminisms in International Perspective*. Boulder, CO: Westview Press.
This book looks at identity politics both theoretically and empirically by examining discourses and movements organized around religious, ethnic, and national identity. Illustrations from around the world are used to reveal the nature of woman as symbol and as political pawn in male directed power struggles. Women are also shown as participants in movements to control women's lives as well as active opponents to those movements. Articles particular to the United States include Hanna Papanek's work on the role of women in the idealized vision of Nazi Germany, Khomeini's Iran, and the anti-abortion movement in the U.S.; Debra Kaufman's analysis of the gender politics involved in American Jewish women's return to Orthodoxy; and Rebecca Klatch's conceptual comparisons of family, feminism, and politics among Right Wing political women in the Republican Party.

686   PHELAN, SHANE. 1989. *Identity Politics: Lesbian Feminism and the Limits of Community*. Philadelphia: Temple University Press.
The author explores liberal philosophical notions of individualism and privacy and the tension that ideology creates for the communitarian ideals often found in lesbian communities. The ideological strains and limitations inherent in each is discussed and contrasted. One area of contention that is presented as

a test case is the issue of lesbian sadomasochism. Feminists of both persuasions consider whether this is an issue of male identified anti-feminist behavior or of individual choice in sexual expression. Phelan finds that the lesbian community has failed to deal with difference and has, instead, constructed an image of "the" lesbian. She argues that individuality is lost in the notion of community.

687   REID, INEZ SMITH. 1975. *Together Black Women*. New York: The Third Press.
This work is the result of a study of attitudes of black women activists towards social issues, the civil rights movement, and women's liberation. Subjects were found to be supportive of the civil rights movement, although not of militancy unless there was no other option. They were not interested in joining the women's movement because they felt it divided their racial alliance with black men, hence, the "together" in the title of the book. In general, they did not feel white women could lead the way for social reform that would help them.

688   REID, PAMELA TROTMAN. 1984. "Feminism Versus Minority Group Identity: Not for Black Women Only." *Sex Roles* 10 (Feb.):247–255.
A report on research that tested hypotheses of why black women have a low rate of participation in the women's movement. Results refuted the following beliefs: 1) that they are more concerned about racism then sex equality (and would weaken the women's movement if they did participate because of this leaning); 2) that they need the movement less since they have a dual oppression which has given them a higher social status than white women; 3) that black matriarchy and black sexism are the cause of their oppression, thus, they have nothing in common with white women. Reid finds instead that class difference is the strongest explanation of lower rates of participation by black women.

689   SIMONS, MARGARET A. 1979. "Racism and Feminism: A Schism in the Sisterhood." *Feminist Studies* 5:384–401.
By examining Simone de Beauvoir's *The Second Sex* (entry 548), Robin Morgan's *Sisterhood is Powerful* (entry 1277), Shulamith Firestone's *The Dialectic of Sex* (entry 560), Kate Millett's *Sexual Politics* (entry 505), and Mary Daly's *Beyond God the Father* (entry 547), Simons presents a critical analysis of racism and ethnocentrism in the women's movement. She finds the lack of minority women in the women's movement is due to racism, not a lack of consciousness on the part of white women.

690   SPELMAN, ELIZABETH V. 1988. *Inessential Woman: Problems in Exclusion in Feminist Thought*. Boston: Beacon Press.
The inessential woman that Elizabeth Spelman refers to is the woman who does not fit into the category of white and middle class—the new "other." Spelman speaks of the exclusiveness of the contemporary women's movement, and the "left out women" who have become the center of feminist division and analysis since the 1980s. This work is a well-written and reasoned

account of feminism's need to eliminate bias within its own ranks and to recognize the significant voices of those women who have felt excluded.

Multiculturalism

691   AFSHAR, HALEH and MARY MAYNARD, eds. 1994. *The Dynamics of Race and Gender: Some Feminist Interventions*. Bristol, PA: Taylor & Francis. An examination of the ways race and gender are interrelated. Sections are divided into: Issues of Theory and Method; Questions of Identity; Racism and Sexism at Work. An overriding framework is the acknowledgement that diversity among women is not static; it is an overlapping and changing phenomenon. The diversities examined are age, class, disability, race, and sexuality.

692   ALBRECHT, LISA and ROSE M. BREWER, eds. 1990. *Bridges of Power: Women's Multicultural Alliances*. Philadelphia, PA: New Society Publishers.
Race, ethnicity, class, age, and sexual orientation constitute social differences that have a long history of dividing women from each other. Efforts at forging bonds have often failed but in recent years examples of successful multicultural alliances can be found, particularly in women's communities. Contributors to this collection reveal innovative ways different groups have celebrated diversity, the results of experimental attempts to break down barriers to connectedness among women, and the variety of cultural sources available which can be utilized to build on women's ability to form community ties among themselves. Contributors include well-known authors such as Gloria Anzaldua, Charlotte Bunch, and Audre Lorde.

693   ANZALDUA, GLORIA. 1987. *Borderlands/La Frontera*. San Francisco: Spinsters/Aunt Lute.
This book takes the reader through Chicana history as well as mythology. In moving into the present, Anzaldua shows the difficulties which continue to exist for her people as well as other minority groups. Possibilities for the future are discussed.

694   ———, ed. 1990. *Making Face, Making Soul: Haciendo Caras*. San Francisco: Aunt Lute Books.
Using essays, scholarly works, poetry, and personal stories, this collection looks at the interconnections of race, class, and gender. This is a book for and about women of color which invites readers to understand multiple meanings of oppression. "Making Faces" is a metaphor for identity construction and one purpose of this book is for Mazaldua and other women of color to reclaim their identity. Authors are attempting to decolonize themselves and express their anger at white people. The women's movement and feminism are frequently criticized for a lack of sensitivity towards women on the margins of society. The question of alliances and unity among women is debated with a number of authors calling for new theories based on diversity rather than attempts to

establish overarching principles. Articles by Lynn Weber Cannon, Bonnie Thornton Dill, Elizabeth Higginbotham, and Maxine Baca Zinn address questions of how the women's movement has failed women of color.

695   BECK, EVELYN TORTON. 1988. "The Politics of Jewish Invisibility." *NWSA Journal: A Publication of The National Women's Studies Association* 1:93–102.

The subject of this article is the absence of Jewish women in Women's Studies texts. With the new emphasis on multiculturalism within feminism and academia, this failure is particularly noted. The author is concerned with the silence surrounding anti-Semitism, which she charges is also the case within The National Women's Studies Association. Torton Beck points out that anti-Semitism is a feminist issue and the effects it has on Jewish women's lives needs to be recognized and addressed. Also mentioned is the feminist transformations of Judaism.

696   BONILLA-SANTIAGO, GLORIA. 1990. *Hispanic Women Leaders in the United States*. New York: Greenwood Press.

In this book the author has provided background information and a well thought out discussion on the relationship of Hispanic women in the United States to the women's movement. The activist work of Hispanic women Bonilla-Santiago covers are labor, politics, education, and the arts. After discussing their social reform efforts, the author allows us to hear the women's own voices as they tell their stories in the last section of the book.

697   BULBECK, CHILLA. 1988. *One World Women's Movement*. Winchester, MA: Pluto Press.

Bulbeck writes of the need to see feminism and women's issues as connected to race and class issues. Black and Third World women argue that, for them, there is no way to make a distinction between these factors in their lives. The author of this book asks white women to come to terms with this fact, even though they do not experience it themselves.

698   CADE, TONI, ed. 1970. *The Black Woman: An Anthology*. New York: American Library.

Cade questions whether all women are simply women. Specifically she is interested in the different experiences and truths of black and white women. This anthology is the result of her feeling that the priorities of the women's movement represent the concerns of white women, and thus, much of feminist literature is irrelevant to black women's lives. The contributors to this work share their thoughts and values through the medium of poetry, essay, and autobiographical stories which reflect their feelings of being black women in white America.

699   CHAL, ALICE. 1981. "An Asian-American Woman's View of the Consciousness-Raising Sessions." *Women's Studies Quarterly* 9 (Sept.):16.

One of the critiques of consciousness-raising (CR) as it was practiced in the 1970s was that the people who gathered into the small CR groups were all alike, and that the experiences they shared were then translated into feminist theory as universal gender experiences. Chal makes the point that there are differences among women by race and ethnicity.

700   ———. 1985. "Toward a Holistic Paradigm for Asian-American Women's Studies: A Synthesis of Feminist Scholarship and Women of Color's Feminist Politics." *Women's Studies International Forum* 8:59–66.

Chal combines the frameworks of feminist theory and scholarship with women of color feminist politics to create a program for studying about Asian-American women.

701   CHOW, ESTHER NGAN-LING. 1987. "The Development of Feminist Consciousness Among Asian-American Women." *Gender & Society* 1:284–299.

A neglected group of women, particularly in discussions of feminism and the women's movement, are Asian-American women. Chow opens this dialogue and discusses how Asian women come to adopt feminism into their consciousness.

702   COCHRAN, JO, J. T. STEWART, and MAYUMI TSUTAKAWA, eds. 1984. *Gathering Ground*. Seattle, WA: Seal Press.

An anthology of artwork and writing by women of color. Three themes are emphasized in this work: self-discovery, community, and cultural awareness.

703   COLE, JOHNETTA, ed. 1986. *All American Women: Lines that Divide, Ties that Bind*. New York: The Free Press.

The articles in this volume challenge the assumption of a common female experience by revealing the diversity that exists in women's lives. While acknowledging the bonds that unite women, Cole points out the race, class, and ethnic differences that belie the ideals of "sisterhood." Among others, articles by Betty Friedan, Audre Lorde, Rosabeth Moss Kanter, Harriette P. McAdoo, Angela Davis, Lillian Rubin, Gloria Joseph, Carol Christ, Geraldine Ferraro, Barbara Sinclair Deckard, Paula Gunn Allen, and Barbara Smith cover women's experiences from numerous academic disciplines, life circumstances, group identities, and political orientations.

704   DILL, BONNIE THORNTON. 1983. "Race, Class, and Gender: Prospects for an All-Inclusive Sisterhood." *Feminist Studies* 9 (March):130–149.

A classic article that set an agenda for an expansion of the topic of race, class, and gender throughout the 1980s. Thornton Dill looks at the ideal of sisterhood that was frequently voiced in the contemporary women's movement. She found that this concept did not apply to her, to other black women or working-class women, because the divisions between them and white middle-class women were too deep and their life experiences could not be converged into one. Rather than thinking of all women together in a universal category,

Dill calls for a multicultural approach which allows for bridges to be built and to focus on coalition work when they have shared interests and common goals.

705   DUBOIS, CAROL ELLEN and VICKI L. RUIZ, eds. 1990. *Unequal Sisters: A Multicultural Reader in U.S. Women's History*. New York: Routledge.
This is a multicultural reader which incorporates racial, ethnic, class, and sexual orientation differences which are often left out of gender analysis. These essays document the diversity among women and contribute to an inclusive women's history. Over half the book focuses on women of color and the ways diversity in women's lives adds to our understanding of gender. Issues such as family, activism, community, and employment are addressed. Contributors include Nancy Hewitt, Rayna Green, Christine Stansell, Kathryn Kish Sklar, Linda Gordon, Meredith Tax, Darlene Clark Hine, Evelyn Nakano Glenn, Amy Swerdlow, and Alice Kessler-Harris. Selected bibliographies on African-American women, Asian-American women, Latinas, Native American women, and the search for sisterhood are useful additions to this collection.

706   FIOL-MATTA, LIZA and MARIAM K. CHAMBERLAIN, eds. 1994. *Women of Color and the Multicultural Curriculum: Transforming the College Classroom*. New York: The Feminist Press.
This book is divided into three sections: Part I, Faculty Development; Part II, Model Undergraduate Curriculum (subdivided into humanities, literature, social science, science, and then further divided into particular disciplines such as history, art, sociology, etc.); and Part III, Focus on Puerto Rican Studies. Except for the last section, the book covers a variety of ethnicities and races. There are contributions from many scholars addressing the issues of multicultural education.

707   FULANI, LENORA, ed. 1988. *The Psychopathology of Everyday Racism and Sexism*. New York: Practice Press.
Women of color speak out on race, gender, and class. Their personal histories and the experiences of their racial/ethnic group form the basis for the stories they tell.

708   GARCIA, ALMA M. 1989. "The Development of Chicana Feminist Discourse, 1970–1980." *Gender & Society* 3 (June):217–238.
During the 1970s Chicana feminist thought emerged. In looking at the relationship between race, class and gender, Chicana feminists raised questions about the position of Chicanas within the Chicano movement, and the relationship between Chicana feminists within the white feminist movement. In addition to exploring these questions, Garcia compares Chicana feminism with black feminism and Asian-American feminism.

709   GONZALES, SYLVIA. 1977. "The White Feminist Movement: The Chicana Perspective." *Social Science Journal* 14 (April):67–76.
A discussion of the status of the Chicana in the white feminist movement as well as in U.S. society in general. The lack of participation in the First

International Women's Year Conference held in Mexico City in 1975 is particularly noted. The position of Chicanas is discussed as: minority group member, low income, members of a male oriented society, a subgroup within the male Chicano movement, and a subgroup within the white feminist movement. Because of these forms of oppression and exclusion, Chicanas have united to form a movement of their own.

710   HARDY-FANTA, CAROL. 1993. *Latina Politics, Latino Politics: Gender, Culture, and Political Participation in Boston*. Philadelphia: Temple University Press.
Hardy-Fanta interviewed Latinos(a) from Puerto Rico, the Dominican Republic, and from Central and South America to examine the culture and political life of this expanding immigrant population. She also participated in community events in order to document the contribution of Latina women as political workers, community organizers, and social movement participants.

711   HO, LIANG. 1982. "Asian-American Women: Identity and Role in the Women's Movement." *Heresies* 4:60–61.
A look at Asian-American women, their self-identity and the identity and role they perceive others give them in the women's movement.

712   HORNO-DELGADO, ASUNCION ELIANA ORREGA, NINA SCOTT ELIANA, and NANCY SAPORTA STERNBACH, eds. 1989. *Breaking Boundaries: Latina Writing and Critical Readings*. Amherst: University of Massachusetts Press.
A good source book for Latina writing and views. The bibliography provides readers with additional readings to go beyond the material presented in this volume.

713   JOSEPH, GLORIA and JILL LEWIS. 1986. *Common Differences: Conflict in Black and White Feminist Perspectives, Second Edition*. Boston: South End Press.
A black author and a white author, Joseph and Lewis examine a variety of issues from their own perspectives. Both women are professors at Hampshire College and this work is the result of a prolonged collaborative effort aimed at mutual learning about their differences. Issues covered include mother/daughter relationships, women's liberation, sexuality, media representation, and sexual socialization. They present a good case for black and white women to work together to understand their specific experiences of oppression and the meaning they employ in their goal of liberation.

714   KADI, JOANNA, ed. *Food for our Grandmothers: Writings by Arab-American & Arab-Canadian Feminists*. 1994. Boston: South End Press.
An anthology of poems, essays, and recipes honoring Arab women from the past and present. Racist and sexist stereotypes of Arab women are challenged, and parallels on the experience of Arab women in North America with other women of color are presented.

715   KANTROWITZ, MELANIE KAYE and IRENA KLEPFISZ, eds. 1986. *The Tribe of Diana: A Jewish Women's Anthology*. Montpelier, VT: Sinister Wisdom Books.
Part of the publishing efforts to bring to the women's movement and general public the cultural history of diverse ethnic and racial groups, this book offers documentation of the historical background and current situation of Jewish women around the world. This is interesting reading as it contains personal accounts of women's lives which encompass wide and varied experiences.

716   KOPACSI, ROSEMARIE and AUDREY FAULKNER. 1988. "The Powers that Might Be: The Unity of White and Black Feminists." *Affilia* 3 (Sept.):33–50.
An essay of possibilities on white and black feminist women working together and understanding each other.

717   LADNER, JOYCE A. 1971. *Tomorrow's Tomorrow: The Black Woman*. Garden City, NY: Doubleday.
Ladner's research for this book led her to the belief that black and white realities are different. She is interested in developing a new conceptual framework to view black women today. Ladner argues for this necessity because racism has segregated the black population from the 'white mainstream' to such an extent that the same values cannot be applied to both groups. The lack of interest in the women's movement by black women is explained by their resistance to being opposed to black men.

718   LINNEKIN, JOCELYN. 1990. *Sacred Queens and Women of Consequence: Rank, Gender, and Colonialism in the Hawaiian Islands*. Ann Arbor: University of Michigan Press.
Most people in the U.S. know very little about the Hawaiian people even though Hawaii is one of the states that makes up the Union. This book reports on Hawaiian women and their social position before their culture was changed by the influences of Western society. In a more general sense, Linnekin provides the reader with an understanding of the meaning and effects of colonialism on indigenous people, particularly women.

719   LOEWENBERG, BERT JAMES and RUTH BOGIN, eds. 1976. *Black Women in Nineteenth Century American Life: Their Words, Their Thoughts, Their Feelings*. University Park: The Pennsylvania State University Press.
A selection of writings from black women leaders of the last century. There are four parts to this reader: Family, Religious Activities, Political and Reformist Movements, and Education. Includes writing from free blacks, those freed from The Emancipation Proclamation, Northern women, Southern women, unknown women and famous women such as Susie King Taylor, Sojourner Truth, Harriet Tubman, Charlotte Grimké, and Ida Wells-Barnett.

720   MARTI, DONALD B. 1991. *Women of the Grange: Mutuality and Sisterhood in Rural America, 1866–1920*. Westport, CT: Greenwood Press.

Farm women are often left out of politics and issues that originate in urban locations. Donald Marti has written a book which shows the activism and shared relationships of women in rural America who are interested in social causes and participate in bringing that about. This book also gives a good foundation in social history of the late 1800s and early 1900s in farming communities.

721   MAZOW, JULIA WOLF, ed. 1980. *The Woman Who Lost Her Name: Selected Writings by American Jewish Women*. San Francisco: Harper and Row.

A collection of writings by Jewish women discussing the search for identity, a sense of alienation, the desire for rebellion, and reconciliation with the past. Well-known feminist and social activist Jewish-American women include: Emma Goldman, Tillie Olsen, Grace Paley, Andrea Dworkin, and Lois Gould.

722   MELHEM, D. H. 1987. *Gwendolyn Brooks: Poetry and the Heroic Voice*. Lexington: University Press of Kentucky.

The poetry of Gwendolyn Brooks bridges art and activism. Brooks voice is one of struggle, black pride and unity, and a call for new leadership.

723   MORAGA, CHERRIE and GLORIA ANZALDUA, eds. 1983. *This Bridge Called My Back: Writings By Radical Women of Color*. New York: Kitchen Table, Women of Color Press.

This book has become a classic anthology in writings for inclusive feminism. The personal critiques of racism within the U.S. women's movement found in this volume have been credited with effecting changes in the movement and contributing to a sense of unity among women of color. African-American, Asian-American, Chicana, Native American, Puerto Rican, and lesbian women speak of their differences and commonalities. Through poems, personal stories, letters, and essays, twenty-nine women of color show how different backgrounds lead to different perspectives on feminism. Contains a forward by Toni Cade Bambara and a lengthy selected bibliography titled "Third World Women in the United States: By and About Us."

724   NIETO, CONSUELO. 1974. "The Chicana and the Women's Rights Movement: A Perspective." *Civil Rights Digest* 6:36–42.

An early assessment of the place of Chicanas in the contemporary women's movement.

725   OMOLADE, BARBARA. 1994. *The Rising Song of African-American Women*. New York: Routledge.

Omolade talks about her multiple identities, with all their contradictions, and shows how they can be life affirming. She discusses black women's lives and the importance of political organizing by black women.

726   PRESTAGE, JEWEL L. 1991. "In Quest of African-American Political
      Women." *Annals of the American Academy of Political and Social
      Science*, (May):88–103.
Prestage discusses the ways African-American women have been active in black
struggles and the women's movement, and the innovative ways they have been
active given their exclusion from traditional political activities. After the mid-
1960s more traditional forms of activism have led to African-American women
having a higher voting average, a higher rate of being elected to public office,
and higher rates of supporting women's issues than white women.

727   ROGOW, FAITH. 1993. *Gone to Another Meeting: The National Council
      of Jewish Women, 1893–1993*. Tuscaloosa: University of Alabama Press.
The National Council of Jewish Women is the oldest national religious organization for Jewish women in the United States. In this book the history of this
organization is traced for the last 100 years. While not a part of the women's
movement per se, such organizations reveal changing directions of women's
activism. Activists are sometimes involved in general social issues, other times
the focus might be religious or ethnic questions.

728   RUIZ, VICKI L. 1988. *Cannery Women, Cannery Lives: Mexican Women,
      Unionization, and the California Food Processing Industry,
      1930–1950*. Albuquerque: University of New Mexico Press.
Biographical stories of a collective of women in the cannery industry talking
about their families, their work experiences, and their union activism.

729   RUIZ, VICKI L. and SUSAN TIANO, eds. 1987. *Women on the United
      States-Mexico Border: Responses to Change*. Winchester, MA: Pandora
      Press.
Ruiz and Tiano are interested in bringing forth the history and present day reality of Mexicana and Chicana women in the southwestern part of the United
States. This is a collection of essays that talk about these women's work, consciousness, culture, contributions to their communities, family life, and migra-
tion history.

730   SANCHEZ, ROSAURA and ROSA MARTINEZ CRUZ, eds. 1977. *Essays on La
      Mujer*. Los Angeles: University of California Press.
This collection consists of twelve articles on the historical position of Chicanas
in the political, economic, and social structures of the United States. Topics
include Chicanas and labor force participation, activism in the student movement, class differences between women, the failure of the women's movement
to address Chicana issues, and cultural nationalism.

731   SCADRON, ARLENE, ed. 1988. *On Their Own: Widows and Widowhood
      in the American Southwest, 1848–1939*. Champaign: University of
      Illinois Press.
Comparative case studies of widowed women in three cultural groups (Native
American, Spanish-speaking, and Anglo women) from mid-eighteenth century

to the eve of World War II. How they managed their lives after the loss of their husband, the cultural support they received, new directions they took, and the identity change they underwent are all seen as part of the process of adaptation and self-empowerment as they become women on their own.

732 SEGURA, DENISE A. and BEATRIZ M. PESQUERA. 1988. "Beyond Indifference and Antipathy: The Chicana Movement and Chicana Feminist Discourse." *Aztlan* 19 (Sept.):69–92.

Based on questionnaire responses (n=101) from Chicanas in higher education, Segura and Pesquera find over 50 percent affirmed there was a Chicana movement separate from the women's movement and the Chicano movement. Four-fifths of the respondents identified themselves as Chicana feminists. Respondents were in agreement on the need to redress historical oppression of Mexican women but did not agree on how to do that, particularly in relationship to perceptions of the centrality of gender oppression, a critique of Chicano culture, and the type of political struggle that is needed.

733 STAPLES, ROBERT. 1973. *The Black Woman in America: Sex, Marriage and the Family*. Chicago: Nelson-Hall.

In examining black women's lives, both in the family and in society, Staples illuminates the ambiguous nature of sexism and racism as it is structured into every aspect of their days. Separate chapters discuss motherhood, sexuality, and the relationships between black men and women. The author devotes one chapter to examining the meaning and lack of connection for African-American women with the Women's Liberation Movement.

734 STERLING, DOROTHY. 1984. *We Are Your Sisters: Black Women in the Nineteenth Century*. New York: W. W. Norton.

A history of African-American women in the nineteenth century showing their lives and their activism in abolition, race consciousness, and gender causes.

735 THOMPSON, BECKY W. and SANGEETA TYAGI, eds. 1994. *Beyond a Dream Deferred: Multicultural Education and the Politics of Excellence*. Minneapolis: University of Minnesota Press.

This anthology consists of articles by scholar/activists who are committed to multicultural education, and social change from within and outside the academy. The intent is to contribute to a re-imagining of national identity which focuses on the diversity of the past and the emerging future. Interdisciplinary in content, the authors provide theoretical insights, reflective voices, and case studies as well as a range of perspectives encompassing feminist, gay, lesbian, and ethnic studies. Contributors include Troy Duster, Evelyn Hu-Dehart, Earl Jackson, Jr., Chandra Mohanty, and Cornel West, among others.

736 UNITED NATIONS. 1980. *Report of the World Conference of the United Nations Decade for Women: Equality, Development and Peace; Copenhagen, 14–30 July 1980*. New York: United Nations.

This is a good resource for those interested in doing comparative work on feminist positions and the women's movement around the world. In 1975 The United Nations Decade for Women began at a conference in Mexico City. In 1980 a mid-decade conference was held in Copenhagen to assess whether progress was being made. This volume documents that meeting in terms of the origins of the conference, decisions made, resolutions passed, attendance, and summaries of general debates. Subsequent conferences for the Decade of Women were held in 1985 in Nairobi, and in Beijing in 1995.

737   WEBBER, KIKANZA N. 1980. "Reflections on Black American Women: The Images of the Eighties." *Western Journal of Black Studies* 4 (Dec.):242–250.

Webber examines the extent of racism that is found in stereotypical images of black women as revealed in examples of academic writing and popular media sources. Five stereotypes are discussed; one that is used to show the importance of race over gender considerations is the "Women's Lib Lackey." The author argues for the priority of fighting racism over sexism and the need for black women to join with black men, rather than white women, to overcome the oppressions in their lives.

738   WHITE, EVELYN C., ed. 1990. *The Black Women's Health Book: Speaking for Ourselves*. Seattle, WA: Seal Press.

This book features essays by women of color on health issues and how they particularly effect ethnic/racial groups. Well-known black activists such as Marian Wright Edelman, Alice Walker, and Faye Wattleton, are contributors to this collection.

739   WILLIS, SUSAN. 1987. *Specifying: Black Women Writing the American Experience*. Madison: University of Wisconsin.

This book is about black women's writing and it looks at that writing from a framework of social change and struggle against the racism, sexism, and poverty they experience in their lives.

740   WOMEN OF COLOR ASSOCIATION. 1991. "Speaking for Ourselves." *Women's Review of Books* 8 (Sept.):27–29.

This is a report from the members of the Women of Color Caucus on why they walked out of the Akron National Women's Studies Association Conference. The authors blame the firing of Ruby Sales, a black woman employed by NWSA, and the way the organization handled the firing as the catalyst for this action. Preliminary work has begun on organizing a National Womanist/Feminist Women of Color Association and a Women of Color Newsletter.

741   ZINN, MAXINE BACA, LYNN WEBER CANNON, ELIZABETH HIGGINBOTHAM, and BONNIE THORNTON DILL. 1986. "The Costs of Exclusionary Practices in Women's Studies." *Signs: Journal of Women in Culture and Society* 11:290-303.

The authors of this piece discuss the importance of including all women in Women's Studies courses, and what it means to leave them out. Because the early stage of the women's movement consisted of mainly white middle-class women, the focus of the movement (and Women's Studies) was also on this group. But that focus created a distorted picture of the movement which kept it from growing because other women felt left out. In order to create the changes feminism calls for, all women need to be involved.

742 ZINN, MAXINE BACA and BONNIE THORNTON DILL, eds. 1994. *Women of Color in U.S. Society*. Philadelphia: Temple University Press.
A collection of articles which address the problems associated with maintaining unity in feminist communities when doing so often means subordinating the experiences of women of color. The contributors are interested in creating a multi-racial feminism. A major point the articles make is that gender is experienced differently depending upon how it intersects with other types of inequalities. The multi-racial feminism the authors speak of does not allow for a singular feminism. Rather, it represents a view of women and men struggling in multiple systems of domination. Contributors include, Linda Grant, Elizabeth Higginbotham, Esther Ngan-Ling Chow, Cheryl Townsend Gilkes, and Carol Stack.

Black Feminism and Black Women's Activism

743 ALMQUIST, ELIZABETH M. 1979. "Black Women and the Pursuit of Equality." Pp. 430–450 in *Women: A Feminist Perspective, Second Edition, edited by Jo Freeman*. Palo Alto, CA: Mayfield Publishing Co.
Almquist points out that black women are concerned about women's issues and are activists in campaigns for women's rights. She argues against the position that black women are only interested in racial issues and points to feminist activists such as Shirley Chisholm and feminist organizations such as the National Black Feminist Organization and Black Women Organized for Action to demonstrate black feminist commitment. Although black women experience a double burden of gender and racial discrimination, Almquist still finds that black and white women are similar to one another and, in the field of employment, she argues that the barriers to equality are stronger along gender lines than racial lines.

744 ANDOLSEN, BARBARA H. 1986. *Daughters of Jefferson, Daughters of Bootblacks: Racism and American Feminism*. Macon, GA: Mercer University Press.
A short book, only 130 pages long, that looks at race relations in the U.S. women's movement. The first four chapters discuss racism in the nineteenth century women's suffrage movement, while chapter five analyzes contemporary perspectives of black women on feminism. This book is written by a middle-class white theologian who believes white feminists need to learn about the perspectives of black women in order to begin a dialogue about issues important to all women. To support her argument, she demonstrates racism in the women's movement when tactics have been used to advance the cause of

women without examining whether those tactics would have a negative effect on the black community.

745   BEAL, FRANCES M. 1969. "Double Jeopardy: To be Black and Female."
       New Generation 51:23–31.
Even though it did not become a primacy issue until the 1980s, questions of race were connected to gender analysis early in the re-emerged women's movement. In this article, Beal deftly describes some of the differences between black and white women who are activists in the movement. She focuses particularly on social and economic situations.

746   BRYAN, DIANETTA GAIL. 1988. "Her-story Unsilenced—Black Female
       Activists in the Civil Rights Movement." *SAGE* 5 (Sept.):60–64.
The lost history of African-American women's participation in the civil rights movement of the 1950s and 1960s is recaptured here. Highlighted is Fannie Lou Hamer, a Mississippi farm worker turned activist as the field secretary for the Student Non-Violent Coordinating Committee (SNCC) and one of the founders of the Mississippi Freedom Democratic Party (MFDP). Her activism for voting rights and political representation in Mississippi is unparalleled, particularly her efforts to seat black delegates at the 1964 Democratic National Convention in Atlantic City. Hamer's work in MFDP is seen in the filmed documentary series "Eyes on the Prize." Another activist highlighted in this article is Diane Nash who helped organize lunch counter sit-ins and trained participants in non-violent civil disobedience in Nashville, Tennessee.

747   COLLINS, PATRICIA HILL. 1990. *Black Feminist Thought: Knowledge,
       Consciousness, and the Politics of Empowerment*. Boston: Unwin
       Hyman.
Drawing upon fiction, oral history, biography, music, everyday conversation, and empirical studies, Collins articulates a black feminist epistemology. Falling within the category of the sociology of knowledge, this work claims a distinct African-American women's consciousness forged by history, social position, and lived experience. A critique of positing a unitary standpoint is the submersion of differences among African-American women and the ways being poor, working class, middle class, or professional affect their experiences in the world. Collins acknowledges the validity of this critique, however she argues that she intentionally focuses on black feminist thought in order to promote it as an area of intellectual inquiry within feminism. Her goal is to push the commonality/diversity debate of identity politics in a direction which will take racial difference seriously.

748   CRAWFORD, VICKI LYNN. 1988. "Grassroots Activists in the Mississippi
       Civil Rights Movement." *SAGE* 5 (Sept.):24–29.
The work of black women in the civil rights movement is often unacknowledged as the leaders who became famous were all black men, mostly ministers. In the 1980s work began to be published which revealed the efforts of women who formed the backbone of local activism, particularly in the South. In this

article the activism of three African-American women in Mississippi are detailed. Annie Devine, Winson Hudson, and Unita Blackwell were able to apply their experience of rural life to the formation of co-operatives to employ black women. They also organized boycotts, marches, and voter registration drives.

749 CRAWFORD, VICKI L., JACQUELINE ANNE ROUSE, and BARBARA WOODS, eds. 1990. *Women in the Civil Rights Movement: Trailblazers and Torchbearers, 1941–1965*. Brooklyn, NY: Carlson Publishing.
The 1987 documentary "Eyes on the Prize" led to a conference on Women in the Civil Rights Movement to highlight the role of African-American women in movements for freedom and justice. The papers in this book were originally presented at that conference, and are part of a series on *Black Women in American History*. Trailblazers are defined as the women who initiated social movement activism and Torchbearers are those who continue the work. As the editors note in the introduction, African-American women have a long history of working for change, beginning with the abolition of slavery to movements concerned with suffrage, temperance, anti-lynching, housing, employment, education, Jim Crow laws, and civil rights legislation. This book focuses on African-American women's activism prior to and during the civil rights movement of the 1950s and 60s and includes writings from both scholars and activists. The articles provide an important contribution to social movement activism often missing in the work of African-American male and white feminist scholars.

750 DAVIS, ANGELA. 1971. *If They Come in the Morning: Voices of Resistance*. New York: Third Press.
A collection of essays in which Davis tells of African-American women activists and the work in which they have involved themselves. Davis stresses the importance of these women because they have become the symbol of resistance to oppressed peoples in other parts of the world.

751 DAVIS, BEVERLY. 1988. "To Seize the Moment—A Retrospective on the National Black Feminist Organization." *SAGE* 5 (Sept.):43–47.
Although the National Black Feminist Organization (NBFO) had a short life, from 1973–1979, it was an important organization for raising the issue of the neglect of black women in both the women's movement and the civil rights movement. Founded by Flo Kennedy, Margaret Sloan and other women, the goal of NBFO was to address the dual oppression of African-American women through both racism and sexism. The organization worked on issues particularly important in black women's lives such as poverty, welfare, public housing, child care, drugs, crime, and prisons.

752 FLEMING, CYNTHIA GRIGGS. 1993. "Black Women Activists and the Student Nonviolent Coordinating Committee: The Case of Ruby Doris Smith Robinson." *Journal of Women's History* 4: (Sept.)65–81.
In this biographical essay, Ruby Doris Smith Robinson is shown as an African-

American activist who sought to define her womanhood through leadership in the civil rights movement. Robinson is described as a powerful woman in the Student Nonviolent Coordinating Committee (SNCC) who had to overcome her middle-class 1950s gender role expectations to ascend to power, but at the same time maintain familial roles of wife and mother. The contrast between African-American female assertiveness that was generally accepted in the black community and the ascendancy of the primacy of male leadership in the civil rights and Black Power movement created dilemmas for African-American women activists. The growing acceptance of the greater victimization of African-American males led to negative assessments of strong African-American women as race loyalty predominated over gender considerations. In learning about Robinson's life, Fleming reveals the pressures on African-American women, the transformation of the valuing of their influence, the different experiences of white and black women activists, and the changing gender assumptions in the civil rights movement.

753 GIDDINGS, PAULA. 1988. *In Search of Sisterhood: Delta Sigma Theta and the Challenge of the Black Sorority Movement*. New York: William Morrow and Co.

At the time of its founding in 1913, Delta Sigma Theta was a black sorority which hoped to create bonds of sisterhood and to have an impact on social issues, particularly women's suffrage. The relationship and tension between African-American suffrage supporters and the women's suffrage movement is discussed. As the organization grew in numbers, members became activists for individual and social change on a broad range of race and gender issues. The author documents the good works, political impact, and feminist consciousness of Delta honorary and active members, including those who achieved high levels of recognition such as Mary McLeod Bethune, Mary Church Terrell, Barbara Jordan, Lena Horne, Constance Clayton, Charlayne Hunter-Gault, Joyce Ladner, and Paula Giddings. Internal conflicts are also revealed around color and class distinctions within the black community. This book demonstrates one of the arguments for separate organizations in the women's movement as Giddings shows that "black women may be among their freest, their happiest, and in some ways, their most fulfilled when they are together in their organizations" (p.9).

754 ———. 1984. *When and Where I Enter: The Impact of Black Women on Race and Sex in America*. New York: Bantam Books.

Black women have been active participants in two major social movements in American history: the civil rights movement and the women's movement. What is often overlooked is the interaction of race and gender which has produced a distinct struggle for African-American women with their own values and concerns. Through the use of diaries, letters, and speeches, Giddings reveals the ways black women have addressed the dual systems of racism and sexism from the seventeenth century on. Discussed are the black women's club movement, the tensions with black male leaders and white feminist leaders, and the individual contributions of women such as Ida B. Wells, Mary McLeod Bethume, and Fannie Lou Hamer.

755 HICKMAN, MARK S. 1989. "Black Feminism: Black Women on the Edge." *Women & Language* 12:5–14.

In the 1960s the civil rights movement was dominated by men and the women's movement was dominated by white middle-class women. Black feminists attempted to address their own issues and ally themselves with both movements through the founding of The National Black Feminist Organization. Even though this organization was short lived, it contributed to an awareness of the lack of inclusiveness in both the civil rights movement and the women's movement.

756 HIGGINBOTHAM, EVELYN BROOKS. 1993. *Righteous Discontent: The Women's Movement in the Black Baptist Church, 1880–1920*. Cambridge, MA: Harvard University Press.

Rather than focusing on what the black church has provided for African-Americans, this book shows the importance of black women in projecting the church as the place where self-help took place in the black community. Left out of high level positions in the National Baptist Convention U.S.A., Baptist women organized separate local and state organizations in the 1880s. In 1900 they established their own national women's convention where they addressed racial equality, women's education, protection of the family, and woman's suffrage. This book reveals the social activism, good works, and feminist thought found in this organization.

757 HOOKS, BELL. 1981. *Ain't I a Woman: Black Women and Feminism*. Boston: South End Press.

This book critiques white feminists for continually drawing analogies between women and blacks which leaves the impression that woman only means white women. The author examines the black experience during slavery to the present, including black male sexism and racism within the women's movement. This book received a great deal of attention for raising important issues, and it also received criticism for ignoring the efforts of anti-racist white feminists and the feminist activism of women of color. hooks early stress on the intertwining of race and gender and the need to incorporate both of these issues into the women's movement has contributed to the current emphasis of race, gender, and class in academic feminism and organizational planning for building a multicultural movement.

758 ———. 1984. *Feminist Theory: From Margin to Center*. Boston: South End Press.

bell hooks builds on her earlier work of citing the failure of the women's movement to build an inclusive feminist political agenda. Her position is that race and class have not been included in the development of feminist thought and that feminists need to go beyond sexism as the focus of oppression. Because the women's movement has been organized by women who are privileged in society, hooks believes activists' goals have been limited by their experiences, thus, the lives and awareness of those who are not privileged—who live on the margin—are rarely acknowledged or included in the development of feminist theory. The focus of her work is the barriers that exist between African-American and Euro-American women which she explores by discussing the implications and differences in the meaning of universal sisterhood, personal and community violence, female/male relations, poverty, power, occupation, education, and family relations.

759 ———. 1989. *Talking Back: Thinking Feminist, Thinking Black.* Boston: South End Press.

This is a collection of hooks' writing which consists of twenty-five pieces which cover almost every issue raised by the black liberation and women's movement since the 1960s. Her writing rings with experience and a frankness that does not fail to challenge. She employs her wit to create an engaging style that urges the reader on.

760 HULL, GLORIA, PATRICIA BELL SCOTT, and BARBARA SMITH, eds. 1982. *All the Women Are White, All the Blacks Are Men, But Some of Us Are Brave: Black Women's Studies*, Old Westbury, NY: Feminist Press.

A volume of writing on the experiences and contributions of black women for the academic field of Black Women's Studies. The authors examine the politics of Black Women's Studies by considering what it is and what it can be. As the title suggests, this work is also intended to speak out about the unconscious assumptions that have operated to keep black women invisible. Contributors cover topics of racism, black feminism, social science myths, literature, health, religion, and education. Articles directly related to feminism and the women's movement include "A Black Feminist's Search for Sisterhood" by Michelle Wallace; "A Black Feminist Statement" by Patricia Bell Scott; and "Racism and Women's Studies" by Barbara Smith. Course syllabi, references, resources, non-print materials, and recommendations for Black Women's Studies are provided. Bibliographies on African-American women, racism and the women's movement, and black poets, writers, playwrights, and composers are also included.

761 JAMES, STANLIE M. and ABENA P. A. BUSIA, eds. 1993. *Theorizing Black Feminisms: The Visionary Pragmatism of Black Women*. New York: Routledge.

This anthology contains writings from black women, mainly academics, on current debates among African-American feminists. Utilizing an interdisciplinary approach, the connecting theme to the articles is a shared belief that black women offer more than a category of multiple oppressions; they are also the agents of a visionary and pragmatic mode of social change. The contributors come from diverse academic fields including anthropology, art, history, literature, political science, and sociology. Contains a foreword by Johnnetta Cole.

762　KING, DEBORAH K. 1988. "Multiple Jeopardy, Multiple Consciousness: The Context of a Black Feminist Ideology." *Signs: Journal of Women in Culture and Society* 14:42–72.

An article that discusses the dual nature of being black and being a woman. King talks about how these two identities can lead to divided loyalties and multiple oppressions. Black feminist ideology follows from these unique awarenesses and experiences.

763　LORDE, AUDRE. 1984. *Sister Outsider*. Freedom, CA: The Crossing Press.

Audre Lorde, a poet laureate of feminism, gathers together fifteen essays and speeches which articulate her views on black feminism. Her writing is personal and draws upon her experiences and identities as a black woman, lesbian, feminist, and mother living in a sexist and racist society. She evocatively explores the homophobia of her black sisters and the racism of white women, and calls for women to accept their differences and identify with each other in order to change the world.

764　MCKAY, NELLIE Y. 1993. "Acknowledging Differences: Can Women Find Unity Through Diversity?" Pp. 267–282 in *Theorizing Black Feminisms: The Visionary Pragmatism of Black Women*, edited by Stanlie M. James and Abena P.A. Busia. New York: Routledge.

McKay notes that after years of seemingly not understanding the complaints of black women and Third World women, white feminists now take seriously the desire to establish a sisterhood amongst all women. She believes this is possible, but still very difficult. McKay points to the example of the Clarence Thomas/Anita Hill hearings to show how race and gender interact for different responses by black and white women. White women were the first to applaud Hill for accusing Thomas of sexual harassment, while "black feminists were faced with the politics of raising voice or remaining silent" (p.278). Ostracized within the black community for speaking out against 'one of their own' and within the feminist community for not supporting Hill fast enough, black women formed a new political organization called African-American Women in Defense of Ourselves. McKay calls for stronger efforts to respect differences while striving to find unity on the things women hold in common.

765　MORRIS, ALDON D. 1984. *The Origins of the Civil Rights Movement: Black Communities Organizing for Change*. New York: The Free Press.

An excellent documentary and sociological history of the civil rights movement from 1953–1963. Originally his doctoral dissertation, this work is well researched with solid analysis of the origins and development of the modern movement for black liberation. Documented are the details of those years, including the boycotts, marches, mass meetings, jailings, violence against the activists, and the nonviolent direct action they took. Morris does justice to black women activists when he describes the important part they played in this movement, as well as the ways they were ignored and denied official leadership roles.

766   RANDOLPH, LAURA. 1991. "The True Pioneers of the Women's
        Movement." *Ebony* 46 (August):96–99.
African-American women have been activists for civil rights and equality for two
centuries. Randolph brings in another perspective on the idea of black women
and feminism.

767   REAGON, BERNICE JOHNSON. 1990. "Women as Culture Carriers in the
        Civil Rights Movement." Pp. 203–218 in *Women in the Civil Rights
        Movement: Trailblazers and Torchbearers, 1941–1965*, edited by Vickie
        L. Crawford, Jacqueline Anne Rouse, and Barbara Woods. Brooklyn, NY:
        Carlson Publishing.
Bernice Johnson Reagon, an activist in the civil rights movement, writes of the
importance of freedom songs in the feeling of unity and purpose for the mass
meetings and protest marches for black liberation. Fannie Lou Hammer, who
she highlights in this piece, was an eloquent and moving contributor to this
African-American oral tradition of cultural transmission.

768   SMITH, BARBARA. 1979. "The Black Women's Issue." *Conditions* 5.
Barbara Smith edits this issue of the journal *Conditions* and dedicates it to
black women's issues. In the introduction she explains what black feminism is
and shows how it is tied to the black experience. Poetry, fiction, essays, photographs, and fiction are part of the materials focusing on themes of family,
being an artist, lesbianism, and feminist organizing. An overriding message is
the desire to connect feminist women of color to each other and to work in
coalitions with other groups.

769   ———. 1983. *Home Girls: A Black Feminist Anthology*. New York:
        Kitchen Table, Women of Color Press.
An anthology of mixed topics that contribute to Black Women's Studies and
that reflect personal and experiential writing. An interesting and useful collection.

770   ———. 1977. *Toward a Black Feminist Criticism*. Freedom, CA: Out
        and Out Books, Distributed by The Crossing Press.
This can be found as a publication in pamphlet form and in the October 1977
issue of *Conditions*. Smith begins by stating the invisibility of black women and
black lesbians to both the women's movement and the lesbian culture. She
cites as an example the lack of critical reviews of black women's literature,
which shows they are not taken seriously. Smith also finds that when reviews
are done, they fail to take into consideration the existence of a historical and
identifiable black woman literary tradition. She calls for both a viable
autonomous black feminist movement and a refocusing of the white feminist
movement as important steps in correcting omissions of the past. Since the
publication of this work, organizing and interest in black women's lives and literary contributions have gained greater recognition.

771 TERRELONGE, PAULINE. 1984. "Feminist Consciousness and Black Women." Pp. 557–567 in *Women: A Feminist Perspective, Third Edition*, edited by Jo Freeman. Palo Alto, CA: Mayfield Publishing Co.

Terrelonge argues that the women's movement has sparked a controversy in Black America because it has raised issues about the status of black females, most particularly the male privilege that exists within African-American culture and the black family. Terrelonge challenges the view that sexism is of less importance than racism in black women's oppression. She also objects to the expectation that the primary roles for black women should be keeping the family together and supporting black males.

772 THE COMBAHEE RIVER COLLECTIVE. 1986. *Black Feminist Organizing in the 1970s and 1980s*. New York: Kitchen Table, Women of Color Press.

The Combahee River Collective dates back to the early days of the contemporary women's movement and has always been a strong voice for understanding issues of race and gender. In this work they discuss the activist work black feminists have done in the 1970s and 1980s.

773 TORREY, JANE W. 1979. "Racism and Feminism: Is Women's Liberation for Whites Only?" *Psychology of Women Quarterly* 4 (Dec.):281–293.

Black women, particularly those involved with the civil rights movement, avoid involvement with white feminists for fear it will split their allegiance to black liberation. Still, black women's problems are different from black men's as well as white women's. Torrey argues that both the black movement and the women's movement need each other, and black women need both movements to succeed.

774 WARE, CELLESTINE. 1970. *Woman Power: The Movement for Women's Liberation*. New York. Tower.

Cellestine Ware analyses the contemporary feminist movement as it emerges and raises questions about the place in it for black women. This is an early work that takes the issue of African-American women's feminism seriously and challenges the women's movement to do the same. Ware was a founder of New York Radical Feminists and an activist in that movement. She is concerned about competition among black and white women in which white women are held up as the ideal, a phenomenon best illustrated by black men's rejection of black women in favor of more "feminine" women. As women grow in strength, Ware warns that white women will experience the same type of rejection by men.

5

Issues

Introduction

The categories in this chapter differ from those in the previous one by their relationship to the women's movement. The topics found in chapter 4, **Feminist Discourse**, are those that are integrated into the meaning of feminism itself. Those that are found in this chapter, **Issues**, are the subject matter of activism, goals, research, policy, contributions, critiques, and schisms.

For instance, the first category, **Race, Class, and Gender** contains entries that cover research and reflections on each of these constructs, as well as their interactions with each other. The connections are strong and, as the entries show, looking at stratification systems through the prism of one component almost always privileges that sector through denial of the others. While there may be instances where it is appropriate to focus on one social group characteristic, more frequently, researchers have to question research on women that takes no note of similarities/differences by race and class, or discussing race without differentiating by gender and class.

Work, Welfare, and Trade Unionism overlaps with the previous topic of **Race, Class, and Gender** but differs by its focus on issues related to poverty, the working-class, the welfare system, welfare rights movements, women and unions, strikes, and union organizing. This is an area where working-class women have often been active; indeed, a history of the labor movement shows some of the most militant strikes have been waged by women workers.

Sex and Pornography constitute a category of issues dealing with women's sexuality, sexual oppression, and the heated debate over sado-masochism among consenting lesbian couples. Pornography is a topic that has raised extreme bitterness among some sectors of the women's movement. The anti-pornography and anti-censorship forces have produced a large quantity of material outlining their position and, unfortunately, attacking the other side. Some of these readings are thoughtful and deeply engaging; others are polemical and disturbing.

Feminist Critique and Contributions includes literary criticism, film, art, writing, scholarly works, non-sexist language, gender and science, family, motherhood, and housework issues. This category captures a wide ranging look at social events and institutions and the ways women have both found fault with them and contributed to change within them.

The entries under **Politics, the Law, and Policy** cover women politicians, women and law, social policy, pensions, affirmative action, pay equity, and comparable worth. The section on **Sexism and Discrimination** includes issues related to women's equality (and inequality), sexual harassment, anti-feminism, the New Right, Right Wing women, and anti-feminism in general.

Religion and Spirituality—the effects on women and the ways women have been involved—make up the last category for chapter 5. Women's spirituality has flourished within the women's movement since the mid-1970s with the re-emergence of followers of the Goddess, the growth of wicca circles, and the drawing together of the interconnections between female "nature," the Earth, and spirituality.

Religious affiliation, particularly the Quaker religion, provided a direct link to activism for many women in the early woman's movement. It is interesting to note that there are both parallels and wide disparities in the impact of religion on women's activism in the nineteenth and twentieth centuries. The contemporary women's movement has a more complex involvement with religious issues where there is a determined religiously connected countermovement, a large segment of the feminist community that is not affiliated with religion at all, women's efforts to change traditional religions from within, and another segment that is creating an energetic and often separatist woman defined spirituality. It matters little what one personally believes (or does not believe) to acknowledge the impact religion and spirituality have had on the women's movement since its inception.

Race, Class, and Gender: Research and Reflections

775   ALLISON, DOROTHY. 1993. "A Question of Class." Pp. 135–155 in *Sisters, Sexperts, Queers: Beyond the Lesbian Nation*, edited by Arlene Stein. New York: Plume.

This article is a personal reflection of the effects of class on the author's life. Allison describes the lack of a feeling of entitlement or a sense of self-importance that arises out of being raised as a member of the "ungrateful poor." Addressing the other identities in her life—lesbian, incest victim, feminist, activist, sadomasochist practitioner—the author maintains that the central fact of her life is being born into a condition of poverty that society finds shameful, contemptible, and deserved. Traditional feminist theory and lesbian community are criticized for their failures to adequately understand and deal with class differences. She also critically examines her own efforts to deny the reality of her experiences in order to disassociate herself from her family to become someone new.

776   ANTHIAS, FLOYA and NIRA YUVAL-DAVIS. 1992. *Racialized Boundaries: Race, Nation, Gender, Colour and Class and the Anti-Racist Struggle.* New York: Routledge.

A theoretical discussion of ideologies and race struggles which emphasize the importance of community and how this fits with current thinking about multiculturalism. These thoughts are then linked with social movement analyses of identity politics.

777   ANTLER, JOYCE and SARI KNOPP, eds. 1990. *Changing Education: Women as Radicals and Conservators*, Albany: State University of New York Press.

The focus of this book is the way education and the impartation of knowledge are gendered phenomena. The effects of culture and how women and men are defined, particularly the varying emphases on similarities and differences, are well covered. This work is interdisciplinary and uses historical sources as well as philosophical debate, theoretical frameworks, and case studies to make important points. There is much useful information here on the topic of women and the cultural development of knowledge systems.

778   BARASH, CAROL, ed. 1987. *The Olive Schreiner Reader: Writings on Women and South Africa.* Winchester, MA: Pandora Press.

This collection draws together Schreiner's reflections on women, race, and suffragists who were jailed for demanding the vote. Her concern with South Africa and the racial divisions in that country continue to raise consciousness about this issue today.

779   BERNARD, JESSIE. 1987. *The Female World from a Global Perspective.* Bloomington: Indiana University Press.

Having written about women within the American context, Bernard branched off to view women from a global perspective. In this work she details the situation of women in various parts of the world, looking for patterns of gender relations.

780   ———. 1971. *Women and the Public Interest: An Essay on Policy and Protest.* New York: Atherton.

Bernard applies a sociological analysis to a study which analyzed the public interest in relationship to women's rights and their place in the labor market. Highlighted in this work is the inter-relationship between sex divisions in the work place and the traditional expectations of women's gender roles.

781   BROD, HARRY and MICHAEL KAUFMAN, eds. 1994. *Theorizing Masculinities.* Thousand Oaks, CA: Sage Publications, Inc.

An interdisciplinary collection of theoretical work on men and gender. Selections from psychology, sociology, and ethnographic studies explore power, feminism, ethnicity, and homophobia. Contributions include "Theorizing Unities and Differences Between Men and Between Masculinities" by J. Hearn and D. L. Collinson; "Masculinity as Homophobia: Fear, Shame, and Silence in the Construction of Gender Identity" by Michael Kimmel; "Men, Feminism, and Men's Contradictory Experiences of Power" by Michael Kaufman; "Postmodernism and the Interrogation of Masculinity" by D. S. Gutterman, and "Weekend Warriors: The New Men's Movement" by Michael Kimmel and Michael Kaufman.

782   BUNCH, CHARLOTTE and NANCY MYRON. 1974. *Class and Feminism: Collection of Essays from The Furies*. Baltimore, MD: Diana Press.
This book consists of seven essays by "The Furies," a 1970s activist women's collective of lesbian feminists. The writers talk about their personal lives and the divisions between working-class and middle-class women. They identify particular problems in overcoming class differences among women, including passivity, unacknowledged privilege, and paternalism.

783   CHISHOLM, SHIRLEY. 1971. "Race, Revolution and Women." *Black Scholar* 3:17–21.
Chisholm sees the Black Revolution and the Women's Liberation Movement as a world-wide revolt affecting all of human societies since racism and sexism are found everywhere. She calls on women and blacks to work together to build a better world.

784   CONNELL, R. W. 1993. "Men and the Women's Movement." *Social Policy* 23 (June):72–78.
Connell makes the point that men, as a group, benefit in power, income, and respect compared to women by an unequal gender order. However, the author also reminds us that men are not a monolithic group. Differences by race, class, and sexual orientation create unequal opportunities and status positions in the social structure among men themselves.

785   CUMMINGS, SCOTT. 1976. "Class and Racial Divisions in the Female Population: Some Practical and Political Dilemmas for the Women's Movement." *Sociological Symposium* 15 (March):99–119.
Attitude surveys and the 1972 election study show that class position and race status, not sex classification, divide the American population on political issues championed by the women's movement. Significant attitudinal differences were found between black and white women and between working-class and professional women.

786   DAVID, DEBORAH S. and ROBERT BRANNON, eds. 1976. *The Forty-Nine Percent Majority: The Male Sex Role*. Reading, MA: Addison-Wesley Publishing Co.
An early reader on the conceptualization of the male gender role in American society. The authors are a sociologist and psychologist respectively, and they bring in a variety of perspectives in this collection of writings on male gender identity and role behavior. Included are writings on the inexpressive male,

homophobia among men, blue collar work, men as parents, why husbands can't say "I love you," conspicuous consumption, masculinity and materialism, the cult of toughness, war, and violence.

787   EPSTEIN, CYNTHIA FUCHS. 1988. *Deceptive Distinctions: Sex, Gender, and the Social Order*. New York: Russell Sage.
A thoughtful analysis of how distinctions between the sexes are exaggerated and manipulated in order to maintain inequality. This is a scholarly book that surveys gender research across disciplines. The author calls for moving beyond socialization models to understand practices of sex/gender differentiation in social control mechanisms such as law, custom, and ideology. These ongoing operational forces are defined as the mechanism for perpetuating sex segregation and unequal gender relations. In discussing the loss of opportunities for women, a caution is voiced about the need to affirm diversities in female and male experiences and the futility of basing conceptions of equality on a male model.

788   FERREE, MYRA MARX and ELAINE J. HALL. 1990. "Visual Images of American Society: Gender and Race in Introductory Sociology Textbooks." *Gender & Society* 4:500–33.
One of the early issues of the contemporary women's movement was the lack (and type) of presentation of girls and women in children's readers. Academics, particularly sociologists, frequently published articles in the 1970s on the effects of this neglect. It is interesting, some twenty years later, to see a content analysis of thirty-three introductory sociology textbooks which shows that only 36 percent of the illustrations are of women. People of color are portrayed in an appropriate or higher percentage than found in the population, and there are many pictorials of people from other societies. The authors argue, however, that the higher representation of blacks appears to be a way of presenting an illusion of equality.

789   FERREE, MYRA MARX. 1983. "The Women's Movement in the Working-Class." *Sex Roles* 9 (April):493–505.
Research into the dimensions of support for feminism among working-class women. Variables tested were attitudes toward the women's movement, traditional vs. non-traditional gender roles, perceptions of discrimination and inequality, and relevance of the movement to them. Those respondents who support the women's movement emphasized the movement's effects on their feelings of self-worth. Those opposed to feminist goals emphasized sexual morality issues and support for traditional gender roles.

790   FILENE, PETER G. 1986. *Him/Her/Self: Sex Roles in Modern America, Second Edition*. Baltimore MD: Johns Hopkins University Press.
A good analysis of how gender roles become defined and institutionalized in social systems. An alternative model is explored by Filene who feels a more flexible and egalitarian ideal is achievable, although probably not for some time.

791   GURIN, PATRICIA and ALLEN TOWNSEND. 1986. "Properties of Gender Identity and their Implications for Gender Consciousness." *British Journal of Social Psychology* 25 (June):139–148.

Research on gender identity using three measures: perceived similarity to other women, sense of common fate, and centrality of gender to sense of self. The sample was a national sample of women in the United States using telephone interviews between 1979 and 1983 (n=929). Findings support the hypothesis that these three variables increase awareness of gender identity with the sense of common fate being the most highly correlated.

792   KAUFMAN, MICHAEL, ed. 1987. *Beyond Patriarchy: Essays by Men on Pleasure, Power, and Change*. New York: Oxford University Press.

In this collection, contributors address relations of power at the personal and political levels and what the patriarchal control of power has meant to the concept "being a man." The premise of the book is that the oppression of women is not just a matter of male/female behavior; rather, it is a structure from which socially constructed notions of masculinity are embedded. Thus, cracking the structure of patriarchy means the individual armor that men acquire must also be cracked. The general approach of the book is to combine an analysis of the oppression of women, gay men, the social structure of domination, and the individual expression of these structures, within an analysis of the ways men are scarred and distorted by the system they help perpetuate for the privileges and power it provides them.

793   LENGERMANN, PATRICIA MADOO and RUTH A. WALLACE. 1985. *Gender in America: Social Control and Social Change*. Englewood Cliffs, NJ: Prentice Hall.

Gender is analyzed through both stability and change in this work on the gendered social system of the United States. Beliefs about gender and the outcome of these beliefs in social organization are covered, along with challenges to traditional thought. Chapter eight covers the contemporary women's movement, both formal organizations and small consciousness-raising groups. In the last chapter the anti-feminist backlash, particularly the Stop ERA and Right-to-Life movement, are critically analyzed. The authors argue that the New Right uses pro-family rhetoric opportunistically in their opposition to gender equality.

794   LEWIN, MIRIAM and LILLI M. TRAGOS. 1987. "Has the Feminist Movement Influenced Adolescent Sex Role Attitudes? A Reassessment after a Quarter Century." *Sex Roles* 15 (Feb.):125–135.

A study of adolescents' sex role attitudes in 1956 are compared with a 1982 sample of lower and middle-class suburban students in the eighth to twelfth grade. The findings showed that the 1982 results were not less stereotypical than the earlier results from the 1950s. Sex differences showed males scoring higher on traditional expectations in both surveys. Females indicated a possible increased level of self-esteem by a score that showed significantly less dissatisfaction with their sex category than they did in the earlier period.

795   LIVINGSTONE, D. W. and MEG LUXTON. 1989. "Gender Consciousness at
       Work: Modification of the Male Breadwinner Norm Among Steelworkers
       and Their Spouses." *Canadian Review of Sociology and Anthropology*
       26 (May):240–275.
A review of the literature on the development and effects of feminist consciousness from liberal, radical, and socialist perspectives. Included are discussions on gender consciousness, role identity, attitudes, and acceptance of
change. Livingstone and Luxton find that despite the impact of changing consciousness and role behavior, male power is still the overriding basis for social
organization among the working-class.

796   LORBER JUDITH. 1994. *Paradoxes of Gender*. New Haven, CT: Yale
       University Press.
Judith Lorber, noted sociologist and founding editor of *Gender & Society*, presents a challenge to established notions of gender in this book. She argues that
gender is a socialized construct, part of our social construction of reality, and
as such it is interpretable and changeable. Further, Lorber identifies gender as
a social institution equal in significance to other social institutions such as the
family, religion, and the economy.

797   LOWE, MARIAN and RUTH HUBBARD, eds. 1983. *Woman's Nature:
       Rationalizations of Inequality*. New York: Pergamon Press.
This collection of articles dispels myths of woman's nature. The myths the
authors discuss are shown to have the function of limiting women's participation in society and to distort how women feel about themselves. The message
this book delivers is that there is no scientific or biological basis to the notion
of woman's nature. They argue this position against the anti-feminists who
wish to restrain women by this belief and the feminists who valorize the "spe-
cialness" of woman's nature.

798   MCADAM, DOUG. 1992. "Gender as a Mediator of the Activist
       Experience: The Case of Freedom Summer." *American Journal of
       Sociology* 5 (March):1211–1240.
McAdam analyses the more than 300 applications from students who volun-
teered to participate in Mississippi Freedom Summer in 1964. He finds gender
played a part in recruitment, the experience, and long term effects following
participation. Specifically, the results showed that females faced greater opposition to their participation, those who did get accepted were confined to
mainly "female roles" of teaching and clerical staffing, and women volunteers
reported less of a behavioral impact than was true for males.

799   MCNEIL, JEAN C. 1975. "Feminism, Femininity, and the Television Series:
       A Content Analysis." *Journal of Broadcasting* 19 (June):259–271.
A report of a study on prime time television on three commercial networks.
Males were found to outnumber female characters by 18 to 1 with 46 percent
of men and 11 percent of women having indeterminate marital status, and 53
percent of men and 19 percent of women having indeterminate parental sta-

tus. The numbers for employed men were 78 percent while only 21 percent of women were shown to be employed and of those who were employed they were shown as having less supervisory positions than men. The women's movement was not mentioned in any of the shows studied.

800   RENZETTI, CLAIRE M. 1987. "New Wave or Second Stage? Attitudes of College Women Toward Feminism." *Sex Roles* 16:255–277.
Survey research of college women's attitudes towards the women's movement. The author was interested in whether positive attitudes towards gender equality equated with positive views of the women's movement, and whether year in school effected the results. Findings show strong support for both sex equality and the women's movement, and that this correlation grows stronger the longer they are in college. In spite of these results, the female students did not favor calling themselves feminists, and there was a strong belief that they could achieve their goals without collective action.

801   ROLLINS, JUDITH. 1985. *Between Women: Domestics and Their Employers*. Philadelphia: Temple University Press.
Empirically grounded research provides the basis for this work on women, labor, and race/ethnic relations. Rollins interviewed twenty domestic workers and twenty employers of domestics. The author also worked as a domestic for a period of time before beginning her interviews. This is interesting research that uncovers issues related to class, status, and dominance among women. Rollins poignantly reveals the indignities of servitude with examples such as becoming an invisible person when employers turn down the heat in the winter when they leave, even though the domestic worker is going to be in the house all day. Employers talk about preferring foreign women workers because they are eager to please and will work for a lower wage. Few of the white middle-class women, even those who considered themselves liberal progressives, seemed aware of the power dynamics embedded in their own employer/employee situations.

802   SINGLETON, CARRIE JANE. 1989. "Race and Gender in Feminist Theory." *SAGE* 6:12–17.
The author examines theories of how race and gender are defined and how women of different races relate to and understand each other. The construction of racism and the ways white women can address this issue are gleaned from the writings of three white women writers: Adrienne Rich, Marilyn Frye, and Elizabeth Spelman. The works of Audre Lorde, bell hooks and Sheila Radford-Hill are used to show how black women writers have worked to make visible black women's lives and their relationship to feminism and the women's movement. These writers find that the relationship between black and white women has not been addressed adequately.

803   ST. PETER, SHIRLEY. 1979. "Jack Went Up the Hill ... but Where Was Jill?" *Psychology of Women Quarterly* 4 (Dec.):256–260.
A study looking at children's picture books as transmitters of gender concep-

tions. Over two hundred pictures are examined which represent titles published before the women's movement, after the women's movement, and those published in a specially defined non-sexist list of books. Findings show a preponderance of sex-typed models with females being underrepresented in all groups.

804   STALLARD, KARIN, BARBARA EHRENREICH, and HOLLY SKLAR. 1983. *Poverty in the American Dream: Women and Children First*. Boston: South End Press.

The authors of this report document changes in the family, economy, and political arena from the end of the 1970s to the early 1980s that have left greater levels of poverty in the United States, particularly for women and children. Interviews with poor women, community activists, and others provide an emotional understanding of what these changes have meant in poor and working-class women's lives.

805   TAVRIS, CAROL. 1973. "Who Likes Women's Liberation—And Why: The Case of the Unliberated Liberals." *Journal of Social Issues* 29:175–198.

A survey which looked at factors related to support or opposition to feminist goals. For men there was a felt threat which led to a hostile response to the Women's Liberation Movement. For women, personal experiences with discrimination were related to support of the movement. Tavris argues that few men really feel threatened, nevertheless, few truly support the movement. She concludes that, even though men may exhibit liberal attitudes, most still maintain traditional behavior.

806   WEILER, KATHLEEN. 1988. *Women Teaching for a Change: Gender, Class and Power*. Granby, MA: Bergin and Garvey.

A look at the opportunities and obstacles in teaching about gender, class, and power. The focus is on feminist teachers in public school settings.

Work, Welfare, and Trade Unionism

807   ABRAMOVITZ, MIMI. 1988. *Regulating the Lives of Women: Social Welfare Policy from Colonial Times to the Present*. Boston: South End Press.

The subject of this book is poor women, public welfare, social security, and family policy. The author looks at the structural roots of white and ethnic/racial women's poverty. This history of realities, policies, and social reform movements in American society help the reader to understand some of the contradictory, yet powerful, forces that effect the lives of poor people. An overall message is the need for greater social support through a fully developed welfare state.

808   BALSER, DIANE. 1987. *Sisterhood and Solidarity: Feminism and Labor in Modern Times*. Boston: South End Press.

This book is about the need for the women's movement to build alliances with unions in order to gain economic power for women. The historical role of women in organized labor and the connection between that activism and feminist goals is examined. The attainment of economic power and its relationship to political power is emphasized, along with new strategies for social change. Placed in the context of the changing relationship between gender and work in the 1980s, Balser argues that these changes can act as a bridge between women in different economic, racial, and ethnic groups.

809   BLEWETT, MARY H. 1988. *Men, Women, and Work: Class, Gender, and Protest in the New England Shoe Industry, 1780–1910*. Champaign: University of Illinois Press.
Taking just one production site, the shoe industry, Blewett weaves a unique tale of the working lives and social change efforts of shoemakers in a period of early industrial development. The author uses written personal accounts from the women and men who worked in this trade to make this a highly interesting book.

810   CAMERON, ARDIS. 1993. *Radicals of the Worst Sort: Laboring Women in Lawrence, Massachusetts, 1860–1912*. Champaign, IL: University of Illinois Press.
This book is about working-class women who actively fought for unionization and gender equality. Cameron calls them the "worst sort" of radicals because they presented a dual challenge to the stratification system when they fought to overcome economic and sexual hierarchies. Focusing on the textile workers' strikes of 1882 and 1912, the author finds that it is female networks and associational life that form the foundation for working-class women's political culture. This work intersects the boundaries of Women's Studies and labor studies, and provides an alternative model for traditional views of women during the progressive era.

811   CANTON, MILTON and BRUCE LAURIE, eds. 1977. *Class, Sex and the Woman Worker*. Westport, CT: Greenwood Press.
An anthology of articles from a conference held at Radcliffe College on the history of American working women. Included is the experience of immigrant working women, women's activism in the trade union movement, the difficulty of managing divided allegiances, and the rise of a class consciousness among Lowell factory workers.

812   COOK, ALICE H., VAL R. LORWIN, and ARLENE KAPLAN DANIELS. 1992. *The Most Difficult Revolution: Women and Trade Unions*. Ithaca, NY: Cornell University Press.
A comparison of labor practices and laws affecting gender and family in five nations—United States, Britain, Germany, Austria, and Sweden. The historical situation of U.S. working women and their participation in unions constitutes an important part of this book.

813   COOPER, PATRICIA. 1988. *Once a Cigar Maker: Men, Women, and the Work Culture in American Cigar Factories.* Champaign: University of Illinois Press.

A look at the work environment and gender differentiation in the cigar factories of the United States before automation nearly eliminated this type of work. Women cigar makers were seen as a threat by the men who practiced this trade and efforts to keep them from union membership were common. The voices of both women and men cigar makers are the heart of this work.

814   DYE, NANCY SCHROM. 1975. "Creating a Feminist Alliance: Sisterhood and Class Conflict in the New York Women's Trade Union League, 1903–1914." *Feminist Studies* 2:24–38.

Founded in 1903 by both middle-class and working-class women, the New York Women's Trade Union League differed from other women's organizations because of its focus on union organizing for women. The League believed in the idea of a sisterhood of women to offset the divisions between women and men that existed. Nevertheless, schisms arose in this organization over program priorities and because of personal animosities. Class conflict was a significant factor in the conflict, but there was also the failure to clearly identify what kind of an organization WTUL was meant to be. Particular members like H. Harot, Harriot Stanton Blatch, and L. O'Reilly illustrate the struggle that emerged between unionism and feminism.

815   ———. 1975. "Feminism or Unionism? The New York Women's Trade Union League and the Labor Movement." *Feminist Studies* 3 (Sept.):111–125.

In the early 1900s the American Federation of Labor (AFL) was not welcoming of women in spite of the increasing numbers of women who were employed. The Women's Trade Union League (WTUL) allied with the AFL even though it often conflicted with it on the issue of women and trade unionism. For the most part, the League organized large numbers of women without AFL support.

816   FERREE, MYRA MARX. 1980. "Working-Class Feminism: A Consideration of the Consequences of Employment." *The Sociological Quarterly* 21 (March):173–184.

This article reports on the results of a survey of married women with school-aged children, 55 percent employed and 45 percent not employed. A feminism scale was administered to test feminist and non-feminist women on their responses to questions of employment status, job satisfaction, home based networks, general life satisfaction, and perceived equity in life opportunities. Results show employment significantly increases levels of feminism. Employed women also report greater satisfaction with their lives than full time homemakers.

817   FONER, PHILIP S. 1979. *Women and the American Labor Movement.* New York: Free Press.

Addressing issues of gender, class, work, and organized labor in the United States, Foner brings a much needed perspective to these discussions with his work on women and the labor movement. The activism and impact of women in the labor movement tells us much about gender relations in society, particularly those related to conceptions of "women's place" that hinder working women's efforts to obtain higher paying jobs and better working conditions. The author also looks at the differences between black and white women in their organizing roles and their placement in segregated employment structures.

818   GABIN, NANCY F. 1990. *Feminism in the Labor Movement: Women and the United Auto Workers, 1935–1975*. Ithaca, NY: Cornell University Press.

Gabin provides a history of women's involvement in the United Auto Workers (UAW) from the 1930s to the 1970s. In 1944 the union set up a Women's Bureau which provided an opening for women's concerns to be voiced. The Bureau allowed women to organize in their own behalf both in the union and in other social arenas. For instance, UAW Women's Bureau members were among the founders of the National Organization for Women (NOW) in 1966. Because unions supported protective labor legislation, UAW members left NOW over the organization's support of the ERA. Later, they were able to convince the UAW to be the first union to support the amendment.

819   GREENWALD, MAURINE WEINER. 1989. *Women, War, and Work: The Impact of World War I on Women Workers in the United States*. Ithaca, NY: Cornell University Press.

This book not only provides important background for integrating women's history with labor history, but also background factors leading up to the re-emergence of the women's movement in the 1960s. Greenwald's research reveals the complex forces that act upon women's lives as well as the responses women make to changing conditions.

820   GRONEMAN, CAROL and MARY B. NORTON, eds. 1987. *To Toil the Livelong Day: America's Women at Work, 1790–1980*. Ithaca, NY: Cornell University Press.

A collection of articles that reveal the ways gender, race, class, and the sexual division of labor affect all women's lives and work opportunities.

821   HARTMANN, SUSAN M. 1982. *The Home Front and Beyond: American Women in the 1940s*. Boston: Twayne Publishers.

Hartmann details women's experiences of paid employment during World War II and the effects that experience had on their desire to continue working at those jobs. After a period of returning to the home at war's end, women's labor force participation began to rise again. The emergence of the women's movement in the late 1960s is shown to be connected to this change in women's traditional role.

822 HAWES, ELIZABETH. 1946. *Hurry Up Please, It's Time*. New York: Reynal & Hitchcock.

Hawes wrote this book as a semi-autobiographical account of her experiences as an educational representative for the UAW-CIO during and immediately after World War II. The problems of unionization, particularly getting equal treatment for women in war plants, is the focus of this work. The conflict between capitalists and labor, gender attitudes, and sectarian disputes within the unions are well highlighted. Other topics include the opposition to the Equal Rights Amendment, male resistance to women's equal pay combined with their fears of lower paid workers taking over the jobs of men, red-baiting, and the work/family burden inherent in women's inability to take active roles in union activism.

823 JANIEWSKI, DOLORES E. 1985. *Sisterhood Denied: Race, Gender, and Class in a New South Community*. Philadelphia: Temple University Press.

The focus of this book is on black and white working women after the Civil War. The author finds that both groups of women were dominated by men of their social group. Over time as urbanization increased, these rural-based women moved into cities where they were able to achieve some level of economic independence. The labor movement became an important arena of activism for them to improve their condition. Janiewski shows that in the city of Durham, where her research takes place, without the participation of women in the labor movement, the city would never have been able to develop as successfully as it did. Women's experiences as workers are well drawn out in this book, and the interplay between race, class, and gender are carefully interwoven throughout the analysis.

824 JENSON, JOAN M. and SUE DAVIDSON, eds. 1984. *A Needle, A Bobbin, A Strike: Women Needleworkers in America*. Philadelphia: Temple University Press.

The garment industry in the United States was the site of some of the most militant strikes in the history of the labor movement. For the most part, these strikes were organized and carried out by working-class ethnic women. This edited volume presents essays which describe the garment industry from its origins up to the present. Analysis of the structure of this industry and some of the historic events that took place within its confines are also examined.

825 KESSLER-HARRIS, ALICE. 1982. *Out to Work: A History of Wage-Earning Women in the United States*. New York: Oxford University Press.

Kessler-Harris centers this book around the transformation of women's work due to wage labor. She argues that this change undermined the ideological belief system of "women's place" because of the contradictions in the need for women's participation in the work force and the traditional concept of a feminine gender role. An overview of working women's experiences since Colonial days is included. The author incorporates discussions of family, sexuality, and feminism throughout the text.

826 ———. 1975. "Where Are the Organized Women Workers?" *Feminist Studies* 3 (Sept.):92–111.
In this article Kessler-Harris looks at the reasons women were not highly unionized in the early decades of this century. She argues that women were kept out of unions by a number of factors, including the resistance of male trade unionists, ideologies of women's place in the home, the negative effects of middle-class reformers in their attempts to speak for working-class women, and ethnic restrictions among many groups of women.

827 KINGSOLVER, BARBARA. 1989. *Holding the Line: Women in the Great Arizona Mine Strike of 1983*. Ithaca, NY: ILR Press, Cornell University.
Generally when people think of strikes, particularly a miner's strike, they think almost solely of men. But there have been articles, books, and films for some time now that demonstrate the part women play in strikes either as strikers themselves or as the backbone of support to allow those who are picketing to continue. This is a movingly written account of women's involvement in the Phelps Dodge copper miners' strike. Kingsolver, who has made stunning films of other strikes, including the coal miners in Harlan County, Kentucky in the 1970s, shows readers the spirit of the women as they contribute to the strike effort and how they were changed in the process.

828 KORNBLUH, JOYCE and MARY FREDERICKSON, eds. 1984. *Sisterhood and Solidarity: Workers' Education for Women, 1914–1984*. Philadelphia: Temple University Press.
Contributors fill in gaps of knowledge which show the efforts on the part of some unions to provide education for women workers. This is a good example of social history that uncovers a world not often documented in typical history tracts

829 LAWRENCE, ELIZABETH. 1994. *Gender and Trade Unions*. Bristol, PA: Taylor & Francis.
Why is women's participation in unions much less than men's? This book explores that question by examining the impact of gender beliefs and gender roles at work and in the family that hinder women's participation in the trade union movement. The impact of feminism on the labor movement is discussed, as are the factors that unite and divide women and men in unions.

830 LEFKOWITZ, ROCHELLE and ANN WITHORN, eds. 1986. *For Crying Out Loud: Women and Poverty in the United States*. New York: Pilgrim Press.
A documentation and call for activism to fight poverty, sexism, racism, and classism. The authors argue that an unequal and discriminatory system creates an economic divide that is immoral and destructive for the entire society. The effects of poverty on women is to perpetuate this state for the next generation. Lefkowitz and Withorn call for the women's movement to claim the elimination of poverty as its mandate for social change.

831   LEHRER, SUSAN. 1987. *Origins of Protective Labor Legislation for Women, 1905–1925*. Albany: SUNY Press.
This book focuses on the social forces, such as feminist groups and those interested in the relations between labor and capital, that led to protective labor legislation for women. Included is the split between the National American Woman Suffrage Association, which favored protective labor legislation, and the National Woman's Party which argued for the Equal Rights Amendment instead. The author examines the impact of middle-class women's participation in the Women's Trade Union League and the subsequent change in the League's form of activism from militant unionism based on women's need for employment to lobbying for women's protection based on their special needs as mothers.

832   LLOYD, CYNTHIA B. and BETH T. NIEMI. 1979. *The Economics of Sex Differentials*. Irvington, NY: Columbia University Press.
A contribution to the list of published books by sociologists on work and Women's Studies. Somewhat dated, but still provides a useful reference source on how U.S. women are disadvantaged across the board in current economic beliefs and practices.

833   LUBIN, CAROL RIEGELMAN and ANNE WINSLOW. 1990. *Social Justice for Women: The International Labor Organization and Women*. Durham, NC: Duke University Press.
The women's movement is often criticized for not placing issues of race and class in a more prominent position. In this book, Lubin and Winslow look at an international labor organization to see what it has done to place women on at least an equal footing with men in priority needs. The authors show how women played an important role in both the American and British trade union movements and in the founding of the International Labor Organization (ILO). Given their input in the early organizational stage, they then discuss the level of concern the ILO has shown for women over the years, and how it dealt with conflicting needs between women from industrialized nations and those from developing nations. A further area of investigation centers on the relationship of the ILO to the women's movement in various countries.

834   MCCOURT, KATHLEEN. 1977. *Working-Class Women and Grass-Roots Politics*. Bloomington: Indiana University Press.
Kathleen McCourt, a sociologist, analyses white working-class women's political activism. Using interview material of twenty-three women from Chicago, the author discusses the communities they work in, the women themselves, the types of community activism they do, and how these involvements have affected their personal lives.

835   MCCREESH, CAROLYN DANIEL. *Women in the Campaign to Organize Garment Workers, 1880–1917*. New York: Garland Publishing.
This book combines the story of strikes and union leaders with the contributions of rank and file women workers to make a more complete account of labor history than is typically found. Working-class women in this book are not

just recipients of other's efforts, they are embedded in the forces of protest and change that occurred.

836   MIES, MARIA, ed. 1988. *Women: The Last Colony*. Atlantic Highlands, NJ: Humanities Press.
The sexual division of labor is the focus of this work which seeks to explain historical modes of production. Beyond understanding the past, the author is interested in applying this knowledge to the global capitalist economy, specifically the growth of exploitation in the Third World where women are usually the most negatively impacted.

837   MILKMAN, RUTH, ed. 1985. *Women, Work and Protest: A Century of US Women's Labor History*. New York: Routledge, Chapman and Hall.
Milkman is a well-known historian of labor history and women's role in it. In this collection she has put together many excellent feminist analyses of the relationship of women to the labor movement in the United States.

838   MILWAUKEE COUNTY WELFARE RIGHTS ORGANIZATION. 1972. *Welfare Mothers Speak Out: We Ain't Gonna Shuffle Anymore*. New York: W. W. Norton.
A full discussion of the welfare system, welfare rights, and myths about people on welfare. Includes survey material from recipients and a review of previous research. Those involved in the struggle for welfare rights are given a voice in this work and new ideas for income distribution are explored.

839   MORRIS, JENNY. 1986. *Women Workers and the Sweated Trades: The Origins of Minimum Wage Legislation*. Brookfield, VT: Gower Press.
A moving history of the exploitation of poor immigrant women in the factories and sweat shops of the United States. The need for a minimum wage was so severe that it is remarkable it took so long to achieve it. An important contribution of this book is the dispelling of the notion that people who work for low wages under poor working conditions are too slow-witted to do "higher-level" work.

840   PAYNE, ELIZABETH ANN. 1988. *Reform, Labor, and Feminism: Margaret Dreier Robins and the Women's Trade Union League*. Champaign: University of Illinois Press.
This book is about Margaret Dreier Robins and other women involved in the Women's Trade Union League. The League was an important voice for working women in the early part of the twentieth century when the male dominated labor movement was not open to them. One of the ways they were able to gain acceptance was their commitment to the values of motherhood and their appeal for protective labor legislation for women because of their special needs.

841   ROBERTS, ELIZABETH. 1988. *Women's Work 1849–1940*. New York: Macmillan Press.
A discussion of issues connected to women and the wage labor market, including the family wage, pay equity, women and unions, and the various conflicts between work and family.

842   ROSE, MARGARET. 1990. "Traditional and Non-traditional Patterns of Female Activism in the United Farm Workers of America, 1962–1980." *Frontiers* 11:26–32.

A look at the part women of Spanish origin have played in the struggles for unionization from the 1950s through the 1970s. In this article Rose focuses on the life of Helen Chavez, wife of Cesar Chavez, to show how Mexicana and Chicana women worked in both the fields and in the home. Their contributions to union efforts and to keeping their families together have been overlooked in studies of migrant farm workers and union organizing.

843   SACKS, KAREN BRODKIN. 1988. *Caring by the Hour: Women, Work and Organizing at Duke Medical Center*. Champaign: University of Illinois Press.

A case study of women union activists, union organizing, contract negotiating, health care workers, employment conditions, and work life. Black women's leadership in the union is highlighted.

844   SEIFER, NANCY. 1976. *Nobody Speaks for Me: Self-Portraits of American Working-Class Women*. New York: Simon and Schuster.

Ten working-class women tell their own stories of political activity, community organizing, and union activism. Women from different regions of the country, rural and urban residents, African-American, Chicana, Jewish, and other ethnic groups are represented in this work.

845   STANSELL, CHRISTINE. 1986. *City of Women: Sex and Class in New York, 1789–1860*. New York: Alfred A. Knopf.

Women's activism takes all forms, and in this book Stansell shows us how working-class women in New York during the late eighteenth and mid-nineteenth centuries organized for improved conditions. The author uses material that reveals a close knit community of women creating change in the tenements where they lived and the sweatshops where they worked.

846   STOPER, EMILY. 1991. "Women's Work, Women's Movement: Taking Stock." *Annals of the American Academy of Political and Social Science* (May):151–162.

In order to overcome the earnings ratio of only 70 percent of what men make, the author discusses the three tactics women can use: affirmative action, pay equity, and work policies to relieve the conflicts between work and family.

847   WARTENBERG, THOMAS E. 1985. "Beyond Babies and Banners: Towards an Understanding of the Dynamics of Social Movements." *New Political Science* 14 (Dec.):157–171.

An analysis of the role social organizations play in the emergence of social movements. Wartenberg uses the case study of the Women's Emergency Brigade (WEB) which formed during the United Auto Worker's strike in Flint, Michigan in the 1930s. The stories of the women, found in the film "With

Babies and Banners" show the new roles, greater confidence, and collective spirit that arose in this autonomous women's group. Wartenberg argues that disbanding WEB after the strike was a way of reducing women's participation in the union.

848 WERTHEIMER, BARBARA MAYER. 1977. *We Were There: The Story of Working Women in America*. New York: Pantheon Books.
A review of the work women have done since Colonial times and the types of opposition they have encountered in their attempts to stretch the boundaries of the work they do. Working women's attempts at unionization are documented, particularly those union activities within the International Ladies Garment Workers' Union.

Sex and Pornography

849 ALDERFER, HANNAH BETH JAKER, and MARYBETH NELSON. 1982. *Diary of a Conference on Sexuality*. New York: Barnard College Women's Center.
This is the record of the Planning Committee of the Bernard Conference "The Scholar and the Feminist IX: Toward a Politics of Sexuality." It was at this 1982 conference that the conflict among feminists on the issue of pornography was first publicly aired. There were more than forty papers presented which addressed a wide diversity of topics on sexuality. The group Women Against Pornography protested the lack of a position which opposed pornography or that considered pornography a major underpinning of patriarchy. The *Diary* details the planning of this conference.

850 BARRY, KATHLEEN. 1984. *Female Sexual Slavery*. New York: New York University Press.
A classic feminist writing on the sexual oppression of women around the world. The practices Barry describes are shocking in their treatment of women and in their revelations about women's position in social systems. This is a powerful and disturbing book.

851 BURSTYN, VARDA, ed. 1985. *Women Against Censorship*. Vancouver: Douglas and McIntyre.
This book contains eleven essays presenting theoretical and personal views opposed to simplistic and reactionary positions on pornography. The various authors express their fears that allowing the State to have the power to determine what is pornographic and what is not is dangerous and could lead to the suppression of feminist and lesbian materials. Included in this work are excerpts from the Minneapolis Ordinance which was the first feminist anti-pornography proposal for women filing legal harm suits against producers of pornographic material.

852   CALIFIA, PAT, LISA DUGGAN, KATE ELLIS, and NAN HUNTER, eds. 1986. *Caught Looking: Feminism, Pornography & Censorship*. New York: Caught Looking.

Most of the articles in this collection have been previously published. The writers are members of the Feminist Anti-Censorship Task Force who have taken a stand against policies of the anti-pornography movement, particularly the legislative solution of Dworkin and MacKinnon. The articles also address issues of sexuality and express the desire to liberate women's sexuality from the oppression it has labored under in American society. Contributors include Pat Califia, Ellen Willis, Paula Webster, Nan Hunter, Carole Vance, Lisa Duggan, Kate Ellis, Barbara O'Dair, and Abelyn Tallman.

853   CALIFIA, PAT. 1982. "A Personal View of the History of the Lesbian S/M Community and Movement in San Francisco." In *Coming to Power*, edited by SAMOIS. Boston: Alyson Publications.

In this book, edited by an S/M lesbian feminist collective, Califia's article discusses the events leading up to the formation of a lesbian sadomasochistic community in San Francisco. The factors she cites are the negative reactions from the women's movement of the late 1960s and early 1970s, and the open hostility of the feminist anti-pornography movement by the late 1970s. Women Against Violence in Pornography and the Media (WAVPM) specifically came into open conflict with this group. When WAVPM hosted the first national conference on anti-pornography, they did not allow SAMOIS members to speak.

854   COWAN, GLORIA, CHERYL CHASE, and GERALDINE B. STAHLY. 1989. "Feminist and Fundamentalist Attitudes toward Pornography Control." *Psychology of Women Quarterly* 13 (March):97–112.

A report on the findings of a study that looked at differences on self-designated feminist and fundamentalist women on the control of pornography. The instrument used in this research was Carole Gilligans 1982 moral reasoning framework. The subjects of this study were interviewed, filled out an 'attitudes towards women' questionnaire, and completed a values scale survey. Fundamentalists and feminists who wanted to control pornography scored high on taking responsibility for the welfare of others. Feminists who were not in favor of controlling pornography scored higher on individual rights and freedom.

855   DWORKIN, ANDREA. 1981. *Pornography: Men Possessing Women*. New York: G. P. Putnam's.

Dworkin takes the position that male sexual violence is a fundamental component of history as we know it and that it is possibly a biologically determined condition. She defines pornography as the core of male supremacy and, thus, the instrument of male power. She is passionate in her writing, using graphic descriptions of violent sexual acts.

856   GRIFFIN, SUSAN. 1981. *Pornography and Silence: Culture's Revenge Against Nature*. New York: Harper & Row.

The contents of pornographic books, magazines, and films are described. The author then analyzes the effects of pornography which she calls a contradiction of natural instincts. Since pornography is against human nature, the effects are detrimental to both sexes. Women are objectified and men are dehumanized. The end result is a negative and dangerous polarization between women and men.

857   HENTOFF, NAT. 1992. *Free Speech For Me—But Not For Thee: How the American Left and Right Relentlessly Censor Each Other*. New York: HarperCollins.

Hentcoff, an uncompromising proponent of free speech, argues against censorship efforts by those who assume a self-righteous protectorship role of public morality. He covers a litany of left and right "politically correct" censorship cases and includes in his examples the Catherine MacKinnon and Andrea Dworkin anti-pornography law passed by the Indianapolis city council (later struck down by a judge). In this illustration, he shows how the right wing and anti-pornography feminists teamed up to prohibit pornography which he claims would have subjected the Bible, some great literature, and even some of Dworkin's work to legal sanctions. Citing another case, he shows the outcome of anti-pornography feminists and fundamentalists activism in a Texas city that resulted in the public library removal of *Our Bodies, Ourselves*.

858   HITE, SHERE. 1994. *Women as Revolutionary Agents of Change: The Hite Reports and Beyond*. Madison: The University of Wisconsin Press.

This book consists of essays and extensive excerpts reprinted from the Hite Reports. Hite's work and the voices of the subjects of her research speak very frankly about their struggles with sexuality, love, friendship, and identity.

859   HOBSON, BARBARA MEIL. 1988. *Uneasy Virtue: The Politics of Prostitution and the American Reform Tradition*. New York: Basic Books.

A critique of the useless efforts to control sexuality. Hobson presents data which reveal the extent of the obsession American society has had over other people's sexual behavior throughout most of its history.

860   JEFFREYS, SHEILA. 1985. *The Spinster and Her Enemies: Feminism and Sexuality, 1880–1930*. Boston: Pandora Press.

Women's sexuality has always been an underlying part of women's activism for autonomy and freedom. In this book, Jeffreys looks at the ways women's sexual and social behavior were controlled by societal attitudes from the Victorian Age to the Roaring '20s.

861   LEDERER, LAURA, ed. 1980. *Take Back the Night: Women on Pornography*. New York: William Morrow and Co.

A collection of thirty-five articles by activists involved in the feminist anti-pornography movement. A common view is articulated by the contributors of the centrality of pornography to women's oppression. Pornography is defined as the ideology of a culture which promotes and condones violence against women; thus, the feminist anti-pornography movement sees itself as working for "preventive medicine." The title of the book represents contributors' commitment to reclaiming women's freedom to walk the streets in safety. Articles by Kathleen Barry, Pauline Bart, Susan Brownmiller, Charlotte Bunch, Phyllis Chesler, Andrea Dworkin, Audre Lorde, Robin Morgan, Adrienne Rich, Diana Russell, Gloria Steinem, and Alice Walker, among others. Since the publication of this book, the feminist debate over pornography intensified and created often hostile division within the women's movement.

862   LEIDHOLDT, DORCHEN and JANICE G. RAYMOND, eds. 1990. *The Sexual Liberals and the Attack on Feminism*. New York: Pergamon Press.
Contributors to this book are active in the feminist anti- pornography movement. The articles focus less on the feminist anti-pornography position than on attacking those feminists who disagree with their ideological foundation and strategic aims. The editors express, in the introduction and title of the book, that those feminists who oppose their anti-pornography work are sexual liberals, not feminists. This work is related to the explosive conflict over pornography that emerged in the late 1970s to early 1980s within the women's movement; however, it presents only one side of that debate. Contributors include Catharine MacKinnon, Andrea Dworkin, Sonia Johnson, Ann Jones, Phyllis Chesler, Pauline Bart, John Stoltenberg, and Mary Daly.

863   LINDEN, ROBIN RUTH, DARLENE R. PAGANO, DIANE E. H. RUSSELL, and SUSAN LEIGH STAR, eds. 1982. *Against Sadomasochism: A Radical Feminist Analysis*. East Palo Alto, CA: Frog in the Well.
Contributors to this anthology are all opposed to sadomasochism. The writings are mainly in the form of essays and personal stories. Although the authors are clear in their negative position on sadomasochism, they are moderate in their level of criticism. The basis for their position is the belief that s/m emerges from patriarchal sexual practices which are opposed to feminist values of equality and mutual respect. Well-known authors include: Robin Morgan, Ti-Grace Atkinson, Alice Walker, Susan Griffin, Kathleen Barry, and Audre Lord. This was an early book in the emerging debate of the 1980s on power in personal relations and the kind of sexual liberation needed to end the oppression of women.

864   RUSSETT, CYNTHIA EAGLE. 1989. *Sexual Science: The Victorian Construction of Womanhood*. Cambridge, MA: Harvard University Press.
Where do our ideas of sexuality and gender come from? Feminists have argued against science, nature, and superhuman powers that have contributed to beliefs of sex limiting sexual capacities. In the publication of this book, Russett has pulled together "scientific" proofs that abounded in the nineteenth century about the inferiority of women's sexuality. This text makes for interesting (almost amusing) reading.

865   SAMOIS. 1982. *Coming to Power: Writings and Graphics on Lesbian S/M*. Boston: Alyson Publications.

One of the most controversial topics within feminism is lesbian sado-masochism. In this book, the ideology and practices of s/m are discussed. Defined as a consensual exchange of power, sadomasochism within the lesbian community is celebrated as a relationship based on absolute trust. Gayle Rubin provides a theoretical framework for understanding lesbian s/m, and Pat Califia outlines the history of the movement. Other contributors provide drawings, photographs, personal accounts, and eroticized fictional stories.

866   SNITOW, ANN, CHRISTINE STANSELL, and SHARON THOMPSON, eds. 1983. *Powers of Desire: The Politics of Sexuality*. New York: Monthly Review Press.

An interesting collection of articles, poems, stories, and oral histories related to women's experiences and views of sex. The combined writings present a dialogue consisting of provocative issues surrounding women, sex, desire, and fantasy. Importantly, the editors discuss the history of how issues of sexuality fit into the socialist and feminist movements of the last two centuries. Sections are divided into six parts: The Capitalist Paradox: Expanding and Contracting Pleasures; Sexual Revolutions; The Institution of Heterosexuality; Domination, Submission, and the Unconscious; On Sexual Openness; and Current Controversies. Contributions include three separate analyses of the historical experiences of African-American women by Rennie Simson, Jacquelyn Dowd Hall, and Barbara Omolade; and "Feminism, Moralism, and Pornography" by Ellen Willis.

867   THORNTON, NEIL. 1986. "The Politics of Pornography: A Critique of Liberalism and Radical Feminism." *Australian and New Zealand Journal of Sociology* 22:25–45.

The relationship between sexuality and pornography are analyzed by examining liberal and radical feminist views. The radical position that pornography causes sexual violence against women is contrasted with the liberal view that pornography is only one of many manifestations of sexism. Thornton criticizes the radical position and concludes that the liberal view more accurately describes what occurs in patriarchal societies. Also the author expresses the view that censorship of pornography would threaten other forms of freedom feminists (and others) do not want to give up.

868   TONG, ROSEMARIE. 1984. *Women, Sex and the Law*. Totowa, NJ: Rowman and Allanheld.

This book provides an analysis of legal theories related to women's crimes and victimizations such as prostitution, rape, pornography, wife battering, and pornography. She explains how all these issues fit under the category of sexuality and how they have been used against women. Tong also addresses the differential attitudes and treatment under the law received by women and men, gays and straights, whites and people of color. This is an insightful book which draws diverse issues into a cogent analytical framework.

869 TREBILCOT, JOYCE. 1983. *Taking Responsibility for Sexuality*. Berkeley, CA: Acacia Books.
This is an essay published in pamphlet form on women taking responsibility for their own sexuality. Trebilcot, noted feminist philosopher, calls for women to consciously think about their sexual identities whether that be lesbian, heterosexual, bisexual, or celibate. The author argues that all women should "come out" by defining their needs and desires rather than assume that sexuality is an inherent unchangeable condition. Trebilcot contends that the act of taking responsibility for our sexuality gives us strength, independence, and understanding; moreover, there is the possibility that it can lessen the heterosexism and lesbophobia that separates women from each other.

870 VALVERDE, MARIANA. 1987. *Sex, Power and Pleasure*. Philadelphia: New Society Publishers.
A look at women's sexuality based on theory and experience. This work is creatively involved in redefining the relationship between pleasure and ethics. In addition to examining the importance of sexual pleasure, serious and controversial social issues connected to sexuality are also examined such as pornography and censorship, and eroticism and power.

871 VANCE, CAROLE S., ed. 1984. *Pleasure and Danger: Exploring Female Sexuality*. Boston: Routlege & Kegan Paul.
The 1982 Barnard Conference on Politics of Sexuality had speakers who presented papers on sex manuals, ethnic women's sexuality, children and sexuality, Victorian era feminism, and pornography. This edited volume is a collection of select papers from that conference. Contributors include Cherrie Moraga, Gayle Rubin, and Kate Millett.

872 WILLIS, ELLEN. 1992. *No More Nice Girls: Countercultural Essays*. Hanover, NH: University Press of New England.
Willis, who was an activist in the early consciousness-raising groups in New York City, has written about women, sexuality, and gender for over twenty years. A teacher of journalism at New York University, Willis previously published most of these essays in *The Village Voice*. This collection covers diverse topics which converge on her main point—that feminism is about personal and sexual freedom. She is a strong advocate for pleasure in one's life. She is also a strong critic of the repressive features of the family and society in achieving that goal for women. Some essays cover debates which have raged within the movement, such as her opposition to the anti-pornography movement and "identity politics" which she opposes because of the multiple, and sometimes contradictory, identities people share. Willis cogently argues against the rise of cultural and group identity as the basis for legitimating one's politics rather than ideological beliefs creating a community based on shared principles.

Feminist Critique and Contributions

873 BARDES, BARBARA and SUZANNE GOSSETT. 1990. *Declarations of Independence: Women and Political Power in Nineteenth Century American Fiction*. New Brunswick, NJ: Rutgers University Press.
This work illustrates the interconnections between women's political struggles for equal relationships with men and the literature that was being written in the nineteenth century. It is an interesting and revealing analysis of how fiction arises within the context of historical periods.

874 BLEIER, RUTH, ed. 1990. *Feminist Approaches to Science*. New York: Pergamon Press.
A collection of essays showing the biases that are often found in the scientific enterprise. These writings debunk the myth of objectivity and show that science is done by people who are rarely value-free. An interesting volume on an important subject.

875 ———. 1984. *Science and Gender: A Critique of Biology and Its Theories on Women*. New York: Pergamon Press.
A number of books were published in the 1980s which criticized science for being gender biased in research and teaching. In this book, Bleier criticizes biology for continuing this tradition. Biology, perhaps more than any other science, involves itself with gender issues; thus, a feminist critique of biology is fundamental to looking at the sciences in general. When you finish reading this book, you will find yourself questioning all kinds of previous assumptions you rarely (if ever) thought about before.

876 BROWN, JOANNE CARLSON and CAROLE R. BOHN, eds. 1990. *Christianity, Patriarchy, and Abuse: A Feminist Critique*. New York: Pilgrim Press.
A critique of religious groups that ignore their own theology to oppose suffering and violence and, in upholding patriarchal models, glorify them instead. Contributors bring varied perspectives to their review of religious doctrines and practices.

877 CANCIAN, FRANCESCA M. 1981. "Mass Media and the Women's Movement: 1900–1977." *Journal of Applied Behavioral Science* 17 (Jan.):9–26.
Cancian finds that news coverage of women greatly increases when there is a strong women's movement. The quality of coverage also varies with the strength of the movement. Coverage was measured from 1900 to 1977 for the *New York Times* and *Reader's Guide*.

878 CHESLER, PHYLLIS. 1972. *Women and Madness*. New York: Avon Books.
Chesler, a feminist psychologist, indicts psychiatric theory and practice (whose practitioners she points out are mostly white, middle-class males) for over-

diagnosing and treating women for depression, anxiety, aggressive behavior, and a stubborn refusal to conform.

879   DE LAURETIS, TERESA. 1984. *Alice Doesn't: Feminism, Semiotics, Cinema*. Bloomington: Indiana University Press.
de Lauretis is a creative thinker and interesting writer. This collection reveals new insights on wide ranging social issues, particularly things that we might not notice if they were not pointed out to us like art, semiotics, and the cinema, to name a few.

880   DONOVAN, JOSEPHINE, ed. 1989. *Feminist Literary Criticism: Explorations in Theory*. Lexington: University Press of Kentucky.
A good introduction and review of feminist critical theory. This is a second edition which includes a new introduction and a lengthy bibliography.

881   EPSTEIN, CYNTHIA FUCHS. 1993. "A New Attack on Feminism." *Dissent* 40 (Dec.):123–124.
A review essay on the following books: Susan Faludi *Backlash: The Undeclared War Against Women* (1991), described as a critique of the media and academic disciplines for failing to recognize the achievements of the women's movement; Carol Tavris *The Mismeasure of Woman: Why Women Are Not the Better Sex, the Inferior Sex, or the Opposite Sex* (1992), a book that reveals the biases of the medical profession, social sciences, and media; and Nancie Caraway *Segregated Sisterhood: Racism and the Politics of American Feminism* (1991), which is described as an attack on white feminists for their racism. Fuchs finds Caraway's approach is overdone and often unfounded.

882   FAUSTO-STERLING, ANNE. 1985. *Myths of Gender: Biological Theories About Women and Men*. New York: Basic Books.
A careful examination of the biological, genetic, evolutionary, and psychological research which reveals a lack of evidence behind commonly promoted ideas about biological sex differences. Fausto-Sterling is a professor of biology and medicine, and as an insider in the field of science, the critique she presents is hard to ignore.

883   FELSKI, RITA. 1989. *Beyond Feminist Aesthetics: Feminist Literature and Social Change*. Cambridge, MA: Harvard University Press.
Feminist literary criticism drawn from American, British, French, and German literary canons. This is a good overview of the theoretical and political issues often debated in the feminist criticism school of thought.

884   FOX, MARY FRANK, ed. 1985. *Scholarly Writing and Publishing: Issues, Problems, and Solutions*. Boulder, Co: Westview Press.
The idea for putting together this collection originated with the Research and Publications Committee of Sociologists for Women in Society (SWS). The contributors share their knowledge of publishing and write about women's special concerns regarding the writing enterprise. The first part of the book consists of how-to articles, e.g., how to revise a journal article, and the art of negotiat-

ing book contracts. The second part discusses problems of writing, e.g., collaborative writing, feelings of isolation, developing a schedule, and setting boundaries.

885   FRANK, FRANCINE WATTMAN and PAULA A. TREICHLER. 1989. *Language, Gender, and Professional Writing: Theoretical Approaches and Guidelines for Nonsexist Usage*. New York: Modern Language Association.
A good guide to using nonsexist language, backed up by solid research and creative thinking.

886   FRASER, NANCY. 1989. *Unruly Practices: Power, Discourse, and Gender in Contemporary Social Theory*. Minneapolis: University of Minnesota Press.
A collection of essays by the author which combines poststructuralism, critical social theory, feminist theory, and pragmatism into a well thought out criticism of late-capitalist political culture. Fraser integrates the thought of contemporary theorists and social movement literature into a cogent analysis of gender relations and feminist oriented theory.

887   GATES, HENRY LOUIS, JR., ed. 1990. *Reading Black, Reading Feminist: A Critical Anthology*. New York: New American Library.
A celebration of the feminist and African-American literary traditions from the pens of top literary critics.

888   GERRARD, NICCI. 1989. *Into the Mainstream: How Feminism Has Changed Women's Writing*. Winchester, MA: Unwin Hyman.
Gerrard sets out to show that women have challenged and changed traditional literary traditions. She brings in the words and life experiences of well-known authors such as Alice Walker and Joyce Carol Oates to prove her points. Discussed in this book are the writers' political beliefs, their ambitions, and the barriers they have experienced in attempting to achieve their career goals.

889   HARDING, SANDRA. 1988. *The Science Question in Feminism*. Ithaca, NY: Cornell University Press.
Harding's work joins the genre of books throughout the 1980s to criticize the scientific field for operating in a male biased manner, but she adds a different twist to her position. She also takes a critical stance to much of the feminist literature that has critiqued and challenged the male paradigm of scientific work. Beyond her analysis of the field of science and the feminist critiques of it, Harding presents her own ideas. In the conclusion, she offers another direction to take for a reconstructed science and theory of knowledge.

890   HEGGER, SUSAN, BARBARA RYAN, and ELISABETH WESTON. 1983. "Women, the Family and Politics." *Issues in Radical Therapy* 11:14–17, 50.
This article looks at the suggested plan by Michael Lerner for the Left to take a pro-family position as a way to offset the Religious Right's takeover of family

issues. Hegger, Ryan, and Weston find Lerner's arguments to consist of male-defined family ideas that fail to recognize the feminist critique of the family. The authors conclude with a challenge to Leftist men to take up the feminist agenda first, and then ask women to join with them on new family issues.

891 HUMM, MAGGIE. 1986. *Feminist Criticism: Women as Contemporary Critics*. New York: St. Martin's Press.
This work is a survey of feminist criticism, particularly literary criticism, written since 1970. Included are myth, black, Marxist-feminist, psychoanalytical, and lesbian criticism. One chapter features the writing of early feminist "pioneers" Simone de Beauvoir, Kate Millett, Betty Friedan, and Germaine Greer. Separate chapters are allocated for Virginia Woolf, Rebecca West, and Adrienne Rich.

892 JACKSON, MARION E., ed. 1989. *Ruth Weisberg: Paintings, Drawings, Prints, 1968–1988*. New York: Feminist Press, City University of New York.
The roots of contemporary feminist art are traced in this book to Weisberg's paintings and drawings. The author discusses her work, art history in general, and the biographical details of her life.

893 JACOBUS, MARY, EVELYN FOX KELLER, and SALLY SHUTTLEWORTH, eds. 1989. *Body/politics: Women and the Discourses of Science*. New York: Routledge, Chapman and Hall.
In varied ways the contributors to this edited volume reveal how often controversies and battlegrounds in science involve the female body. Many of the pieces are real eye openers.

894 KASS-SIMON, G. and PATRICIA FARNES, eds. 1989. *Women of Science: Righting the Record*. Bloomington: Indiana University Press.
This is a collection of scientists writing about scientists. The motivation for organizing these articles is to make clear that women are highly suited to scientific work and to dispel the notion that they are not. Secondly, the authors want to recover the names and contributions of women who went before them.

895 KELLER, CATHERINE. 1988. *From a Broken Web: Separatism, Sexism and Self*. Boston: Beacon Press.
Offering a critique of patriarchy, Keller provides feminist criticism on a wide range of issues. Much of the material has been covered before, but it is a story that can be told many times.

896 KELLER, EVELYN FOX. 1985. *Reflections on Gender and Science*. New Haven, CT: Yale University Press.
Evelyn Fox Keller is one of the most widely known scientists who has challenged the academic world to look closely at the gender bias embedded in the very framework of empirical research. She questions concepts such as objectivity and reason representing male characteristics while subjectivity and feeling are considered female. And, she asks readers to consider the effect such

beliefs have on the process of scientific inquiry. After raising these important questions, Fox Keller proposes ways to remove biased generalizations to develop gender free science.

897 KIMBALL, GAYLE, ed. 1981. *Women's Culture: The Women's Renaissance of the Seventies*. Metuchen, NJ: Scarecrow Press.
A collection of original essays on the topic of creative energy. The outpouring of writing, poetry, music, and other artistic endeavors that emerged in the women's movement of the seventies allows for some wonderful reflections on that period, aptly named by Kimball, "the women's renaissance." The first section has an interesting dialogue between Kimball and Robin Morgan on the ways cultural feminism holds revolutionary change potential. What's most interesting about this discussion is that they both agree it does—rather than one arguing for the revolutionary potential and the other arguing that separatism creates exclusivity and political apathy. In various other sections the art, music, literature, spirituality, feminist groups, and dreams are discussed. This volume reveals the impact feminism has had on women's creativity.

898 LONDON, BETTE. 1990. *The Appropriated Voice: Narrative Authority in Conrad, Forster and Woolf*. Ann Arbor: University of Michigan Press.
Through a combination of feminist theory, narrative theory, cultural criticism, and ethnographic ethics, London provides a critique of the categories usually employed by those who engage in revisionist criticism. The importance of the debate on narrative interpretation is covered in her analysis.

899 LUEPNITZ, DEBORAH ANNA. 1990. *The Family Interpreted: Feminist Theory in Clinical Practice*. New York: Basic Books.
This is a good book in the genre of family therapy framed within a feminist perspective. Luepnitz does a particularly good job of explaining the ways people change.

900 MALOS, ELLEN, ed. 1980. *The Politics of Housework*. New York: Schocken Books.
One of the most valuable contributions this collection makes is an introduction that provides a survey of the history of housework debates. There are also some interesting individual essays which cover the various wages for housework campaigns and theoretical positions on the relation of domestic labor to capital. Classic pieces found that are hard to find today make this a valuable historic and current reference source for those still interested in this debate. Authors include: Margaret Benston, Mariarosa Dalla Costa, Selma James, and Pat Mainardi, among others.

901 MEESE, ELIZABETH and ALICE PARKER. 1989. *The Difference Within: Feminism and Critical Theory*. Philadelphia: John Benjamins.
A gathering of wide-ranging discussions on the work of authors such as Alice Walker, Frances Harper, William Faulkner, and Toni Morrison. Much of the writing is theoretically based, both from feminist and critical theory perspectives.

902   MULVEY, LAURA. 1989. *Visual and Other Pleasures*. Bloomington:
       Indiana University Press.
A collection of essays written by Mulvey, a British film maker and film theorist.
The essays look at the effects of feminism on the film culture of the 1970s and
1980s.

903   NOCHLIN, LINDA. 1988. *Women, Art, and Power*. New York: Harper &
       Row.
Nochlin gathers together essays on women artists and women who have made
their careers in art history. Nochlin herself is an important figure in feminist art
history.

904   PARKER, ROZIKA and GRISELDA PILOCK, eds. 1987. *Framing Feminism:
       Art and the Women's Movement*. Winchester, MA: Pandora Press.
The effects of the women's movement on art is demonstrated. Parker and
Pilock create a vivid record of the ways feminism has imparted a new woman's
view which is articulated in a wide variety of artists' work.

905   RAVEN, ARLENE, CASSANDRA LANGER, and JOANNA FRUEH, eds. 1989.
       Feminist Art Criticism: An Anthology. Ann Arbor: UMI Research Press.
A collection of writings on feminist art criticism ranging from 1970 to the present. Essays focus on sexuality, language, spirituality, and women in the arts.

906   RICH, ADRIENNE. 1976. *Of Woman Born: Motherhood as Experience
       and Institution*. New York: W. W. Norton.
Taking on the sacrosanct topic of motherhood, Rich argues that motherhood
is embodied in patriarchal culture and in the structural arrangements of power
and powerlessness. She distinguishes between motherhood as experience
(which she finds transforming) and the institution of motherhood which
restricts women's autonomy and creates prohibitions to reproductive freedom. In this anniversary edition, Rich provides an extensive new foreword that
places this work in the context of the events that have transpired in the ten
years since the original publication came out.

907   ROSSER, SUE V. 1990. *Female-Friendly Science: Applying Women's
       Studies Methods and Theories to Attract Students*. Elmsford, NY:
       Pergamon Press.
In this book, Rosser draws together literature from a number of fields to consider ways of making science more gender neutral, friendly, relevant, inclusive,
and meaningful. Feminist theory and Women's Studies pedagogy are a large
part of the foundation she suggests for the study and teaching of science.

908   ————, ed. 1990. *Feminism Within the Science and Health Care
       Professions: Overcoming Resistance*. Elmsford, NY: Pergamon Press.
Contributors to this anthology discuss and challenge the science and health
care industries through critique, suggestion, and thoughtful consideration.
The goal is to create ways of integrating feminist principals into traditional
practices that are resistant to change.

909   ROSSITER, MARGARET W. 1982. *Women Scientists in America: Struggles and Strategies to 1940*. Baltimore, MD: Johns Hopkins University Press.
The experience of women scientists in the United States until World War II is documented in this book. It is a shameful record of senseless discrimination that crushed women's aspirations and drained the country of needed intellectual and creative scientific development. In light of the forces against them, women scientists' efforts to change their situation and make science more available to women is all the more admirable.

910   ROTHMAN, SHEILA M. 1978. *Woman's Proper Place: A History of Changing Ideals and Practices, 1870 to the Present*. New York: Basic Books.
This book reflects an understanding of the principles and consequences of American social policy toward women. It is a historical look at competing claims and clashes of interests. Rothman found that underlying the opposing perspectives lay diverse judgements of what constitutes woman's proper place. Invariably conflicts arose over the models and ideals that were believed inherent in shaping women's lives, particularly those connected to family obligations. Current issues over day care, abortion, and the ERA fall into this category as do earlier issues of suffrage, education, divorce, and birth control. Rothman argues that the debate is not always the same as every generation advances particular definitions of woman's place and the public and private policies needed to promote that definition. This work traces those changes over time.

911   SANDERS, MARLENE and MARCIA ROCK. 1988. *Waiting for Prime Time: The Women of Television News*. Champaign: University of Illinois Press.
Although not overtly involved in an organized component of the women's movement, many women are located in careers which offer positions of power for effecting women's position in society. Women in the news media are an important part of this stratum, and in this book a history of the underground women's movement at the networks is documented.

912   SCHIEBINGER, LONDA. 1989. *The Mind Has No Sex? Women in the Origins of Modern Science*. Cambridge, MA: Harvard University Press.
The gender politics of science is the focus of this book. Schiebinger discusses this topic through a historical account of how much science itself has played a part in establishing the concepts and limitations of gender categories. Another important feature is Schiebinger's recognition of the women of science who are mainly unknown.

913   SPALLONE, PAT and DEBORAH I. STEINBERG, eds. 1987. *Made to Order: The Myth of Reproductive and Genetic Progress*. New York: Pergamon Press.
A collection of papers selected from a conference concerned with the direction science is taking in genetic engineering. The conference was titled Feminist International Network of Resistance to Reproductive and Genetic Engineering.

An example of one area of concern is the critical analysis of in-vitro fertilization which is defined in this volume as the medical control of women's bodies.

914   THORNE, BARRIE, CHERIS KRAMARAE, and NANCY HENLEY, eds. 1983.
       Language, Gender and Society. Cambridge, MA: Newbury Publishing.
In this edited volume contributors take a close look at sociolinguistics. There are two sections to this book: selected papers on language and gender; and a lengthy annotated bibliography of research on sex similarities and differences in language, speech, and nonverbal communication.

915   THORNE, BARRIE and MARILYN YALOM, eds. 1982. *Rethinking the Family:*
       Some Feminist Questions. New York: Longman.
A collection of twelve selected articles which critically evaluate the charge from the religious and political Right that feminists are anti-family. The editors divide the concept of family into component parts—sexual division of labor, sexuality, and socialization. Next they make a distinction between the levels of power among household members, and challenge the conception of the autonomous nuclear family by showing how the state intervenes into the family arena. Other topics that are covered in this volume include: welfare, reproductive freedom, mothering, the interconnection between the public and private realm, and marital property reform. Contributors include: Rayna Rapp, Nancy Chodorow, Michelle Z. Rosaldo, Eli Zaretsky, Sara Ruddick, Renate Bridenthal, and Linda Gordon.

916   TREBILCOT, JOYCE, ed. 1984. *Mothering: Essays in Feminist Theory*.
       Totowa, NJ: Rowman & Allanheld.
Trebilcot writes in her preface that even though she decided long ago that she would not be a mother, she realizes the importance that mothering plays for every woman in patriarchy, and thus, the centrality of understanding mothering for feminist theorizing. The essays in this collection which analyze patriarchy, recognize woman-identified values, and conceive of strategies for change are framed by an understanding that mothering in a feminist future will be defined by women. Examples of selections are: Azizah al-Hibri "Reproduction, Mothering, and the Origins of Patriarchy;" Pauline Bart "Review of Chodorow's The Reproduction of Mothering;" and Sara Ruddick "Maternal Thinking."

917   TUANA, NANCY, ed. 1989. *Feminism and Science*. Bloomington: Indiana
       University Press.
The articles in this volume question the objectivity of research and inquiry within the sciences and, more particularly, the level of gender bias that works against women's entry and promotion within the scientific enterprise. Both the ways science is affected by this bias and the ways it continues to be maintained are examined.

918   YAEGER, PATRICIA S. 1988. *Honey-Mad Women: Emancipatory*
       Strategies in Women's Writing. New York: Columbia University Press.

This book looks at the way literature can transform ideologies to create social change. Yaeger argues that women's writing intentionally fills this role. Examples are shown of women writers who attempt to emancipate themselves, other women, and society in general.

919   ZIPES, JACK. 1987. *Don't Bet on the Prince: Contemporary Feminist Fairy Tales in North America and England*. New York: Metheun.
This is an excellent reconstruction and critical response to classical fairy tales. Sixteen tales are retold with a new perspective.

Politics, the Law, and Policy

920   ACKER, JOAN. 1989. *Doing Comparable Worth: Gender, Class, and Pay Equity*. Philadelphia: Temple University Press.
An ethnographic study of the state of Oregon's attempt to evaluate state employees' occupational positions and remuneration in order to remedy pay inequities between male and female employees. Although unions resisted wage redistribution and managers manipulated figures in evaluating jobs, gender based pay inequities were identified. Acker deftly shows how seemingly objective technical measurement scales can be turned into political tools to thwart pay equity along gender lines. Feminist activists and union women are credited with achieving a partial victory after an initial defeat in their efforts to advance the concept and practice of comparable worth evaluations. This book was the winner of the 1989 Jessie Bernard Award from the American Sociological Association.

921   BERGMANN, BARBARA. 1986. *The Economic Emergence of Women*. New York: Basic Books.
Bergmann addresses the question of how to achieve sex equality in the work place, home, parenting, and other realms. Policy recommendations are well thought out and clearly stated. It is hard to ignore the message of this book.

922   BLUM, LINDA M. 1991. *Between Feminism and Labor: The Significance of the Comparable Worth Movement*. Berkeley: University of California Press.
Blum provides a historical context for studying grass roots efforts of the comparable worth movement. She uses two case studies from California which integrate class and gender concerns. The inclusion of comparable worth policies into feminist politics is important because it incorporates a working-class issue into a movement that is often accused of being middle-class. The long-term emphasis on affirmative action has often meant that middle-class women were able to move into positions typically held by middle-class men, but comparable worth re-evaluates and raises the value of work that is primarily done by women who are not managers and professionals. Blum argues that the comparable worth movement enhances and enlarges the women's movement.

923   CARABILLO, TONI and JUDITH MEULI. 1988. *The Feminization of Power*.
       Arlington, VA: The Fund for the Feminist Majority.
Carabillo and Meuli have been activists in the women's movement since 1967
and, at the time of this writing, were officers of the Fund for the Feminist
Majority, a feminist political organization headed by Eleanor Smeal (former
national president of NOW). Carabillo and Meuli provide an overview of the
political power structure in the United States, women in public office, feminist
initiatives on the political level, and individual brief descriptive pieces of
women legislators beginning with Jeannette Rankin (the first, in 1916) to current members. Appointed women, state politicians, and national woman's
rights leaders of the past (Sojourner Truth, Elizabeth Cady Stanton, Susan B.
Anthony, Carrie Chapman Catt, Jane Addams, Margaret Sanger, Alice Paul, and
Eleanor Roosevelt) are also profiled to show the wide range of contributions
women have made in the course of American politics.

924   CARD, EMILY. 1980. "Women, Housing Access and Mortgage Credit."
       Signs: Journal of Women in Culture and Society 5:215–219.
An examination of the ways the Equal Credit Opportunity Act have affected
women's ability to get credit. Past practices are discussed, particularly those
that created barriers to women becoming homeowners.

925   CHARLTON, SUE ELLEN M., JANA EVERETT, and KATHLEEN STAUDT, eds.
       1989. *Women, The State, and Development*. Albany: State University of
       New York Press.
The role of policy on the state level and the ideologies which define gender are
the issues covered in this collection of articles. The articles focus on questions
such as how much power the state should have over people's lives, the boundaries between the public and private, who has the right to determine the lines
separating women's right to privacy over their reproductive lives and the interest of the state in creating policy for the social good of all.

926   COOLE, DIANA. 1988. *Women in Political Theory: From Ancient
       Misogyny to Contemporary Feminism*. Boulder, CO: Lynne Reinner
       Publishers.
Political theory has focused on the participation of men, often leaving women
out all together. In this book, Coole brings women into the center of political
thought by examining the history of women's erasure from the political arena.

927   CRITES, LAURA L. and WINIFRED L. HEPPERLE, eds. 1987. *Women, the
       Courts, and Equality*. Newbury Park, CA: Sage.
An investigation into whether judges in courts of law are affected by tradi-
tional beliefs about gender in making their rulings with regard to women.
The articles in this anthology find the Courts are gender biased by tradition-
al gender expectations. The book is divided into four sections: Women's
Rights and the Supreme Court; Women as Victims; Women as Judges,
Lawyers, Administrators, and Jurors; Overcoming Gender Bias in the Courts.

928 DECROW, KAREN. 1975. *Sexist Justice*. New York: Random House/Vintage
Books.

Karen DeCrow is a lawyer and former president of the National Organization
for Women. In this book she presents a feminist analysis of the legal and political system. Specific examples of sexism in the government are provided, and
extensive coverage is given to the Fourteenth Amendment, the Equal Rights
Amendment, and abortion laws.

929 FREEMAN, JO. 1980. "Women and Urban Policy." *Signs: Journal of
Women in Culture and Society* 5:4–21.

Freeman makes the case that urban areas create special problems for women
with housing being a primary consideration. Further, she finds a need for a
new way to organize work to allow women more autonomy and freedom to
select hours that fit with other demands on their time. Suggestions the author
offers are four day weeks, flex time, and part time work.

930 GELB, JOYCE. 1989. *Feminism and Politics: A Comparative Perspective*.
Berkeley: University of California Press.

A comparative analysis of feminism and the women's movement in the United
States, Britain, and Sweden. The findings show the autonomy of the U.S. movement allows it greater freedom to impact the political process than the Left-
identified feminist movement in Britain. Additionally, the more heterogeneous
and less ideologically oriented U.S. movement has experienced greater
increases in size and has had a stronger impact on the populace. In Sweden,
an all-encompassing state which promotes equality has tempered the rise of a
feminist presence, particularly in the electoral/political arena.

931 GELB, JOYCE and MARIAN LEIF PALLEY. 1979. "Women and Interest
Group Politics: A Comparative Analysis of Federal Decision-Making."
Journal of Politics 41 (May):362–392.

Gelb and Palley report on their study of the degree of success feminist groups
achieve in changing government policies. Their findings show the importance
of having broad based support, a compelling issue, and a high level of cooper-
ation from various sectors of society.

932 GOLDSTEIN, LESLIE FRIEDMAN. 1994. *Contemporary Cases in Women's
Rights*. Madison: University of Wisconsin Press.

A collection of groundbreaking recent court decisions that affect women.
Abortion, sexual harassment, rape, surrogate motherhood, pornography, and
custody rights are examined for legal and social perspectives through excerpts
of the U.S. courts.

933 GREGORY, JEANNE. 1986. *Sex, Race, and the Law: Legislating for
Equality*. Newbury Park, CA: Sage Publications.

This book is a good source for learning about the issues and problems embedded in equal rights legislation from a legal perspective. The major focus of this
work is employment provisions, although other areas are addressed.

934   HARRISON, CYNTHIA. 1989. *On Account of Sex: The Politics of Women's Issues, 1945–1968*. Berkeley: University of California Press.
A good reference source for legislators, historians, political scientists, and Women's Studies scholars who are interested in understanding the ways public policy has been shaped in a feminist direction.

935   HARTMANN, SUSAN M. 1989. *From Margin to Mainstream: American Women and Politics Since 1960*. New York: Alfred A. Knopf.
A chronicle of how American women moved from the margins of the political system in the 1960s to the mainstream of political activism by the 1980s. The reactivation of the women's movement is credited with pressuring the government to address issues related to women's needs, such as ERA, child care, abortion, and the appointment of women to public office. Organizations on the left and right of the political spectrum are included, as are the effects of class and race on women's political behavior. From campaigning for issues to voter registration and women running for office, this book demonstrates that feminist activism has played a vital role in shaping the electoral process and political agenda over the last twenty-five years.

936   HILL, M. ANNE and MARK R. KILLINSWORTH, eds. 1989. *Comparable Worth: Analysis and Evidence*. Ithaca, NY: ILR Press.
A compilation of data and knowledge which can serve as a source book for those interested in knowing the background arguments for and against comparable worth.

937   KANN, MARK E. 1983. "Legitimation, Consent, and Anti-feminism." *Women and Politics* 3 (March):1–19.
Kahn traces the history of contract theory and finds that the idea of a social contract was never one developed with the idea of including women as equal participants in the contract. The author of this article finds this exclusion to have been true for early philosophers as well as the signers of the U.S. Constitution.

938   KEYFITZ, NATHAN. 1981. "Equity Between the Sexes: The Pension Problem." *Journal of Policy Analysis and Management* 1 (Sept.):133–135.
The issue of pension policy has found its way into the sex equity debate and the findings and implications are rather startling. The feminist position on this issue is that policies surrounding pensions (and social security as well) are based on a male model of working life. Pensions are based on years of employment and women have historically spent a significant number of their working lives out of the paid employment field. No money is contributed to women's pension for the work they do in the home, and thus, women do not build up a pension for their retirement years anywhere near the extent that men do. Pensions are also based on amounts earned, once again leaving women in a lower payout level in old age. The proposal on how to address this situation, including the suggestion of giving both sexes the same expected lifetime benefit for a specified amount of initial payments is debated.

939 KLEIN, ETHEL. 1984. *Gender Politics: From Consciousness to Mass Politics.* Cambridge, MA: Harvard Press.

A well-documented source for examining women's role in the political process and the ways women's participation are changing. Contains public opinion surveys, census data, and public policy information. Klein asks two questions: what are the common concerns that mobilize women, and how do these concerns shape political activism.

940 LEVENESS, FRANK P. and JANE P. SWEENEY, eds. 1987. *Women Leaders in Contemporary U.S. Politics.* Boulder, CO: Lynne Rienner Publishers.

LeVeness and Sweeney discuss the careers of nine women holding important political positions. The authors acknowledge that women are rarely found in strategic elected or appointed offices in the U.S. political system, but for those women who do succeed, they are interested in uncovering what factors contribute to that occurrence. The nine women, which include Shirley Chisholm and Sandra Day O'Connor, tell us how they chose the path they did. The authors then attempt to explain what other factors intervened to increase their chances of success.

941 LEWIS, JANE, ed. 1983. *Women's Welfare: Women's Rights.* London: Croom Helm.

Collection of essays on how social policy in family and employment practices affect women. Good descriptions and analysis that refute many of the stereotypes common in American society about women and poverty.

942 MANDLE, JOAN D. 1986. "The Women's Movement and Electoral Politics: Where Do We Go From Here?" *Socialist Review* 16 (March):25–39.

What happens to a feminist candidate's ideals when that candidate has to appeal to a wide range of voters? Mandle discusses this risk as the women's movement increasingly puts its resources into political races. She recommends the movement gain the support of multicultural women in order to provide a wider base to retain their electability potential.

943 MCGRATH, WILMA E. and JOHN W. SOULE. 1974. "Rocking the Cradle or Rocking the Boat: Women at the 1972 Democratic National Convention." *Social Science Quarterly* 55 (June):141–150.

A description and analysis of women's role at the 1972 Democratic Convention, the effects of their presence on rules of delegates, and the ideological differences between the women and men present.

944 MUELLER, CAROL. 1982. "Feminism and the New Women in Public Office." *Women and Politics* 2 (Sept.):7–21.

A look at women legislators and public officials which reveals that there has been an increase in the numbers of female elected officials who can be defined as feminist and who support feminist legislation.

945   ———, ed. 1988. *The Politics of the Gender Gap: The Social Construction of Political Influence*. Newbury Park, CA: Sage Publications.

There are various paths women desiring political power can take to achieve that goal. This book describes those processes within the electoral system. The expectation of a continuing, even increasing, gender gap in voting behavior is predicted. The effects on women's political influence, though, requires more strategic planning than merely greater numbers at the polls.

946   NAFFINE, NGAIRE. 1991. *Law and the Sexes: Explorations in Feminist Jurisprudence*. New York: Allen & Unwin.

With the rise of women lawyers and the increase in legal challenges raised by the women's movement, the author of this book surmises it is time to examine the legal system itself. Naffine applies a critical look at legal studies and feminist jurisprudence and finds that the legal tradition represents the model of white middle-class men. Gender issues brought before the courts are, therefore, lacking in neutrality. The author argues that gender, race, and class equity require philosophical changes in the legal system before objective decisions can be applied in court cases.

947   NICHOLAS, SUSAN CARY, ALICE M. PRICE, and RACHEL RUBIN. 1986. *Rights and Wrongs: Women's Struggle for Legal Equality, Second Edition*. New York: Feminist Press at the City University of New York.

A guide to women and the law which reveals how the law affects women's private and work related lives. New material in this edition includes a discussion of the failure of the Equal Rights Amendment, sexual harassment, domestic violence, sex discrimination, affirmative action, comparable worth, and the growing numbers of women in poverty.

948   O'BRIEN, DAVID M. 1986. *Storm Center: The Supreme Court in American Politics*. New York: W. W. Norton.

A narrative of the history, structure, processes, and landmark cases of the Supreme Court. Includes Webster v. Reproductive Health Services (1989), Roe v. Wade (1973), Brown v. Board of Education (1954), Texas v. Johnson (1989), and many more.

949   REMICK, HELEN, ed. 1984. *Comparable Worth and Wage Discrimination: Technical Possibilities and Political Realities*. Philadelphia: Temple University Press.

Background information and some suggested solutions on wage discrimination affecting women.

950   RIDDIOUGH, CHRISTINE R. 1981. "Women, Feminism and the 1980 Elections." *Socialist Review* 56:37–54.

A report on the effects of feminist political organizing and women candidates in the 1980 general election in the United States. Riddiough presents interesting analyses to understand what led to the outcome of that election and what needs to be done to change the direction of conservative politics that emerged.

951 SLIPMAN, SUE. 1986. *Helping Ourselves to Power: A Handbook for Women on the Skills of Public Life*. New York: Pergamon Press.
A practical manual for women interested in challenging the current social structure by becoming part of it to change it. Many of the examples Slipman uses are from Britain, but the general understanding of skill development for public office applies to the United States as well. The author begins this guide with a discussion of why women need power and ends it with strategies for gaining power.

952 WARE, SUSAN. 1981. *Beyond Suffrage: Women in the New Deal*. Cambridge, MA: Harvard University Press.
What happened to women activists after the achievement of suffrage in 1920? This book looks at women's contributions to New Deal policies during the depression years of the 1930s. With roots going back to the suffrage campaign, other reform movements and social welfare activities, a network of women influenced government policy during this era. The focus of this work is how that network came into being, and the ways it contributed to social welfare initiatives as well as New Deal politics in general. A group profile and short individual biographies of the twenty-eight women making up this distinctive network of political activists are included.

953 WITT, LINDA, KAREN M. PAGET, and GLENNA MATTHEWS. 1993. *Running as a Woman: Gender and Power in American Politics*. New York: Free Press.
The authors of this book chronicle the political progress of women from the time Jeannette Rankin became the first woman elected to Congress shortly before women obtained the right to vote up to the 1992 elections when women representatives in the Senate tripled (from two to six) and increased their figures in the House from twenty-nine to forty-eight. The televised Thomas/Hill Senate hearings which dramatically revealed the all male bastion of power and the ill treatment women could expect from them is cited as the catalyst for political action by women, particularly the record number of women running for office. The authors pool their expertise—political science, history and journalism—to piece together women politicians' stories of their experiences in a readable account of how 'political woman' arrived.

954 WOLGAST, ELIZABETH. 1988. *Equality and the Rights of Women*. Ithaca, NY: Cornell University Press.
A general discussion of women in society, what equality would consist of, and what issues are included in the concept of women's rights. A particular focus of this book is on affirmative action.

Sexism, Discrimination, and Anti-Feminism

955   BIRD, CAROLINE (WITH SARA WELLES BRILLER). 1971. *Born Female: The
       High Cost of Keeping Women Down*. New York: Pocket Books.
This is a revised edition of a 1968 book in which Bird charges sexism as the
cause for women being underprivileged. Although it may seem ancient to people in the 1990s, her illustrations provide a look at the way things were in the
late 1960s and why the contemporary women's movement expressed so much
anger in that emergent stage. Examples include the requirement of higher
marks for females to enter college than for males; a wage disparity of almost 50
percent for the same job; and the practice of male college graduates taking
aptitude tests for job interviews while female graduates took typing tests.

956   BLEE, KATHLEEN M. 1987. "Gender, Ideology, and the Role of Women in
       the 1920s Klan Movement." *Sociological Spectrum* 7:73–97.
The female branch of the Ku Klux Klan, Women of the Ku Klux Klan (WKKK),
consisted of white, Protestant, United States born women who were conservative, racist, and—supporters of women's rights in political and economic
life. In this article, Blee examines the development of an ideology of gender
equality in the 1920s Klan movement which was full of contradictions and
limitations.

957   BRADY, DAVID W. and KENT L. TEDIN. 1976. "Ladies in Pink: Religion and
       Political Ideology in the Anti-ERA Movement." *Social Science Quarterly*
       56:564–575.
This was an early study of social characteristics of anti-ERA activists. Brady and
Tedin identify religion and family as the sources of anti-feminist orientations in
the women they observed and interviewed.

958   BROWN, RUTH MURRAY. 1984. "In Defense of Traditional Values: The
       Anti-feminist Movement." *Marriage and Family Review* 7
       (Sept.):19–35.
This study found that anti-ERA activists were conservative Catholics, fundamentalist Protestants, Orthodox Jews, and Mormons. They also tended to be
less educated, more rural, and older than pro-ERA activists. This study consisted of a questionnaire that was sent to pro and anti factions in Oklahoma. In
answer to the question "How important is religion in your life," 96 percent of
anti-ERA activists said "very important" compared to only 53 percent of pro-
ERA activists. Other reported beliefs show antis feel the husband should be
head of the family, women should not be employed, and women's responsibilities lie with the home and family. In addition, antis disapproved of alcohol,
smoking, drugs, and sexual permissiveness.

959   BURRIS, VAL. 1983. "Who Opposed the ERA? An Analysis of the Social
       Basis of Anti-feminism." *Social Science Quarterly* 64 (June):305–317.
In this article Burris locates three reasons for opposition to the Equal Rights
Amendment: the lack of making ERA a priority among non-feminist political

groups; geographic differences in support of women's equality; and the growing strength of the Right Wing backlash in the country as a whole.

960   CONOVER, PAMELA JOHNSTON and VIRGINIA GRAY. 1983. *Feminism and
       the New Right: Conflict Over the American Family*. New York: Praeger.
An exploration of the conflict over abortion and the ERA focusing on the New
Right and other anti-feminist groups that organized in the late 1970s around
their opposition to the feminist agenda. Conover and Gray show how this
backlash emerged after gains were made by the women's movement. Since
that time there has been a continuing struggle over the role of women and the
place of the family in society. Both the feminist and pro-family movements are
analyzed from the perspective of social movement organizing and interest
group theory. Issues, symbols, and forms of mobilization are also discussed.

961   DIAMOND, SARA. 1990. *Spiritual Warfare: The Politics of the Christian
       Right*. Boston. South End Press.
To know more about where the Religious Right is coming from in its opposition to feminism, read this book. Diamond shows the tradition, thinking, motivation, and political clout the Christian Right has gained throughout the 1980s.

962   EISENSTEIN, ZILLAH R. 1982. "The Sexual Politics of the New Right:
       Understanding the 'Crisis of Liberalism' for the 1980's." Pp. 77–98 in
       Feminist Theory: A Critique of Ideology, edited by Nannerl O. Keohane,
       Michelle Z. Rosaldo, and Barbara C. Gelphi. Chicago: University of
       Chicago Press.
In this article Eisenstein analyzes the problems a powerful Political Right can
bring, what that means for liberal politics, and the possibilities for containment
of the anti-woman agenda the Right proposes.

963   GORDON, LINDA and ALLEN HUNTER. 1977. "Sex, Family and the New
       Right: Anti-feminism as a Political Force." *Radical America* 11/12
       (November):8–25.
The authors of this article argue forcefully for the position that the New Right
is not just a backlash against feminism and gay liberation. Gordon and Hunter
identify the attack on the culture and politics of sex and family as a reassertion
of the patriarchal family and male dominance.

964   HOFF, JOAN. 1991. *Unequal Before the Law: A Legal History of U.S.
       Women*. New York: New York University Press.
A look at the status of women in the legal system of the United States throughout its history. The author shows that women have never had equality and full
citizenship under the law. From the American Revolution to the present, the
Constitution has failed to include women on an equal basis with men.

965   KLATCH, REBECCA E. 1987. *Women of the New Right*. Philadelphia:
       Temple University Press.
This work contributes to research on New Right politics and the women involved
in this movement. Scholarly research in the form of participant-observation,

interviews, and content analysis of publications form the basis of Klatch's conclusion that Right Wing women are not homogeneous. The author shows that there are two major branches of followers, social conservative women who are part of the religious right which focuses on the differences between women and men, and laissez-faire women who adopt a classical liberalist position based on the similarities between the sexes. The author claims that even though social conservative women are opposed to feminist principles, their belief system places them in a position of supporting their definition of women's interest, whereas laissez-faire women fail to recognize their interests as women.

966   KRYZANOWSKI, LAWRENCE and ELIZABETH BERTIN-BOUSSU. 1981. "Equal Access to Credit: Lenders' Attitudes Toward an Applicant's Sex and Marital Status." *International Journal of Women's Studies* 4:213–232.

Although not an issue today as it once was, this work brings to mind the kinds of discriminatory treatment women have historically (and sometimes still do) receive at the hands of lenders. Marital status is the second variable of interest in this study.

967   MARSHALL, SUSAN E. 1985. "Ladies Against Women: Mobilization Dilemmas of Anti-feminist Movements." *Social Problems* 32 (April):348–362.

A comparison of the anti-suffrage movement in 1912–1918 with the anti-ERA movement of 1972–1982. Marshall looks at the resource mobilization potential in these two periods. She finds that both movements sharply defined themselves as different from feminist activists. This created a dilemma for them as they moved into the public/political arena to express their opposition to women's equal rights.

968   MARSHALL, SUSAN E. and ANTHONY M. ORUM. 1986. "Opposition Then and Now: Countering Feminism in the Twentieth Century." *Research in Politics and Society* 2:13–34.

A comparison of anti-feminist social movements during the early twentieth century suffrage campaign and the contemporary women's movement of the 1970s and 1980s. Anti-feminist ideology, tactics, membership, and organizational structures are analyzed within the framework of the women's movement of each time period. In examining historical documents, Marshall and Orum found resource mobilization concepts to apply, as well as pressure effects from public opinion and symbolic meanings.

969   MORRISON, TONI, ed. 1992. *Race-ing Justice, En-gendering Power: Essays on Anita Hill, Clarence Thomas, and The Construction of Social Reality*. New York: Pantheon Press.

Focusing on Anita Hill's testimony at the U.S. Senate Judiciary Committee's confirmation hearings of Clarence Thomas to the Supreme Court, the articles in this collection bring critical analysis to the process and outcome of those hearings. The sexual harassment charges she brought to the committee and the treatment she received there were catalysts for renewed activism among feminist supporters, particularly in the political arena. Contributors include Cornel West, Patricia Williams, Nellie McKay, Kimberle Crenshaw, and Paula Giddings.

970   MUELLER, CAROL. 1983. "In Search of a Constituency for the New Religious Right." *The Public Opinion Quarterly* 47 (June):213–229.
Is there really a moral "majority?" Mueller looks at this question in relationship to the opposition developed in the 1970s to women's liberation, gay and lesbian rights, and reproductive freedom. Responses to survey questions from the General Social Surveys of 1972–1980 are compared to responses on questions of spending priorities. Results show no conservative trend on feminist issues. Mueller concludes that differences on these issues are not new, they have existed since the early part of this century.

971   PHELPS, TIMOTHY M. and HELEN WINTERNITZ. 1992. *Capitol Games: Clarence Thomas, Anita Hill and the Story of a Supreme Court Nomination*. New York: HarperCollins Publishers.
Because the Supreme Court confirmation hearing of Clarence Thomas led to widespread viewing of a televised debate on sexual harassment, research on this hearing has become part of the understanding of racism, feminism, and the women's movement in the 1990s. The treatment Professor Anita Hill received from an all-white all-male panel after filing charges of sexual harassment by Judge Thomas led to more women running for office than at any other time in history. Four new women senators were elected, two of whom would ascend to the Senate Judiciary Committee in order to participate in future confirmation hearings. The hearing itself and subsequent opinion polls revealed the widely divergent views on sexual harassment held by women and men, as well as the race loyalty towards Thomas (but not to Hill) that predominated in the black community. Filings of sexual harassment charges increased and discussions were held in the mass media which legitimated the issue as one that would have to be taken more seriously in the future. This book provides the background story of the Committee, factions, motives, and fears that underlie this infamous event.

972   RUTH, SHEILA. 1983. "A Feminist Analysis of the New Right." *Women's Studies International Forum* 6:345–351.
Ruth argues that the family movement of the 1970s—including the New Right, the Religious Right, and the Moral Majority—used religion as a cover for their true leanings of militarism, patriarchy, and fascism.

Religion and Spirituality

973   ANDERSON, SHERRY RUTH and PATRICIA HOPKINS. 1991. *The Feminine Face of God: The Unfolding of the Sacred in Women*. New York: Bantam Books.
This book presents sensitive portraits of the meaning and effects of leading spiritual lives. Presented within a feminist perspective, the work is based on

over 100 interviews of women in the United States who are involved in spiritual renewal activities.

974   ATKINS, CLARISSA W., CONSTANCE H. BUCHANAN, and MARGARET R.
       MILES. 1987. *Shaping New Vision: Gender and Values in American Culture, Volume II of the Harvard Women's Studies in Religion Series.* Ann Arbor: UMI Research Press.
The impact of religious thought on the meaning of gender and values is analyzed in this work. Of particular interest are the interpretations the authors provide of issues raised by the women's movement.

975   BRANDE, ANN. 1989. *Radical Spirits: Spiritualism and Woman's Rights in Nineteenth Century America.* Boston: Beacon Press.
This book reveals that spiritualism played a part in the formation of the early woman's rights movement of the nineteenth century. Brande's analysis is lucid and her research is solid. It is surprising that it has taken so long for the connection of last century's feminist spiritualism to emerge since the connection with the contemporary women's culture is very strong. Interesting topic on a not often thought about component of women's activism in that era.

976   DEXTER, MIRIAM ROBBINS. 1990. *Whence the Goddesses: A Source Book.* New York: Pergamon Press.
This is a book about the history of goddesses, including the characteristics, powers, and functions among them. The focus is on ancient Europe and those areas in which Indo-European peoples resided.

977   GADON, ELINOR W. 1989. *The Once and Future Goddess.* San Francisco: Harper & Row.
Gadon delves into ways of reconstructing human relations to allow people to feel empowered over their life direction. A reasonable prescription and an interesting discussion along the way.

978   GIMBUTAS, MARITA. 1989. *The Language of the Goddess.* San Francisco: Harper & Row.
A good source for learning more about the Goddesses that were part of the culture of prehistoric Europe.

979   GRANT, JACQUELYN. 1990. "Civil Rights Women: A Source for Doing Womanist Theology." Pp. 39–50 in *Women in the Civil Rights Movement: Trailblazers and Torchbearers, 1941–1965,* edited by Vickie L. Crawford, Jacqueline Anne Rouse, and Barbara Woods. Brooklyn, NY: Carlson Publishing.
An exploration of the religious and spiritual influences of women involved in the civil rights movement. Grant looks at individual women's attachments to religious institutions and their religious philosophy.

980   LEVACK, BRIAN P., ed. 1993. *Articles on Witchcraft, Magic and Demonology*. Hamden, CT: Garland Publishers.
This is a twelve volume anthology of scholarly articles from contributors in the fields of history, legal studies, psychology, anthropology, sociology, art history, and literature. The articles focus on the historical process of witch-hunting in Europe and America between 1450 and 1750 when 100,000 (or more) women were tried as witches. Many approaches are taken in an effort to explain why these persecutions occurred. Two volumes within this series are of particular interest to Women's Studies scholars in the United States: Witchcraft in Colonial America and Witchcraft, Women, and Society.

981   LORENTZEN, ROBIN. 1991. *Women in the Sanctuary Movement*. Philadelphia: Temple University Press.
Women involved in religious-based political movements, such as the sanctuary movement, played a role in developing a feminist activist consciousness. Lorentzen examines that connection in this book, along with the history of activism in the sanctuary movement. The tensions between women and men in the sanctuary movement comprise an interesting segment of this work. The author uses interview material to show how mainly white, middle-class homemakers and nuns mobilize themselves and others to intervene on behalf of refugees.

982   PLASKOW, JUDITH and CAROL P. CHRIST, eds. 1989. *Weaving the Visions: New Patterns in Feminist Spirituality*. San Francisco, CA: Harper and Row.
This book is similar to an earlier book by the same authors, *Womanspirit Rising* (1979), and covers many previously raised themes in woman centered spirituality, e.g., personal experience, nature, and the importance of connections to others. In this sequel there are more minority voices which represents greater diversity of religious beliefs and ethnic groups than the first book. Contributors cover both traditional and non-traditional religions, including Judaism, Christianity, Black Christianity, Native American beliefs, Wicca, Haitian Voodoo, and Asian-American spiritualities.

983   RABUZZI, KATHRYN ALLEN. 1988. *Motherself: A Mythic Analysis of Motherhood*. Bloomington: Indiana University Press.
A book on women's spirituality focusing on the mother. In this work motherhood is not idealized as a way of confining women but is presented as a replacement for androcentric myths. In choosing gynocentric myths based on a model of the Goddess, Rabuzzi claims women will achieve a state of inner peace and power.

984   RUTH, SHEILA. 1994. *Take Back the Light: A Feminist Reclamation of Spirituality and Religion*. Lanham, MD: Rowman & Littlefield.
Sheila Ruth, a pioneer in the field of Women's Studies, writes about feminism and spirituality. She calls for feminist women to reclaim, in their own image and vision, religion in their life.

985   SPRETNAK, CHARLENE, ed. 1982. *The Politics of Women's Spirituality: Essays on the Rise of Spiritual Power within the Feminist Movement*. Garden City, NY: Anchor Press/Doubleday.
A collection of essays that are active, revolutionary, and politically aware. Contributors cover a wide range of issues within a spiritual framework which represents their attitude toward life. Part One is titled Discovering a History of Power and includes a section on "What the Goddess Means to Women." Part Two, titled Manifesting Personal Power, covers consciousness, energy, action, and self-images of strength. Part Three, Transforming the Political, is concerned with the unity of politics and spirituality and applications of spirituality as a political force. Half of the selections are considered classics and the other half are new essays. Contributors include Margot Adler, Phyllis Chesler, Carol P. Christ, Mary Daly, June Jordan, Robin Morgan, Marge Piercy, Adrienne Rich, Ntozake Shange, Starhawk, Gloria Steinem, and many others.

986   STAMBAUGH, SARA. 1988. *The Witch and the Goddess in the Stories of Isak Dinensen: A Feminist Reading*. Ann Arbor: UMI Research Press.
Stambaugh presents an alternative to fundamentalist Christianity which she argues is detrimental to human society and particularly hostile to women. Instead, she proposes Isak Dinensen's ideas of a deity that shows a strong feminine side but who represents women and men equally.

987   STARHAWK. 1982. *Dreaming the Dark: Magic, Sex and Politics*. Boston: Beacon Press.
Starhawk is a witch who writes of the Goddess and a spirituality that can lead us to a better world, one without an ethos of competition, winning, and controlling other people and the world around us. By combining feminism, paganism, and politics, the author reveals ways of creating anti-authoritarian structures and social processes that lead to power within ourselves rather than power over others.

988   ———. 1989. *The Spiral Dance: A Rebirth of the Ancient Religion of the Great Goddess, Tenth Anniversary Edition*. New York: HarperCollins Publishers.
When this book was first published, it transformed the women's spirituality movement. Starhawk presented information which defined witchcraft as a Goddess-worshiping religion. Further she analyzed the growth, suppression, and modern day re-emergence of this female centered religion. In this anniversary edition she discusses how changes in the last decade have affected her original thought.

989   STONE, MERLIN. 1991. *Ancient Mirrors of Womanhood: A Treasury of Goddess and Heroine Lore From Around the World*. Boston: Beacon Press.
As in her first edition of this book (1979), Stone is interested in reclaiming the Goddess tradition which reveals women as strong and powerful people. Drawing upon historical and archaeological evidence of Goddess worship, she

makes the case that ancient people in diverse cultures believed that the Goddess was the creator of the world. Including evidence from every continent across race and ethnic boundaries, Goddess worship is revealed as a way of seeing and being that exists within a person and that expresses itself as an inclusive process of interconnection. The author argues that Goddess reclamation, which is tied to the re-emergence of feminist thought and the growth of a women's spirituality movement, leads to an understanding that all creatures, nature, and people belong to the same family of life on earth.

990   WESSINGER, CATHERINE, ed. 1993. *Women's Leadership in Marginal Religions: Explorations Outside the Mainstream*. Champaign/Urbana: University of Illinois Press.

This anthology examines women's leadership roles in the religions of the Shakers, Pentecostalism, Spiritualism, Christian Science, Theosophicalism, New Thought, Unity, Hindu, Buddhism, African-American spirituality, the Women-Church movement among Roman Catholics, Mormonism, and the feminist spirituality movement. The articles cover the nineteenth and twentieth centuries and focus on the factors within these religious groups that have supported women taking leadership positions. A major theme of this work is that religions that have emphasized spiritual inspiration have been open to allowing women a leadership role and, concomitantly, as women became empowered within these religions, they were able to express their desires for equality. Contributors come from the academic disciplines of history, folk lore, and theology.

6

Guide to the Sources

Introduction

In this, the last chapter of this collection, the listings consist of referencing information to assist students of the women's movement in their search for data sources. The first category, **Bibliographies**, shows where to begin to look for books, articles, and newspaper clippings. Some of the bibliographies are specific to a particular topic or social group; others are generalized collections of materials related to women and women's interests.

Funding Sources is included to assist students and researchers in finding the funding necessary to do in-depth research on women. Many of these listings are specific allocations for women researchers.

The selections under **Library Collections, Archives, Catalogs, and Museums** advise where to look for primary data. Personal papers, photographs, organizational archives, historic sites, and the finding materials to locate these sources are found in the materials listed in this section. The next category, **Primary Documents**, contains published sources of primary materials, such as letters, diaries, and speeches of women activists.

Reference Materials is a generic term which includes dictionaries, encyclopedias, online resources, indexes, abstracts, workshops, directories, and general reference sources. All of these references provide aids to the research and learning process.

The last category is a listing of **Anthologies and Texts**. The anthologies shown here are collections of writings that tend to cover many areas of feminism and the women's movement. Those that focus on only one topic can be found listed in that topical category rather than in the anthologies listing. The texts are those which have been specifically designed to be used in the classroom as an introductory text book, mainly for courses on Women's Studies or Sex and Gender. These two sources, anthologies and texts, cover feminist material in a thorough manner. Many of them provide a substantial record of the origin and transformation of the women's movement over time.

Bibliographies

991 ADDIS, PATRICIA K. 1983. *Through a Women's I: An Annotated Bibliography of American Women's Autobiographical Writings, 1946–1976*. Metuchen, NJ: Scarecrow Press.
A good resource for locating autobiographical works by a wide variety of American women. The authors listed in this reference work were published after World War II up until the mid-1970s.

992 BALLOU, PATRICIA K. 1986. *Women: A Bibliography of Bibliographies, Second Edition*. Boston: G. K. Hall.
The bibliographies listed cover a broad range of geographical areas and topics related to women. Included are sections on feminism, activism, and various categories of women such as lesbian, black, elderly, and working-class.

993 BUHLE, MARI JO. 1983. *Women and the American Left: A Guide to Sources*. Boston: G. K. Hall.
Socialist feminism and women's activism in the Left in the United States is the focus of this bibliographical sourcebook and research guide.

994 CABELLO-ARGANDONA, ROBERTO JUAN GOMEZ-QUINONES, and PATRICIA HERRERA DURAN. 1976. *The Chicana: A Comprehensive Bibliographic Study*. Los Angeles: Aztlan Publications.
A listing of nearly 500 articles, books, and periodicals on Chicanas. Much of the material is on general topics of Chicanas in the United States, folk culture, family, history, politics, labor, and economics. Some of the references are annotated, but most are not. One section is on the Chicana and women's liberation.

995 COMMON WOMEN COLLECTIVE. 1976. *Women in U.S. History: An Annotated Bibliography*. Cambridge, MA: Common Women Collective.
This reference work provides a broad range of information on the literature of women in the United States, particular ethnic and racial groups of women, autobiographies, and issues of sexuality. Social reform efforts constitute one section which covers abolition, feminism, suffrage, and temperance.

996 DAVIS, LENWOOD G. 1975. *The Black Woman in American Society: A Selected Annotated Bibliography*. Boston: G. K. Hall.
Includes reports, pamphlets, government documents and speeches, major collections on black history, national organizations, black women newspaper editors, publishers and elected officials. One section provides statistics for black women in rural and urban areas. Strong on early nineteenth century black women. All entries are annotated.

997 DUPREE, SHERRY SHERROD. 1993. *The African-American Holiness Pentecostal Movement: An Annotated Bibliography*. Hamden, CT: Garland Publishing.
A comprehensive guide to the African-American Pentecostal church in the

United States. This bibliography is a reference text and an introduction to this religious movement and women's part in it. Entries include organizations, individuals, gospel groups, singers, books, articles, interviews, newspaper articles, and church documents.

998   FRANKLIN, MARGARET LADD, ed. 1975. *The Case for Women Suffrage: A Bibliography*. New York: National College Equal Suffrage League (reprint: Washington, D.C.: Zenger Publishing Co.).
Listing of congressional documents, books, leaflets, periodical articles, and suffrage journals. This is a thorough reference source for the suffrage movement up to 1913.

999   GARBER, LINDA, ed. 1993. *Lesbian Sources: A Bibliography of Periodical Articles 1970–1990*. New York: Garland Press.
Periodical articles from significant feminist and lesbian journals are indexed from the field of lesbian studies. This useful reference work includes some 3500 entries covering a broad range of lesbian concerns. The material is cross-referenced and cross-listed in more than 100 categories; however, the entries are not annotated and there is no subject index beyond the heading that the material is listed under. Chronological material is listed under the category of history which is broken down by century. Lesbian culture is covered as well as specific topics such as domestic partnership, lesbian identity, and Butch/Femme roles. Subject categories also include biographical and autobiographical articles.

1000 GOODFRIEND, JOYCE D. 1987. *The Published Diaries and Letters of American Women: An Annotated Bibliography*. Boston: G. K. Hall.
A collection of diaries, journals, and letters of mostly privileged American women. There are some selections of Jewish and black women, although Goodfriend notes that the overabundance of such works come from women with the leisure to write about their daily lives. However, efforts to diversify the collection are enhanced by the inclusion of a wide range in age, occupational, and regional groups. There are some seventeenth century entries, the eighteenth century is covered, and a good many are from the nineteenth century. Entries go up to the early 1980s. Most of the selections are from unknown women, however, there are some of well-known women, including abolitionist and suffragist activists Angelina and Sarah Grimké.

1001 GREEN, RAYNA. 1983. *Native American Women: A Contextual Bibliography*. Bloomington: Indiana University Press.
Books, articles, dissertations, and bibliographies. An excellent history of the literature on Native American women is found in the preface. All entries are fully annotated.

1002 GREENWOOD, HAZEL, ed. 1976. *The Equal Rights Amendment: A Bibliographic Study*. Westport, CT: Greenwood Press.
Publications and resources pertaining to the Equal Rights Amendment prior to

1976. Some anti-ERA material is included, but the bibliography is focused on pro-ERA literature.

1003   HABER, BARBARA. 1978. *Women in America: A Guide to Books, 1963–1975*. Boston: G. K. Hall.
This annotated bibliography covers the years just preceding the emergence of the contemporary women's movement and the early years when much of the theoretical development was occurring. Haber does a good job of covering the classic works that came out of that time period and providing a thorough description of what these writings contain. The section on feminism includes developing feminist thought and activism within the different sectors of the movement. An appendix covering the years 1976–1979 was published through University of Illinois in 1981.

1004   HUMM, MAGGIE. 1987. *An Annotated Critical Bibliography of Feminist Criticism*. Boston: G. K. Hall.
In this work, Maggie Humm selects articles and books from England and the United States over the last twenty years which have strongly impacted feminist thought. There are over 800 annotations placed within eight categories: Theory and Sexual Politics; Literary Criticism; Sociology, Politics and Economics; Arts, Film, Theater, Media, Music; Psychology; History; Anthropology and Myth; Education and Women's Studies. Religion and women's spirituality are missing, however, the categories covered are well chosen and thorough.

1005   HUNTER, ALLEN and JAMES O'BRIEN. 1972. "Reading About the New Left." *Radical America* 6:73–94.
This is a brief bibliography of work, mostly produced in the 1960s, on the New Left, the student movement, and the Women's Liberation Movement.

1006   KEMMER, ELIZABETH J. 1977. *Rape and Rape Related Issues: An Annotated Bibliography*. New York: Garland Publishing.
Rape literature published between 1965 and 1976. Good introduction to the early foundation of rape crisis centers and the violence against women segment of the contemporary women's movement. All entries are thoroughly developed.

1007   KENNEDY, SUSAN ESTABROOK. 1981. *America's White Working-Class Women: A Historical Bibliography*. New York: Garland Publishing.
Six subject areas: general items, pre-industrial America; industrialized America; modern America; and recent America (post-1940). Over 1,000 entries that are annotated.

1008   KINNARD, CYNTHIA D. 1986. *Anti-feminism in American Thought: An Annotated Bibliography*. Boston: G. K. Hall.
While this bibliography is on anti-feminism rather than feminism or the women's movement, the annotations reveal the strength and rationale for resistance to women's efforts for change. Many of the arguments used against

suffrage during the nineteenth century were still being used in the 1980s against the Equal Rights Amendment. Kinnard maintains it is essential to know the resistance and to maintain pressure regardless of the political gains made because every time feminist activism declines, anti-feminism makes gains. Each section is prefaced with an introduction to the context of that subject matter.

1009   KRICHMAR, ALBERT. 1972. *The Women's Rights Movement in the United States 1848–1970: A Bibliography and Sourcebook*. Metuchen, NJ: Scarecrow Press.
This is a partially annotated bibliography of women's movement publications from 1848 to 1970 covering books, periodical articles, dissertations, pamphlets, and government documents from the Women's Bureau. Also included is a guide to the sources of manuscript collections which was gathered from the National Union Catalog of Manuscript Collections and inquiry replies from historical societies, and public, state, and academic libraries. There are separate sections in this reference work covering biography, women's liberation serial publications, and reference sources.

1010   ———. 1977. *The Women's Movement in the Seventies: An International English-Language Bibliography*. Metuchen, NJ: Scarecrow Press.
Picking up where he left off in his first volume on the women's movement, Krichmar provides a listing of publications from 1970 to 1976. There is a strong emphasis on periodical citations.

1011   LOEB, CATHERINE, SUSAN E. SEARING, and ESTHER F. STINEMAN. 1987. *Women's Studies: A Recommended Core Bibliography, 1980–1985*. Littleton, CO: Libraries Unlimited.
A thorough annotated bibliography covering the field of Women's Studies. This edition is a supplement to the 1979 publication under the same title. Sections on the women's movement, feminism, and Women's Studies periodicals are included.

1012   MAGGIORE, DOLORES, ed. 1992. *Lesbianism: An Annotated Bibliography and Guide to the Literature 1976–1991*. Metuchen, NJ: Scarecrow Press.
This is an update of a 1988 edition of this reference work. The new material is appended to reprints of previously printed entries. It is a useful reference tool providing annotated entries for books and articles on lesbianism covering a wide range of topics drawn from diverse sources. Lesbian topics include identity, history, aging, youth, minorities, coupling, mothering, custody cases, alcoholism, and heterosexism in theory and practice.

1013   MCCULLOUGH, RITA I., ed. 1991. *Sources: An Annotated Bibliography of Women's Issues*, Manchester, CT: Knowledge, Ideas & Trends, Inc.
An annotated bibliography on women's issues in the United States. Useful for Women's Studies on a wide array of areas, including reference information on the women's movement.

1014 MOORE, GLORIA and RONALD MOORE. 1986. *Margaret Sanger and the Birth Control Movement: A Bibliography, 1911–1984*. Metuchen, NJ: Scarecrow Press.

This bibliography was compiled from computer searches conducted between 1982 and 1984 under the subject headings of Margaret Sanger, Birth Control, and Contraception (history of). Additional references come from the New York Call, 1910–1916 (microfilm); 1953–1975 Population Council Annual Reports, and Woman Rebel (1914). The location of special collections are noted for American Birth Control League Papers (Houghton Library, Harvard University); Margaret Sanger Collection (Katharine Dexter McCormick Library, Planned Parenthood Federation of American, 810 Seventh Ave., New York City 10009); Margaret Sanger Papers (Library of Congress); Margaret Sanger Papers, Sophia Smith Collection (Smith College); Planned Parenthood Federation of America Papers, Sophia Smith Collection (Smith College).

1015 MULDOON, MAUREEN. 1980. *Abortion: An Annotated Indexed Bibliography*. New York: E. Mellen Press.

A source of early writing on abortion which provides the historical background of arguments in the debate before and after Roe v. Wade through the 1970s.

1016 MUMFORD, LAURA. 1989. *Women's Issues: An Annotated Bibliography*. Pasadena, CA: Salem Press.

Annotated references to women's issues that cover a wide spectrum.

1017 NORDQUIST, JOAN. 1992. *The Feminist Movement: A Bibliography*. Santa Cruz, CA: Reference and Research Services.

This is a small publication but lists the major works on the Feminist Movement of the twentieth century. There are also sections on the woman's movement in the nineteenth century, issues of race in the movement, and the sexuality debates (includes sadomasochism and pornography). Not annotated.

1018 ———. 1992. *Violence Against Women: A Bibliography*. Santa Cruz, CA: Reference and Research Services.

A bibliography of more than 1,000 citations on violence against women. Material comes from feminist, small, and alternative presses, and activist organizations that are not usually available in standard bibliographies. Information can be found on battered women, rape, and sexual harassment. This sixty-eight page reference source is not annotated.

1019 OAKES, ELIZABETH and KATHLEEN SHELDON. 1978. *A Guide to Social Science Resources in Women's Studies*. Santa Barbara, CA: Clio Books.

Annotated entries covering anthropology, economics, history, psychology, sociology, contemporary feminist thought, journals, and bibliographies.

1020 PAPACHRISTOU, JUDITH. 1985. *Bibliography on the History of Women in the Progressive Era*. Bronxville, NY: Sarah Lawrence College Women's Studies Publication.

A bibliography covering woman's rights activism and politics during the late 1800s and the early part of the twentieth century.

1021 REDFERN, BERNICE, ed. 1989. *Women of Color in the United States: A Guide to the Literature*, New York: Garland Press.
This bibliography lists and annotates 636 works on African-American, Asian-American, Hispanic-American, and Native American women. The selections bring together the significant recent publications for each of these racial/ethnic groups. Redfern's organization of this work provides access to scattered sources which are difficult to find, including articles from anthologies, journal articles, dissertations, and monographs.

1022 RITCHIE, MAUREEN. 1980. *Women's Studies: A Checklist of Bibliographies*. London: Mansell.
Non-annotated entries mainly from 1964–1979 publications.

1023 ROSENBERG, MARIE and LEN BERGSTROM. 1975. *Women and Society: A Critical Review of the Literature with a Selected Annotated Bibliography*. Beverly Hills, CA: Sage Publishing.
Over 3,000 books, articles, and periodicals are listed in this reference guide. Included are biographical dictionaries, women's organizations, and collections on women in libraries. The most represented areas are political science, history, and sociology. Not all the citations are annotated, although most have a brief description.

1024 ROWBOTHAM, SHEILA, ed. 1973. *Women's Liberation and Revolution*. Bristol, England: Falling Wall Press.
Although Rowbotham has done much of her research on the Women's Liberation Movement and socialist feminism in England, she includes sources on the American movement in this annotated bibliography.

1025 SCHMITZ, BETTY. 1985. *Integrating Women's Studies into the Curriculum: A Guide and Bibliography*. Old Westbury, NY: The Feminist Press.
A good deal of useful information can be found in this resource for Women's Studies.

1026 SELLEN, BETTY CAROL and PATRICIA A. YOUNG. 1987. *Feminists, Pornography, & the Law: An Annotated Bibliography of Conflict, 1970–1986*. Hamden, CT: Library Professional Publications.
This is an annotated bibliography about the anti-pornography debate. Material is drawn from computer data bases, periodical indexes, newspaper indexes, and references in articles, books, and other bibliographies. Detailed in the Introduction are: the history of the anti-pornography movement, the formation of Women Against Pornography in 1979, Take Back the Night marches, the legislative solution of Andrea Dworkin and Catharine MacKinnon, the 1982 Barnard Conference, and the formation of the Feminist Anti-Censorship Task Force (FACT). The authors take a neutral stance and include entries covering all positions in the debate. Their purpose is to help people form a thoughtful response to the complicated issues of women's equality, sexual freedom and free speech.

1027 SIMS-WOOD, JANET L. 1980. *The Progress of Afro-American Women: A Selected Bibliography and Research Guide*. Westport, CT: Greenwood Press.

A listing of thirty-three categories from feminism to slave narratives. Includes books, journal articles, theses and dissertations. Not annotated.

1028 SOLTOW, MARTHA JANE and MARY K. WERY. 1976. *American Women and the Labor Movement, 1825–1975: An Annotated Bibliography*. Metuchen, NJ: Scarecrow Press.

Included is information on women and trade unions, strikes, legislation, labor leaders, the National Women's Trade Union League, the Coalition of Labor Union Women, and autobiographical materials. The annotations are extensive and there are sections on archival sources, indexes, and Women's Bureau materials. A good number of sources are listed from labor newspapers such as *Union Wage* and *Life and Labor*.

1029 STINEMAN, ESTHER. 1979. *Women's Studies: A Recommended Core Bibliography*. Littleton, CO: Libraries Unlimited.

Over 1,700 books in twenty-five subject areas. Each entry is described and evaluated. Also included are annotated entries on feminist periodicals.

1030 SWEENEY, PATRICIA E., ed. 1990. *Biographies of American Women: An Annotated Bibliography*. Oxford: Clio Press Ltd.

For those interested in biography of American women, this is a useful reference source. It is an annotated bibliography with over a thousand entries. Additionally, there are listings (or sometimes complete essays) of memoirs, portraits by family and friends, books, and dissertations. Data sources go back to the 1800s and up to the present.

1031 TIMBERLAKE, ANDREA, LYNN WEBER CANNON, REBECCA F. GUY, and ELIZABETH HIGGINBOTHAM, eds. 1988. *Women of Color and Southern Women: A Bibliography of Social Science Research, 1975 to 1988*. Memphis, TN: Center for Research on Women, Memphis State University.

This reference work lists citations from books, chapters in books, published papers, dissertations, and papers presented at meetings on women of color and Southern women. There are six major subject headings: Culture; Education; Employment; Family; Health; and Political Activism/Social Movements. The racial-ethnic categories listed under each heading are African-American; Asian-American; Latina; Native American; Comparative Research on Women of Color; and The South. The citations included were selected from the Research Clearinghouse online database of social science and historical research on women of color and Southern women since 1975. Each year an annual supplement is published which contains approximately 900 additional citations.

1032   TINGLEY, ELIZABETH and DONALD F. TINGLEY. 1981. *Women and
       Feminism in American History: A Guide to Information Sources.*
       Detroit, MI: Gale Research Co.
This reference work contains an annotated bibliography on works related to
women and feminism. There is also a section which provides a guide to major
repositories of archival collections divided by region of the country.

1033   WATSON, G. 1989. *Feminism and Women's Issues: An Annotated
       Bibliography and Research Guide.* New York: Garland Publications.
A useful source on the women's movement, feminism, and a wide variety of
women's issues.

Funding Sources

1034   AAUW American Fellowships. American Association of University
       Women, Educational Foundation. 1111 16th St., NW, Washington, D.C.
       20006.
Postdoctorate fellowships for women, doctoral degree in any field, with no
restrictions on the place of study or age of the researcher. Selection criteria is
based on scholarly excellence of proposal and the applicant's commitment to
helping women through service in their community or profession and/or
research projects. Nine post-doctoral fellowships are available from $20,000 to
$25,000. Application deadline is November 15 for the following fellowship year
beginning July 1. For more information, phone (202)728-7603.

1035   ACLS Fellowships. American Council of Learned Societies, Office of
       Fellowships and Grants, 228 E. 45th Street, New York, NY 10017-3398.
Postdoctorate fellowship to enable scholars to devote time to research.
Minorities and women are encouraged to apply. Fellowships do not exceed
$20,000 and are intended as salary replacement. Request applications in writ-
ing and provide the following information: date of highest degree; citizenship;
academic position; field of specialization; proposed subject of research; date
for beginning and ending award period; specific award program for which
application is requested. Completed application forms must be postmarked no
later than October 1. Awards are for 6-12 months between July 1 of the award
year and December 31 of the following year. Three years must have elapsed
before the end of the last supported research leave and July 1 of the fellowship
year. Phone (212)697-1505 for more information.

1036   ACLS Grants for East European Studies. American Council of Learned
       Societies, Fellowships for Postdoctoral Research, 228 E. 45th St., New
       York, NY 10017-3398.
Postdoctorate fellowships of up to $25,000 to do full-time research concerned
with Eastern Europe for at least six months. Must be U.S. citizen with three
years past the last funded research period. Request applications in writing;

deadline for application form is November 15. Contact the Office for Fellowships and Grants at (212)697-1505.

1037   ACLS Grants-in-Aid. American Council of Learned Societies, Office of Fellowships and Grants, 228 E. 45th St., New York, NY 10017-3398.
Postdoctorate grants to assist with the expenses of research projects. Must be U.S. citizen or permanent legal resident. Grants will not exceed $3000 and may be used for travel and maintenance away from home necessary to gain access to data collection. Grants for computer equipment, books, or other non-expendable items are usually not allowed. Application form must be requested in writing providing the following information: highest academic degree held and date received; country of citizenship or permanent legal residence; academic or other position; field of specialization; proposed subject of research of study; proposed date for which application is requested. Completed application must be postmarked by November 1. Decisions are announced in late April. Fellowships are for a 12-month period beginning May 1. For more information, call (212)697-1505.

1038   ASA/NSF Small Grants. American Sociological Association. 1722 N Street, N.W., Washington, D.C. 20036.
Two grant rounds per year with deadlines June 15 and November 15. The grants support basic research activity—either projects or conferences that bring scholars together. Requests must show relevance to issues of basic research in sociology. Clear statements of theoretical/conceptual background, methodology, and the potential contribution of the project should be provided. Restricted to postdoctoral research. The upper limit of each award is $2,500. Proposals should include a cover sheet with 100-200 word statement of the research question, a text of no more than three single-spaced pages (with no appendices), a budget statement, a bibliography and vita. Both the title and author(s) should appear on the cover page. Send eight complete and individually bound copies of the entire packet. Call (202)833-3410.

1039   Bunting Fellowship. Mary Ingraham Bunting Institute of Radcliffe College, 34 Concord Avenue, Cambridge, MA 02138.
Postdoctorate professional development fellowship for women scholars, creative writers, and visual artists. Scholars must hold a Ph.D. or appropriate terminal degree for at least two years prior to appointment. Award is for a $21,500 stipend for a one year appointment, July through June. Ten awards are made each year. When applying, provide the names of three recommenders on the application sheet. Application must be postmarked by October 15. Notification in April. Call (617)495-8212 for more information.

1040   Directory of Financial Aid for Women. Reference Service Press, 1100 Industrial Road, Suite 9, San Carlos, CA 94070.
This 1993 publication contains over 1700 cross-referenced entries on scholarships, fellowships, grants, and awards for women from high school to postdoctoral level. Order direct (415)594-0743.

1041   Fellowships and Grants for Training and Research. Social Science
       Research Council, 605 Third Avenue, New York, NY 10158.
A listing of fellowships and research grants available from the Social Science
Research Council.

1042   Financial Aid for Research and Creative Activities Abroad. Reference
       Service Press, 1100 Industrial Road, Suite 9, San Carlos, CA 94070.
Directory with over 1200 references to funding opportunities for high school
students, undergraduates, graduate students, postdoctorates, professionals
and other individuals involved in research or creative activities abroad. Order
direct (415)594-0743.

1043   Financial Aid for Graduate and Professional Education. 1993. Princeton,
       NJ: Peterson's Guides.
Gives information on how and when to apply for fellowships, assistantships,
grants, loans, work-study, and tuition remission.

1044   Fulbright Scholar Program. Council for International Exchange of
       Scholars, 3007 Tilden Street, N.W., Suite 5M, Washington, D.C. 20008-
       3009.
Fulbright lecturing and research awards in other countries have a deadline of
August 1. Contact the above address for a catalog of host countries, topics and
disciplines desired, and instructions for applying.

1045   Grants for Postdoctoral Study. Peterson's Guides, Box 2123, Princeton,
       NJ 08543.
Lists information on more than 700 research, teaching, and writing programs
in the United States. Order direct from (800)225-0261.

1046   Grants for Women and Girls. 1992. New York: The Foundation Center.
A listing of nearly 3500 grants of $10,000 or more to nonprofit organizations for
education, research, and service for women and girls.

1047   National League of American Pen Women Scholarships for Mature
       Women. The National League of American Pen Women, Inc., 1300 17th
       St., N.W., Washington, D.C. 20036.
Professional development scholarship to further the creative goals of women
thirty-five years of age or older. There are three $1000 awards given in even
numbered years in Art, Letters, and Music. Applicants must submit a letter stating they will be thirty-five or over by the application deadline, a $5.00 fee, and
a self-addressed stamped envelope. They must also submit slides, manuscripts,
or musical compositions by the January 15 deadline in even-numbered years.
Awards are made by April.

1048   National Endowment for the Humanities. Division of Fellowships and
       Seminars. Room 316, 1100 Pennsylvania Avenue, N.W., Washington, D.C.
       20506.
Through its fellowships and summer stipend programs, NEH supports

advanced study and research in the humanities. There are a number of different programs with varying deadlines, e.g., Summer Stipends for $4000 have an October 1 deadline; Travel to Collections Grants for $750 have a July 15 and January 15 deadline; NEH Fellowships up to $30,000 have a May 1 deadline; the Interpretive Research Program awards range from $10,000–$150,000 for up to three years and have an application deadline of October 15. The rules, awards, and deadlines can change. Contact the above address for further information and application packet. Phone (202)606-8438.

1049   National Humanities Fellowship Program. National Humanities Center, PO Box 12256, Research Triangle Park, NC 27709-2256.
The Center offers 35-40 fellowships for advanced study in history, philosophy, languages, literature, classics, religion, history of the arts, and other fields in the liberal arts. Scholars from any nation or discipline may apply. Fellowships are for the academic year, September through May. Stipends are individually determined. Application deadline is October 15.

1050   SCHLACHTER, GAIL ANN. 1993. *Directory of Financial Aids for Women 1993–1995, Ninth Edition*. San Carlos, CA: Reference Service Press.
A sourcebook on scholarships, fellowships, loans, awards, internships, and state sources of funding directed primarily at individuals. For other publications of interest to grant seekers, see also *Finding Funding. Grant-Getting Tips for Women* by Phyllis Holman Weisbard which can be requested from the University of Wisconsin-Madison, Office of Women's Studies Librarian.

1051   SCHLACHTER, GAIL ANN *AND* SANDRA E. GOLDSTEIN. 1994. *Directory of Financial Aid for Minorities, 1993–1995*. San Carlos, CA: Reference Service Press.
A directory listing over 2,000 references to scholarships, fellowships, grants, loans, awards, and internships available to African-Americans, Native Americans, Asian-Americans, and Hispanic-Americans.

1052   SCHLACHTER, GAIL ANN. 1987. *How To Find Out About Financial Aid*. San Carlos, CA: Reference Service Press.
Guide to print and online directories listing fellowships, scholarships, loans, grants, awards, and internships available to undergraduate and graduate students, and postdoctoral researchers.

1053   Sociology Program of the National Science Foundation. National Science Foundation, 1800 G Street NW, SES Room 336, Washington, D.C. 20550.
Supports research on problems of human social organization, demography, and processes of individual and institutional change. The Sociology Program encourages theoretically focused empirical investigations aimed at improving the explanation of social processes and social structure. The Program recognizes the theoretical and methodological diversity of the discipline and invites proposals for basic research regardless of theoretical perspective and/or

research methodology. Proposal deadlines are August 15 and January 15. Phone (202)357-7802.

1054   The Grants Register. 1994. New York: St. Martin's Press.
A reference source on more than 200 granting institutions. Awards are listed from regional, national, and international sources. This publication covers the years 1993–1995.

1055   The Henry A. Murray Research Center. Radcliffe College, 10 Garden Street, Cambridge, MA 02138.
Visiting scholar grants for postdoctoral research drawing on the center's data resources. Application deadline is April 1. Call (617)495-8140.

1056   The National Guide to Funding for Women and Girls. 1993. New York, NY: Foundation Center.
Provides information on over 3000 grants for funding in the categories of child care, health care, civil rights, homelessness, education, legal defense, employment, rape, family planning, and other subject areas.

1057   The Woodrow Wilson Center Awards. The Woodrow Wilson Center, The Fellowship Office, Washington, D.C. 20560.
Approximately 40 fellowships annually in an international competition for project proposals with a strong emphasis on the humanities and social sciences. The average yearly stipend is approximately $36,000. Application deadline is October 1. Phone (202)357-2841.

Library Collections, Archives, Catalogs, and Museums

1058   ALA Gay & Lesbian Task Force Clearinghouse, c/o American Library Association, Office of Library Outreach Services, 50 E. Huron, Chicago, IL 60611.
Library Collection on homosexuality, lesbianism, feminism, gay rights. Holdings are more than 2000 books, pamphlets, and periodicals. For more information, call (312)944-6780.

1059   Alice Paul Centennial Foundation, P.O. Box 472, Moorestown, New Jersey 08057.
Historic preservation project to save "Paulsdale," childhood home of Alice Paul, militant suffragist and author of the Equal Rights Amendment. The Foundation has restored Paul's home in Mt. Laurel, NJ, had it registered on the National Register for historic buildings, and converted part of it into a conference center for women and girls. Memorabilia of Paul, her law degrees, pictures, and a full set of the journal *The Suffragist* (published by the National Woman's Party from 1913–1920) are housed here. Phone (609)231-1885.

1060   American Friends Service Committee, Women's Program, 1501 Cherry Street, Philadelphia, PA 19102.

The American Friends Service Committee has files, bibliographies, and listings of contacts for researching or addressing violence against women. Phone (215)241-7044.

1061 ASH, LEE, ed. 1993. *Subject Collections: A Guide to Special Book Collections and Subject Emphasis as Reported by University, College, Public and Special Libraries, and Museums in the United States and Canada, Seventh Edition, Revised and Enlarged.* New Providence, NJ: R. R. Bowker.
A listing by subject of collections held in libraries throughout the country.

1062 Atlanta University Library, Atlanta University, Atlanta, GA 30314.
This library has a large collection of papers related to the history of black women, including organizations such as the Association of Southern Women for the Prevention of Lynching.

1063 Bancroft Library, University of California, Berkeley, CA 94708.
This Library has a large holding of materials on women's rights leaders, including Charlotte Perkins Gilman, Alice Paul, Carrie Chapman Catt, Harriot Stanton Blatch (daughter of Elizabeth Cady Stanton), Jeannette Rankin, and Mary Ritter Beard. The Bancroft Library has an extensive oral history project on activist women from suffrage to the current women's movement.

1064 Bethune Museum and Archives for Black Women's History, 1318 Vermont Ave., N.W., Washington, D.C. 20005.
Contains the largest manuscript collection of materials on black women in the country. Includes both organizational and individual collections. Over 300 photos are housed here. Phone (202)332-1233.

1065 BISHOP, BEVERLY D. and DEBORAH W. BOLAS. 1983. *In Her Own Write: Women's History Resources in the Library and Archives of the Missouri Historical Society.* St. Louis, MO: Missouri Historical Society.
A guide to the research materials available on women who played significant roles in social movements such as suffrage, prohibition, abolition, and social welfare. Holdings comprise letters, diaries, legal and financial documents, speeches, reports, and manuscripts. Organizational holdings include those of the League of Women Voters, and The Equal Suffrage League. Holdings on activist women include materials on Susan B. Anthony, Carol Bates (Missouri Welfare League), Thekla Bernays (suffrage in St. Louis), Alice Stone Blackwell, Carrie Chapman Catt, Virginia Minor, Carrie Nation (temperance), Kate Richards O'Hare (socialism), Elizabeth Cady Stanton, and Lucy Stone.

1066 Black Women in Church and Society, Research/Resource Center, Interdenominational Theological Center, 671 Beckwith St. S.W., Atlanta, GA 30314.
Contains 250 volumes on feminism, women's movements, women in ministry, and liberation theology. Phone (404)527-7740.

1067   Center for the American Woman & Politics Library, Eagleton Institute,
       Rutgers University, Wood Lawn Neilson Campus, New Brunswick, NJ 08901.
Major collection on women and American politics and government. The
Center is also a research and education center. Over 700 books, 2000 papers,
newspaper clippings, and pamphlets, and 75 journals. Phone (908)932-9384.

1068   Chicago Historical Society, Library and Archives, Clark St. at North Ave.,
       Chicago, IL 60614.
History of women in Illinois, Chicago, and the United States; women's clubs;
women's rights; suffrage; temperance movement; women union leaders,
biographies of Chicago women; archives of the Chicago Women's Liberation
Union; and more than 500,000 prints, photographs and posters on Chicago.
Phone (312)642-4600.

1069   Clearinghouse on Family Violence Information, PO Box 1182,
       Washington, D.C. 20013.
Holdings of more than 700 books and articles on all types of family violence,
including parent abuse, spouse abuse, elder abuse, and sibling abuse. Phone
(703)385-7565.

1070   Collections on the Women's Movement, New York City Public Library,
       New York, NY.
Holdings for collections of a number of suffragists and other women reform-
ers. Large holding for Lillian Wald of the Henry Street Settlement House in New
York.

1071   Commission on Civil Rights, National Clearinghouse Library, 1121
       Vermont Ave. N.W., Washington, D.C. 20425.
Over 65,000 books and 1,000 periodicals on civil rights, education, sex discrimination, law, sociology, and economics. Phone (202)376-8110.

1072   Cornell University, New York State School of Industrial and Labor
       Relations, 15 E. 26th St., New York, NY 10010-1565.
Over 6000 books and 125 journals on labor relations, industrial relations, col-
lective bargaining, women and work. A special collection of Trade Union
Women is housed here. Phone (212)340-2845.

1073   Freedom Information Service (FIS), PO Box 3568, Jackson, MS 39207.
The FIS Deep South People's History Project houses research holdings on
workers, blacks, grass roots organizations, and reprints of items on women's
liberation. Phone (601)352-3398.

1074   Friends Historical Library Peace Collection, Swarthmore College, 500
       College Avenue, Swarthmore, PA 19081-1399.
The Peace Collection at Swarthmore College houses some papers of a number
of feminist activists including Jane Addams and Alice Paul. There are also organizational papers of the Women's International League for Peace and Freedom
here. Other holdings in the Friends Library include collections on Quaker faith

and history, genealogy, social concerns, abolition, race relations, women's rights, peace, prison reform, and temperance. Special collections on Friends Meeting records (4000 volumes of manuscripts); Quaker manuscripts (277 collections); Lucretia Mott manuscripts (7 boxes); Elias Hicks manuscripts (12 boxes). Publications on the Library: Guide to the Manuscript Collections of Friends Historical Library of Swarthmore College (1982); and Guide to the Records of Philadelphia Yearly Meeting (1989). Phone (215)328-8496. Access library holdings on internet: mchijiol@cc.swarthmore.edu.

1075   General Federation of Women's Clubs. Women's History and Resource Center, 1734 N St. N.W., Washington, D.C. 20036.
Contains collections on women's clubs, history, issues, and home life. Houses the archives for the General Federation of Women's Clubs from 1890 to the present. Also houses the Collection on the UN Decade for Women, 1975–1985. Phone (202)347-3168.

1076   Interdenominational Theological Center, Research/Resource Center, 671 Beckwith St. S.W., Atlanta, GA 30314.
Contains 250 volumes on feminism, women's movements, women in ministry, and liberation theology in a collection known as "Black Women in Church and Society." Phone (404)527-7740.

1077   International Planned Parenthood Federation, Western Hemisphere Region, Library, 902 Broadway, 10th Floor, New York, NY 10010.
Over 5000 books and audio-visual programs, 200 journals on family planning. Phone (212)995-8800.

1078   June Mazer Lesbian Collection, Connexus Women's Center, 626 N. Robertson Blvd., West Hollywood, CA 90069.
Houses subjects of lesbian history, organizations, writing, culture, and thought. Special Collections include Margaret Cruikshank Collection and Lillian Faderman Collection. Phone (213)659-2478.

1079   Kinsey Institute for Research in Sex, Gender & Reproduction, Library and Information Service, 313 Morrison Hall, Indiana University, Bloomington, IN 47405.
Subject matter includes research on gender, reproduction, erotica, sexual behavior and sexual attitudes. Phone (812)855-7686.

1080   Lambda, Inc., Barnes Library, Box 55913, Birmingham, AL 35255.
A library on gay and lesbian literature. Special Collections include the Alabama Gay Archives, and books/records from the entertainment fields. Phone (205)326-8600.

1081   Lesbian and Gay Archives, c/o Naiad Press, Inc., Box 10543, Tallahassee, FL 32302.
Literature on women, lesbians, and gays. Over 18,000 books and 1,000 periodicals. Phone (904)539-5965.

1082   Lesbian Herstory Educational Foundation, Inc., Box 1258, New York, NY
         10116.
Archival holdings on lesbian history and culture. Special collections include
manuscripts, oral histories, lesbian organizations, biographical collection, art
and music, buttons and t-shirts, and photographs. Phone (212)874-7232.

1083   Library of Congress, Public Service and Collections, 10 First Street S.E.,
         Washington, D.C. 20540.
The Library of Congress has a Manuscript Division, a Prints and Photographs
Division, and a Microform Reading Room at this location (202)707-5325. The
Rare Books and Special Collections Division is located in the Thomas Jefferson
Building (202)707-5434. Women leaders and activists for widely divergent caus-
es have their papers housed in the Library of Congress. Mary Baker Eddy,
founder of the Christian Science Religion, and many feminists such as Ida
Huster Harper, Margaret Sanger, Elizabeth Cady Stanton, and Alice Paul have
collections here. Organizational papers include the National Woman's Party,
National League of Women Voters, American Anti-slavery Society, and the
Women's Trade Union League. The scrapbooks of Susan Brownell Anthony
(1820–1906) in microform are located in the rare book collection. Includes
newspaper clippings, programs, handbills, posters, journal extracts, trial
reports, personal letters (some handwritten) documenting the history of
woman's suffrage. The scrapbooks cover 1848–1900.

1084   The Manuscript Inventories and the Catalogs of Manuscripts, Books and
         Periodicals for the Arthur and Elizabeth Schlesinger Library on the
         History of Women in America, Second Revised and Enlarged Edition.
         1984. Boston: G. K. Hall.
The volumes in this edition list the holdings in this library on the history of
women in America, including facsimiles of the card catalog of books, periodicals, and the manuscript holdings.

1085   Margaret Sanger Center, Planned Parenthood New York City, Abraham
         Stone Library, 380 Second Ave., New York, NY 10010.
Over 6000 books and 3000 periodicals, plus a large collection of reprints and
newspaper clippings on abortion, adolescent sexuality, sex, family living,
demography, women's health, and infertility. Phone (212)677-6474.

1086   Medical College of Pennsylvania, Archives and Special Collections on
         Women in Medicine, 3300 Henry Ave., Philadelphia, PA 19129.
Collections on health care, women physicians, Medical College of Pennsylvania
archives (this was the first women's medical college in the United States), black
women physicians, Asian-American women physicians, and an oral history project (43 interviews). Phone (215)842-7124.

1087   Midwest Women's Historical Collection, University of Illinois-Chicago
         Circle, Chicago, Illinois.
Houses the papers of Jane Addams and Hull House, the National Black

Feminist Organization, and the state chapter papers of the National Women's Political Caucus and Abortion Rights Association.

1088 Minnesota Historical Society, Women's Collections, St. Paul, MN.
Houses collections on the Minnesota League of Women Voters and the Minnesota Woman Suffrage Association.

1089 MURDOCK, MARY ELIZABETH, ed. 1975. *Catalog of the Sophia Smith Collection, Women's History Archive*. Boston: G. K. Hall.
A listing of the manuscript and periodical collection on women's history in the Sophia Smith Collection, Smith College Library, Northampton, MA. This is a seven volume guide: volumes 1 and 2 list author catalogs; volumes 3, 4, and 5 contain a subject catalog, volumes 6 and 7 detail manuscript collections. Vol. 7 also contains photograph listings.

1090 National Abortion Federation Resource Center, 1436 U St., N.W., Suite 103, Washington, D.C. 20009.
Resources on contraception, abortion, sexuality, health, medicine, sexually transmitted diseases, sociology. Phone (202)667-5881.

1091 National Association for the Advancement of Colored People, NAACP Legal Defense and Educational Fund, Law Library, 99 Hudson St., 16th Floor, New York, NY 10013.
Collection on civil rights law, discrimination against blacks and against women. Phone (212)219-1900.

1092 National Center on Women and Family Law, Information Center, 799 Broadway, Rm. 402, New York, NY 10003.
Collection on laws regarding battered women, marital rape, rape, divorce, child custody, single mothers, child support, and child snatching. Phone (212)674-8200.

1093 National Clearinghouse on Marital and Date Rape, 2325 Oak St., Berkeley, CA 94708.
Subjects of holdings include rape, cohabitation, marital rape and prosecution. Collection includes over 1000 files of briefs, testimony, reports, research studies, newsletters, and dissertations. Phone (510)524-1582.

1094 National Women's Christian Temperance Union, Frances E. Willard Memorial Library, 1730 Chicago Ave., Evanston, IL 60201.
This library holds a collection on the history of the temperance movement, biographies of temperance leaders, social reform history, and history of the women's movement. Phone (708)864-1396.

1095 National Women and Media Collection, Western Historical Manuscript Collection, University of Missouri-Columbia, 23 Ellis Library, Columbia, MO 65201.
Included in this collection are histories of blacks, women, politics, and social reform in Missouri. Phone (314)882-6028.

1096 National Women's Health Network, Women's Health Information
       Service Library, 1325 G St., N.W., Washington, D.C. 20005.
This library houses information on women and health, abortion, breast cancer,
childbirth, menopause, birth control, cervical cancer, osteoporosis, pregnancy,
sexually transmitted diseases, teen pregnancy, toxic shock syndrome, and
women and alcohol. Phone (202)347-1140.

1097 Northwestern University, Special Collections—Women's Collection,
       University Library, 1935 Sheridan Road, Evanston, IL 60208-2300.
Houses collections on the Women's Liberation Movement since the 1960s
including the Chicago Women's Liberation Union, national NOW until 1975,
radical feminist groups, socialist feminist groups, and the Equal Rights
Amendment. Phone (708)491-3635.

1098 Oberlin College Library, Archives and Collections, 420 Mudd Center,
       Oberlin, OH 44074-1532.
Houses subject areas of higher education, women's history, nineteenth century reform, black education, abolition movement, and temperance. Phone
(216)775-8014.

1099 ONE, Inc., Blanche M. Baker Memorial Library, 3340 Country Club Drive,
       Los Angeles, CA 90019.
Subject areas include the homophile movement, gay liberation movement,
women's and lesbian studies. Phone (213)735-5252.

1100 Papers of Eleanor Roosevelt, The Franklin D. Roosevelt Library, Hyde
       Park, NY 12538.
Archival collections of Eleanor Roosevelt's papers, housed in the Franklin D.
Roosevelt Library in Hyde Park, New York.

1101 Papers on the President's Commission on the Status of Women,
       1961–1964. The John F. Kennedy Library, Waltham, MA 02118.
An important collection of primary documents from the Commission on the
Status of Women including the debates on the ERA.

1102 Pennsylvania Historical Society, 1300 Locust Street, Philadelphia, PA
       19107.
Substantial holdings of a number of activists and groups involved in abolition,
suffrage, and women's rights. Archives of the state and local League of Women
Voters. Phone (215)732-6200.

1103 Picture Catalog of the Sophia Smith Collection. 1972. Smith College
       Collection, Northampton, MA.
A catalog with reproductions of photographs housed in the Sophia Smith
Collection on Women in America. Included in this listing are sections on abo-
lition, biography, social reform, and woman's rights.

1104 Radcliffe College, Arthur and Elizabeth Schlesinger Library on the
       History of Women in America, 10 Garden St., Cambridge, MA 02138.

One of the largest collections on women's history and the women's movement in the country. The Women's Rights Collection began in 1943 with the donation of suffragist Maud Wood Park's papers. Schlesinger Library holds extensive collections on the early woman's movement, suffrage, women's organizations, the contemporary women's movement, and history of women in America. Special collections: Woman's Rights; Blackwell family; Charlotte Perkins Gilman; Emma Goldman; Jeannette Rankin; Alice Paul; National Organization for Women; National Women's Political Caucus; National Woman's Party; and the Black Women Oral History Project. Also houses a large photo collection. Phone (617)495-8647.

1105 ———. Henry A. Murray Research Center, 10 Garden St., Cambridge, MA 03138.

Subject areas of interest: women and social change, work, education, careers, mental health, political participation, family, and aging. A large collection of data sets of computer accessible social science research studies. Phone (617)495-8140.

1106 Rockefeller Archive Center, 15 Dayton Ave, Pocantico Hills, North Tarrytown, NY 10591.

Holdings include materials on philanthropy, the Rockefeller family, medicine, social sciences, medicine, arts, humanities, black history, labor, politics, religion, social welfare, and women's history. Phone (914)631-6017.

1107 Seneca Falls Historical Society, Jessie Beach Watkins Memorial Library, 55 Cayuga Street, Seneca Falls, NY 13148.

Holdings on the Women's Rights Collection from 1848 to the present. Phone (315)568-8412.

1108 Sewall-Belmont House, 144 Constitution Avenue, N.E., Washington, D.C. 20002.

This is the headquarters of the National Woman's Party (NWP). Tours are available where artifacts from the suffrage movement are exhibited. Phone (202)546-3989.

1109 Smithsonian Institute, Museum of American History, Division of Political History, National Women's History Collection, Washington, D.C. 20560.

Holdings for the National American Woman Suffrage Association, large collection of material objects from the woman's rights movement beginning from 1848, political images of women, posters, and women's political organizations. Phone (202)357-2008.

1110 Sophia Smith Collection, Smith College, Women's History Archive, Northampton, MA 01063.

An important archival library on women's history in the United States, this collection began in 1942 and is named after the founder of the college. The library has extensive holdings on women activists and the organizations they belong to, including two of the college's graduates, Betty Friedan and Gloria Steinem.

Holdings cover women's history, birth control, social work, woman suffrage, women's rights, and the women's movement. Over 200 collections of personal papers and manuscript holdings on, among many others, Margaret Sanger, Ida Tarbell, Susan B. Anthony, Jane Addams, Carrie Chapman Catt, Planned Parenthood, and the Garrison family. Recently, Neilson Library, the main library of Smith College, added two microfilm publications to its holdings: *Women, Emancipation and Literature: The Papers of Harriet Martineau, 1802–1876* (17 reels); and *Women, Suffrage and Politics: the Papers of Sylvia Pankhurst, 1882–1960* (37 reels). The Sophia Smith Collection can be reached by phone at (413)585-2970.

1111   Southern Regional Council, Inc., Reference Library, 60 Walton St., N.W., 2nd Floor, Atlanta, GA 30303-2199.
Materials on civil rights, poverty, politics, suffrage. Phone (404)522-8764.

1112   Stanford University Library, Stanford University, Palo Alto, CA 94303.
Holdings for Kate Douglas Wiggins, leader in the kindergarten movement, and Alice Park, birth control leader.

1113   State Historical Society of Wisconsin, Archives, Collections, and Holdings, 816 State Street, Madison, WI 53706-6534.
Holdings on American history, labor, radical movements, reform, ethnic groups, women, some suffragists papers, and the records of the Women's Peace Party.

1114   Susan B. Anthony House, 17 Madison Street, Rochester, NY 14608.
A museum of Susan B. Anthony's furniture, artifacts, and mementos of other suffragists.

1115   Syracuse University Library, Syracuse University, Syracuse, NY 13220.
Contains the holdings of the Garrit Smith Collection on the abolitionist movement and includes papers on Susan B. Anthony, Elizabeth Cady Stanton (cousin to Smith), Lucy Stone, Victoria Woodhull, and Sojourner Truth.

1116   Temple University, Central Library System, Contemporary Culture Collection, 13th & Berks Sts., Philadelphia, PA 19122.
Holdings on social change, peace, fringe politics, alternative life styles, gays, and feminism. Special collections on the counterculture, peace movement, feminist publications from the nineteenth and twentieth centuries, and Liberation News Service archive. Phone 215-787-8667.

1117   The National Archives for Black Women's History, Washington, DC 20560.
Archival holdings include letters of African-American leaders, photographs, and the organizational records of the National Council of Negro Women.

1118   The National Gay and Lesbian Task Force, Papers for the First Twenty Years, Cornell University's Human Sexuality Collection, Ithaca, NY 14850.

Cornell University established a Human Sexuality Collection in 1989 with support from David B. Goodstein, publisher of *The Advocate*. The collection includes gay and lesbian history and works on the politics of pornography. The papers of the National Gay and Lesbian Task Force add an important dimension to the collection.

1119   UMI Research Collections, 300 North Zeeb Road, Ann Arbor, Michigan. UMI Research Collections handles multiple topic microfilm collections of interest to scholars of the women's movement and women's rights. For instance, they have microfilm collections on Women's Rights and on Leaders of Social and Political Reform. They can be contacted for information or a catalog.

1120   University of Michigan Library, University of Michigan, Ann Arbor, MI 48106.
Holdings for abolitionists, including Sarah and Angelina Grimké, and American Association of University Women.

1121   University of Missouri-St. Louis, Western Historical Manuscript Collection, Thomas Jefferson Library, 8001 Natural Bridge Road, St. Louis, MO 63121.
Houses materials on women's history, African-American history, socialism, peace, social reform, and labor. Special collections of the Socialist Party of Missouri, Oral History Projects, League of Women Voters of Missouri, Sierra Club (Ozark Chapter), Nuclear Weapons Freeze Campaign, St. Louis Labor Council, Amalgamated Clothing and Textile Workers, and papers of Harriet Woods. Phone (314)553-5143.

1122   U.S. Department of Labor, Women's Bureau, Reference Library on Women and Women's Employment, 230 S. Dearborn St., 10th Floor, Chicago, IL 60604.
The Women's Bureau works to improve the status of women in employment through programs within the Department of Labor. Holdings include works on affirmative action, equal opportunity, career information, women's employment and training. Phone (312)353-6985.

1123   Vassar College Library, Special Collections, Box 20, Poughkeepsie, NY 12601.
Holdings on women's history with papers of Alma Lutz, Elizabeth Cady Stanton, Susan B. Anthony, and woman's suffrage collection. Phone (914)437-5799.

1124   Women Artists News/Midmarch Arts, Archives, Grand Central Station, Box 3304, New York, NY 10163.
Collections on art, women artists, women in art, women's organizations, and exhibitions. Phone (212)666-6990.

1125 Women's Action Alliance, Inc., Library, 370 Lexington Ave., Suite 603, New York, NY 10017.
Subjects of interest include women's issues, sex discrimination, employment, affirmative action, reproductive freedom, women's organizations and centers. Special collections: files of national women's organizations and women's centers throughout the United States. Phone (212)779-2846.

1126 Women's Christian Temperance Union, Frances E. Willard Memorial Library, 1730 Chicago Ave., Evanston, IL 60201.
This library holds a collection on the history of the Temperance Movement, the Women's Christian Temperance Union (WCTU), biographies of temperance leaders, social reform history, and history of the women's movement. Phone (708)864-1396.

1127 Women's Health Resources, 1003 W. Wellington, Chicago, IL 60657.
Manuscripts and papers on women's health, battered women, breast cancer, mental health, disabilities, nutrition, stress, and occupational health. Phone (312)525-1177.

1128 Women's History and Resource Center, General Federation of Women's Clubs, 1734 N St., N.W., Washington, D.C. 20036.
Contains collections on women's clubs, history, issues, and home life. Houses the archives for the General Federation of Women's Clubs from 1890 to the present. Also houses the Collection on the UN Decade for Women, 1975–1985. Phone (202)347-3168.

1129 Women's History Research Center, Women's History Library, 2325 Oak Street, Berkeley, CA 94708.
Subjects of interest: women's health, mental health, women and the law, black and Third World women, women artists, films by and about women. Phone (510)524-1582.

1130 Women's International League for Peace and Freedom, The University of Colorado Library, Boulder, CO 80302.
Contains papers from the Women's International League for Peace and Freedom.

1131 Women's Movement Archives, Women's Educational Center, Inc., 46 Pleasant Street, Cambridge, MA 02139.
A collection of Boston area women's liberation groups: Bread and Roses (1969–1971); Female Liberation (1970–1974); Cell 16 (1968–1975); The Women's Center (1971 to the present). Phone (617)354-8807.

1132 Women's Project of New Jersey, 34 Maynard Court, Ridgewood, NJ 07451.
Biographical histories and exhibits of New Jersey women. There are additional documents available at the Women's Archives, Rutgers University. Phone (201)652-4440.

1133 Women's Resource and Action Center, Sojourner Truth Women's Resource Library, 130 N. Madison, Iowa City, IA 52242.

Subject area of interest is feminism and race. Special Collections include the complete holdings of *Ain't I A Woman* (feminist periodical 1970–1973). Phone (319)335-1486.

1134 Women's Resource Center Library, 250 Golden Bear Center, University of California, Berkeley, CA 94720.

Holdings on Women's Studies, women and work, comparable worth, women of color. Special collections on women in American history, lesbian history, women's movement magazines of the 1970s. Phone (510)643-8367.

1135 WOMEN'S RESOURCES GROUP. *Library and Information Sources on Women: A Guide to Collections in the Greater New York Area.* New York: The Feminist Press.

A directory of the holdings on women at more than 170 libraries and information centers in New York City, Westchester County, Long Island, and New Jersey. Each entry provides access information, a description of the materials, and the size of the collection. Sponsored by the Greater New York Metropolitan Area Chapter of the Association of College and Research Libraries and the Center for the Study of Women and Society of the Graduate School and University Center of the City University of New York.

1136 Women's Rights National Historical Park, PO Box 70, Seneca Falls, NY 13148.

A memorial park to commemorate the first woman's rights convention held in Seneca Falls in 1848. Preservation includes the Wesleyan Chapel where the convention was held, the home of Elizabeth Cady Stanton, and the McClintock House where the "Declaration of Sentiments" was written. Phone (315)568-2991.

Primary Documents

1137 ANDERSON, JUDITH ed., 1984. *Outspoken Women: Speeches by American Women Reformers, 1635–1935.* Dubuque, IA: Kendall Hunt.

A collection of reprints of speeches by forty American women reformers. Included are speeches by Anne Hutchinson, Susan B. Anthony, Alice Paul, Mary McLeod Bethune, Dorothea Dix, Jane Addams, Mary Baker Eddy, and Sojourner Truth.

1138 BARLETT, ELIZABETH ANN, ed. 1988. *Sarah Grimké: Letters on the Equality of the Sexes and Other Essays*, New Haven, CT: Yale University Press.

This collection of letters and essays by Sarah Grimké, a pioneering figure in the abolition and feminist movements, is an important resource for understanding the origins of the woman's rights movement. Her Letters on the Equality of the

Sexes documents a well developed philosophical position supporting equality for women because they are moral beings. The letters cover the condition of women, laws which negatively affect women, the lack of educational and employment opportunities, opposition to slavery, and the subjugation of women through marriage. The introduction by Barlett provides biographical information and an analysis of Grimké's evolving feminism.

1139 BEASLEY, MAURINE. 1988. *The White House Press Conferences of Eleanor Roosevelt*. New York: Garland Publishers.
Eleanor Roosevelt was a reformer who worked behind the scenes for much of the legislation that was passed in the 1930s to provide benefits for poor and working-class people. Beasley has gathered approximately one hundred transcripts of Roosevelt's women-only press conferences over a twelve year period beginning in 1933.

1140 BELL, SUSAN GROAG and KAREN M. OFFEN, eds. 1983. *Women, the Family, and Freedom: The Debate in Documents*. Stanford, CA: Stanford University Press.
A collection of over 250 documents on defining women's place in society. Philosophers, educators, scientists, writers, politicians, religious leaders, and others argue about what rights women should be allowed to have in marriage, motherhood, education, the political realm, the law, and the work place. We hear from famous people like Flora Tristan, Frederich Engles, Olive Shreiner, George Bernard Shaw, Sigmund Freud, and Virginia Woolf. And we gain insights from the public documents of past eras, such as the Napoleonic Code and various newspaper accounts of women's events, such as the 1848 Seneca Falls convention. The editors provide informative introductions to each section and include documents from other countries which add to the impact of the message the selections contain. Once you get past the depressing thought of how long the question of women's rights has been debated, the reading becomes quite fascinating.

1141 BUHLE, MARIJO and PAUL BUHLE, eds. 1978. *The Concise History of Woman Suffrage: Selections from the Classic Work of Stanton, Anthony, Gage and Harper*. Urbana: University of Illinois Press.
A collection of the documentation and writing on the suffrage movement by leaders and activists Elizabeth Cady Stanton, Susan B. Anthony, Matilda Josyln Gage, and Ida Husted Harper. Buhle and Buhle have condensed the six volume record these four women put together over the course of forty years into this more manageable text.

1142 CAMPBELL, KARLYN KOHRS, ed. 1993. *Women Public Speakers in the United States, 1800–1925: A Bio-Critical Sourcebook*. New York: Greenwood Press.
This is the first volume of a planned two volume work on women orators discussing the issues of their times. This volume consists of thirty-seven women who were speakers and activists prior to 1925. Entries consist of essays which

analyze each woman's rhetoric and the public discourse to which they contributed. A chronological list of their major speeches and resources for biographical accounts of their lives are provided at the end of each essay. The selections include a broad range of professions and activities these women engaged in as they challenged restricted views of women's place. Most entries are of well-known activists such as Antoinette Brown, the first ordained woman minister, educator Emma Willard, anti-lynching activist Ida B. Wells-Barnett, labor organizer Mother Jones, race and woman's rights speaker Sojourner Truth, and suffragist Susan B. Anthony. Other entries cover peace, temperance, and general themes of social justice.

1143 CEPLAIR, LARRY, ed. 1989. *The Public Years of Sarah and Angelina Grimké*. Irvington, NY: Columbia University Press.
An important collection, given the fact that most of these essays are out of print and unavailable. The Grimké sisters' writing provides insights into the development of feminist thought, women's history, the abolition movement, the woman's rights movement, and the lives of these two social movement activists of the nineteenth century.

1144 COSS, CLARE, ed. 1989. *Lillian D. Wald: Progressive Activist*. New York: The Feminist Press.
A collection of letters and speeches Lillian Wald wrote on a variety of issues. Wald who was active in the Settlement House Movement entered into many arenas to fight for justice and better conditions for women and poor people in the United States.

1145 DUBOIS, ELLEN CAROL, ed. 1981. *Elizabeth Cady Stanton, Susan B. Anthony: Correspondence, Writings, Speeches*. New York: Schocken Books.
A good primary source for learning, through their own words, about the thoughts of these two dynamic and long lasting leaders of the early woman's movement.

1146 GREENE, DANA, ed. 1980. *Lucretia Mott: Her Complete Speeches and Sermons*. New York: Edwin Mellen Press.
Lucretia Mott is well known to Women's Studies scholars, and she was well known during her activist days in the 1800s. A Quaker minister, Mott was involved in the abolition movement, founding the first Female Abolitionist Society in Philadelphia. She was a co-organizer of the first woman's rights convention held in Seneca Falls, New York in 1848. She was recognized for her contributions to the woman's movement in 1923 when Alice Paul named the Equal Rights Amendment the Lucretia Mott Amendment and had it introduced into Congress under that name. In this edited volume, Dana Greene has collected Mott's sermons and speeches which reflect her philosophy of reform. In reading her own words it becomes clear that she was a deeply religious woman. In addition, she was fervent in her political and feminist ideals. Some interesting examples of her writing include "The Principles of the Co-

Equality of Woman With Man" (1853), and "Place Woman in Equal Power"
(1878).

1147 ———. 1983. *Suffrage and Religious Principle: Speeches and Writings
    of Olympia Brown.* Metuchen, NJ: Scarecrow Press.
This collection serves as a good primary source for arguments used during the
suffrage campaign. It is also important for understanding Olympia Brown's
commitment and principles.

1148 GROAG, SUSAN and KAREN M. OFFEN, eds. 1983. *Women, the Family,
    and Freedom: The Debate in Documents.* Palo Alto, CA: Stanford
    University Press.
This collection of documents on "the woman question" comes in two volumes.
Vol. I covers 1750–1880 and Vol. II covers 1880–1950. There are more than 250
primary documents found in these works. Included are writings from philosophers, political figures, scientists, and religious leaders along with news
accounts and public documents.

1149 HULL, GLORIA T., ed. 1984. *Give Us Each Day: The Diary of Alice
    Dunbar-Nelson.* New York: W. W. Norton & Co.
Alice Dunbar-Nelson was a poet and activist in the woman's suffrage movement, the crusade against lynching, and the black women's club movement.
Her edited diaries covering the years 1921–1931 show her to be a newspaper
publisher, public speaker, and social activist with diverse interests.

1150 KRADITOR, AILEEN S., ed. 1968. *Up From the Pedestal: Selected Writings
    in the History of American Feminism.* New York: Quandrangle/The
    New York Times Book Co.
An anthology of documents on American feminism. Kraditor has selected documents representing the principal emphases of the feminist movement in particular periods. Sections consist of: Part I—The Question of Spheres—which
begins with a selection by Anne Bradstreet in 1642 and ends with a speech by
Lucy Stone in 1855. Part II—The Argument Becomes Specific—covers Emma
Hart Willard on education in 1819 through Charlotte Perkins Gilman on economics in 1898. Part III—Woman and Government—begins with the
Declaration of Sentiments and Resolutions of the Seneca Falls Convention of
1848 and ends with Predictions of the Results of Women's Enfranchisement
from 1852–1914. The last section—Unfinished Business—begins in 1931 with
Senate Hearings on the ERA and ends in 1966 with the NOW Statement of
Purpose.

1151 LASSER, CAROL and DEAHL MERRILL, eds. 1987. *Friends and Sisters:
    Letters Between Lucy Stone and Antoinette Brown Blackwell, 1846–93.*
    Champaign: University of Illinois Press.
This is an interesting and important collection of the letters of two women who
were related by marriage and ideals. For those interested in the early woman's
rights movement, the suffrage movement, and the abolition movement, these

letters provide a good background to some of the feelings of those committed to these causes as well as some of the controversial issues that arose. This volume contains the complete correspondence between Stone and Blackwell.

1152   LERNER, GERDA, ed. 1973. *Black Women in White America: A Documentary History*. New York: Vintage Books Series, Random House.
The documents in this collection date from a Bill of Sale for a slave in 1811 to Fannie Lou Hamer's address on "The Special Plight and the Role of Black Women" before the NAACP in the early 1970s. The material is varied and includes letters, papers on the National Club Movement, and writings on the concerns of black women and race pride. It took Lerner four years to collect these historical documents which constitute a comprehensive survey of the black experience in America. The author also provides important background notes and a biographical section outlining additional sources.

1153   ———. 1977. *The Female Experience: An American Documentary*. Indianapolis, IN: Bobbs Merrill Educational Publishing.
A collection of primary source material by American women on their lives, values, political environment, social institutions, protests and reform movements. This compilation includes letters, papers, and diaries, over half of which had not been published previously. A broad range of women's lives are documented in these sources which include contributions from early woman's rights activists Frances E. Willard, Rose Schneiderman, Lucy Stone, Charlotte Perkins Gilman, Emma Willard, Susan B. Anthony, Anna Howard Shaw, Elizabeth Cady Stanton, Victoria Woodhull, and Sarah Grimké. Some contemporary writings are included, as well as organizational documents from such diverse groups as Ladies' Relief Society, Shirt Sewers' Cooperative Union, National Women's Trade Union League, National Association for Repeal of Birth Control Laws, Rape Crisis Center Collective, and Speaking Out on Prostitution.

1154   MILLSTEIN, BETH and JEANNE BODIN, eds. 1977. *We, the American Women: A Documentary History*. New York: J. S. Ozer.
Reprinted primary material on women's reform activities in abolition, woman's rights, suffrage, and the modern women's movement.

1155   MOYNIHAN, RUTH BARNES, CYNTHIA RUSSETT, and LAURIE CRUMPACKER. 1993. *Second to None: A Documentary History of American Women*. Lincoln: University of Nebraska Press.
This collection contains source material on women in America. The first volume covers the sixteenth century to 1865 and consists of 153 selections including selections on Native Americans, Hispanic, African-American, and Euro-American women. Volume Two covers material after the Civil War, from 1865 to the present, and includes 122 selections. Selections range from a writing by Elizabeth Cady Stanton to the testimony of Anita Hill at the Thomas/Hill Hearings.

1156 RAKOW, LANA and CHERIS KRAMARAE, eds. 1990. *The Revolution in Words: Righting Women, 1868–1871*. New York: Routledge.
When the early woman's movement split after the Civil War, the National Woman Suffrage Movement was founded by Elizabeth Cady Stanton and Susan B. Anthony. With funding from woman's suffrage supporter Parker Pillsbury, they began publishing *The Revolution*. Although it lasted less than three years, *The Revolution* is a gold mine of writing on women's issues of the day, particularly suffrage. Elizabeth Cady Stanton was a major contributor to the writing of this periodical.

1157 SPRINGER, MARLENE. 1990. *The Web They Wove: Correspondence Among Nineteenth Century Women of Letters*. Ann Arbor: UMI Research Press.
A collection of personal letters between influential women of the nineteenth century. Topics addressed in these private letters include woman's rights, marital and other types of personal relationships, money, independence, professional work, and religion. The letters offer an interesting glimpse into what life was like for activist white middle-class women of that era.

1158 STANTON, ELIZABETH, SUSAN B. ANTHONY, and MATILDA JOSLYN GAGE. 1881, 1886, 1902, 1922. *The History of Woman Suffrage, Volumes I-VI*.
The most complete documentation of the woman suffrage movement is found in the six volume work *The History of Woman Suffrage*. The first three volumes were assembled by Elizabeth Cady Stanton, Susan B. Anthony, and Mathilda Joslyn Gage in 1881 and 1886. Volume IV was edited by Susan B. Anthony and Ida Husted Harper, published in 1902. Volumes V and VI were edited by Harper and published in 1922. Minute details of the suffrage campaigns including speeches, travels, political strategies, newspaper articles, pamphlets, conventions, dates, and committees are included in these works, particularly the first three volumes. Found in major research libraries.

1159 WALKER, ROBBIE JEAN, ed. 1992. *The Rhetoric of Struggle: Public Address by African-American Women*. Hamden, CT: Garland Publications.
This work analyses the rhetoric found in thirty-six speeches by African-American women from the 1830s to the 1980s. Walker explores mythic and cultural messages, and provides the full text of the speeches. The speeches are primary sources of data for researchers interested in understanding the work of these African-American women activists.

1160 WOLOCH, NANCY, ed. 1992. *Early American Women: A Documentary History, 1600–1900*. Belmont, CA: Wadsworth Publishing.
This is a good resource for primary documents from the mid-1600s to the early 1900s on a wide range of issues related to women's lives. Examples of documents include: William Penn (1682) "A Quaker Family;" Emma Willard (1815) "Matrimonial Risks;" Angelina Grimké Weld (1839) "The Cruel Mistress;" Sarah Grimké (1837) "Reply to the Massachusetts Clergy;" Antoinette Brown, (1848)

"A New Era in Women's History;" "Moments of Emancipation, Accounts of Former Slaves" (1865–1937); Leonara Barry (1888) "A Labor Organizer;" Frances A. Willard (1885) "Women and Politics;" Jane Addams and Ellen Gates Starr (1895) "The Clubs of Hull House;" Elizabeth Cady Stanton and Susan B. Anthony (1882) "Political Lessons;" and Charlotte Perkins Gilman (1903) "The Ills of the Home."

1161 WOMEN'S RIGHTS CONVENTIONS, SENECA FALLS AND ROCHESTER. 1969. New York: Arno Press.

This is a reprint of the 1870 edition which was published under the title "Proceedings of the Woman's Rights Conventions Held at Seneca Falls and Rochester, New York." This work includes proceedings of the Seneca Falls convention held on July 19 and 20, 1848; and the proceedings of the woman's rights convention held at the Unitarian Church in Rochester, New York on August 2, 1848. This publication can be found at the Library of Congress.

Reference Materials

1162 ATKINSON, STEVEN and JUDITH HUDSON, eds. 1992. *Women Online: Research in Women's Studies Using Online Databases*. Binghamton, NY: Haworth Press.

Guide to online research in Women's Studies. This publication also provides information on investigating interdisciplinary topics and locating feminist scholarship. The book has three sections: Disciplines (Humanities and Social Science); Format of the Material (non-bibliographic and cited reference databases); and Topics (e.g., Lesbian Studies and Women of Color).

1163 Barnard College. Workshop on Autobiography/Biography. Barnard College of Columbia University, 3009 Broadway, New York, NY 10027.

This is a summer writing workshop from the annual series "Writers on Writing at Barnard." Afternoon and evening classes with campus housing available. Phone (212)854-7489. The focus on Autobiography/Biography is connected to the growing interest in feminist circles to make women's lives public.

1164 BARRER, MYRA E., ed. 1975. *Women's Organizations and Leaders, 1975–1976*. Washington, D.C.: Today Publishing and News Service.

Even though the information is now dated, this is an interesting listing because it includes many leaders of the feminist movement at that time. There are over 8,000 listings of women's organizations in this reference source.

1165 BATAILLE, GRETCHEN M., ed. 1993. *Native American Women: A Biographical Dictionary*. New York: Garland Press.

This is the first biographical dictionary on Native American women. It includes historical and contemporary figures, tribal identities, and communal roles. The biographies are presented in 1-2 page entries on more than 200 women representing over ninety tribes. An account of their lives from their own perspective is verified by each Native American woman's signature at the end of the essay. There are references provided for each entry and indices by time, period, place of birth, and general subject matter. While this sourcebook is important in its own right, it also plays a part in understanding some of the practices that have been adopted from Native American culture within the women's culture of the contemporary women's movement.

1166   BRENNA, SHAWN, ed. 1993. *Women's Information Directory: A Guide to Organizations, Agencies, Institutions, Programs, Publications, Services, and Other Resources Concerned with Women in the United States*. Detroit, MI: Gale Research.

National, regional, state, and local organizations, battered women's services, displaced homemaker programs, women's centers, Women's Studies programs, research centers, women's colleges, library and museum collections, publishers, journals, newsletters, booksellers, governmental agencies, women-owned businesses, consultants, scholarships, awards, videos, electronic resources and other directories are all included in this extensive resource guide on women. The information was compiled from researchers at Gale Research as well as previous Gale reference sources. Additional assistance was provided from the resources of the National Council for Research on Women, the National Women's Studies Association, and Working Woman, Inc. This work provides a comprehensive resource guide to individual researchers and centers interested in general issues concerning women and feminist activism.

1167   BROWN, LOULOU, HELEN COLLINS, PAT GREEN, MAGGIE HUMM, and MEL LANDELLS. 1994. *The International Handbook of Women's Studies (WISH)*. Hertfordshire, England: Harvester Wheatsheaf.

A handbook that lists programs around the world for Women's Studies. Included are courses, research centers, training, research resources, and publications.

1168   BUHLE, MARI JO, PAUL BUHLE, and DAN GEORGAKAS. 1990. *Encyclopedia of the American Left*. Hamden, CT: Garland Publishers.

This reference work focuses on the radical Left, including socialist feminism. Included in this encyclopedia are individual biographies, histories of political organizations, essays on social movements, descriptions of periodicals, definitions of concepts, and analyses of key events. Includes subject and name indices, cross-referencing, and over 100 illustrations. This work received a CHOICE Outstanding Academic Book award and a Library Journal Best Reference Book award.

1169   BULLOUGH, VERN L., OLGA CHURCH, and ALICE P. STEIN, eds. 1989. *American Nursing: A Biographical Dictionary*. New York: Garland Publishers.

The contents of this reference work goes well beyond nursing. A very useful collection for people interested in health care, reform, and women's activism. Information is found on nearly 200 activists, writers, reform workers, educators, feminist activists, Settlement House workers, health care practitioners, and many others who have involved themselves in some way to change American society to benefit women, the poor, and the oppressed.

1170 BURNHAM, LINDA, ed. 1992. *Women of Color: Organizations & Projects: A National Directory*. Berkeley, CA: Women of Color Resource Center.
The Women of Color Resource Center provides information to social change activists for organizing on behalf of women of color. In this guide, reference material and descriptions of special projects are provided on organizations focused on women of color, defined as African/African-American/Afro-Caribbean, Arab/Arab-American, Asian/Asian-American/Pacific Islander, Indigenous/Native American/Hawaiian/Alaskan, Latina, and women of multiple heritages. Approximately 200 listings are found in this directory which was compiled from responses to a questionnaire sent to 2500 organizations.

1171 BUTCHER, PATRICIA SMITH. 1989. *Education for Equality: Women's Rights Periodicals and Women's Higher Education, 1849–1920*. New York: Greenwood Press.
A resource guide to periodicals on women's rights and women's education.

1172 CAPEK, MARY ELLEN S., ed. 1987. *A Women's Thesaurus: An Index of Language Used to Describe and Locate Information By and About Women*. New York: Harper and Row.
Contains more than five thousand terms related to women which are helpful for cataloging and making use of existing catalogs. In addition, this work stimulates rethinking of definitions pertaining to women's experiences, their work roles, social environments, issues, and history. A project of The National Council for Research on Women and the Business and Professional Women's Foundation, this book is an important resource for developing article and discussion topics. It also contributes to the ongoing efforts of the women's movement to change the language that is used to describe women and their lives.

1173 CARDINALE, SUSAN. 1982. *Anthologies By and About Women: An Analytical Index*. Westport, CT: Greenwood Press.
All entries were published after 1960. Organized by subject, gives list of table of contents, editor, contributor, and keyword indices. Useful to access literature that is difficult to locate.

1174 CARTER, SARAH and MAUREEN RITCHIE. 1990. *Women's Studies: A Guide to Information Sources*. London: Mansell Publishing Ltd.
A comprehensive bibliographical survey of sources in Women's Studies from 1978–1989. Included are language reference works, monographic and serial sources, and a selection of periodicals and organizations. There are three parts to the Guide: General Material, with reference sources and bibliographies; Women in the World, which contains sections on international feminism; and Special Subjects, which includes the arts, media, black women, education, history, law and politics, lesbians, literature and language, mind and body, science,

mathematics and technology, society and the environment, spirituality, mythology and religion, travel, leisure, sport, and women in the labor market. A section on men's studies is tacked on at the end. Brief introductions are provided for the different sections. Within sections there are separate headings for bibliographies, archival collections, library sources, periodicals, databases, organizations and groups.

1175   CASTILLO-SPEED, LILLIAN, ed. 1992. *Chicanas and Hispanic-American Women*. Berkeley: University of California Chicano Studies Library Publications Unit.
This reference source provides citations on women of Mexican heritage in the United States. It is a useful tool for guiding researchers to material on this ethnic group which covers both general and specialized publications. There is a subject index which includes topics, people, places, books, plays, and poems totaling over 1,000 citations. Entries provide bibliographic information, descriptors, and alternative subject terms. Also included are citations indexed under blacks, Cubanos, Latin-Americans, and Puerto Ricans. There are 183 entries under the term feminism.

1176   CLARDY, ANDREA FLECK. 1993. *Words to the Wise: A Writer's Guide to Feminist and Lesbian Periodicals and Publishers*. Ithaca, NY: Firebrand Books.
The fourth edition of this resource material consists of fifty-two pages of annotated listings of feminist and lesbian presses and periodicals. Also included is a list of academic and trade presses with an interest in women's publishing and a description of supplementary resources. This edition has been issued as Firebrand Sparks Pamphlet #1 and can be obtained from Firebrand Books, 141 The Commons, Ithaca, NY 14850.

1177   CLARK, JUDITH FREEMAN. 1987. *Almanac of American Women in the Twentieth Century*. New York: Prentice-Hall.
This work provides a historical background for learning about women's lives in the twentieth century. The almanac is arranged by decade and includes biographical sketches of notable women, including activists integral to the events of that time period.

1178   CONWAY, JILL K. 1988. *The Female Experience in Eighteenth and Nineteenth Century America: A Guide to the History of American Women, Volume I*. New York: Garland Publishers.
Reference work that has proven itself to be useful to Women's Studies scholars.

1179   DALY, MARY *AND* JANE CAPUTI. 1987. *Webster's First New Intergalactic Wickedary of the English Language*. Boston: Beacon Press.
A source book of words, essays, messages, and information for feminist women, particularly those of the lesbian and radical variety. The authors of this often humorous "wickedary" had a lot of fun putting this together. The reader most likely will share in the fun.

1180 DANKY, JAMES P., ed. 1982. *Women's Periodicals and Newspapers from the Eighteenth Century to 1981*. Boston: G. K. Hall.
A guide to nearly 1500 periodical and newspaper titles relating to women up to July 1981. The scope of the guide includes literary, political, and historical journals as well as general newspapers and feature magazines. It represents many phases of women's thought and action from the eighteenth century to the contemporary women's movement.

1181 *Electronic Discussion Groups on Women*.
Electronic discussion groups allow subscribers to the BITNET and INTERNET systems to share interests and resources on discussion topics. Many of them include information on feminism and the women's movement. For additional information on resources that provide user information and a list of bulletin board groups available to join, refer to Brendan P. Kehoe, Zen and the Art of the Internet: A Beginner's Guide, Second Edition. (Prentice-Hall 1992); and/or E. Krol The Whole Internet User's Guide & Catalog (O'Reilly & Associates 1992).

WMST-L (to subscribe, send the one-line message "subscribe wmst-l firstname lastname" to listserv@umdd on BITNET or listserv@umdd.umd.edu on INTERNET). The Women's Studies List is meant to serve academic and professional needs of Women's Studies faculty, administrators, librarians, and students. Information is exchanged about teaching, research, funding sources, developing Women's Studies programs, and a variety of feminist related topics. Announcements about conferences, calls for papers, job opportunities, and publications are often exchanged.

FEMAIL is an internationally focused discussion group for feminists from different cultures to discuss shared interests. Subscription requests should be addressed to "femail-request@lucerne.eng.sun.com" or "femail-request%hpldlh@hplabs.hp.com" (quotation marks are not needed, they are only provided here for ease in identifying what needs to go in the subscription request).

FEMINIST discusses issues of interest to librarians and researchers. This list is owned by the Feminist Task Force of the American Library Association and topics such as racism, pornography, censorship, ethnicity, and sexism are frequently discussed. Address subscriptions to listserv@mitvma.

FEMISA is a discussion group for people interested in gender issues, feminist thought, and international relations. The list owner is Deborah Stienstra in the Department of Political Science at the University of Winnipeg (stienstr@uwpg02.uwinnipeg.ca). To subscribe to this list, send the single line message "sub femisa firstname lastname" to listserv@mach1.wlu.ca.

1182 *Feminist Periodicals: A Current Listing of Contents*. Women's Studies Librarian, University of Wisconsin-Madison, 430 Memorial Library, 728 State Street, Madison, WI 53706.
An excellent resource for keeping up on the latest publications. This is a quarterly that provides a table of contents of over one hundred feminist magazines

and journals. This publication is available by subscription and includes Feminist Collections (essays and listings of books, resources, information) and New Books on Women (a semi-annual bibliography). Phone (608)263-5754.

1183 FRANK, IRENE and DAVID BROWNSTONE. 1993. *The Women's Desk Reference*. New York: Viking/Penguin Books.
An A-to-Z encyclopedia of women's issues, events, books, and politics. A good sourcebook which includes recent events such as the Tailhook Scandal and Anita Hill Hearings. Wide variety of topics included, e.g., Title VII of the 1964 Civil Rights Act, rape, battered women, statistics on working women, feminist organizations, and individual brief biographies of activist women.

1184 *Guide to Women's Studies*. New York Commission on the Status of Women, New York.
New editions come out on a regular basis, each filled with comprehensive information supplied by educational institutions.

1185 HARRISON, CYNTHIA ELLEN. 1975. *Women's Movement Media: A Source Guide*. New York: R. R. Bowker.
While much of the information in this reference book is out of date, the listings are useful for providing an overall view of the accumulation of resources that the contemporary women's movement had provided by the mid-1970s. Included are listings of women's groups, publications, governmental agencies, location of ephemeral materials, community organizations, films, speakers, records, radio shows, bookstores, and feminist products.

1186 HERNANDEZ, AILEEN C. 1992. *National Women of Color Organizations: A Report to the Ford Foundation*. New York: Ford Foundation Publications.
An overview of Asian-Pacific, African-American, Hispanic, and Native American women. A directory listing of women of color organizations is included. Can be obtained through the Ford Foundation Publications, 320 East 43rd Street, New York, NY 10017. Phone (212)573-4814.

1187 HILL, RUTH EDMONDS. 1991. *The Black Women Oral History Project: From the Arthur and Elizabeth Schlesinger Library on the History of Women in America, Radcliffe College*. Westport, CT: Meckler.
Information is provided on the Black Women Oral History Project that has been sponsored by the Schlesinger Library.

1188 HILL, RUTH EDMONDS and PATRICIA MILLER KING. 1991. *Guide to the Transcripts of the Black Women Oral History Project*. Westport, CT: Meckler.
This work is a companion to The Black Women Oral History Project by Ruth Edmonds Hill. This publication has information on the transcripts themselves.

1189 HINDING, ANDREA and ROSEMARY RICHARDSON (compilers and editors). 1972. *Archival and Manuscript Resources for the Study of*

Women's History: A Beginning. St. Paul: University of Minnesota
Libraries.
This is a small part of a much larger published work by Andrea Hinding on
manuscript holdings on women.

1190 HINDING, ANDREA, ed. 1979. *Women's History Sources: A Guide to
Archives and Manuscript Collections in the United States*. New York:
Bowker.
A very useful guide for finding archival and manuscript collections on women
throughout the United States.

1191 HINE, DARLENE CLARK, ed. 1993. *Black Women in America: A
Historical Encyclopedia*. Brooklyn, NY: Carlson Publishing.
This is a comprehensive reference source which focuses on African-American
women's lives. This two-volume work provides a portrait of the culture and
social involvements of black women in America. There are over 800 essays contributed by 400 people. Of these, more than 600 are biographies. Topical issues
include slavery, the abolition movement, feminism, the National Association of
Colored Women, religion, infanticide among slave women, the black middle
class, and black women's activism in numerous social causes. Biographical
essays reveal black American life and the involvement of black women in the
suffrage and civil rights movements. Well-known contemporary women such
as Rosa Parks and Toni Morrison, as well as historical figures such as Phyllis
Wheatley and Harriet Tubman, are included; but also lesser-known women
who worked to improve the position of African-American women and men are
part of this encyclopedia. Frederick Douglass, W. E. B. DuBois, and Booker T.
Washington are highlighted because of their support for woman's suffrage and
improved educational opportunities. Information on the largest repositories
and holdings on black women are provided, such as the Bethune Museum and
Archives in Washington, D.C. and the Moorland-Springarm Research Center at
Howard University.

1192 HOWARD, ANGELA, ZOPHY KAVENIK, and FRANCES KAVENIK, eds. 1989.
Dictionary of American Women's History. New York: Garland
Publishing.
A good resource which contains essays and bibliographies covering terms, con-
cepts, organizations, events, and individual women who have contributed to
American society. Material dates from 1607 to the present and includes minor-
ity and ethnic women's history in the United States.

1193 HUMM, MAGGIE. 1990. *Dictionary of Feminist Theory*. Columbus: Ohio
State University Press.
This reference work provides definitions of terms and issues in contemporary
feminism. The entries contain citations and commentaries, and include categories for black women, lesbians, and radical feminists.

1194   JAMES, EDWARD T., JANET WILSON JAMES, and PAUL S. BOYER, eds. 1971.
       Notable American Women 1607–1950: A Biographical Dictionary.
       Cambridge, MA: Belknap Press of Harvard University Press.
Over 1200 women are included in this biographical source material on women
who have contributed to the social good in a wide range of categories in the
United States. Most of these women were born before 1900 and their activist
work ended by 1920; all had died by 1950. The subjects are alphabetically listed with approximately one page per listing. Additional reference sources are
appended to each biography and an occupational index is provided at the back
of the book.

1195   JOAN, POLLY and ANDREA CHESMAN. 1978. *Guide to Women's
       Publications*. Paradise, CA: Dustbooks.
Guide to women's journals and newspapers up to 1978. Lists feminist journals,
women's newspapers, presses, distribution and directories.

1196   JOHNSON, JOHN W., ed. 1992. *Historic U.S. Court Cases, 1690–1990: An
       Encyclopedia*. Hamden, CT: Garland Publishers.
This is a collection of essays on landmark court cases beginning in 1690 which
chronicles U.S. legal history. The more than eighty lawyers, historians, and
political scientists who wrote the essays discuss the issues involved in these
cases and their importance to the judicial system. Sections in this work are
devoted to race, gender, ethnicity, and civil liberties. An index provides ease in
finding needed information on particular issues.

1197   KEESING'S REFERENCE PUBLICATIONS COLLECTION. 1988. *Women's
       Movements of the World*. Phoenix, AZ: Oryx Press.
Contains over 1500 detailed profiles of women's movement organizations
around the world. Each entry provides name, address, telephone number,
acronym, English translation of the organization's name, office holders with
specific titles, year founded, ideological orientation, membership requirements, a detailed description of organizational aims, brief history, current activities, publications, and affiliations.

1198   KRAMARAE, CHERIS and PAULA A. TRIECHLER. 1985. *A Feminist
       Dictionary*. London: Pandora Press.
A unique compilation of feminist terms and concepts. Language is defined
from a woman's perspective with selections that are sometimes humorous and
eccentric. Much of this work is serious and the dictionary contains a wealth of
historic and more recent quotes from feminists. This dictionary emancipates
readers from "man-made" and often sexist language.

1199   LEONARD, ARTHUR S., ed. 1993. *Sexuality and the Law: An
       Encyclopedia of Major Legal Cases*. Hamden, CT: Garland Publishers.
This easy to read reference source provides information about significant court
decisions on sexuality, sexual identity, sexual behavior, sexual orientation,
pornography, domestic relations, and reproductive freedom. Cases come from

the U.S. Supreme Court as well as appellate and trial court decisions. Explanations of legal and scientific terms are provided.

1200 MAGGIO, ROSALIE. 1990. *The Nonsexist Word Finder: A Dictionary of Gender Free Usage*. Boston: Beacon Press.
A useful source for learning how to change sexist terms into more suitable gender neutral forms.

1201 MCKEE, KATHLEEN BURKE, ed. 1977. *Women's Studies: A Guide to Reference Sources*. Storrs: University of Connecticut Library.
A collection of information on the resources for doing research on women in the 1970s. McKee lists handbooks, guides, catalogs, directories, and periodicals focusing on women.

1202 MULDOON, MAUREEN. 1991. *The Abortion Debate in the United States and Canada: A Source Book*. Hamden, CT: Garland Publishers.
An examination of abortion and its social, legal, religious, and moral implications. Surveys of public views about abortion are included. Major advocacy groups with information on their origins, activities, and official positions constitute one section. The chapter on legal issues provides a chronological description of major court decisions. Each section is followed by an annotated bibliography.

1203 *National Women's History Project*, 7738 Bell Road, Windsor, CA 95492. This is the group that provides resources on the history of women for the annual celebration of Women's History Month (March). Published sources, decorative pieces, information on films, and other materials are available for planning activities and educational events. They also do workshops and publish a catalog of films, books, and posters which can be purchased. Phone (707)838-6000.

1204 NORDQUIST, JOAN, ed. *The Left Index*. Santa Cruz, CA: Reference and Research Services.
A quarterly reference source with an author/subject index to periodicals of the Left. Material covers a wide range of topics and disciplines on social, political, and economic issues. Feminist, radical, and multicultural perspectives are found throughout the listings. A major focus is on modern/postmodern debates in philosophy and social theory.

1205 PETERSON, DEENA, ed. 1975. *A Practical Guide to the Women's Movement*. New York: Women's Action Committee.
Annotated list of women's periodicals and listing of women's organizations from the contemporary women's movement up to 1975.

1206 PROJECT ON THE STATUS AND EDUCATION OF WOMEN. *A Guide to Nonsexist Language*. Washington, D.C.: Association of American Colleges.
Guide for choosing alternative terms for sexist language.

1207 PURVIS, JUNE, ed. *Studies on Women Abstracts*. Oxfordshire, England: Carfax Publishing Co.
This is a reference publication which comes out six times a year as an international abstracting service. Material is included which covers teaching, studying, and researching in the generalized area of Women's Studies and women's activism.

1208 SALEM, DOROTHY C., ed. 1993. *African-American Women: A Biographical Dictionary*. Hamden, CT: Garland Publishing.
Nearly 300 black women involved in social reform, politics, and the professions from the colonial times to the present are featured in this reference source. Entries are written in essay form and cover each woman's childhood, education, career, significant achievements, and contributions to social change. An annotated bibliography that cites manuscript collections and secondary sources is provided.

1209 SICHERMAN, BARBARA and CAROL HURD GREEN, eds. 1980. *Notable American Women: The Modern Period, A Biographical Dictionary*. Cambridge, MA: Belknap Press of Harvard University Press.
This work follows the 1971 biographical dictionary of Edward James which listed notable American women who died before 1950. Each entry tells of the woman's life and achievements and provides references for further information.

1210 SMITH, JESSIE CARNEY. 1992. *Notable Black American Women*. Detroit, MI: Gale Research.
A reference work on the lives of famous and lesser-known black women in the United States. Entries include a wide variety of occupations and social callings such as teachers, journalists, doctors, workers, sharecroppers, singers, and activists. Some 200 people contributed to the 500 entries which make up this 1200+ page book. Well-known feminist and civil rights activists from the nineteenth and twentieth centuries, such as Harriet Tubman and Rosa Parks, are found in this extensive biographical source book.

1211 STRUNIN, MARION HARRIS. 1974. *American Women: A Research Guide to U.S. Government Sources*. Los Angeles: University of California, School of Library Services.
This is a useful guide for learning how to find and obtain publications from government sources. A survey of federal publications that are likely to have information on women is provided. The method and guidelines this book provides is timeless so that even as some of the annotations on monographic materials are outdated, this reference work remains applicable for current usage.

1212 *Studies on Women Abstracts*. Oxfordshire, England: Carfax Publishing.
Originating in 1983 this bimonthly abstracting journal offers full abstracts of Women's Studies books and articles from feminist sources and traditional disciplines.

1213 TELGEN, DIANE and JIM KAMP, eds. 1993. *Notable Hispanic-American Women*. Detroit, MI: Gale Research.
This is a follow-up to the 1992 publication *Notable Black American Women*. This reference work fills a void on historical and contemporary women who reside in the United States and identify their descent as being from Mexico, Puerto Rico, Cuba, Spain, or any Spanish-speaking country of Central or South America. There are close to 300 entries which are drawn from interviews, books, and articles. Photographs add an important element to this collection. Included are Hispanic-American women's activism in civil rights, women's rights, and other social movements.

1214 TEN-YEAR REVIEW OF PERIODICAL LITERATURE ON WOMEN AND WORK IN ENGLISH. 1989. *Journal of Women's History* 1. (March):138-169.
A listing of history articles on women, biography, crafts, trades, home-based work, domestics, factory work, family, farm women, frontier women, housework, legal issues, the military, minority and ethnic women, unions, professions, and volunteer work.

1215 THE WOMEN ORGANIZERS COLLECTIVE. 1990. *Women Organizers: A Beginning Collection of References and Resources*. New York: Hunter College School of Social Work.
Reference source for articles and sources on women organizers.

1216 THOMAS, EVANGELINE. 1983. *Women Religious History Sources: A Guide to Repositories in the United States*. New York: R. R. Bowker.
Archival sources of women's religious communities in the United States. Entries are listed by state with sublistings by city and community name. A short description of the history and archival collections for each entry are included.

1217 *Tuning In To The Movement: Feminist Periodicals*. 1974. Pittsburgh, PA: KNOW, Inc.
KNOW, Inc. provided reprints of classic papers from the contemporary women's movement in the early organizing years. This reference work lists publications, newsletters, pamphlets, women's presses, and bookstores involved in that enterprise.

1218 TUTTLE, LISA. 1986. *Encyclopedia of Feminism*. New York: Facts On File.
This work provides information ranging from a paragraph to a few pages on leaders, activists, events, organizations, books, and concepts of the nineteenth and twentieth centuries' women's movement.

1219 UGLOW, JENNIFER S. 1982. *The International Directory of Women's Biography*. New York: Macmillan.
Most of the entries are for North America, Europe and the British Commonwealth.

1220   VAUX, TRINA. 1983. *Guide to the Women's History Resources in the Delaware Valley Area.* Philadelphia: University of Pennsylvania Press.
Commissioned by the Mayor's Commission for Women of Philadelphia, this is an excellent guide to research materials available in the Philadelphia area. Institutions and their holdings are listed with details of special collections. A list of notable women from the area and a bibliography are included.

1221   *Violence Against Women.* Philadelphia, PA: American Friends Service Committee, Women's Program.
The American Friends Service Committee has files, bibliographies, and listings of contacts for researching or addressing violence against women.

1222   WALKER, BARBARA G. 1988. *The Women's Dictionary of Symbols and Sacred Objects.* New York: HarperCollins Publishers.
This is a useful reference source for learning about feminist history and the relevance of symbols to western civilization. Sacred and esoteric symbols are focused on, but also included are magical, holy, ritualistic, sexual, natural and supernatural objects and ideas. Many illustrations are incorporated which heighten the understanding and interest of the entries.

1223   WALLS, DAVID, ed. 1993. *The Activist's Almanac: The Concerned Citizen's Guide to the Leading Advocacy Organizations in America.* New York: Simon & Schuster/Fireside.
This work provides a profile of 105 national organizations in several social movements including peace, civil rights, women, gay and lesbian, aging, disability, and multi-issue progressive groups. Information is provided on the history, goals, membership, organizational structure, and publications from these organizations. An extensive bibliography is included.

1224   *Who's Who of American Women.* Chicago: Marquis Who's Who.
Published biennially since 1958, entries are listed alphabetically and contain the following information on each submitted name: education, marital status, occupation, political activities, awards, honors, organizational memberships, clubs, and publications. These entries consist of women who are still alive and who have achieved success in a wide variety of areas, including politics and social movement activism.

1225   *Who's Who of American Women.* 1993. New Providence, NJ: Reed Reference Publishing.
Now in its eighteenth edition, this 1993–1994 edition contains 27,500 entries on biographical information on better-known American women of achievement.

1226   WILLIAMSON, JANE. 1979. *New Feminist Scholarship: A Guide to Bibliographies.* Old Westbury, NY: Feminist Press.
Although only containing references prior to 1978, this guide to bibliographies directs the reader to the sources of work done in this period of the contemporary women's movement.

1227 *Women Studies Abstracts*. Rush, NY: Rush Publishing.
In existence since 1972 this quarterly is a journal index for Women's Studies. Articles come from both scholarly and popular periodicals, plus selected books, documents, and unpublished materials. Approximately 1,000 references are included in each issue, although most are not annotated.

1228 *Women's Studies Index*. Boston: G. K. Hall.
Since 1989, this annual index to women's periodicals has provided citations on Women's Studies from over eighty diverse American publications. Feminist periodicals and newsjournals are covered such as Women's Studies International Forum, Resources for Feminist Research, and Off Our Backs, as well as commercial magazines such as Family Circle and Glamour. This is a thorough and important index for research on women even though the publication time lags behind the sources by about a year.

1229 WOMEN'S ACTION COALITION. 1993. *WAC STATS: The Facts About Women*. New York: New Press, distributed by W. W. Norton.
This is the second updated and revised edition of this useful booklet which consists of a collection of statistics and other types of information about women. The Women's Action Coalition, an activist feminist group located in New York City, is responsible for compiling this work. It is a wonderful source for checking current data on topics such as AIDS, art, reproductive freedom, abortion, work, global issues, and gender conditions.

1230 ZOPHY, ANGELA HOWARD, ed. 1993. *Biographical Dictionaries of Minority Women*. Hamden, CT: Garland Publishing.
Entries provide information on the lives and social contributions of minority women in America. Personal sketches and a guide to source material are included.

1231 ZOPHY, ANGELA HOWARD and FRANCES M. KAVENIK, eds. 1990. *Handbook of American Women's History*. Hamden, CT: Garland Publishing.
Winner of CHOICE Outstanding Academic Book and RASD Outstanding Reference Source awards, this encyclopedic handbook on American women is a reference source containing facts, definitions, and bibliographic materials on concepts, events, movements, organizations, and individuals. A bibliography of primary and secondary sources on each subject is provided. The emphasis is on history, however there is also good coverage on more recent women, events, and issues that contribute to an understanding of the contemporary women's movement.

Anthologies and Texts

1232 ABEL, ELIZABETH and EMILY K. ABEL, eds. 1983. *The Signs Reader: Women, Gender, and Scholarship*. Chicago: University of Chicago Press.
This is a collection of some of the most influential articles printed in the first

five years of *Signs: A Journal of Women in Culture and Society*. Since its founding in 1975, *Signs* has been an important interdisciplinary journal for publishing feminist scholarship and it has also served as a forum for the discussion of controversial issues. Representative of some of the still timely articles included in this anthology are Adrienne Rich's "Compulsory Heterosexuality and Lesbian Existence;" Catherine MacKinnon's "Feminism, Marxism, Method, and the State: An Agenda for Theory;" and Diane Lewis's "A Response to Inequality: Black Women, Racism and Sexism."

1233 ADAMS, ELSIE and MARY LOUISE BRISCOE. 1971. *Up Against the Wall, Mother: On Women's Liberation*. Beverly Hills, CA: Glencoe Press.
An anthology of writings related to women's position in society and attempts to change it. Both historical and contemporary selections are included. Sections include: The Traditional View of Women; The Nature of Woman; Adjustment for Survival; and Toward Freedom.

1234 ADELSTEIN, MICHAEL E. and JEAN G. PIVAL, eds. 1972. *Women's Liberation*. New York: St. Martin's Press.
A collection of essays that look at significant issues connected to changing expectations of the role of women since the re-emergence of the women's movement. Many of the topics have two opposing views presented. Selections include essays from Betty Friedan, Caroline Bird, Germaine Greer, Ashley Montagu, Margaret Mead, and Gloria Steinem.

1235 ANDERSEN, MARGARET L. and PATRICIA HILL COLLINS, eds. 1992. *Race, Class, and Gender: An Anthology*. Belmont, CA: Wadsworth.
The focus of diversity and inclusiveness is well represented by the contributors of this anthology. Gender, class, and race are seen as interlocking systems which are examined through personal experience and institutional analysis. There are fifty-four pieces ranging from 4-19 pages written by authors representing a rainbow of race and ethnic groups. The question of privilege and the complexity of both privilege and oppression for people who are located in multiple group positions are discussed. Social institutions such as the family, work, and education are examined for the ways that race, class, and gender are incorporated into them. The final section of the book contains articles on political activism and empowerment. Articles on a Chinese immigrant woman's transformation ("From Housewife to Housing Advocate"), the growth of an older women's movement, Native American women's consciousness, and coalition politics demonstrate types of activism not typically thought of as part of the feminist movement's efforts for social change.

1236 ANDERSEN, MARGARET L. 1993. *Thinking About Women: Sociological Perspectives on Sex and Gender, Third Edition*. New York: Macmillan.
An interdisciplinary text on sex and gender which contains a review of feminist scholarship grounded in sociological theory and research. Race and class are integrated throughout the book. An introduction introduces sociological and feminist perspectives.

1237 ANDOLSEN, BARBARA HILKERT, CHRISTINE E. GUDORF, and MARY D. PELLAUER, eds. 1989. *Women's Consciousness, Women's Conscience: A Reader in Feminist Ethics*. New York: Harper & Row.
This reader explores moral, ethical, and religious dimensions of feminism. The contributors provide diverse discussions on these topics which lead readers to explore areas of thought not often raised within the discourse of feminism.

1238 BABCOX, DEBORAH and MADELEINE BELKIN, eds. 1971. *Liberation Now! Writings From the Women's Liberation Movement*. New York: Dell Publishing.
A collective attempt to record the thoughts and politics of the developing Women's Liberation Movement. The selections are meant to represent the spectrum of views within the movement and cover job discrimination, sexuality, day care, revolution, housework, and social class. Included are: "Why Women's Liberation?" by Marlene Dixon; "The Next Great Moment in History is Ours" by Vivian Gornick; "What It Would Be Like If Women Win" by Gloria Steinem; "Job Discrimination and What Women Can Do About It" by Alice Rossi; "Marriage and Love" by Emma Goldman; "Double Jeopardy: To Be Black and Female" by Frances Beal; "Colonized Women: The Chicana" by Elizabeth Sutherland; "The Woman Identified Woman" by Radicalesbians; "The Myth of the Vaginal Orgasm" by Anne Koedt; and many other classic pieces.

1239 BACKHOUSE, CONSTANCE and DAVID H. FLAHERTY, eds. 1992. *Challenging Times: The Women's Movement in Canada and the United States*. Montreal: McGill-Queen's University Press.
This anthology presents analysis and sometimes answers to questions about the nature of feminism, the interaction and conflicts between different sectors of the women's movement, and the prospects for the future. Many of the contributors have been activists in the movement and have helped shape the history and direction of North American feminism. Entries from the United States include those by Naomi Black, Sara Evans, Jean O'Barr, and Catharine MacKinnon.

1240 BOLES, JANET K., ed. 1991. *American Feminism: New Issues for a Mature Movement*. Newbury Park, CA: Sage Publications.
This collection is part of the series Annals of the American Academy of Political and Social Science, Volume 515. Selected articles cover anti-feminism in the 1980s, media treatment of women, and African-American feminists' contributions to the women's movement.

1241 BONEPARTH, ELLEN, ed. 1982. *Women, Power, and Policy*. New York: Pergamon Press.
A good collection of writings on public policy issues related to women. The range of the articles indicates the depth of sex/gender concerns and how they have affected public awareness, the political arena, and social movement agendas.

1242   BOOKMAN, ANN and SANDRA MORGEN, eds. 1988. *Women and the Politics of Empowerment*. Philadelphia: Temple University Press.
The editors put together this collection of readings out of a symposium on U.S. Women and Resistance in the Workplace and the Community. Their interest is to support and further the struggles of working-class women, white and black. Articles include: "Making Your Job Good Yourself: Domestic Service and the Construction of Personal Dignity" by Bonnie Thornton Dill; "Building in Many Places: Multiple Commitments and Ideologies in Black Women's Community Work" by Cheryl Townsend Gilkes; "Working-Class Women, Social Protest, and Changing Ideologies" by Ida Susser; "Vending on the Streets: City Policy, Gentrification, and Public Patriarchy" by Roberta M. Spalter-Roth; and "Communities, Resistance, and Women's Activism: Some Implications for a Democratic Polity" by Martha Ackelsberg.

1243   BUTLER, JUDITH and JOAN W. SCOTT, eds. 1992. *Feminists Theorize the Political*. New York: Routledge.
By bringing together a diverse collection of writings on feminism and the post-structuralist challenge, the editors of this volume reveal the politicized nature of feminist theory. A variety of perspectives address wide-ranging concerns including anti-discrimination laws, violence against women, reproductive freedom, and the politics of exclusion and hierarchy.

1244   CHAFETZ, JANET SALTZMAN. 1978. *Masculine, Feminine or Human? An Overview of the Sociology of Gender Roles, Second Edition*. Itasca, IL: F. E. Peacock.
This is the second edition of an early text on the sociology of gender roles. Past and present roles are described and prescriptions for change are offered.

1245   CONWAY, JILL K., SUSAN C. BOURQUE, and JOAN W. SCOTT, eds. 1989. *Learning About Women: Gender, Politics, and Power*. Ann Arbor: The University of Michigan Press.
This anthology looks at the ways feminist ideology and activism have affected power, politics, gender equality, scientific thought, and women's opportunities over the last two decades.

1246   COOKE, JOANNE, CHARLOTTE BUNCH-WEEKS, and ROBIN MORGAN, eds. 1969. *The New Women: An Anthology of Women's Liberation*. Greenwich, CT: Fawcett Publications.
This is a diverse collection of radical feminist writing. Includes poems, an exploration of women in Leftist politics and the roles of American women, Marlene Dixon on women's liberation, Del Martin and Phyllis Lyon on lesbianism, Naomi Weinsstein's classic article on "Kinder, Kuche, Kirche," Charlotte Bunch on issues and actions of the Women's Liberation Movement, and a position statement by W.I.T.C.H. Originally published in *Motive Magazine*, these writings reveal some of the early thinking of the Women's Liberation Movement.

1247 COOPER, JAMES L. and SHEILA MCISAAC COOPER, eds. 1974. *The Roots of American Feminist Thought*. Boston: Allyn and Bacon.
This collection gathers seven of the most significant early works of the feminist movement: Mary Wollstonecraft, an enlightenment rebel; Sarah Grimké, radical sectarian; Margaret Fuller, romantic idealist; John Stuart Mill, utilitarian liberal; Charlotte Gilman, evolutionary socialist; Margaret Sanger, romantic irrationalist; Suzanne LaFollette, radical libertarian.

1248 CYRUS, VIRGINIA, ed. 1993. *Experiencing Race, Class, and Gender in the United States*. Mountain View, CA: Mayfield Publishing Co.
A text which looks at the topic of American multiculturalism. The interdisciplinary nature of this collection provides a broad perspective on race, class, gender, and power. Individual stories, data, and analysis are all included in the diversity making up this reader. There are three themes: identity and the ways race, class and gender shape experience; power which reveals the connections between social forces and individual lives; and change which introduces strategies for change and people who have contributed to the process of social change, including Mother Jones, Carmen Domingues, and Anne Moody. Subsections deal with ethnic and racial identity, gender identity, economics, stereotypes, prejudice, power, heterosexism, violence, and taking action.

1249 DIAMOND, IRENE and LEE QUINBY, eds. 1988. *Feminism and Foucault: Reflections of Resistance*. Boston: Northeastern University Press.
Utilizing post-structuralist analysis to examine feminist theory and Foucault's writings, the authors look for common themes in philosophy, literary criticism, social theory, political theory, and religion. The essays show an activist orientation that is sometimes overlooked.

1250 DORENKAMP, ANGELA G., JOHN F. MCCLYMER, MARY M. MOYNIHAN, and ARLENE C. VADUM, eds. 1985. *Images of Women in American Popular Culture*. New York: Harcourt Brace Jovanovich Publishers.
An anthology of stories, advertising copy, poems, magazine articles, advice literature, marriage manuals, political manifestos, and newspaper columns that reveal the way popular culture portrays American women. The selections cover the last two centuries and are interdisciplinary in content. Over 100 selections are included with a wide range of interest and viewpoints. Includes contributions from well-known feminists such as Betty Friedan, Shulamith Firestone, Elizabeth Cady Stanton, Charlotte Perkins Gilman, Adrienne Rich, Susan Brownmiller, Gloria Steinem, Anne Moody, and many other lesser-known figures from a wide variety of fields.

1251 ENGLISH, JANE, ed. 1977. *Sex Equality*. Englewood Cliffs, NJ: Prentice-Hall.
A philosophical approach to the question of sex equality from the advent of the written word to the present. Selections include writings from Plato, Aristotle, Rousseau, Locke, John Stuart Mill, Simone de Beauvoir and Friedrich Engels in

the first section titled "The Philosophical Background." The second section "Contemporary Arguments" contains selections from Alison Jaggar, Joyce Trebilcot, and Christine Pierce. In the last section "The Popular Debate" there are selections from Sam Ervin, Jr., Ruth Bader Ginsburg, Steven Goldberg, Naomi Weisstein, and Robin Lakoff.

1252   EPSTEIN, CYNTHIA FUCHS and WILLIAM J. GOODE, eds. 1971. *The Other
        Half: Roads to Women's Equality*. Englewood Cliffs, NJ: Prentice-Hall.
A wide-ranging collection of articles on issues concerned with achieving women's equality. Related to the women's movement are selections covering American feminist programs, proposals for the future, and excerpts of writings from Kate Millett, Alice Rossi, the National Organization for Women, and Redstockings.

1253   FERREE, MYRA MARX and BETH B. HESS, eds. 1987. *Analyzing Gender:
        A Handbook of Social Science Research*. Newbury Park, CA: Sage.
The focus of the articles in this collection is the social structural effects on the experience and meaning of gender. There are five sections: Gender and Ideology; Social Control of Female Sexuality; Gender Stratification; Gendered Worlds; and Gender and the State.

1254   FREEMAN, JO, ed. 1994. *Women: A Feminist Perspective, Fifth Edition*.
        Mountain View, CA: Mayfield Publishing Co.
Beginning in 1975, Freeman has come out with editions of this anthology on various aspects of feminist issues. This latest edition has sections on: Body Politics; Relationships, Family and the Life Cycle; Work and Occupations; Words and Images (new section); Institutions of Social Control; Feminism in Perspective; Feminism and Diversity (new section). The section on Feminism in Perspective covers the early and contemporary women's movement, African-American feminism, anti-feminism, and men's response to feminism. The section on Feminism and Diversity examines the intersections of race, gender, and class and the diversity of feminist thought found among black, Chicana, and Jewish women. The work is interdisciplinary in scope and features classic as well as new articles from a diverse array of authors.

1255   FRIEDMAN, SCARLETT and ELIZABETH SARAH, eds. 1982. *On the Problem
        of Men: Two Feminist Conferences*. London: The Women's Press.
The contributors of this edited volume are British feminists and the articles are drawn from two conferences on feminism. The subjects they cover and the theories they use are similar to those found in the United States, although in some instances they voice even stronger criticisms of men than what might typically be found in the States. The authors feel that the thoughts and experiences they report on are universal.

1256   GARSKOF, MICHELE HOFFNUNG, ed. 1971. *Roles Women Play: Readings
        Toward Women's Liberation*. Belmont, CA: Brooks/Cole.
An early anthology on the contemporary women's movement and feminist

issues. Essays include contributors Naomi Weisstein, Marlene Dixon, Jo Freeman, and Ellen Cantarow.

1257 GERGEN, MARY MCCANNEY, ed. 1989. *Feminist Thought and the Structure of Knowledge*. New York: New York University Press.
An anthology which focuses on examining the effects of feminism on the social sciences. The contributors come from many disciplines and represent an international view. Traditional ways of thinking about the social sciences and the ways these disciplines conduct their teaching and research are challenged.

1258 GLAZER-MALBIN, NONA and HELEN YOUNGELSON WAEHRER. 1972. *Woman in a Man-Made World: A Socioeconomic Handbook*. Chicago: Rand McNally.
An early Women's Studies reader that looked at the social position of women in the United States. Glazer-Malbin, a sociologist, and Waehrer, an economist, put these articles together out of their frustration in trying to find adequate material on women's position in the economy and on the sociology of women. Sections of the book are: Part I, General Perspectives—includes historical and theoretical perspectives; Part II, Determinants of Differences between Women and Men—looks at psychological, sociological, and economic factors; Part III, Sex and Social Roles—focuses on marriage and work; Part IV, Myths About Women; and Part V, Toward Sex Equality.

1259 GORNICK, VIVIAN and BARBARA K. MORAN, eds. 1971. *Women in Sexist Society: Studies in Power and Powerlessness*. New York: Basic Books.
This collection of articles addresses issues that the contemporary women's movement has called into question. The authors are interested in promoting empirical research agendas and theoretical advancement to explicate sexism in social relations. By better understanding women's place in the world, the authors hope to contribute to developing attitudes and policies for change. This work contains some of the earliest theoretical discussions within the contemporary women's movement on sexist language and prostitution.

1260 GOULD, CAROL C. and MARX W. WARTOFSKY, eds. 1976. *Woman and Philosophy: Toward a Theory of Liberation*. New York: G. P. Putnam.
An anthology outlining philosophic views of the women's movement and particular feminist issues that the movement has raised.

1261 GRIFFIN, GABRIELLE, SASHA ROSENEIL, MARIANNE HESTER, and SHIRIN RAI, eds. 1994. *Stirring It: Challenges for Feminism*. Bristol, PA: Taylor & Francis.
Contributors debate the challenges of politics and action for feminism and Women's Studies, particularly in the areas of the women's movement, women's position in society, and the political arena. The politics of women's cultural production is discussed, and critiques of heterosexuality and monogamy are raised. A good illustration of the diversity in topics and tone found in Women's Studies.

1262   HABER, BARBARA, ed. 1983. *The Women's Annual, 1982–1983*. Boston:
       G. K. Hall & Co.
A collection of articles covering a variety of feminist issues. Included are:
"Feminist Theory: The Meaning of Women's Liberation" by Kathleen Barry;
"Politics and Law" by Peggy Simpson; "Violence Against Women" by Freada
Klein; and "Work" by Karen Sacks.

1263   HEWITT, NANCY A. and SUZANNE LEBSOCK, eds. 1993. *Visible Women:
       New Essays on American Activism*. Champaigne/Urbana: University of
       Illinois Press.
A century of women's political activism (1830 to 1930) is explored by leading
historians of women's and American history. Diverse forms of activism from a
wide spectrum of racial, ethnic, and class groups are presented. Along with
descriptive information, the authors attempt to analyze and conceptually clar-
ify the issues such diversity raises. Some of the groups covered in this collection are housewives, Native American women, African-American women, social
feminists, and suffragist activists. There are fifteen contributors to this volume,
including well-known writers Ellen Carol DuBois, William Chafe, Sara Evans,
Mari Jo Buhle, Nancy Hewitt, and Darlene Clark Hine.

1264   HIRSCH, MARIANNE and EVELYN FOX-KELLER, eds. 1990. *Conflicts in
       Feminism*. New York: Routledge.
A collection of twenty essays by academic feminist theorists on conflicts within the women's movement. Hirsch and Fox-Keller establish in the introduction
that feminism is both a political movement and a theoretical venture, and that
conflict is inherent in intellectual and activist endeavors. The editors asked
contributors to consider how conflicts within feminism have been acted out
and how they could be reconciled in a better way. Fitting into this framework,
the essays cover substantive issues and discuss ways of developing a discourse
for difference that would maintain diverse positions without creating irrecon-
cilable divisions. Internal debates on ERA, pornography, reproductive technologies, sexual orientation, workplace equality, methodology, race, class, and
ethnicity are included. Also includes, "A Conversation about Race and Class" by
Mary Childers and bell hooks; and "Race, Class, and Psychoanalysis? Opening
Questions" by Elizabeth Abel.

1265   HUBER, JOAN, ed. 1973. *Changing Women in a Changing Society*.
       Chicago: University of Chicago Press.
An early anthology covering diverse topics including the origins of the
Women's Liberation Movement. There is a chapter on feminist texts which
reviews seventeen well-known publications. Contributors include Jessie
Bernard, Jo Freeman, Myra Komarovsky, Cynthia Fuchs Epstein, Diane Scully,
and Pauline Bart. Huber and many of the contributors are sociologists and
their writing is framed within that tradition. This work was originally published
in the *American Journal of Sociology*, V.78, No. 4 (January 1973).

1266 HUMM, MAGGIE, ed. 1992. *Modern Feminisms: Political, Literary, Cultural*. New York: Columbia University Press.

Humm has put together over seventy excerpts from pivotal feminist writings according to their historical period and thematic focus. An entry on each author and introduction to each section is provided. This collection of inter-disciplinary texts provides an overview of feminism's history, theoretical writings, and chronology of twentieth century politics.

1267 JAGGAR, ALISON and PAULA S. ROTHENBERG, eds. 1984. *Feminist Frameworks: Alternative Theoretical Accounts of the Relations Between Men and Women, Second Edition*. New York: McGraw-Hill.

A collection of writings on feminist thought and practice. Each section includes an introduction to "the problem," which is followed by selected readings from alternative feminist frameworks, concluding with an examination of practice and the implications of the various theories. An improvement over the 1978 edition is the inclusion of articles by women of color. This is a well-done text which provides essential coverage and comparative views from the anti-feminist position as well as from liberal, Marxist, radical feminist, and socialist feminist perspectives.

1268 JAGGAR, ALISON and SUSAN R. BORDO, eds. 1989. *Gender/Body/Knowledge: Feminist Reconstructions of Being and Knowing*. New Brunswick, NJ: Rutgers University Press.

Contributors to this collection have written essays from a strong interdisciplinary framework. The overall effect is a feminist challenge to traditional conceptions of knowledge that have been accepted as unquestioned truths in their domination of Western intellectual thought.

1269 KANTOR, HANNAH, SARAH LEFANU, SHAILA SHAH, and CAROLE SPEDDING, eds. 1984. *Sweeping Statements: Writings From the Women's Liberation Movement, 1981–1983*. London: The Women's Press.

An anthology of feminist writings from British periodicals, particularly *SpareRib* and *Feminist Review* and some smaller publications. All are listed with subscription information in a separate section. The selections cover a two year period from 1981 to 1983 and are grouped into eight topical sections: Violence Against Women; Forever Working; Racism; No Nukes; Up Against the State; Sex and Sexuality; Our Bodies; and Challenges. Feminist activism, theory, and issues are well covered in these selections.

1270 KAPLAN, ALEXANDRA G. and JOAN P. BEAN, eds. 1976. *Beyond Sex-Role Stereotypes: Readings Toward a Psychology of Androgyny*. Boston: Little, Brown and Co.

The concept of androgyny, highly popular in the mid-1970s, states that women and men can retain the best qualities of their gender expectations and take on the best qualities of the other sex. This combination supposedly defines a model of well being that is superior to sex specific limitations. The ideal of androgyny began to be questioned with the rise of the women's culture, separatism, and radical lesbian essentialist ideology. This reader covers more than androgyny as it looks at sex and gender in many lights. Some of the readings are interesting because they are so obviously dated, others remain relevant to our time.

1271 KAUFFMAN, LINDA S., ed. 1993. *American Feminist Thought at Century's End: A Reader*. Cambridge, MA: Blackwell Publishers.
A collection of writings from feminist writers on current social issues. This work shows how far feminist thought has evolved in connecting strategies for change with theory and practice. Topics are far-ranging such as sex equality under the law, feminist politics, international feminism, sexuality, and gender conceptions under new biological and technological advances. Contributors include Catharine MacKinnon, bell hooks, Gayle Rubin, Sandra Harding, Judith Stacey, Barrie Thorne, Evelyn Fox-Keller, Joan Wallach Scott, Angela Davis, Gloria Anzaldua, and Jean Bethke Elshtain.

1272 KEOHANE, NANNERL O., MICHELLE Z. ROSALDO and BARBARA C. GELPI, eds. 1982. *Feminist Theory: A Critique of Ideology*. Chicago: University of Chicago Press.
A collection of writings providing views from liberal, Marxist, socialist, and radical feminism on theoretical issues related to sexuality, power, literary criticism, and political thought. Drawn from a number of issues of *Signs: Journal of Women in Culture and Society*, these essays explore relationships between family and the state, psychology and politics, and masculinity and objectivity.

1273 KOURANY, JANET A., JAMES P. STERBA, and ROSEMARIE TONG, eds. 1992. *Feminist Philosophies: Problems, Theories, and Applications*. Englewood Cliffs, NJ: Prentice-Hall.
This anthology is meant to be an introductory text to Women's Studies. The first part of the book contains articles which address issues relevant to women's inequality. Topics covered are gender socialization, sexuality, reproduction, self-images, the world of work, the domestic scene, and cultural invisibility. In the second section, theoretical considerations of women's position in patriarchal society detail the origins and solutions to this condition. The philosophical perspectives represented in this section are divided into liberal, radical, psychoanalytic, Marxist/socialist, and postmodern feminist positions. The last two readings address the need for feminism to accommodate women's diversity without losing their gender commonality.

1274 MACCANNELL, JULIET FLOWER, ed. 1990. *The Other Perspective in Gender and Culture: Rewriting Woman and the Symbolic*. Irvington, NY: Columbia University Press.
Original essays by well-known feminists discuss the way gender is embedded in social institutions and cultural practices. In general the writing is optimistic in concluding that patriarchal definitions of gender are giving way to newer views expressed by women.

1275　MARTIN, WENDY, ed. 1972. *The American Sisterhood: Writings of the Feminist Movement from Colonial Times to the Present*. New York: Harper and Row.

The editor of this anthology is interested in showing the feminist connections of the past to the thinking and activism found in the contemporary women's movement. There are forty-six selections that are evenly divided between writings that occurred before 1969 and those that occurred since that time. Even though there is a wide spectrum of issues covered, they fall into two major themes which constitute sections of this book: Political, Legal and Economic Questions; and Social, Sexual, and Psychological Questions. Includes selections from Elizabeth Cady Stanton, Crystal Eastman, Gloria Steinem, Fannie Wright, Margaret Sanger, Matina Horner, and Robin Morgan.

1276　MILLMAN, MARCIA and ROSABETH MOSS KANTER, eds. 1975. *Another Voice: Feminist Perspectives on Social Life and Social Science*. Garden City, NY: Anchor/Doubleday.

Two noted sociologists have put together a book of readings questioning the methods and perspectives of the social sciences and suggesting ways to change them to incorporate a feminist view. Selections include: Thelma McCormack "Toward a Non-sexist Perspective on Social and Political Change;" Judith Lorber "Women and Medical Sociology: Invisible Professionals and Ubiquitous Patients;" Gaye Tuchman "Women and the Creation of Culture;" Lena Wright Myers "Black Women and Self-Esteem;" Arlie Russell Hochschild "The Sociology of Feeling and Emotion: Selected Possibilities;" and Arlene Kaplan Daniels "Feminist Perspectives in Sociological Research."

1277　MORGAN, ROBIN, ed. 1970. *Sisterhood is Powerful: An Anthology of Writings From the Women's Liberation Movement*. New York: Vintage Books.

Important writings, with over fifty contributors, from the early years of the contemporary U.S. women's movement are included in this classical anthology. Most of the articles, position papers, poems, and photographs are from the small group sector of the movement. The revolutionary spirit and principles of the radical feminist position of this time period are well documented. Includes a section on women in the black liberation movement with selections by Frances Beal, Eleanor Holmes Norton, and the Black Women's Liberation Group of Mount Vernon, NY.

1278　NEWHOUSE, NANCY R., ed. 1986. *Hers: Through Women's Eyes*. New York: Harper and Row.

Beginning in 1977 the New York Times instituted a "Hers" column with different contributors weekly writing on whatever they wished. The idea was to create a forum for women to write about women, gender, sex, feminism, activism, social change, or their personal lives. The essays selected for inclusion in this collection were chosen because of the revelation and provocative punch they contained. These writings allow a view of the thoughts of many adherents of feminist thinking from the end of the 1970s to the mid-1980s.

1279 OLDFIELD, SYBIL, ed. 1994. *This Working-Day World: A Social, Political and Cultural History of Women's Lives, 1914–1945*. Bristol, PA: Taylor & Francis.
A collection of essays on women's activities in colleges, institutes, and political militancy. Specific topics in women's cultural history include art, medicine, fiction, political radicalism, and personal lives.

1280 PHILLIPS, ANNE, ed. 1987. *Feminism and Equality*. New York: New York University Press.
Phillips has included articles in this volume that were written in the mid-1970s to the mid-1980s. These writings, some of which are chapters from books, are centered on the meaning of feminism and of equality. A number of the selections have become classical works which are frequently cited and found in other anthologies. The focus of this collection is the attempt to create an encompassing definition of feminism that includes all groups. There is a heavy emphasis on socialist feminism and overt criticisms of U.S. liberal feminism. Phillips provides a 20+ page introduction which outlines and discusses each article. Selections include writings by Juliet Mitchell, Michele Barrett, bell hooks, Zillah Eisenstein, Carole Pateman, Ellen DuBois, Jean Bethke Elshtain, Sally Alexander, and Denise Riley.

1281 RICHARDSON, DIANE and VICTORIA ROBINSON, eds. 1993. *Thinking Feminist*. New York: Guilford Publications, Inc.
This compilation is a text providing a survey of feminist thought. The editors have selected works which give a comprehensive overview of past, present, and developing feminist theory covering the major themes and issues of Women's Studies.

1282 RICHARDSON, LAUREL and VERTA TAYLOR, eds. 1993. *Feminist Frontiers III: Rethinking Sex, Gender, and Society*. New York: McGraw-Hill.
A feminist interdisciplinary reader combining scholarly research articles, personal stories, cartoons, poems, and essays covering the range of issues appropriate for an undergraduate introduction to Women's Studies. Topics covered include: the women's movement; non-sexist language; visual images; spirituality; female sexual mutilation; violence against women; religion; socialization; science; health; law; family; intimacy; politics; inequality; racism; class; ethnicity; work; and the future of feminism.

1283 RIES, PAULA and ANNE J. STONE, eds. 1992. *The American Woman 1992–93: A Status Report*. New York: W. W. Norton & Co.
A volume in the annual series on the status of the American woman by the Women's Research and Education Institute. This issue provides the latest statistical information on the social, economic, and political position of women in American society. Essays discuss the status of women in the family, health, education, and employment fields. This, the fourth edition of this series, focuses on women in politics and highlights political women such as Governor Ann Richards, Senator Nancy Kassebaum, and Representative

Maxine Waters. This series covers a broad spectrum of women, feminism, and social activism.

1284 RISMAN, BARBARA J. and PEPPER SCHWARTZ, eds. 1989. *Gender in Intimate Relationships: A Microstructural Approach.* Belmont, CA: Wadsworth Publishing Co.
A collection of articles which look at gender roles from a sociological perspective. The overarching framework of the articles is the position that women and men are shaped by social settings—gender is not determined; it is changeable. Contributors include Francesca Cancian, Lillian Faderman, Michael Kimmel, Alice Echols, Judith Lorber, Laurel Richardson, Mary Zimmerman, Joan Spade, Rosanna Hertz, Kathleen Gerson, and Robert Staples covering gender related topics of love, lesbianism, men and feminism, friendship, couples, sexuality, abortion, baby care, dual-career couples, single heads of households, and black families.

1285 RIX, SARA E., ed. 1987. *The American Woman 1987–88: A Report in Depth.* New York: W. W. Norton & Co.
This is the first issue in a series of annual reports on the status of women in American society prepared under the auspices of the Women's Research and Education Institute (WREI), the non-partisan research arm of the bipartisan Congressional Caucus for Women's Issues. The report provides essays and statistical data on women in the economy, women and politics, the family, women of color, and a wide variety of gender issues. This book is reflective of the types of inquiries WREI received from researchers on women's issues, and serves as a comprehensive and useful resource on women and the changes in their lives. Of particular interest to scholars of the women's movement and feminist activism are "Women in Twentieth Century America: An Overview" by Sara M. Evans and "The Women's Movement in Recent American Politics" by Marian Lief Palley.

1286 ———. 1988. *The American Woman, 1988–89: A Status Report.* New York: W. W. Norton & Co.
The second annual report to the bipartisan Congressional Caucus for Women's Issues on women in the United States regarding their social, economic, and political status. Topics covered include women in relationship to the economy, family, politics, the arts, military, media, sports, and science. In addition, there are selections that address specific issues of ethnic women and women of color. Updated statistical portraits of women are found in the appendix. Articles related to the women's movement are "A Richer Life: A Reflection on the Women's Movement" by Cynthia Harrison; and "The Political Woman" by Ruth B. Mandel.

1287 ———, ed. 1990. *The American Woman, 1990–91: A Status Report.* New York: W. W. Norton & Co.
In this, the third year of this series, contributors examine women in relationship to housing, child care, employment policies, medical school, business,

contingent work, television, and the arts. Articles representing portraits of African-American, Hispanic, Asian, Pacific, and Native American women are found in this volume. Articles pertaining specifically to the women's movement are "Flourishing in the Mainstream: The U.S. Women's Movement Today" by Sarah Harder; "Women and the Peace Movement" by Kate McGuinness; and "The Emergence and Growth of Women's Studies Programs" by Mariam Chamberlain.

1288   ROSALDO, MICHELLE ZIMBALIST and LOUISE LAMPHERE, eds. 1974. *Woman, Culture and Society*. Stanford, CA: Stanford University Press.
The purpose of this anthology is to broaden comparative cultural conceptions of social life by addressing women's lives with the same interest that anthropology has focused on men. A sampling of the types of selections are "Family Structure and Feminine Personality" by Nancy Chodorow; "Women in Politics" by Jane Fishburne Collier; "Sex Roles and Survival Strategies in an Urban Black Community" by Carol B. Stack; "Female Status in the Public Domain" by Peggy Sanday; and "Engels Revisited: Women, the Organization of Production, and Private Property" by Karen Sacks.

1289   ROSSI, ALICE S., ed. 1988. *The Feminist Papers: From Adams to de Beauvoir*. Boston: Northeastern University Press.
This is an updated version, with new preface, of a 1973 publication of diverse writings going back to colonial days. Rossi reveals, through chronological placement, women's understandings of their place in society, freedom, autonomy, rights, and justice. The evolution of feminist thought and the social activism that springs from that ideological base is also revealed. Rossi provides useful scholarly remarks as an introduction to each section of the book. Selected writings include works from Abigail Adams, Mary Wollstonecraft, Margaret Fuller, John Stuart Mill, Susan B. Anthony, Elizabeth Cady Stanton, Friedrich Engels, Emma Goldman, Margaret Sanger, Jane Addams, Virginia Woolf, Margaret Mead, and Simone de Beauvoir.

1290   ROSZAK, BETTY and THEODORE ROSZAK, eds. 1969. *Masculine/ Feminine: Readings in Sexual Mythology and the Liberation of Women*. New York: Harper and Row.
This is an interesting early anthology which contains writings that argue for and against feminism. The authors include blatant misogynist work from psychology (Freud) and anthropology (Lionel Tiger), progressive men's views (George Bernard Shaw, Havelock Ellis, Gunnar Myrdal), and feminist voices ranging from de Beauvoir, Alice Rossi, and Marlene Dixon to such pieces as the 'SCUM Manifesto' and a position piece from the radical feminist group Redstockings of the Women's Movement.

1291   ROTHENBERG, PAULA S. 1994. *Race, Class, and Gender in the United States: An Integrated Study, Third Edition*. New York: St. Martin's Press.
A study of racism and sexism within the context of class. In this second edition Rothenberg has included more writings on heterosexism and homophobia,

and these concerns are reflected throughout the book. There are many selections (some one page or less) with many different forms of presentation. Contributors include: Audre Lorde, Gloria Anzaldua, Cherrie Moraga, bell hooks, Maya Angelou, Richard Wright, Ruth Hubbard, Marilyn Frye, Letty Cottin Pogrebin, Ntozake Shange, the Anti-Suffragists Selected Papers, and court decisions in Dred Scott v. Sanford, Bradwell v. Illinois, Plessy v. Ferguson, Brown v. Board of Education of Topeka, Roe v. Wade.

1292 RUTH, SHEILA, ed. 1994. *Issues in Feminism, Third Edition*. Mountain View, CA: Mayfield Publishing Co.

Ruth's text serves as an introduction to the field of Women's Studies. Interdisciplinary in scope, this work features both contemporary and classic feminist writing. In this edition a sharper focus on diversity is provided and opposing views from anti-feminists are included. Aside from the interesting selection of articles, a strong point for this text is its organizational framework. Ruth's introductory essays for each chapter outline the articles, place the material in context, and articulates the themes, concepts and issues to be covered. The first chapter "An Introduction to Women's Studies" is an excellent beginning for new students to this field. It is followed by sections titled Part I Consciousness: Concepts, Images, and Visions; Part II Sexism Realized: Women's Lives in Patriarchy; and Part III Women Move. The third section includes work on feminist activism, events, and documents.

1293 SALPER, ROBERTA, ed. 1972. *Female Liberation: History and Current Politics*. New York: Alfred A. Knopf.

Varied and interesting collection of documents on feminist activism in the women's movement from the nineteenth and twentieth centuries. Includes essays and writings from Mary Wollstonecraft, Charlotte Perkins Gillman, Emma Goldman, Marlene Dixon, Roxanne Dunbar, Meredith Tax, the Fourth World Manifesto, and a personal essay on Salper's changing consciousness.

1294 STAMBLER, SOOKIE, ed. 1970. *Women's Liberation: Blueprint for the Future*. New York: Ace.

There were many fine collections which came out of the early writing of the contemporary women's movement. Many of these anthologies are unheard of and hard to find, but contain writings from feminist activists who went on to become well-known. These articles contain their thoughts as they were being formulated and create a foundation for understanding the direction these writers and parts of the movement took in the late 1970s and early 1980s. Included in this anthology are writings by Susan Brownmiller, Kate Millett, and Rita Mae Brown.

1295 SUNSTEIN, CASS R., ed. 1990. *Feminism and Political Theory*. Chicago: The University of Chicago Press.

Papers in this edited volume are organized around four themes: Justice and Rights; Equality and Inequality; Sexuality Issues in Public vs. Private Arenas; Trust and Responsibility. The authors are interested in bridging feminist thought with political theory. By utilizing critique, reconstruction, and new assessments of political theory, the authors question traditional understandings of issues affecting individual and community lives. Contributors include Susan Moller Okin, Catharine A. MacKinnon, Virginia Held, Carole Pateman, among others.

1296   SWERDLOW, AMY and HANNA LESSINGER, eds. 1983. *Class, Race, and Sex: The Dynamics of Control.* Boston: G. K. Hall.
Swerdlow and Lessinger have put together a collection of papers which originated at the 1980 and 1981 Scholar and Feminist Conferences at Barnard College. Papers address race, class, sex, ethnicity, welfare, lesbianism, difference, black families, women and work, and the New Right. Includes, Bonnie Thornton Dill on the concept of sisterhood between women of different races (with a review of the literature), and Cheryl Gilkes on the feminism among black women even though racism is their principal struggle. Also, "The Social Enforcement of Heterosexuality and Lesbian Resistance in the 1920s" by Lisa Vogel; "The Feminist Theology of the Black Church" by Evelyn Brooks; "Issues of Race and Class in Women's Studies: A Puerto Rican Woman's Thoughts" by Angela Jorge.

1297   TANNER, LESLIE B., ed. 1970. *Voices from Women's Liberation.* New York: New American Library.
This anthology contains selections by women of the past and present who have spoken out on the need for women's liberation. The militant voices heard in this volume are strong and frank. They cover marriage, motherhood, politics, work, legal rights, suffrage, African-American women, male chauvinism, and sexuality. Selections include historical writings from Abigail Adams, Frances Wright, Mary Wollstonecraft, the Grimké sisters, Elizabeth Cady Stanton, Susan B. Anthony, Elizabeth Blackwell, Lucretia Mott, Harriet Martineau, Sojourner Truth, Lucy Stone, Carrie Chapman Catt, Florence Kelley, and the First Woman's Rights Convention. Contemporary offerings include the Redstockings, Carol Hanisch, Kathie Sarachild, Anne Koedt, Evelyn Reed, Linda Gordon, Robin Morgan, Betsy Warrior, Margaret Benston, Naomi Weisstein, Ellen Willis, Roxanne Dunbar, Lisa Leghorn, Pat Mainardi, Beverly Jones, Judith Brown, and Shulamith Firestone.

1298   THE QUEST STAFF. 1981. *Building Feminist Theory: Essays from Quest.* New York: Longman.
A collection of articles previously published in *Quest: A Feminist Quarterly.* The journal was founded in 1974 by feminist activists in the Washington, D.C. area who were interested in addressing questions of race, class, and lesbianism. The selections incorporated in this work come from the first three volumes and include "Fundamental Feminism: Process and Perspective," by Nancy Hartsock; "Beyond Either/Or: Feminist Options" and "Not for Lesbians Only," by Charlotte Bunch; "Who Wants a Piece of the Pie?," by Marilyn Frye; "An Open Letter to the Academy," by Michelle Russell; and "Patriarchy and Capitalism," by

Linda Phelps. The history of the journal (1974–1981) is recounted by Charlotte Bunch in the introduction.

1299 THOMPSON, MARY LOU, ed. 1970. *Voices of the New Feminism*. Boston: Beacon Press.

Thompson put together this anthology in the hope that it would encourage others to examine the ideas which inspired these contributors to write on the social revolutionary potential of the contemporary women's movement. All of the authors do not agree with each other, but that is what Thompson wants to portray in encouraging dialogue among a wide spectrum of women. Some of the pieces are reprints and others are written for this book. Included are: Betty Friedan, "Our Revolution is Unique"; Roxanne Dunbar, "Female Liberation as the Basis for Social Revolution"; Alice Rossi, "Sex Equality: The Beginnings of Ideology"; Pauli Murray, "The Liberation of Black Women"; Martha Griffiths, "Women and Legislation"; Mary Daly, "Toward Partnership in the Church"; Caroline Bird, "The Androgynous Life"; and Shirley Chisholm, "Women Must Rebel."

1300 WEST, UTA, ed. 1975. *Women in a Changing World*. New York: McGraw-Hill.

It is interesting to note that this book about problems arising out of feminist consciousness was written in 1975. Since the movement has continued to be a vital contender for social change, any effects at this early date would only be partial responses to feminist demands. Still, the issues the contributors raise are quite relevant to women in the 1990s. The question of motherhood, whether or not to have children and how to raise them while maintaining a career, is even more pressing today than it was then. Also discussed are marriage, love, loneliness, and the possibility of financially supporting men who give back very little to the women who support them except perhaps drug and alcohol problems. Reading this book almost twenty years after it was published points out how deeply the dynamics of sex/gender relations penetrate every corner of public/private life. Contributors include Caryl Rivers, Mary Daly, Uta West, Doris Lessing, Elizabeth Janeway, Grace Paley, and Donald Barthelme.

1301 ZAK, MICHELE WENDER and PATRICIA A. MOOTS. 1983. *Women and the Politics of Culture*. New York: Longman.

An introductory text for Women's Studies which combines classic readings with more recent commentary. Many of the selections are organized around the theme of sexual economy and oppressive sexual arrangements. Contributors include Friedrich Engels, Simone de Beauvoir, John Stuart Mill, Sigmund Freud, Jean Jacques Rousseau, Susan Brownmiller, Virginia Woolf, Mary Wollstonecraft, Susan B. Anthony, Elizabeth Cady Stanton, Betty Friedan, Shulamith Firestone, and Charlotte Bunch.

Subject Index

1848 Woman's Rights Convention, 25, 26, 33, 40, 64, 74, 159, 369, 381, 1009, 1107, 1136, 1140, 1161

1920s feminism, 28, 63, 65, 73, 83, 84, 183, 188, 358, 956

1960s social movement activism, 56, 89, 97, 111–114, 120, 127, 147, 219, 268, 271, 281, 376, 422, 464, 476, 559, 578, 651, 653, 726, 746, 755, 853, 935, 955, 1005

1972 Democratic Convention, 943

Abbott, Edith, 386, 393

abolition, 3, 15, 18, 70, 130, 369, 371, 374, 378, 381, 392, 401, 409, 415, 425, 426, 438, 440, 629, 675, 754, 995, 1000, 1074, 1102, 1103, 1115, 1120, 1143, 1146, 1151, 1154 1191

abortion, 7, 103, 106, 107, 111, 131, 141, 142, 169, 174, 206–227, 447, 491, 568, 629, 634, 667, 685, 793, 925, 928, 932, 935, 948, 960, 1015, 1085, 1087, 1090, 1096, 1196, 1199, 1202, 1254, 1292

Abzug, Bella, 135

academia, 8, 14, 16, 153, 307–331, 385, 449, 457, 504, 611, 613, 624, 625, 632, 650, 884, 907, 1257, 1276

ACT UP, 228, 297

Addams, Jane, 23, 29, 37, 45, 245, 246, 332, 365, 384–386, 923, 1074, 1087, 1110, 1137

advertising, 532, 1250

affirmative action, 112, 846, 922, 936, 949, 954, 1122, 1125

African-American women (*see also* black women; black feminism; women of color), 91, 356, 367, 372, 376, 402, 414, 435, 725, 726, 778, 997, 1027, 1062, 1159, 1208, 1240

ageism, 151, 532, 572, 1254

AIDS, 228, 243, 297, 1229

Akron National Women's Studies Association (1990), 740

Akron Woman's Rights Convention (1852), 372, 392

Alaskan women, 1170

alliances, 627, 692, 694, 808

American Association of University Women (AAUW), 1034, 1120

American Friends Service Committee (AFSC), 75, 253, 1060, 1221

American Woman Suffrage Association
     (AWSA), 39, 366, 473, 409
anarchism, 359, 377, 389, 436, 496, 582,
     588, 636
androgyny, 279, 541, 1270, 1299
Anthony, Susan B., 25, 45, 365, 371, 1083,
     1110, 1114, 1115, 1123, 1137,
     1141, 1142, 1145, 1153, 1156,
     1158, 1160, 1289, 1297, 1301
anthropology, 314, 316, 329, 418, 513,
     523, 605, 762, 980, 1004, 1019,
     1288, 1290
anti-abortion, 169, 212, 214, 215, 218,
     685, 960
anti-ageism, 151
anti-authoritarian, 987
anti-censorship, 851, 852, 857, 867, 1026
anti-discrimination laws, 1243
anti-Dowry violence, 231
anti-ERA, 68, 176, 184, 196, 199, 200–203,
     629, 822, 957, 959, 967
anti-feminism (*see also* New Right;
     Religious Right; backlash), 16,
     27, 68, 81, 118, 155, 156, 398,
     465, 510, 793, 797, 893, 937,
     958, 960, 963, 967, 968, 972,
     1008, 1267, 1290, 1292
anti-lynching, 382, 400, 749, 754, 1062,
     1142
anti-nuclear, 140, 250, 258, 306, 638
anti-politics, 682
anti-pornography, 230, 508, 849, 851–854,
     857, 861, 862, 872, 1026
anti-racism, 93, 758, 776
anti-rape (*see also* violence against
     women), 238
anti-religious, 90, 91
anti-Semitism, 673, 677, 695
anti-slavery (*see also* abolition), 3, 76,
     369, 415, 420, 425, 438, 439,
     629, 1083
anti-suffrage, 967, 968, 1291
anti-violence, 287
anti-war, 18, 113, 131, 140, 253, 258, 261,
     478
Arab-American women, 714, 1170
archives, 1057, 1064, 1065, 1068, 1075,
     1080, 1081, 1086, 1098, 1102,
     1113, 1117, 1124, 1128, 1131,
     1132, 1190, 1191

art, 338, 423, 897, 902, 1124
Asian-American women, 700, 701, 703,
     705, 708, 711, 723, 982, 1021,
     1031, 1051, 1086, 1170
autobiography, 72, 153, 288, 332–361,
     478, 485, 495, 496, 532, 533,
     618, 625, 639, 653, 654, 696,
     698, 728, 892, 991, 995, 999,
     1028, 1149, 1163

Baptist women, 756
Baby M Case, 225, 557
backlash (*see also* anti-feminism), 106,
     107, 150, 169, 207, 321, 882,
     959, 961, 963
Baker, Ella, 61, 424
Barnard Conference, 849, 871, 1026,
     1163, 1296
Barnett, Ida B. Wells (*see also* Ida B.
     Wells; Ida B. Wells-Barnett),
     361, 386, 428, 729, 1142
battered women, 231, 232, 242, 488,
     1018, 1092, 1127, 1183
   battered women's movement, 229,
     231, 232, 240, 241, 244
   services, 1166
   shelters, 106, 236, 240, 244
Beard, Mary Ritter, 411, 1063
Besant, Annie, 1
Bethune, Mary McLeod, 402, 753, 1137
Bethune Museum and Archives, 1064,
     1191
biography, 10, 59, 103, 187, 262, 362–445,
     531, 752, 840, 903, 912, 923,
     952, 999, 1024, 1030, 1068,
     1082, 1094, 1126, 1132,
     1143–1144, 1151, 1152, 1163,
     1165, 1169, 1177, 1183, 1191,
     1194, 1208, 1209, 1210, 1219,
     1214, 1218, 1219, 1224, 1225,
     1230, 1231
biology (*see also* essentialism), 467, 513,
     560, 614, 797, 875, 882
birth control (*see also* contraception), 7,
     215, 221, 237, 447, 569, 910,
     915, 924, 925, 1085, 1096, 1153
birth control movement, 1, 7, 70, 207,
     211, 365, 377, 387, 389, 394,
     425, 1014, 1110, 1112

black (*see also* African-American)
    church, 360, 756, 1296
    community, 354, 752, 753, 756, 765, 971, 1288
    family, 733
    feminism, 132, 354, 374, 421, 572, 675, 676, 680, 690, 702,716, 743–774, 802, 887, 1254, 1277, 1296
    liberation (*see also* civil rights movement; Black Power),341, 344, 363, 464, 595, 759, 765, 767, 773, 1277
    Marxist revolution, 351
    nationalism, 363
    Panthers, 376
    Power, 111, 344, 376, 621, 630, 682, 752
    studies, 312
    women (*see also* African-American women; women of color), 197, 333, 348, 382, 435, 452, 461, 678, 687, 688, 698, 717, 719, 733, 734, 737-739, 743–774, 783, 996, 1064, 1066, 1104, 1117, 1152, 1187, 1188, 1191, 1210
    Women's Club Movement, 361, 754, 1149
    women's studies, 311, 312, 680, 760, 769
Blackwell, Alice Stone, 45, 1065
Blackwell, Antoinette Brown, 1151
Blackwell, Elizabeth, 22, 336, 394, 1104, 1297
Blatch, Harriot Stanton, 36, 45, 337, 814, 1063
Bloomer costume, 25, 261, 381
Bly, Robert, 488
bodybuilders, 532
boycotts, 348, 748, 765
Bread & Roses, 172
Breckinridge, Sophonisba, 393
British feminism, 35, 167, 526, 883, 1219, 1255, 1269
British suffrage movement, 35, 47, 48
Brooklyn Welfare Action Council, 657
Brown, Antoinette, 1142, 1151
Brown, Olympia, 380, 1147
Bryant, Louise, 569
Burns, Lucy, 45, 48, 380
Butch/Femme, 283, 290, 300, 999
Butler, Josephine, 394

capitalism, 82, 241, 264, 318, 472, 519, 555, 556, 560, 563, 568, 586, 588, 660, 1298
CARASA (Committee for Abortion Rights and Against Sterilization Abuse), 298
cartoons, 914, 1282
catalogs, 1084, 1089, 1172, 1201, 1257
Catt, Carrie Chapman, 29, 39, 45, 395, 427, 923, 1064, 1065, 1110, 1297
Cell 16, 172, 1131
censorship, 230, 278, 870, 1181
Chaflin, Tennessee, 366
charity (*see also* philanthrophy), 433
chauvinism (*see also* sexism), 472, 1297, 1298
Chicago Women's Liberation Union (CWLU), 170, 577, 1068, 1097
Chicana (*see also* Mexicana), 568, 693, 729, 730, 842, 844, 994, 1175
Chicana feminism, 708, 709, 723, 724, 732, 1238, 1254
child care, 106, 107, 224, 390, 561, 751, 935, 1056, 1254, 1287
child custody, 488, 1092
child labor, 53, 65, 73
children, 17, 19, 107, 212, 219, 225, 295, 379, 456, 477, 484, 803, 804, 871
Children's Bureau, 19
Children's Defense Fund, 390
Chisholm, Shirley, 135, 339, 340, 743, 940
cinema (*see also* films; film criticism), 879
civil disobedience (*see also* direct action), 140, 195, 251, 256, 260, 263, 406, 747
civil rights movement, 61, 88, 113, 131, 147, 253, 333, 341, 348, 356, 357, 360, 376, 412, 421, 423, 424, 630, 637, 644, 645, 653, 666, 682, 687, 746, 748, 749, 752, 754, 755, 765, 767, 770, 773, 783, 798, 979, 1152, 1191
Civil War, 378, 440, 443
class (*see also* race, class, and gender; working class; socialist feminism), 6, 112, 132, 140, 159, 189, 276, 283, 362, 471, 498, 499, 516, 524, 549, 550, 566, 652, 655, 775–806, 920, 922

classic feminist writings, 80, 138, 296, 331, 370, 470, 476, 486, 507, 530, 535, 542, 548, 573, 581, 583, 584, 588, 704, 723, 850, 900, 985, 1003, 1141, 1217, 1238, 1247, 1255, 1266, 1277, 1280, 1292, 1301
clinic escorts, 208
Club Movement, 12, 1152
Coalition of Labor Union Women, 1028
collective consciousness, 509, 641
colonialism, 498, 718
Combahee River Collective, 555
comics, 914
Commission on the Status of Women, 131, 192, 1101, 1184
communes, 630
communism, 346, 519
community (*see also* lesbian community; black community), 33, 194, 208, 210, 254, 266, 267, 272, 300, 301, 326, 381, 421, 495, 636, 669, 692, 705, 756
community organizing, 65, 72, 119, 299, 396, 435
comparable worth (*see also* pay equity), 920, 922, 936, 947, 949, 1134
comparative analysis of
feminism, 101, 546
pro and anti ERA activists, 202
social movements, 154, 644, 647, 655, 666
women's movements, 48, 623, 627–629, 634, 641, 736, 930
competition theory, 152, 281
conflicts in feminism, 23, 81, 91, 95, 98, 109, 111, 123, 159, 160, 161, 183, 188, 231, 259, 292, 297, 321, 491, 564, 686, 740, 753, 841, 815, 849, 852, 853, 862, 910, 1026, 1239, 1264
Congress of Racial Equality (CORE), 356
Congressional Union (CU), 380
consciousness-raising (CR), 89, 98, 110, 112, 119, 120, 122, 131, 146, 165, 583, 584, 665, 699, 793, 872
contemporary women's movement, 7, 29, 55–57, 60, 61, 63, 65, 68, 70, 72, 85, 86, 88, 89–175, 450, 451, 460, 464, 465, 470, 506, 994, 1003–1005, 1010, 1017, 1023, 1026, 1084, 1097, 1104, 1131, 1150, 1154, 1164, 1170, 1172, 1180, 1185, 1186, 1197, 1205, 1213, 1217, 1218, 1226, 1229, 1231
contraception (*see also* birth control), 206, 214, 215, 648, 1014, 1090
countermovement (*see also* anti-feminism; backlash), 88, 169, 199, 629
court cases, 557, 932, 947, 948, 1196
COYOTE (Call Off Your Old Tired Ethics), 136
Craft, Ellen, 439
credit (*see* equal credit)
Cuba, 154, 1213
Cubanos, 1175
cultural feminism (*see also* lesbian feminism; feminist community; separatism), 111, 267, 280, 302, 306, 462, 495, 539, 602, 636, 656, 682, 692, 693, 897

Daly, Mary, 343, 467, 530, 562
Davies, Emily, 395
Davis, Katharine Bement, 393
Day, Dorothy, 66, 425, 569
de Beauvoir, Simone, 391
Delta Sigma Theta, 402, 753
Democratic National Committee, 444
Democratic Party, 412, 421
Denett, Mary Ware, 1
Depression Years, 56, 408, 594
deviant women, 36, 662
direct action activism and groups (*see also* civil disobedience), 159, 193, 195, 251, 254, 298, 345, 635, 637, 765
disability rights movement, 94, 116, 129, 691
discrimination, 16, 313, 557, 787, 836, 846, 909, 920, 924, 949, 955–972
discussion lists (*see* online)
displaced homemakers, 1166
diversity (*see* multiculturalism)
division (see, conflict; identity politics)

Dix, Dorothea, 365, 1137
domestic abuse (*see* battering; battered
    women's movement; violence
    against women)
domestic partnership, 999
domestic relations, 1199
domestic violence (*see* battering; bat-
    tered women's movement; vio-
    lence against women)
doner insemination, 300
Douglass, Frederick, 1191
dress reform (*see also* Bloomer), 32, 261
drugs, 751
DuBois, W.E.B., 53, 66
Dunbar-Nelson, Alice, 1149
Dworkin, Andrea, 857
early feminist thought, 3, 14, 21, 31, 35,
    36, 41, 42, 55, 58, 646, 500, 515,
    590
early social reform, 1–21
early woman's rights movement, 22–34
ecofeminism, 250, 252, 258, 264, 266,
    306, 343
Eddy, Mary Baker, 1083, 1137
educated women, 86, 313
education, 12, 514, 735, 838
    feminist (*see also* women's studies),
        311, 9, 14
    higher (*see also* academia), 8, 14, 16,
        29
    medical, 336
    multicultural, 735
    reform, 17, 88, 777, 1206
electronic resources (*see* online)
employment (*see also* work), 816, 920,
    933, 941, 1122
encampment (*see also* peace), 251, 368
    Greenham Common, 256, 306
    Seneca, 248, 259, 263, 267, 306
encyclopedia of
    court cases, 1196
    black women, 1191
    feminism, 1218
    the Left, 1168
    sexuality, 1199
    women, 1183
English feminism (*see* British)
environment (*see* ecofeminism)
ephemeral materials (*see* library collections)

equal credit, 924, 966
equal pay (*see* comparable worth; pay
    equity)
equal rights (*see* equality)
Equal Rights Amendment (ERA), 29, 68,
    81, 87, 103, 106, 107, 114, 122,
    131, 173, 176–205, 359, 368,
    379, 405, 406, 416, 491, 556,
    568, 627, 1002, 1101, 1264, 1285
equality, 416, 479, 629, 933
essentialism, 449, 462, 467, 480, 537, 578,
    675
ethics, 221, 286, 650, 1237
ethnicity, 413, 537, 557, 569, 621, 677,
    685, 692, 694, 702, 703, 722,
    735, 801, 807, 836, 1264
exclusion, 690, 730, 741, 1243
fairy tales, 553, 919
family, 29, 68, 107, 114, 453, 476, 560,
    563, 671, 890, 899, 910, 915,
    1092, 1140, 1148, 1284
family planning (*see also* birth control),
    1, 214, 215
farm women, 71
farm workers, 61
farm workers union (*see also* United
    Farm Workers' Union), 842
fast (dietary), 345, 406
feminism between suffrage and the con-
    temporary women's movement,
    65, 81, 87, 444, 822
    between the wars, 62, 69, 73, 83, 177,
    183, 248, 358
feminist
    critique, 770, 891, 1004
    history, 10, 83, 88, 111, 411, 1143,
        1289
    meaning, 55, 530, 534, 539, 1222
    men, 494, 497, 528
    methods, 611, 664
    movement comparisons (*see also*
        comparative social
    movements), 622, 623, 627–269, 631,
        634, 641, 646, 648, 661, 663
    Party, 414
    pedogogy, 311
    perspectives, 101, 122, 130, 249, 250,
        277, 490, 501, 521, 614, 673,
        713, 865, 1254, 1276

feminist (*cont.*)
  philosophy, 280, 309, 481, 1267
  relations, 148, 267, 239
  research, 316, 605, 610, 613
  scholarship, 307, 314, 316, 322, 330,
      490, 526, 571, 580, 602, 620,
      642, 643, 700, 880, 883, 888,
      918, 1226
  sociology, 617, 632, 665
  theory, 151, 220, 222, 241, 276, 280,
      304, 314, 446, 501, 530, 536,
      537, 540–596, 620, 632, 747,
      758, 802, 880, 901, 1193, 1272,
      1273, 1298
  therapy, 899
  thought, 58, 65, 96, 105, 114, 117,
      128, 137, 153, 254, 279, 296,
      311, 334, 430, 446–541, 624,
      662, 673, 679, 690, 777, 787,
      790, 819, 850, 860, 869, 872,
      878, 886, 892, 954, 1004,
      1140, 1247, 1257, 1260, 1268,
      1271, 1276, 1278, 1129, 1185,
      1203
film (*see also* cinema), 48, 746, 827, 847
film criticism, 902, 1004
Firestone, Shulamith, 467
Flynn, Elizabeth Gurley, 347
foot binding, 553
free love, 366
Freud, Sigmund, 472, 532
Friedan, Betty, 103, 135
Fuller, Margaret, 365, 590
fundamentalism, 475
funding, 1034–1057

gay and lesbian studies (*see also* cate-
      gories under lesbian), 270
Gay and Lesbian Task Force, 1118
gay history and collections, 1058, 1080,
      1081, 1099, 1116, 1118
gay/lesbian movement, 271, 278, 287,
      293, 303
gay men and lesbians, 289, 297, 299
gay theory (*see also* Queer theory), 285
gender
  analysis, 455, 456, 463, 480, 489, 501,
      523, 640, 787

discourse, 370, 449, 453, 466, 525,
      532, 535, 540, 609, 674, 796,
      886, 969
  cross-cultural comparisons, 112, 571
  and education, 8, 654, 777
  and health, 116, 228
  ideology, 447, 472, 537, 791, 882, 956
  inequality, 376, 385, 512, 793, 797,
      920, 927, 933, 1251
  and language, 885, 914, 1200
  and law, 946, 1196
  and peace, 247, 257
  politics, 198, 939, 943, 945, 953, 1245
  and power, 806
  race and class (*see* race, class, and
      gender)
  roles, 20, 128, 290, 319, 359, 363, 454,
      790, 794, 1244, 1256
  studies, 659, 662, 788, 789, 794, 798,
      799, 800, 803, 1235, 1236, 1244,
      1253, 1282, 1284
  and violence, 237, 287
  and work, 233, 795, 808, 809, 812,
      813, 818, 819, 820, 826, 829, 848
gender-free science, 875, 889, 893, 896,
      912,
General Federation of Women's Clubs,
      1075, 1128
genetics, 913
Gethi, Angela, 255
Gilman, Charlotte Perkins, 29, 45, 349,
      364, 386, 425, 1063, 1104, 1153
global feminism (*see also*, international
      feminism), 451, 490, 512, 648,
      685, 736, 779, 836, 1167, 1219
goddess (*see also* spirituality), 976, 977,
      978, 983, 986, 987, 988, 989
Goldman, Emma, 1, 359, 389, 394, 436,
      590, 1104
government publications, 1211
grassroots activism, 394, 748
Greenham Common Peace Encampment
      (*see* encampments)
Greer, Germaine, 103, 398
Griffin, Susan, 467
Grimké, Angelina, 415, 1000
Grimké, Charlotte, 440
Grimké, Sarah, 425, 1000, 1138, 1153
Grimké sisters, 25, 1120, 1143

guide to the sources (*see* Section VI,
     especially Reference Materials)

Hammer, Fannie Lou, 421, 754, 767
harassment (*see* sexual harassment)
Harlem Writers Guild, 333
Harper, Ida Huster, 1083
Hawaiian women, 718
Haymarket Square, 582
Haywood, Bill, 359
health and the health care movement
     (*see also* women's health move-
     ment), 387, 390, 490, 614, 738
     908, 1086, 1096, 1105, 1127,
     1129, 1169
Hedda Nussbaum Case, 557
hierarchy, 1243
higher education (*see also* academia),
     886, 147, 1171
Hill, Anita (*see also* Hill Thomas
     Hearings; Thomas Hill
     Hearings), 953, 969, 971, 1155
Hill-Thomas Hearings, 414, 557, 704
Hispanic-American women (*see also*
     Chicanas; Latinas), 731, 1175
leaders, 696, 1213
historic site, 1059, 1107, 1108, 1114, 1136
history of
     black women, 1064, 1117, 1152,
          1188
     feminism, 20, 23, 28, 29, 58, 65, 83,
          88, 101, 109, 130, 144, 154, 159,
          163, 177, 500, 531, 590, 1032,
          1104, 1275
     misogyny, 24
     reproductive freedom, 7, 219, 227,
          1014
     sexuality, 853, 864, 1118
     U.S. society in general, 362, 382, 459,
          570, 615
     welfare, 484
     women, 22, 27, 56, 60, 63, 64, 68, 70,
          77, 82, 124, 910, 964, 995, 1020,
          1190, 1153–1155, 1160, 1178,
          1189, 1190, 1192, 1203, 1231
     and education, 8, 16, 86
     and politics, 34, 54, 62, 76, 79, 84
     and work, 57, 69, 234, 825, 837

holdings (*see* Section VI, Library
     Collections)
homemakers, 476, 1166, 1263
homophobia, 263, 461
HOTDOG (Humanitarians Opposed to
     Degrading Our Daughters), 200
housework, 900, 1238
housing, 924, 929
Hull House, 29, 384, 388, 1087
humor, 1179

identity, 36, 126, 127, 203, 259, 281, 284,
     291, 292, 301, 509, 516, 522, 583,
     609
identity politics, 159, 160, 272, 283, 300,
     321, 323, 492, 636, 656,
     673–690, 699, 704, 711, 716,
     724, 740, 744, 747, 753, 764,
     773, 1264
ideological purity, 138, 160
ideology, 21, 36, 99, 157, 159, 170, 184,
     202, 225, 541, 651, 666, 762,
     956, 957, 1272
illegal abortion, 219
images (*see also* media; advertising), 251,
     319, 737, 788, 1250
immigrants, 67
imprisonment, 345
inclusiveness, 684
index, 1015, 1172, 1173, 1204, 1228
individualism, 168
inequality, 63, 237, 313, 328, 501, 525,
     527, 537, 797
interest group, 125, 931
intra-movement group relations, 159
international feminism (*see also* global
     feminism), 255, 490, 512, 736,
     779, 833
International Ladies Garment Workers
     Union (ILGWU), 848
International Women's Year (IWY), 92,
     107, 173, 175, 556
interviews, 133, 195, 834
Irish-American, 67
Irwin, Inez Haynes, 358, 569

Jewish feminism, 695, 1254

Jewish women, 420, 685, 715, 721, 727
Johnson, Sonia, 195, 405, 406, 495
journalism, 182

Kelley, Abby, 29, 45, 438
Kelley, Florence, 386, 444
Kellor, Frances, 393
Kennedy, Flo, 414, 751
King, Martin Luther, 333
Ku Klux Klan, 956

labeling theory, 662
labor (*see also* work; trade unionism;
        Women's Trade Union League;
        Coalition of Labor Union
        Women; minimum wage
legislation; protective labor legislation)
    activism, 382, 384, 388, 389, 397,
        582
    education, 828
    history, 837
    Knights of, 66
    movement, 66, 70, 367, 569, 808, 815,
        817, 823, 826, 833, 1028, 1142
    organizing, 253, 347, 420, 425, 445
    unions, 728, 810, 818, 824, 827, 842
language, 315, 430, 490, 650, 914, 1172,
        1179, 1254, 1259
    non-sexist, 885, 1198, 1200, 1206
Latinas, 91, 710, 712, 1175
laws, 5, 68, 107, 142, 181, 190, 192, 209,
        216, 223, 227, 479, 491, 501,
        512, 558, 576, 812, 868,
        920–954, 964, 971, 1026, 1092,
        1129, 1153, 1199, 1243, 1262
leaders, 29, 45, 96, 103, 409, 696, 940,
        1119, 1164
leadership, 120, 273, 752, 990
League of Women Voters, 62, 1083, 1088,
        1121
Left Wing (*see also* New Left), 66, 671,
        857, 993, 1168, 1204
legal rights, 479, 491, 947, 964, 1196,
        1199, 1297
legislation (*see* protective labor; mini-
        mum wage; abortion)
legislators, effects of women, 944
lesbian, 88, 103, 109, 111, 122, 123,
        269–306, 343, 354, 430, 450,
        451, 495, 552, 763, 775, 782
    AIDS activism, 228
    community, 282, 283, 286, 290, 292,
        686, 775, 865
    feminism, 259, 263, 869
    and gay liberation movement (*see*
        gay/lesbian movement)
    parenting, 295, 305
    sadomasochism, 853, 865
    studies, 735, 999, 1012, 1058, 1078,
        1079–1082, 1176
    theory, 573, 681
Lewis, Sarah Evans, 382
liberal feminism, 111, 115, 123, 131, 135,
        159, 477, 479, 556, 589, 862,
        1239, 1252, 1273, 1280
liberalism, 323, 458, 589, 686, 867, 962
library collections, 1058–1136
lifestyle, 529
lifestyle politics, 682
literary criticism, 505, 880, 883, 887, 919
literature, 417, 540, 885, 986, 1266
love, 366, 466, 486, 552, 858, 1300
Lutz, Alma, 1123
lynching (*see* anti-lynching)

MacKinnon, Catherine, 587
male dominance (*see* patriarchy)
male gender role (*see also* masculinity),
        786, 795
marches, 159
marriage, 29, 359, 399, 453, 454, 472,
        486, 495, 535, 733, 915, 1238,
        1297, 1300
Marxism, 519, 543, 570, 588
Marxist feminism, 498, 574, 586, 592
masculinity (*see also* male gender role),
        488, 781
mass movement sector, 120, 131, 1239
The Masses, 569
materialism, 574, 519
matriarchy, 462
Mead, Margaret, 365
media (*see also* images), 182, 306, 476,
        490, 799, 853, 877, 911, 1095,
        1185, 1240, 1250
medical/medicine, 233, 336, 650, 1086
men's movement, 236, 488

methodology, 311, 597–620, 658, 664, 1264, 1276
   auto/biography, 371, 597–600, 606, 607, 609, 618–620, 1163
   oral history, 603–605
Mexicana (*see also* Chicana), 728, 729, 824
midwife, 233, 234, 413
militancy, 20, 35, 44, 48, 416, 1279
militarism, 249, 517
Millett, Kate, 103, 355, 398
minorities, 1051
misogyny, 16, 233, 376, 472, 475, 505, 511, 553, 926
Mitchell, Juliet, 467
Montgomery Bus Boycott, 348, 749, 765
Moorland-Springarm Research Center, 1191
moral development, 316, 482, 483
moral reasoning, 854
morality, 6, 114, 233
Mormons for ERA, 205, 405
Moskowitz, Belle, 429
Mother Jones, 66, 420, 425, 1142
motherhood, 68, 114, 218, 225, 268, 430, 447, 4553, 486, 906, 932, 983, 1297, 1300
mothering, 449, 456, 557, 906, 915, 916
mothers, 17, 19, 221, 476, 484, 838
   single, 484
Mott, Lucretia, 25, 33, 369, 381, 1074, 1146
movement analysis, 150, 281, 636
movement publications, 206
movement sectors, 1239
Ms. Magazine, 144, 532
multiculturalism, 283, 320, 321, 323, 516, 673, 677, 690, 691–742, 1261
Murray, Pauli, 357
museums, 1061, 1064, 1109, 1191
myth, 134, 472, 488, 511, 573, 882, 913, 983, 1290

NAACP (National Association for the Advancement of Colored People), 53, 1091
NARAL (National Abortion Rights Action League), 1285

NAWSA (National American Woman Suffrage Association), 395, 409, 427, 831, 923, 1109
NBFO (National Black Feminist Organization), 751, 755, 1087
National Congress of Mothers, 17
National Consumer's League, 444
National Council of Negro Women, 402
NOW (National Organization for Women), 90, 91, 97, 98, 103, 107, 111, 120, 122, 131, 135, 143, 159, 166, 170, 173, 198, 200, 269, 357, 406, 414, 477, 490, 556, 818, 928, 968, 1097, 1104, 1252, 1285, 1292
National Welfare Rights Organization, 657
National Woman Suffrage Association, 29
National Woman's Party (NWP), 29, 44, 65, 81, 87, 183, 188, 380, 416, 441, 831, 923, 1083, 1104, 1108, 1285
National Women's Political Caucus (NWPC), 135, 159, 1087, 1104, 1285
National Women's Studies Association (NWSA), 150, 324, 695, 740
nationalism, 363, 685
nationality, 457
Native American women, 420, 731, 1001, 1165, 1235, 1263
nature, 264, 480, 567, 797, 856
network analysis, 15
New Deal, 444, 952
New Jersey, 43, 78, 1132
New Left, 90, 113, 131, 172, 275, 464, 559, 645, 653, 671, 1005
New Social Movement Theory, 637, 652, 656, 670, 682
Nightingale, Florence, 394
non-profit organizations, 1046
non-violent activism (*see also* direct action; civil disobedience), 245–268, 635, 742
Norton, Caroline, 394
nurses, 46, 233, 234, 394, 1169

older women, 404, 1235
Olmsted, Mildred Scott, 255, 368
online, 1162, 1181

oppression, 471, 523, 544, 549, 560, 592, 850
oral history (*see* methodology)
organizational documents, 1153
organizational structure, 170
organizations, 119, 149, 164, 170, 727, 1023, 1104, 1125, 1164, 1166, 1168, 1170, 1186, 1205, 1223
origins of first wave feminism, 22–34, 35, 58
origins of contemporary women's movement, 31, 70, 122, 131, 584
outreach, 91

pacifism (*see also* peace), 59, 255, 256, 262, 263, 265, 396, 407, 569
Pankhurst, Sylvia, 52, 1110
Parent Teachers Association, 17
Parks, Rosa, 1191
Parsons, Elsie Clews, 569
Parsons, Lucy Gathering, 367, 382
patriarchy, 24, 60, 225, 276, 287, 462, 463, 472, 488, 501, 505, 519, 523, 525, 537, 555, 563, 566, 569, 594, 640, 792, 876
Paul, Alice, 29, 44, 45, 187, 193, 416, 1059, 1063, 1074, 1083, 1104, 1137
pay equity (*see also* comparable worth), 841, 846, 920
peace (*see also* encampments; Women's International League for Peace and Freedom), 75, 88, 245–268, 736, 1074, 1113, 1116
    activism, 65, 368, 383, 384, 397, 425, 517
    movement, 61, 131, 345, 647, 653
pensions, 938
periodical sources, 206, 999, 1084, 1171, 1176, 1180, 1182, 1205, 1214, 1217, 1228
Philadelphia area, 1220
philanthropy, 6, 58
philosophy, 213, 280, 298, 304, 309, 343, 458, 471, 481, 547, 557, 560, 562, 567, 869, 1251, 1260, 1267
photographs, 1103
picture books, 803
policy, 19, 68, 94, 112, 120, 125, 139, 150, 179, 181, 192, 223, 231, 390,

512, 627, 641, 780, 807, 920–954, 1241
political
    candidates, 406, 950
    correctness, 321, 676
    office, 59
    organizations, 119, 1168
    science, 316, 546
    theory, 469, 474, 926, 1295
    women, 590, 726
politicians, 191, 395, 940
politics, 5, 6, 9, 24, 34, 39, 49, 54, 59, 61, 66, 79, 84, 88, 105, 120, 127, 135, 145, 175, 178, 180, 191, 204, 218, 220, 339, 340, 407, 421, 429, 444, 503, 509, 834, 890, 920-954, 961, 962, 1067, 1295
politics of difference, 676
poor women and poverty, 19, 32, 57, 66, 72, 356, 390, 452, 655, 657, 717, 751, 775, 804, 807, 830, 836, 838, 839
popular culture, 147, 182, 1250
pornography (*see also* anti-pornography), 136, 174, 271, 447, 566, 849, 851, 852, 854, 866, 867, 868, 870–872, 1026, 1273
Porter, Polly, 444
post-feminism, 162, 527
postmodern, 473, 479, 669
power, 2, 76, 96, 121, 165, 168, 224, 376, 396, 457, 510, 594, 774, 792, 806, 873, 923, 951, 953, 1241, 1245, 1259
praxis, 240, 558, 886, 920
pregnancy, 215, 224
prejudice, 16, 313, 435, 909, 924
President's Commission on the Status of Women, 1101
primary sources, 1137–1161
prison, 345, 347, 350, 393, 441
prison reform, 5
privacy, 447
pro-choice movement, 169, 667
pro-family movement, 465, 960
professional women, 911
Progressive Era, 4, 8, 49, 359, 1020
prostitutes' rights movement, 136
protective labor legislation (*see also*

labor), 29, 65, 81, 177, 188, 192, 393, 818, 831
protest, 79, 88, 154, 261, 630, 635, 780, 809, 837, 909, 1242
psychoanalysis, 448, 456, 473, 507
psychoanalytical feminism, 455, 581
psychology, 116, 201, 203, 316, 463, 474, 482, 483, 489, 504, 538, 573, 878, 899, 1270
publishing, 109, 324, 884, 1195
Puerto Rican Studies, 706, 1175

Quaker activism, 33, 34, 75, 257, 369, 381, 438, 1146
queer theory, 681

race, class, and gender, 132, 312, 692, 702, 704, 707, 737, 744, 775–806, 1235, 1248, 1291, 1296,
racial groups, 808
racism, 66, 333, 348, 357, 372, 382, 435, 673, 707, 717, 754, 956
racism in the women's movement, 91, 93, 141, 310, 414, 675, 678, 689, 744, 773
radical feminism, 89, 90, 98, 107, 110, 111, 115, 120, 126, 131, 159, 165, 172, 279, 280, 406, 422, 547, 552, 560, 565, 571–573, 584, 867, 872, 1238, 1277
Rankin, Jeannette, 59, 407, 953, 1063, 1104
rape (*see also* violence against women), 11, 141, 230, 237, 238, 447, 583, 678, 861, 868, 932, 1006, 1018, 1093, 1243, 1254, 1292
rape crisis centers, 236, 1153
Reconstruction, 440
Reed, John, 359
reform, 3, 6, 10, 15, 18, 73, 75, 231, 419, 428, 433, 840, 1098, 1103, 1112, 1119, 1137
  prison, 5, 393
  prostitution, 11, 20, 859
religion and
  anti-feminism, 24, 472, 475, 511
  progressive activism, 34, 66

feminist critique, 90, 108, 157, 210, 399, 547, 876
women, 500, 715, 756, 978, 986, 997, 1146, 1147, 1216
Religious Right, 957, 961, 970
reproductive freedom, 1, 7, 206–227, 555, 556, 925, 1077, 1199, 1243, 1273
reproductive politics, 893, 913
reproductive technologies, 1264
Republicans, 191
resource mobilization, 152, 205, 637
revolution, 154, 264, 351, 451, 471, 491, 507, 560, 582, 584, 588, 595, 635, 783, 812, 858, 1024, 1156
Rich, Adrienne, 467, 531
Right Wing, 450, 685, 959
Right Wing women, 956, 965
Right-to Life, 793
Robeson, Esland Goode, 382
Robins, Margaret Dreier, 29, 388, 840
Robinson, Jo Ann Gibson, 348
Robinson, Ruby Doris Smith, 752
Roosevelt, Eleanor, 365, 379, 1100, 1139
rural women, 720
Russia, 587
sadomasochism, 300, 686, 853, 863, 865
SAMOIS, 853, 865
sanctuary movement, 981
Sanger, Margaret, 217, 342, 365, 377, 387, 394, 1014, 1083, 1085, 1110
schisms in feminism, 323, 675, 1264
Schlafly, Phyllis, 398
Schlesinger Library, 1084, 1104, 1187, 1188
scholarly research, 787
scholarly writing, 884
scholarship, 307, 314, 316, 322, 324, 330, 580, 602, 642, 643, 700, 888, 918, 1047, 1226, 1232
science, 614, 797, 874, 875, 882, 889, 893, 894, 896, 907–909, 912, 917
Sears Case, 557
segregation, 717
Senate Judiciary Committee, 971
Seneca Falls Convention (*see* 1848 Convention)
Seneca Women's Peace Encampment (*see* encampments)

separatist feminism, 279, 280, 288, 291,
    302, 306, 451, 495, 496, 578,
    681, 895
settlement movement, 4, 29, 332, 383,
    384, 385, 393, 1144, 1160, 1169
sex workers, 228
sexism, 16, 66, 74, 107, 142, 153, 157,
    233, 249, 263, 313, 328, 357,
    376, 385, 435, 472, 475, 517,
    528, 532, 560, 625, 650, 707,
    895, 928, 973–990
sexual harassment, 447, 868, 932, 947,
    969, 971, 1018
sexual orientation, 471, 480, 1264
sexual politics, 270, 505
sexuality, 11, 136, 165, 214, 222, 271, 278,
    298, 355, 457, 486, 495, 501,
    579, 849, 858, 860, 864, 866,
    868–872, 1026, 1079, 1199, 1249
single women, 454, 484, 860
small group, 89, 110, 120, 131, 355, 565,
    682, 1239
Smeal, Eleanor, 143
social change, 8, 38, 61, 69, 159, 179, 735,
    793, 795, 883, 1105, 1285
social construction, 480, 945
social feminism, 13, 49, 73, 393, 459,
    1263
social justice causes, 379, 833
social movement
    analysis, 9, 105, 159, 281, 621–672,
        682, 847
    strategies, 91, 112, 135, 150, 159, 163,
        208, 641, 945
    tactics, 35, 112, 150, 159, 641
social norms, 795
social science, 291, 457, 610, 650, 1019,
    1031, 1253, 1257, 1276
social work, 4, 385
socialism, 65, 123, 346, 359, 362, 397, 545,
    561, 568, 587, 596, 671, 822,
    1168
socialist feminism, 35, 52, 98, 107, 111,
    115, 122, 127, 147, 149, 172,
    241, 318, 349, 364, 366, 367,
    465, 498, 519, 542, 545, 554,
    555, 559, 563, 566, 569, 574,
    575, 577, 581, 585, 587, 593,
    595, 890, 993
socialist feminist unions (see also

Chicago Women's Liberation
    Union), 95, 127, 170
socialization, 142, 456
sociology, 9, 114, 153, 281, 291, 316, 370,
    385, 386, 456, 617, 621–672,
    788, 1038, 1053, 1236, 1244
songs, 767
Sophia Smith Collection, 1089, 1103,
    1110
sorority, 753
Southern Christian Leadership
    Conference (SCLC), 333
Southern women, 84, 1031
speeches, 432, 1137, 1142, 1145–1147
spiritualism, 306, 975
spirituality (see also Goddess), 259, 360,
    703, 973–990
Stanton, Elizabeth Cady, 25, 33, 45, 394,
    399, 420, 425, 437, 500, 1083,
    1115, 1123, 1145, 1153, 1156
statistics, 1229, 1285, 1286
status politics, 9
Steinem, Gloria, 103, 532
Steward, Maria, 432
Stone, Lucy, 45, 373, 409, 590, 1115,
    1151, 1153
Stop ERA, 793
strikes (see also labor activism; unions),
    834, 827, 847
Strong, Anna Louise, 425
structure, 119, 121, 122, 170
student movement, 630, 1005
suffrage, 2 25, 27, 32, 59, 84, 85, 130, 627,
    998, 1147, 1156,
suffrage movement, 23, 26, 28–30, 35–53,
    159, 253, 337, 350, 371–373,
    380, 395, 399, 408, 416, 427,
    441, 629, 1084, 1104, 1141, 1158
Supreme Court, 971
Supreme Court decisions, 209, 216, 948
surrogate motherhood, 221, 557, 932
symbolism, 100, 186, 636, 960, 1220

Take Back the Night, 861, 1026
technology, 225, 521
temperance movement, 2, 9, 66, 1094,
    1126, 1160
Terrell, Mary Church, 428, 439
"the woman question," 575, 593, 640

theory of knowledge, 889
Third World women, 836, 1129
Thomas-Hill Hearings (*see also* Hill-Thomas), 414, 557, 764, 971
Thompson, Mattie Proctor, 382
time, 446
trade union women (*see also* labor union women), 1072
trade unionism (*see also* labor movement), 841, 15, 29, 411, 728, 807–848
trade unions, 1153
trashing, 138, 355
Truth, Sojourner, 372, 392, 401, 426, 1115, 1133, 1137, 1142
Tubman, Harriet, 378, 425, 1191

underground railroad, 378
unions (*see* labor movement; trade unions)
United Auto Workers (UAW), 847
United Auto Worker's Women's Bureau, 818
United Farm Workers Union, 253
United Nation's Conference Report, 737
United Nations Decade for Women, 1075, 1128
unity, 716, 764

violence against women, 107, 136, 228–244, 475, 855, 856, 861, 1018, 1026, 1060, 1069, 1092, 1221, 1254, 1262, 1294
voluntary women's associations, 18
Vorse, Mary Heaton, 397, 569
voter registration drives, 748

wage discrimination (*see also* sexism; inequality), 846, 920, 949
Wald, Lillian D., 383, 1070, 1144
welfare, 49, 88, 235, 400, 428, 484, 807, 830, 952, 1106
Wells, Ida B. (*see also* Ida B. Wells-Barnett), 382, 439, 675, 754,
Wells-Barnett, Ida B. (*see also* Ida B. Wells), 361, 428
widows, 731

Willard, Emma, 365, 1142, 1153
Willard, Frances, 66, 1094, 1126, 1153
WITCH [Women's International Terrorist Conspiracy from Hell), 1246
witch hunts, 553
witchcraft, 259, 980, 988
witches, 234, 986
Wittig, Monique, 681
Wollstonecraft, Mary, 442, 515, 590
Woman's Peace Party, 245
woman's rights, 22–34, 369, 380, 399, 975, 1084, 1104, 1138, 1142, 1263
Women Against Censorship, 851
Women Against Pornography, 849
Women Against Violence in Pornography and the Media, 853
women and economics, 499, 563, 900
women and politics, 5, 54, 88, 168, 196, 209, 212, 255, 339, 395, 400, 447, 832, 841, 873, 886, 935, 937, 943, 1067, 1249, 1254
women of color, 91, 197, 228, 344, 351, 413, 492, 578, 657, 675, 683, 693, 694, 696, 700, 702, 703, 706, 711, 713, 714, 723, 729, 740, 742, 757–759, 768, 769, 778, 836, 1021, 1031, 1152, 1170, 1186
women physicians (*see also* Elizabeth Blackwell), 1086
Women Strike for Peace, 268
Women's Christian Temperance Union (WCTU), 2, 9, 66, 183, 1126
women's clubs (*see also* Club Movement; Black Women's Club Movement), 12, 18, 183, 1075, 1128, 1160
women's community (*see* lesbian community)
women's culture (*see* lesbian)
Women's Emergency Brigade, 847
Women's Equity Action League (WEAL), 1285
women's health movement, 228, 233, 234, 239, 243, 387, 1096, 1169
Women's International League for Peace and Freedom (WILPF), 245, 246, 255, 368, 384, 1130

women's liberation movement (*see also* contemporary women's movement), 122, 126, 1238, 1246, 1269, 1277
Women's Political Council, 348
women's property rights, 33
women's studies (*see also* academia), 307–331, 514, 571, 616, 680, 700, 735, 741, 760, 907, 974, 1011, 1019, 1022, 1025, 1029, 1162, 1167, 1174, 1184, 1201, 1228
Women's Trade Union League (WTUL), 388, 1028, 1083, 1153
women's ways of knowing, 449, 907

Woodhull, Victoria, 366, 1115, 1153
working-class (*see also* labor; Marxism, socialism; trade unions; work), 19, 52, 445, 795, 813, 826, 487, 586, 728, 789, 810, 811, 814–816, 824, 827, 834, 844, 1007
working-class women (*see also* socialist feminism; WTUL), 74, 352, 431
World War II, 56, 75, 476

young women, 201, 527
Young Women's Christian Association (YWCA), 75

Author Index

ABBOTT, SIDNEY, 269
ABEL, ELIZABETH, 1232, 1264
ABEL, EMILY K., 1232
ABELOVE, HENRY, 270, 363
ABRAMOVITZ, MIMI, 807
ACKER, JOAN, 920
ACT UP/NY WOMEN AND AIDS BOOK
    GROUP, 238
ADAM, BARBARA, 446
ADAM, BARRY D., 271
ADAMS, DAVID, 229
ADAMS, ELSIE, 1233
ADDAMS, JANE, 37, 245, 246, 332, 1137
ADDIS, PATRICIA K., 991
ADELSTEIN, MICHAEL E., 1234
ADLER, KAREN S., 363
AFSHAR, HALEH, 691
AIKEN, SUSAN HARDY, 307
AISENBERG, NADYA, 308
ALAN GUTTMACHER INSTITUTE, 206
ALBRECHT, LISA, 692
ALDERFER, HANNAH, 849
AL-HIBRI, AZIZAH Y., 309, 588
ALLEN, ANITA L., 447
ALLEN, JEFFNER, 272
ALLEN, PAMELA, 89
ALLEN, POLLY WYNN, 364
ALLEN, SHEILA, 621
ALLISON, DOROTHY, 775
ALMQUIST, ELIZABETH M., 743

ALONSO, HARRIET HYMAN, 247, 248
ALPERN, SARA, 597
ALTBACH, EDITH HOSHINO, 542
ANDERSEN, MARGARET L., 1235, 1236
ANDERSON, JUDITH, 1137
ANDERSON, SHERRY RUTH, 573
ANDOLSEN, BARBARA H., 744, 1237
ANGELOU, MAYA, 333
ANTHIAS, FLOYA, 621, 776
ANTICOGLIA, ELIZABETH, 365
ANTLER, JOYCE, 777
ANZALDUA, GLORIA, 693, 694, 723
APPLEWHITE, HARRIET B., 546
APTHEKER, BETTINA, 55, 310
ARLING, EMANIE NAHM, 360
ARRINGTON, THEODORE S., 1766
ASCHER, CAROL, 598
ASH, LEE, 1061
ASHBAUGH, CAROLYN, 367
ASSITER, ALISON, 543
ATKINS, CLARISSA W., 974
ATKINSON, STEVEN, 1162
ATKINSON, TI-GRACE, 90

BABCOX, DEBORAH, 1238
BACK, KURT W., 1
BACKHOUSE, CONSTANCE, 1239
BACON, MARGARET HOPE, 368, 369
BADER, ELEANOR J., 91

BAKER, ANDREA J., 273
BALLOU, PATRICIA K., 992
BALSER, DIANE, 808
BANKS, OLIVE, 35, 622
BANNER, LOIS, 56
BANNISTER, ROBERT C., 370
BARASH, CAROL, 778
BARDES, BARBARA, 873
BARLETT, ELIZABETH ANN, 1138
BARRER, MYRA E., 1164
BARRETT, MICHELE, 544
BARRY, KATHLEEN, 371, 599, 600, 850
BARUCH, ELAINE HOFFMAN, 448
BASSNETT, SUSAN, 623
BATAILLE, GRETCHEN M., 1165
BAXANDALL, ROSALYN, 57
BEAL, FRANCES M., 745
BEASLEY, MAURINE, 1139
BECK, EVELYN TORTON, 695
BECKER, SUSAN D., 177
BELENKY, MARY FIELD, 449
BELL, SUSAN GROAG, 1140
BERG, BARBARA J., 58
BERGMANN, BARBARA, 921
BERNARD, HOLLINGER F., 335
BERNARD, JAQUELINE, 372
BERNARD, JESSIE, 624, 625, 779, 780
BERRY, MARY FRANCES, 178
BETHUNE, MARY MCLEOD, 1137
BILLINGTON, ROSAMUND, 36
BIRD, CAROLINE, 92, 955
BISHOP, BEVERLY D., 1065
BJORKMAN, FRANCES, 37
BLACKMAR, BETSY, 362
BLACKWELL, ALICE STONE, 373
BLACKWELL, ELIZABETH, 336
BLATCH, HARRIOT STANTON, 337, 437
BLEE, KATHLEEN M., 956
BLEIER, RUTH, 874, 875
BLEWETT, MARY H., 809
BLUM, LINDA M., 922
BLUMBERG, RHODA LOIS, 88
BOARD, JOHN C., 59
BOGGS, CARL, 626
BOLES, JANET, 179, 180, 617, 1240
BONEPARTH, ELLEN, 1241
BONILLA-SANTIAGO, GLORIA, 696
BOOKMAN, ANN, 1242
BORDIN, RUTH, 2
BOSTON WOMEN'S HEALTH BOOK
    COLLECTIVE, 243

BOUCHIER, DAVID, 628
BOULDING, ELISE, 60
BOURNE, JENNY, 93
BOYD, MELBA JOYCE, 374
BOYLAN, ESTHER, 94
BRADY, DAVID W., 957
BRADY, KATHLEEN, 735
BRANDE, ANN, 975
BRENNA, SHAWN, 1166
BREWER, ROSE, 692
BROCK-UTNE, BIRGIT, 249
BROD, HARRY, 781
BRODY, MICHAL, 274
BROWN, BARBARA A., 181
BROWN, ELAINE, 376
BROWN, JOANNE CARLSON, 876
BROWN, LOULOU, 1167
BROWN, RITA MAE, 275, 1294
BROWN, RUTH MURRAY, 958
BROWNMILLER, SUSAN, 230, 1250, 1294,
    1301
BRYAN, DIANETTA GAIL, 746
BUCK, MACKY, 95
BUECHLER, STEVEN M., 38, 629
BUHLE, MARI JO, 545, 993, 1141, 1168
BULBECK, CHILLA, 697
BULKIN, ELLY, 673
BULLOUGH, VERN L., 1169
BUNCH, CHARLOTTE, 96, 311, 450, 451,
    782, 1246, 1298
BURNHAM, LINDA, 452, 1170
BURRIS, VAL, 959
BURSTYN, VARDA, 851
BURTON, GABRIELLE, 453
BUSH, DIANE MITSCH, 231
BUTCHER, PATRICIA SMITH, 1171
BUTLER, JOHNELLA E., 312
BUTLER, JUDITH, 674, 1243
BUTLER, MATILDA, 182

CABELLO-ARGANDONA, ROBERTO, 994
CADE, TONI, 698
CALDECOTT, LEONIE, 2250
CALIFIA, PAT, 852, 853
CAMERON, ARDIS, 810
CAMPBELL, KARLYN KOHRS, 3, 1142
CANCIAN, FRANCESCA M., 877, 1285
CANNON, LYNN WEBER, 694, 741, 1031
CANTAROW, ELLEN, 61
CANTON, MILTON, 811

CAPEK, MARY ELLEN, 1172
CARABILLO, TONI, 97, 923
CARAWAY, NANCIE, 675
CARBY, HAZEL V., 676
CARD, EMILY, 924
CARDEN, MAREN LOCKWOOD, 98, 99, 630
CARDINALE, SUSAN, 1173
CARLSON, AVIS, 62
CARROLL, BERNICE A., 546
CARTER, SARAH, 1174
CASSELL, JOAN, 100
CASTILLO-SPEED, LILLIAN, 1175
CASTRO, GINETTE, 101
CATALDO, MIMA, 251
CATT, CARRIE CHAPMAN, 39
CAVIN, SUSAN, 277
CEPLAIR, LARRY, 1143
CHAFE, WILLIAM H., 63, 102
CHAFETZ, JANET SALTZMAN, 631, 632, 633, 1244
CHAL, ALICE, 699, 700
CHAMBERLAIN, MARIAM K., 313, 706
CHAMBERS-SCHILLER, LEE, 454
CHARLTON, SUE ELLEN M., 925
CHESLER, ELLEN, 377, 488
CHESLER, PHYLLIS, 878
CHICAGO, JUDY, 338
CHISHOLM, SHIRLEY, 339, 340, 783
CHODOROW, NANCY, 455, 456
CHOW, ESTHER NGAN-LING, 701
CLARDY, ANDREA FLECK, 1176
CLARK, JUDITH FREEMAN, 1177
CLARK, SEPTIMA POINSETT, 341
CLOUGH, PATRICIA TICINETO, 457
COCHRAN, JO, 702
COHEN, MARCIA, 103
COLE, JOHNETTA, 703
COLLARD, ANDREE, 252
COLLINI, STEFAN, 458
COLLINS, PATRICIA HILL, 747, 1235
COMBAHEE RIVER COLLECTIVE, 555, 772
CONLON, FAITH, 677
CONNELL, R. W., 784
CONOVER, PAMELA JOHNSTON, 960
CONRAD, EARL, 378
CONWAY, JILL K., 342, 1178, 1245
COOK, ALICE H., 812
COOK, BLANCHE WIESEN, 379
COOKE, JOANNE, 1246
COOLE, DIANA, 926

COONEY, ROBERT, 253
COOPER, JAMES L., 1247
COOPER, PATRICA, 813
COOTE, ANNE, 104
COSS, CLARE, 1144
COSTAIN, ANNE N., 105
COTE, CHARLOTTE, 380
COTT, NANCY F., 22, 64, 65, 183, 459
COWAN, GLORIA, 854
CRAIG, ROBERT H., 66
CRAWFORD, VICKI L., 748, 749
CRITES, LAURA L., 927
CROCKER, RUTH HUTCHINSON, 4
CROMWELL, OTELIA, 381
CROWDER, RALPH L., 382
CRUIKSHANK, MARGARET, 278
CUMMINGS, SCOTT, 785
CURTHOYS, ANN, 460
CYRUS, VIRGINIA, 1248

DAHLERUP, DRUDE, 634
DALY, MARY, 678, 680, 343, 547, 1179, 1299, 1300
DANIELS, DORIS GROSHEN, 383
DANKY, JAMES P., 1180
DAVID, DEBORAH S., 786
DAVIS, ALLEN FREEMAN, 384
DAVIS, ANGELA, 344, 461, 678, 750, 1271
DAVIS, BEVERLY, 751
DAVIS, ELIZABETH GOULD, 462
DAVIS, FLORA, 106
DAVIS, LENWOOD G., 996
DAVIS, NANETTE J., 232
DAVIS, SUSAN E., 207
DE BEAUVOIR, SIMONE, 334, 548
DE LAURETIS, TERESA, 679, 879
DECKARD, BARBARA SINCLAIR, 107
DECROW, KAREN, 928
DEEGAN, MARY JO, 385, 386
DELPHY, CHRISTINE, 549
DEMING, BARBARA, 254, 345
DENNIS, PEGGY, 346
DEUTCHMAN, IVA E., 184
DEXTER, MIRIAM ROBBINS, 976
DIAMOND, IRENE, 1249
DIAMOND, SARA, 961
DILL, BONNIE THORNTON, 694, 704, 741, 742, 1242, 1296
DILORIO, JUDITH, 208
DIMOCK, PETER, 362

DINER, HASIA R., 67
DINNERSTEIN, DOROTHY, 307, 463
DIXON, MARLENE, 550, 1238, 1246, 1256, 1290, 1293
DOELY, SARAH BENTLEY, 108
DONEGAN, JANE B., 233
DONOVAN, JOSEPHINE, 551, 880
DORENKAMP, ANGELEA G., 1250
DOUGLAS, CAROL ANNE, 109, 552
DOUGLAS, EMILY TAFT, 387
DREIER, MARY E., 388
DREIFUS, CLAUDIA, 110
DRINNON, RICHARD, 389
DUBOIS, CAROL ELLEN, 40, 41, 314, 705, 1145
DUCILLE, ANN, 680
DUPREE, SHERRY SHERROD, 997
DWORKIN, ANDREA, 553, 855, 1026
DYE, NANCY SCHROM, 814

ECHOLS, ALICE, 111, 464, 1285
EDELMAN, MARIAN WRIGHT, 390
EHRENREICH, BARBARA, 234, 465, 554
EICHENBAUM, LUISE, 466
EICHLER, MARGRIT, 601
EISENSTEIN, HESTER, 112, 467
EISENSTEIN, ZILLAH R., 185, 468, 555, 556, 588
ELSHTAIN, JEAN BETHKE, 469
ENGLISH, JANE, 1251
EPSTEIN, BARBARA, 635, 636
EPSTEIN, CYNTHIA FUCHS, 787, 881, 1252
ESTERBERG, KRISTIN G., 281
EVANS, MARY, 315, 391
EVANS, SARA, 68, 113, 382, 1239, 1263
EYERMAN, RON, 637

FADERMAN, LILLIAN, 282, 1284
FARGANIS, SONDRA, 114, 557, 558
FARNHAM, CHRISTIE, 316
FARRAR, ANNE, 559
FAUSET, ARTHUR HUFF, 392
FAUSTO-STERLING, ANNE, 882
FAUX, MARIAN, 209
FELSKI, RITA, 883
FELSTINER, MARY LOWENTHAL, 470
FERGUSON, ANN, 471

FERRARO, BARBARA, 210
FERREE, MYRA MARX, 115, 788, 789, 816, 1253
FIGES, EVA, 472
FILENE, PETER G, 790.
FINE, MICHELLE, 116
FIOL-MATTA, LIZA, 706
FIRESTONE, SHULAMITH, 560, 1250, 1297, 1301
FISHER, BERENICE, 117
FITZPATRICK, ELLEN, 393
FLAX, JANE, 473
FLEMING, CYNTHIA GRIGGS, 752
FLEXNER, ELEANOR, 23
FLYNN, ELIZABETH GURLEY, 347
FONER, PHILIP S., 817
FONOW, MARY MARGARET, 602
FORSTER, MARGARET, 394
FOSTER, CATHERINE, 255
FOWLER, M. G., 474
FOWLER, ROBERT BOOTH, 395
FOX, MARY FRANK, 884
FRANK, FRANCINE WATTMAN, 885
FRANK, IRENE, 1183
FRANKLIN, MARGARET LADD, 998
FRANZEN, TRISHA, 283
FRASER, NANCY, 886
FREEDMAN, E. B., 284
FREEDMAN, ESTELLE B., 5
FREEMAN, BONNIE COOK, 118
FREEMAN, JO, 119, 120, 121, 122, 186, 317, 638, 929, 1254
FREID, MARILYN GERBER, 211
FRENCH, MARILYN, 475
FRIEDAN, BETTY, 476, 477, 1234, 1250, 1299, 1301
FRIEDMAN, SCARLETT, 1255
FRITZ, LEAH, 123, 478, 561
FRUG, MARY JOE, 479
FRY, AMELIA R., 187
FRYE, MARILYN, 562
FULANI, LENORA, 707
FUSS, DIANA, 285, 480

GABIN, NANCY F., 818
GADON, ELINOR W., 977
GAGE, MATILDA JOSLYN, 24
GARBER, LINDA, 999
GARCIA, ALMA M., 708

GARLAND, ANNE WITTE, 396
GARNER, LES, 42
GARRISON, DEE, 397
GARROW, DAVID J., 348
GARRY, ANN, 481
GARSKOF, MICHELE HOFFNUNG, 1256
GATES, HENRY LOUIS, JR., 887
GATLIN, ROCHELLE, 124
GEIDEL, PETER, 188
GEIGER, SUSAN, 603
GELB, JOYCE, 125, 930, 931
GERGEN, MARY MCCANNEY, 1257
GERRARD, NICCI, 488
GERTZOG, IRWIN N., 43
GIDDINGS, PAULA, 753, 754
GILL, SANDRA K., 189
GILLIGAN, CAROL, 482, 483
GILMAN, CHARLOTTE PERKINS, 349, 563,
   1063, 1150, 1153, 1160, 1247, 1250
GIMBUTAS, MARITA, 978
GINSBURG, FAYE D., 212
GINSBURG, RUTH BADER, 190, 1251
GINZBERG, LORI D., 6
GLAZER, NONA Y., 318
GLAZER-MALBIN, NONA, 1258
GLUCK, SHERNA, 350, 604
GLUCK, SHERNA BERGER, 69, 605
GOERTZEL, TED G., 398
GOETTING, ANN, 639
GOLDSTEIN, LESLIE FRIEDMAN, 932
GONZALES, SYLVIA, 709
GOODFRIEND, JOYCE D., 1000
GORDON, LINDA, 7, 484, 963, 1297
GORDON, LYNN D., 8
GORNICK, VIVIAN, 485, 1259
GOULD, CAROL C., 1260
GRANT, JACQUELYN, 979
GRANT, JUDITH, 564
GREEN, RAYNA, 1001
GREENE, DANA, 1146, 1147
GREENWALD, MAURINE WEINER, 819
GREENWOOD, HAZEL, 1002
GREER, GERMAINE, 486, 1234
GREGORY, JEANNE, 933
GRIFFIN, GABRIELLE, 1261
GRIFFIN, SUSAN, 856
GRIFFITH, ELISABETH, 399
GROAG, SUSAN, 1148
GRONEMAN, CAROL, 820
GRUBER, JAMES E., 487

GURIN, PATRICIA, 791
GURKO, MIRIAM, 25
GUSFIELD, JOSEPH R., 9

HABER, BARBARA, 1003. 1262
HAGAN, KAY LEIGH, 488
HALL, JACQUELYN DOWD, 400, 606
HALPERIN, DAVID M., 270
HAMMER, JALNA, 235
HANCOCK, BRENDA ROBINSON, 126
HANDBERG, ROGER, 191
HANISCH, CAROL, 565, 1297
HANSEN, KAREN, 127, 566
HARDING, SANDRA, 889, 1271
HARDY-FANTA, CAROL, 710
HARE-MUSTIN, RACHEL T., 489
HARFORD, BARBARA, 256
HARRIS, ADRIENNE, 257
HARRISON, BEVERLY WILDUNG, 213
HARRISON, CYNTHIA, 192, 934, 1185
HARTMANN, SUSAN M., 821, 935
HAWES, ELIZABETH, 822
HEGGER, SUSAN, 890
HEIDE, WILMA SCOTT, 490
HEILBRUN, CAROLYN G., 607
HENNESSY, ROSEMARY, 681
HENSLEY, FRANCES, 26
HENTOFF, NAT, 857
HERNANDEZ, AILEEN C., 1186
HERSON, LIZ, 128
HERTHA, PAULI, 401, 426
HEWITT, NANCY A., 1263
HICKMAN, MARK S., 755
HIGGINBOTHAM, ELIZABETH, 694, 741,
   1031
HIGGINBOTHAM, EVELYN BROOKS, 741,
   756, 1031
HILL, M. ANNE, 936
HILL, RUTH EDMONDS, 1187, 1188
HILLYER, BARBARA, 129
HINDING, ANDREA, 1189, 1190
HINE, DARLENE CLARK, 1191
HIRSCH, MARIANNE, 1264
HITE, SHERE, 858
HO, LIANG, 711
HOAGLAND, SARAH LUCIA, 286
HOBSON, BARBARA MEIL, 859
HOFF, JOAN, 964
HOFF-WILSON, JOAN, 193, 491

HOLE, JUDITH, 130
HOLT, RACKHAM, 402
HOOKS, BELL, 132, 488, 757, 758, 759
HOPE, CAROL, 133
HORNO-DELGADO, ASUNCION, 712
HOROWITZ, HELEN LEFKOWITZ, 403
HUBER, JOAN, 1265
HUCKLE, PATRICIA, 404
HULL, GLORIA, 760, 1149
HUMM, MAGGIE, 891, 1004, 1193, 1266
HUNTER, ALLEN, 1005
HUNTER COLLEGE WOMEN'S STUDIES
    COLLECTIVE, 319
HURTADO, AIDA, 492
HYMOWITZ, CAROL, 70

ILES, TERESA, 608
INGRAHAM, SARAH R., 10
IRWIN, INEZ HAYNES, 44, 569

JACKSON, MARION E., 892
JACOBUS, MARY, 893
JAGGAR, ALISON, 567, 1267, 1268
JAMES, EDWARD T., 1194
JAMES, STANLIE M., 761
JANEWAY, ELIZABETH, 134, 493
JANIEWSKI, DOLORES E., 823
JAQUITH, CINDY, 135
JARDINE, ALICE, 494
JEFFREYS, SHEILA, 11, 860
JENNESS, LINDA, 568
JENNESS, VALERIE, 136, 287
JENSON, JOAN M., 71, 824
JOAN, POLLY, 1195
JOFFE, CAROLE, 214
JOHNSON, JOHN W., 1196
JOHNSON, SONIA, 405, 406, 495
JOHNSTON, JILL, 288
JONES, BEVERLEY, 137
JONES, ELISE F., 215
JONES, HETTIE, 351
JONES, MARGARET C., 569
JOREEN, 138, 573
JOSEPH, GLORIA, 713
JOSEPHSON, HANNAH, 407
JUSTICE, BETTY, 139
KADI, JOANNA, 714
KAHN, KAREN, 140

KAHN, KATHY, 72
KAMEN, PAULA, 141
KANDAL, TERRY R., 640
KANN, MARK E., 937
KANTOR, HANNAH, 1269
KANTROWITZ, MELANIE KAYE, 715
KAPLAN, ALEXANDRA G., 1270
KASS-SIMON, G., 894
KATZ, JONATHAN NED, 289
KATZENSTEIN, MARY FAINSOD, 641
KAUFFMAN, L. A., 682
KAUFFMAN, LINDA S., 1271
KAUFMAN, MICHAEL, 792
KEAN, HILDA, 408
KEESING'S REFERENCE PUBLICATIONS
    COLLECTION, 1197
KELLER, CATHERINE, 895
KELLER, EVELYN FOX, 896, 1264
KELLY, JOAN, 570
KEMMER, ELIZABETH J., 1006
KENNEDY, ELIZABETH LAPOVSKY, 290,
    314
KENNEDY, MARY, 320
KENNEDY, SUSAN ESTABROOK, 1007
KEOHANE, NANNERL O., 1272
KERR, ANDREA MOORE, 409
KESSLER-HARRIS, ALICE, 321, 825,
    826
KEYFITZ, NATHAN, 938
KHOSLA, PUNAM, 236
KIMBALL, GAYLE, 897
KIMMEL, MICHAEL S., 497
KING, DEBORAH K., 762
KINGSOLVER, BARBARA, 827
KINNARD, CYNTHIA D., 1008
KLATCH, REBECCA E., 965
KLEIN, DORIE, 237
KLEIN, ETHEL, 939
KLEIN, RENATE D., 571
KLEIN, VIOLA, 27
KOEDT, ANNE, 572, 573
KOEN, SUSAN, 258
KOLBERT, KATHRYN, 216
KOMAROVSKY, MIRRA, 642, 643
KOMISAR, LUCY, 142
KOPACSI, ROSEMARIE, 716
KORNBLUH, JOYCE, 828
KOURANY, JANET A., 1273
KRADITOR, AILEEN S., 45, 1150
KRAMARAE, CHERIS, 322, 1198

KRASNIEWICZ, LOUISE, 259
KRICHMAR, ALBERT, 1009, 1010
KRIEGER, SUSAN, 291, 292
KRYZANOWSKI, LAWRENCE, 966
KUHN, ANNETTE, 574
KUHN, MAGGIE, 410
KYLE, PATRICIA A., 1766

LADER, LAWRENCE, 217
LADNER, JOYCE A., 717
LANDRY, DONNA, 498
LANE, ANN J., 411
LANGER, ELINOR, 194
LANGER, HOWARD J., 143
LANGLOIS, KAREN, 195
LARCOM, LUCY, 352
LARUE, LINDA, 644
LASSER, CAROL, 1151
LAUBY, MARY, 229
LAWRENCE, ELIZABETH, 829
LEDERER, LAURA, 861
LEFANU, SARAH, 1269
LEFKOWITZ, ROCHELLE, 830
LEGHORN, LISA, 499
LEHRER, SUSAN, 831
LEIDHOLDT, DORCHEN, 862
LEIDNER, ROBIN, 323
LEMONS, STANLEY J., 73
LENGERMANN, PATRICIA MADOO, 793
LENIN, V. I., 575
LENSINK, JUDY NOLTE, 307, 353
LEONARD, ARTHUR S., 1199
LERNER, GERDA, 74, 500, 1152, 1153
LEVACK, BRIAN P., 980
LEVENESS, FRANK P., 940
LEVINE, SUZANNE, 144
LEVY, DARLENE G., 546
LEWENSON, SANDRA BETH, 46
LEWIN, MIRIAM, 794
LEWIS, JANE, 941
LEX, LOUISE M., 145
LIDDINGTON, J., 47
LIEBERMAN, MORTON A., 146
LIEBLICH, AMIA, 609
LINDEN, ROBIN RUTH, 863
LINDEN-WARD, BLANCHE, 147
LINNEKIN, JOCELYN, 718
LIVINGSTONE, D. W., 795
LLOYD, CYNTHIA B., 832

LOCKE, MAMIE E., 412
LOEB, CATHERINE, 1011
LOEWENBERG, BERT JAMES, 719
LOGAN, ONNIE LEE, 413
LONDON, BETTE, 898
LORBER, JUDITH, 796
LORDE, AUDRE, 354, 763, 1291
LORENTZEN, ROBIN, 981
LOVE, BARBARA, 269
LOWE, MARIAN, 797
LOWY, BEVERLY, 414
LUBIN, CAROL RIEGELMAN, 833
LUEPNITZ, DEBORAH ANNA, 899
LUKER, KRISTIN, 218
LUMPKIN, KATHARINE DU PRE, 415
LUNARDINI, CHRISTINE A., 416
LYNN, SUSAN, 75

MACCANNELL, JULIET FLOWER, 1274
MACKENZIE, MIDGE, 48
MACKINNON, CATHARINE A., 501, 576
MAGGIO, ROSALIE, 1012, 1200
MALOS, ELLEN, 900
MANDLE, JOAN D., 148, 942
MANSBRIDGE, JANE J., 196
MARCUS, ERIC, 293
MARCUS, JANE, 417
MARK, JOAN, 418
MARSHALL, SUSAN E., 197, 967, 968
MARTI, DONALD B., 720
MARTIN, GLORIA, 577
MARTIN, PATRICIA YANCEY, 149
MARTIN, THEODORA PENNY, 12
MARTIN, WENDY, 1275
MATHES, VALERIE SHERER, 419
MATHEWS, G. DONALD, 198
MATTHEWS, GLENNA, 76, 953
MATTHEWS, NANCY A., 238
MAZOW, JULIA WOLF, 721
MCADAM, DOUG, 645, 798
MCALLISTER, PAM, 260, 261, 262
MCCLAIN, EDWIN W., 502
MCCLUSKEY, AUDREY, 683
MCCOURT, KATHLEEN, 834
MCCREESH, CAROLYN DANIEL, 835
MCCULLOUGH, RITA I., 1013
MCDANIEL, JUDITH, 263
MCDERMOTT, PATRICE, 324
MCDONAGH, EILEEN LORENZI, 49

MCGLEN, NANCY, 199, 646
MCGRATH, WILMA E., 943
MCKAY, NELLIE Y., 764
MCKEE, KATHLEEN BURKE, 1201
MCNEIL, JEAN C., 799
MEESE, ELIZABETH, 901
MELHEM, D. H., 722
MERCHANT, CAROLYN, 264
MERRIAM, EVE, 426
MEYER, DAVID S., 647
MEYERDING, JANE, 265
MIES, MARIA, 836
MILES, ANGELA, 578, 684
MILES, ROSALIND, 77
MILKMAN, RUTH, 837
MILLER, JEAN BAKER, 503, 504
MILLER, MARGARET I., 200
MILLER, PATRICIA G., 219
MILLETT, KATE, 355, 505, 579
MILLMAN, MARCIA, 1276
MILLS, KAY, 421
MILLS, SARA, 580
MILLSTEIN, BETH, 1154
MINNICH, ELIZABETH, 325
MITCHELL, JULIET, 506, 507, 581
MLOTT, SYLVESTER, 201
MOGHADAM, VALENTINE M., 685
MOODY, ANNE, 356
MOON, TERRY, 582
MOORE, GLORIA, 1014
MORAGA, CHERRIE, 723
MORGAN, ROBIN, 422, 508, 583, 648,
    1246, 1275, 1277, 1297
MORGEN, SANDRA, 239
MORRIS, ALDON D., 649, 765
MORRIS, JENNY, 839
MORRISON, TONI, 969
MOSER, CHARLOTTE, 423
MOYNIHAN, RUTH BARNES, 1155
MUELLER, CAROL, 202, 424, 509, 944, 945,
    970
MULDOON, MAUREEN, 1015
MULVEY, LAURA, 902
MUMFORD, LAURA, 1016
MURDOCK, MARY ELIZABETH, 1089
MURRAY, PAULI, 357
MURRAY, SUSAN B., 240
MURRIN, MARY R., 78
MYRON, NANCY, 294
NAFFINE, NGAIRE, 946

NEBRASKA SOCIOLOGICAL FEMINIST
    COLLECTIVE, 650
NELSON, BARBARA J., 150
NELSON, KRISTINE, 510
NEWHOUSE, NANCY R., 1278
NICHOLAS, SUSAN CARY, 947
NICHOLS, CAROLE, 50
NIELSEN, JOYCE MCCARL, 610
NIES, JUDITH, 425
NIETO, CONSUELO, 724
NOCHLIN, LINDA, 903
NODDINGS, NEL, 511
NORDQUIST, JOAN, 1017, 1018, 1204
NORRIS, PIPPA, 512

OAKES, ELIZABETH, 1019
OAKLEY, ANN, 506, 513
O'BARR, JEAN FOX, 325, 326
OBERSCHALL, ANTHONY, 651
O'BRIEN, DAVID M., 948
O'BRIEN, MARY, 220
O'BRIEN, JAMES, 1005
OFFE, CLAUS, 652
OFFEN, KAREN M., 1140
OLDFIELD, SYBIL, 1279
O'MALLEY, SUSAN GUSHEE, 61, 514
OMOLADE, BARBARA, 725
O'NEILL, WILLIAM L., 28, 29
OPPENHEIMER, MARTIN, 653
ORLANS, KATHRYN P. MEADOW, 654
OVERALL, CHRISTINE, 221

PAPACHRISTOU, JUDITH, 30, 1020
PARKER, ALICE, 901
PARKER, KATHERINE, 499
PARKER, ROZIKA, 904
PASCOE, PEGGY, 13
PAULI, HERTHA, 426
PAYNE, ELIZABETH ANN, 840
PECK, MARY, 427
PEEBLES-WILKINS, WILMA, 428
PERRY, ELISABETH ISREALS, 429
PERSONAL NARRATIVES GROUP, 620
PETCHESKY, ROSALIND POLLACK, 222
PETERSON, DEENA, 1205
PHELAN, SHANE, 686
PHELPS, TIMOTHY M., 971
PHILLIPS, ANNE, 1280

PILOCK, GRISELDA, 904
PIVEN, FRANCES FOX, 655
PLANT, JUDITH, 266
PLASKOW, JUDITH, 982
PLATKE, DAVID, 656
PLUTZER, ERIC, 223, 226
POLLACK, SANDRA, 295, 311
POPE, JACQUELINE, 657
POSTON, CAROL H., 515
PRATT, MINNIE BRUCE, 516, 673
PRESTAGE, JEWEL L., 726
PRINCE-EMBURY, SANDRA, 184, 203
PURVIS, JUNE, 1207

QUEST STAFF, 1298

RABUZZI, KATHRYN ALLEN, 983
RAKOW, LANA, 1156
RAMAZANOGLU, CAROLINE, 658
RANDOLPH, LAURA, 766
RAVEN, ARLENE, 905
REAGON, BERNICE JOHNSON, 767
REARDON, BETTY A., 517
REDFERING, DAVID L., 518
REDFERN, BERNICE, 1021
REDSTOCKINGS, 584
REED, EVELYN, 519
REID, INEZ SMITH, 687
REID, PAMELA TROTMAN, 688
REINHARZ, SHULAMIT, 151, 609, 611
REITER, RAYNA R., 523
REMICK, HELEN, 949
RENDELL, JANE, 31
RENZETTI, CLAIRE M., 800
RICH, ADRIENNE, 296, 430, 520, 906, 1232
RICHARDSON, DIANE, 1281
RICHARDSON, DOROTHY, 431
RICHARDSON, LAUREL, 659, 1282
RICHARDSON, MARILYN, 432
RICHARDSON, ROSEMARY, 1189
RIDD, ROSEMARY, 79
RIDDIOUGH, CHRISTINE R., 950
RIES, PAULA, 1283
RISMAN, BARBARA J., 1284
RITCHIE, MAUREEN, 1022
RIX, SARA E., 1285, 1286, 1287
ROBERTS, ELIZABETH, 841
ROBERTS, HELEN, 613

ROBINSON, VICTORIA, 1281
ROGOW, FAITH, 727
ROLLINS, JUDITH, 801
ROSALDO, MICHELLE ZIMBALIST, 1272, 1288
ROSE, MARGARET, 842
ROSENBERG, MARIE, 1023
ROSENBERG, ROSALIND, 14
ROSENFELD, RACHEL A., 152, 325
ROSENTHAL, NAOMI, 15
ROSSER, SUE V., 614, 907, 908
ROSSI, ALICE, 153, 1289
ROSSITER, MARGARET W., 909
ROSZAK, BETTY, 1290
ROSZAK, THEODORE, 1290
ROTHENBERG, PAULA S., 1267, 1291
ROTHMAN, BARBARA KATZ, 224, 225
ROTHMAN, DAVID, 16
ROTHMAN, SHEILA M., 16, 910
ROTHSCHILD, JOAN, 521
ROUSE, JACQUELINE ANNE, 433, 748, 749
ROWBOTHAM, SHEILA, 154, 362, 585, 586, 1024
ROWLAND, ROBYN, 155, 156, 522
RUBIN, GAYLE, 523
RUBIN, RACHEL, 947
RUDDICK, SARA, 434, 598
RUETHER, ROSEMARY RADFORD, 157, 488
RUIZ, VICKI L., 705, 728, 729
RUPP, LEILA J., 80, 81, 602, 615
RUSSETT, CYNTHIA EAGLE, 864
RUSSO, ANN, 32
RUTH, SHEILA, 158, 972, 984, 1292
RUTHCHILD, ROCHELLE, 587
RYAN, BARBARA, 159, 160, 223, 226, 660, 890
RYAN, MARY P., 82

SACKS, KAREN, 524, 843
SALEM, DOROTHY C., 1208
SALPER, ROBERTA, 1293
SAMOIS, 865
SANCHEZ, ROSAURA, 730
SANDAGE, DIANE, 161
SANDERS, MARLENE, 911
SARAH, ELIZABETH, 661, 1255
SARGENT, LYDIA, 588
SCADRON, ARLENE, 731
SCHAEF, ANNE WILSON, 525

SCHARF, LOIS, 83
SCHECHTER, SUSAN, 241
SCHIEBINGER, LONDA, 912
SCHLACHTER, GAIL ANN, 1050, 1051, 1052
SCHMITZ, BETTY, 1025
SCHNEER, JONATHON, 362
SCHNEIDER, BETH E., 162
SCHRAMM, SARAH, 163
SCHRAMM, SARAH SLAVIN, 327
SCHULMAN, SARAH, 297
SCHUR, EDWIN M., 662
SCHWARTZ, PEPPER, 1284
SCHWARTZ-SHEA, PEREGRINE, 267
SCOTT, ANNE FIROR, 18, 84
SCOTT, JOAN W., 1243, 1245
SCOTT, KESHO YVONNE, 435
SEALANDER, JUDITH, 164
SEARING, SUSAN E., 616, 1011
SEGAL, LYNNE, 526
SEGURA, DENISE A., 732
SEIFER, NANCY, 844
SELLEN, BETTY CAROL, 1026
SHAW, SHEILA, 1269
SHOWALTER, ELAINE, 358
SHULMAN, ALIX KATE, 165
SICHERMAN, BARBARA, 1209
SIDEL, RUTH, 527
SIMEONE, ANGELA, 328
SIMON, RITA J., 663
SIMONS, MARGARET A., 298, 309, 689
SIMS-WOOD, JANET L., 1027
SINGLETON, CARRIE JANE, 802
SKOCPOL, THEDA, 19
SLAVIN, SARAH, 204
SLIPMAN, SUE, 951
SMITH, BARBARA, 673, 760, 768, 769, 770
SMITH, DENNIS, 664
SMITH, DOROTHY E., 164, 665
SMITH, PAUL, 494
SMITH-ROSENBERG, CARROLL, 20
SNITOW, ANN, 866
SNODGRASS, JON, 528
SOCHEN, JUNE, 85, 166, 529
SOLOMON, BARBARA MILLER, 86
SOLOMON, IRVIN D., 666
SOLOMON, MARTHA, 436
SOLTOW, MARTHA JANE, 1028
SOPER, KATE, 589
SPALLONE, PAT, 913

SPEDDING, CAROLE, 1269
SPELMAN, ELIZABETH V., 690
SPENDER, DALE, 167, 322, 329, 530, 531, 590
SPRETNAK, CHARLENE, 488, 985
SPRINGER, MARLENE, 1157
ST. PETER, SHIRLEY, 803
STACEY, JUDITH, 506
STACEY, MARGARET, 168
STAGGENBORG, SUZANNE, 169, 170, 667
STALLARD, KARIN, 804
STAMBAUGH, SARA, 986
STAMBLER, SOOKIE, 1294
STANLEY, LIZ, 73, 602, 617, 618, 619
STANLIE, M. JAMES, 761
STANSELL, CHRISTINE, 845, 866
STANTON, ELIZABETH CADY, 437, 1141, 1145, 1158
STANTON, THEODORE, 437
STAPLES, ROBERT, 733
STARHAWK, 488, 987, 988
STEIN, ARLENE, 300
STEINEM, GLORIA, 532, 533, 591, 1234, 1238, 1250, 1275
STERLING, DOROTHY, 438, 439, 734
STEVENS, DORIS, 441
STEVENSON, BRENDA, 440
STEWARD, MARY, 668
STIMPSON, CATHARINE R., 534
STINEMAN, ESTHER, 1011, 1029
STOLOFF, CAROLYN, 171
STONE, MERLIN, 989
STOPER, EMILY, 846
STRUNIN, MARION HARRIS, 1211
SUNSTEIN, CASS R., 1295
SUNSTEIN, EMILY W., 442
SWARTZ, GERALD, 443
SWEENEY, PATRICIA E., 940, 1030
SWERDLOW, AMY, 268, 1296
SWITZER, M'LISS, 242
SYFERS, JUDY, 535, 573

TANNER, LESIE B., 1297
TAVRIS, CAROL, 805
TAX, MEREDITH, 172
TAYLOR, VERTA, 81, 87, 301, 302, 602, 1282

TELGEN, DIANE, 1213
TERRELONGE, PAULINE, 771
THIBAULT, GISELE MARIE, 330
THOMAS, EVANGELINE, 1216
THOMPSON, BECKY W., 735
THOMPSON, E. P., 362
THOMPSON, MARK, 303
THOMPSON, MARY LOU, 1299
THORNE, BARRIE, 195, 914, 1271
THORNTON, NEIL, 867
TICKNER, LISA, 51
TIMBERLAKE, ANDREA, 1031
TINGLEY, DONALD, 1032
TINGLEY, ELIZABETH, 1032
TONG, ROSEMARIE, 536, 868, 1273
TORREY, JANE W., 773
TOURAINE, ALAIN, 669, 670
TREBILCOT, JOYCE, 304, 869, 916
TRIBE, LAURENCE H., 227
TRIMBERGER, ELLEN KAY, 359, 671
TUANA, NANCY, 917
TUCHMAN, GAYE, 21
TUTTLE, LISA, 1218

UGLOW, JENNIFER S., 1219
UMI RESEARCH COLLECTIONS, 1119
UNITED NATIONS, 736

VALVERDE, MARIANA, 870
VANCE, CAROLE S., 871
VAUX, TRINA, 1220
VOGEL, LISE, 388, 592, 593

WADE-GAYLES, GLORIA, 360
WALBY, SYLVIA, 537
WALKER, BARBARA G., 1222
WALKER, ROBBIE JEAN, 1159
WALLS, DAVID, 1223
WALSH, MARY ROTH, 538
WALSH, VAL, 320
WANDERSEE, WINIFRED D., 173
WARE, CELLESTINE, 774
WARE, SUSAN, 444, 952
WARTENBERG, THOMAS E., 594
WATERS, MARY ALICE, 595

WATSON, BARBARA BELLOW, 331
WATSON, G., 1033
WEBBER, KIKANZA N., 737
WEIKE, DAVID THOREAU, 445
WEILER, KATHLEEN, 806
WEINBAUM, BATYA, 596
WELLMAN, JUDITH, 33
WELLS-BARNETT, IDA B., 361
WERTHEIMER, BARBARA MAYER, 848
WESSINGER, CATHERINE, 990
WEST, GUIDA, 88
WEST, UTA, 1300
WESTON, ELISABETH, 890
WESTON, KATH, 305
WHARTON, CAROL S., 244
WHITE, EVELYN C., 738
WHITE, KENDALL O., 205
WHITTIER, NANCY, 301, 647
WIDGERY, DAVID, 52
WILLIAMSON, JANE, 1226
WILLIS, ELLEN, 174, 872
WILLIS, SUSAN, 739
WITT, LINDA, 953
WOLFF, JANET, 539
WOLGAST, ELIZABETH, 954
WOLOCH, NANCY, 1160
WOMEN OF COLOR ASSOCIATION, 740
WOMEN'S RESOURCES GROUP, 1135
WOOD, JAMES L., 672
WOODS, BARBARA, 748, 749
WOOLF, VIRGINIA, 540

YAEGER, PATRICIA S., 918
YATES, GAYLE GRAHAM, 541
YELLIN, JEAN FAGAN, 53
YOUNG, ALISON, 306
YOUNG, LOUISE M., 34
YOUNG, NANCY, 133
YOUNG, PATRICIA A., 1026

ZAK, MICHELE WENDER, 1301
ZAMITI-HORCHANI, MALIKA, 175
ZINN, MAXINE BACA, 694, 741, 742
ZIPES, JACK, 919
ZOPHY, ANGELA HOWARD, 1192, 1230, 1231

Title Index

A Question of Class, 775

Abortion: An Annotated Indexed Bibliography, 1015

Abortion and the Politics of Motherhood, 218

Abortion and Woman's Choice: The State, Sexuality and Reproductive Freedom, 222

Abortion Debate in the United States and Canada: A Source Book, 1202

Abortion II: Making the Revolution, 217

Abortion: The Clash of Absolutes, 227

Academic Women, Working Towards Equality, 328

Acknowledging Differences: Can Women Find Unity Through Diversity?, 764

Activist's Almanac: The Concerned Citizen's Guide to the Leading Advocacy Organizations in America, 1223

Affirmation by Negation in the Women's Liberation Movement, 126

African-American Holiness Pentecostal Movement: An Annotated Bibliography, 997

African-American Women: A Biographical Dictionary, 1208

Against Our Will: Men, Women and Rape, 230

Against Sadomasochism: A Radical Feminist Analysis, 863

Against the Tide: Pro-Feminist Men in the United States, 1776–1990, A Documentary History, 497

Ahead of Her Time: Abby Kelley and the Politics of Anti-slavery, 438

Ain't I a Woman: Black Women and Feminism, 757

Ain't Nowhere We Can Run: A Handbook for Women on the Nuclear Mentality, 258

Alderson Story: My Life as a Political Prisoner, 347

Alice Doesn't: Feminism, Semiotics, Cinema, 879

Alice Paul and the ERA, 187

All-American Women: Lines that Divide, Ties that Bind, 703

All Said and Done, 334

All Sides of the Subject, 608

All the Women Are White, All the Blacks Are Men, But Some of Us Are Brave: Black Women's Studies, 760

Almanac of American Women in the Twentieth Century, 1177

Althusser and Feminism, 543

Always a Sister: The Feminism of Lillian D. Wald, 383

Always In Your Face: Flo Kennedy, An
    Activist Forever, 414
Always Leading Our Men in Service and
    Sacrifice: Amy Jacques Garvey,
    Feminist Black Nationalist, 363
Amazon Odyssey, 90
American Feminism: A Contemporary
    History, 101
American Feminism: New Issues for a
    Mature Movement, 1240
American Feminist Thought at Century's
    End: A Reader, 1271
American Heroine: The Life and Legend
    of Jane Addams, 384
American Nursing: A Biographical
    Dictionary, 1169
American Sisterhood: Writings of the
    Feminist Movement from Colonial
    Times to the Present, 1275
American Woman 1987–88: A Report in
    Depth, 1285
American Woman 1988–89: A Status
    Report, 1286
American Woman 1990–91: A Status
    Report, 1287
American Woman 1992–93: A Status
    Report, 1283
American Woman: Her Changing Social,
    Economic, and Political Roles,
    1920–1970, 63
American Women: A Research Guide to
    U.S. Government Sources, 1211
American Women and the Labor
    Movement, 1825–1975: An Annotated
    Bibliography, 1028
American Women in the 1970s: On the
    Move, 173
American Women Since 1945, 124
America's White Working-Class Women: A
    Historical Bibliography, 1007
America's Working Women: A
    Documentary History, 1600 to the
    Present, 57
Analyzing Gender: A Handbook of Social
    Science Research, 1253
Anatomy of Freedom: Feminism, Physics,
    and Global Politics, 508
Ancient Mirrors of Womanhood: A
    Treasury of Goddess and Heroine
    Lore from Around the World, 989

Angela Davis, An Autobiography, 344
Annotated Critical Bibliography of
    Feminist Criticism, 1004
Another Voice: Feminist Perspectives on
    Social Life and Social Science, 1276
Anthologies By and About Women: An
    Analytical Index, 1173
Anti-feminism in American Thought: An
    Annotated Bibliography, 1008
Anti-feminists and Women's Liberation: A
    Case Study of a Paradox, 118
Anti-Politics of Identity, The, 682
Anti-Violence Activism and the
    (In)Visibility of Gender in the
    Gay/Lesbian and Women's Movement,
    287
Appropriated Voice: Narrative Authority
    in Conrad, Forster and Woolf, 898
Archival and Manuscript Resources for
    the Study of Women's History, 1189
Are We There Yet? A Continuing Story of
    Lavender Woman, A Chicago Lesbian
    Newspaper, 1971–1976, 274
Articles on Witchcraft, Magic and
    Demonology, 980
Asian-American Women: Identity and
    Role in the Women's Movement, 711
Asian-American Women's View of the
    Consciousness-Raising Sessions, 699
Attitudes Toward the Equal Rights
    Amendment: Influence of Class and
    Status, 189
Autobiography of an American
    Communist: A Personal View of a
    Political Life, 1925–1975, 346

Barbara Deming: We Are All Part of One
    Another, 265
Battered Women: Implications for Social
    Control, 232
Beauty, the Beast and the Militant
    Woman: A Case Study in Sex Roles
    and Social Stress in Jacksonian
    America, 20
Becoming a Feminist: The Social Origins
    of 'First Wave' Feminism, 35
Beginning to See the Light: Pieces of a
    Decade, 174
Belle Moskowitz: Feminine Politics and

the Exercise of Power in the Age of Alfred E. Smith, 429

Between Feminism and Labor: The Significance of the Comparable Worth Movement, 922

Between Myth and Morning: Women Awakening, 134

Between Women: Biographers, Novelists, Critics, Artists and Teachers Write About Their Work on Women, 598

Between Women: Domestics and Their Employers, 801

Between Women: Love, Envy, and Competition in Women's Friendships, 466

Beyond a Dream Deferred: Multicultural Education and the Politics of Excellence, 735

Beyond Babies and Banners: Towards an Understanding of the Dynamics of Social Movements, 847

Beyond Feminist Aesthetics: Feminist Literature and Social Change, 883

Beyond God the Father: Toward a Philosophy of Women's Liberation, 547

Beyond Indifference and Antipathy: The Chicana Movement and Chicana Feminist Discourse, 732

Beyond Methodology: Feminist Scholarship as Lived Research, 602

Beyond Patriarchy: Essays by Men on Pleasure, Power, and Change, 792

Beyond Separate Spheres: Intellectual Roots of Modern Feminism, 14

Beyond Sex-Role Stereotypes: Readings Toward a Psychology of Androgyny, 1270

Beyond Suffrage: Women in the New Deal, 952

Bibliography on the History of Women in the Progressive Era, 1020

Biographical Dictionaries of Minority Women, 1230

Biographies of American Women: An Annotated Bibliography, 1030

Biography and the Search for Women's Subjectivity, 599

Biting the Hand That Feeds Them: Organizing Women on Welfare at the Grass Roots Level, 657

Black Feminism: Black Women on the Edge, 755

Black Feminist Organizing in the Seventies and Eighties, 772

Black Feminist Thought: Knowledge, Consciousness, and the Politics of Empowerment, 747

Black Foremothers: Three Lives, 439

Black Movement and Women's Liberation, 644

Black Studies and Women's Studies: Search for a Long Overdue Partnership, 312

Black Woman: An Anthology, 698

Black Women in America: Sex, Marriage and the Family, 733

Black Women in American Society: A Selected Annotated Bibliography, 996

Black Women: A Neglected Dimension in History, 382

Black Women Activists and the Student Nonviolent Coordinating Committee: The Case of Ruby Doris Smith Robinson, 752

Black Women and the Pursuit of Equality, 743

Black Women in America: An Historical Encyclopedia, 1191

Black Women in Nineteenth Century American Life: Their Words, Their Thoughts, Their Feelings, 719

Black Women in White America: A Documentary History, 1152

Black Women Oral History Project: From the Arthur and Elizabeth Schlesinger Library on the History of Women in America, Radcliffe College, 1187

Black Women's Health Book: Speaking for Ourselves, 738

Blood, Bread and Poetry: Select Prose 1979–1985, 520

Blue Book, Woman Suffrage: History, Arguments, and Results, 37

Body/politics: Women and the Discourses of Science, 893

Bonds of Womanhood: 'Woman's Sphere' in New England, 1780–1835, 64

Boots of Leather, Slippers of Gold: The History of a Lesbian Community, 290

Borderlands/La Frontera, 693

Born Female: The High Cost of Keeping Women Down, 955

Born For Liberty: A History of Women in America, 68

Breaking Boundaries: Latina Writing and Critical Readings, 712

Bridges of Power: Women's Multicultural Alliances, 692

Building Domestic Liberty: Charlotte Perkins Gilman's Architectural Feminism, 364

Building Feminist Theory: Essays from *Quest*, 276

Called to Account: The Story of One Family's Struggle to Say No to Abuse, 242

Cannery Women, Cannery Lives: Mexican Women, Unionization, and the California Food Processing Industry, 1930–1950, 728

Capitalist Patriarchy and the Case for Socialist Feminism, 555

Capitol Games: Clarence Thomas, Anita Hill and the Story of a Supreme Court Nomination, 971

Caring by the Hour: Women, Work and Organizing at Duke Medical Center, 843

Carrie Catt: Feminist Politician, 395

Carrie Chapman Catt: A Biography, 427

Case for Woman Suffrage: A Bibliography, 998

Catalog of the Sophia Smith Collection, Women's History Archive, 1089

Caught Looking: Feminism, Pornography & Censorship, 852

Century of Struggle: The Woman's Rights Movement in the United States, 23

Challenge of Feminist Biography: Writing the Lives of Modern American Women, 597

Challenging Authority: Civil Disobedience in the Feminist Anti-militarist Movement, 140

Challenging Times: The Women's Movement in Canada and the United States, 1239

Challenging Years: The Memoirs of Harriot Stanton Blatch, 337

Change and Continuity in the American Women's Movement, 1848–1930: A National and State Perspective, 26

Changes of Heart: Reflections of Women's Independence, 128

Changing Education: Women as Radicals and Conservators, 777

Changing Our Minds: Feminist Transformations of Knowledge, 307

Changing the Future: American Women in the 1960s, 147

Changing Women in a Changing Society, 1265

Chicana: A Comprehensive Bibliographic Study, 994

Chicana and the Women's Rights Movement: A Perspective, 724

Chicanas and Hispanic American Women, 1175

Christianity, Patriarchy, and Abuse: A Feminist Critique, 876

City of Women: Sex and Class in New York, 1789–1860, 845

Civil Rights Women: A Source for Doing Womanist Theology, 979

Class and Feminism: A Collection of Essays from *The Furies*, 782

Class and Racial Divisions in the Female Population: Some Practical and Political Dilemmas for the Women's Movement, 785

Class, Race, and Sex: The Dynamics of Control, 1296

Class Roots of Feminism, 524

Class, Sex and the Woman Worker, 811

Close to Home: A Materialist Analysis of Women's Oppression, 549

Clyde Connell: The Art and Life of a Louisiana Woman, 423

Collective Consciousness, Identity Transformation, and the Rise of Women in Public Office in the United States, 509

Collective Identity in Social Movement Communities, 301

Coming of Age in Mississippi, 356

Coming to Power: Writings and Graphics on Lesbian S/M, 865

Common Differences: Conflict in Black and White Feminist Perspectives, 713

Communes and Protest Movements in the U.S., 1960–1975: An Analysis of Intellectual Roots, 630

Comparable Worth: Analysis and Evidence, 936

Comparable Worth and Wage Discrimination: Technical Possibilities and Political Realities, 949

Compulsory Heterosexuality and Lesbian Existence, 296

Concise History of Woman Suffrage: Selections from the Classic Work of Stanton, Anthony, Gage and Harper, 1141

Conditions: Five, The Black Women's Issue, 768

Conflicts in Feminism, 1264

Confronting Rape: The Feminist Anti-Rape Movement and the State, 238

Consequences of Professionalization and Formalization in the Pro-Choice Movement, 667

Conservative Policies and Women's Power, 510

Contemporary Cases in Women's Rights, 932

Contemporary Feminist Thought, 467

Contemporary U.S. Women's Movement: An Empirical Example of Competition Theory, 152

Contested Lives: The Abortion Debate in an American Community, 212

Contradictions in an Ideology: The Nineteenth Century Doctrine of Separate Spheres, 21

Controversy and Coalition: The New Feminist Movement, 115

Costs of Exclusionary Practices in Women's Studies, 741

Creating a Feminist Alliance: Sisterhood and Class Conflict in the New York Women's Trade Union League, 1903–1914, 814

Creation of Feminist Consciousness: From the Middle Ages to 1870, 500

Crusade for Justice: The Autobiography of Ida B. Wells, 361

Curious Courtship of Women's Liberation and Socialism, 596

Dangers of Education: Sexism and Origins of Women's Colleges, An Anthology of Nineteenth Century Sources, 16

Daring to Be Bad: Radical Feminism in America, 1967–1975, 111

Daughters of Jefferson, Daughters of Bootblacks: Racism and American Feminism, 744

Death of Nature: Women, Ecology, and the Scientific Revolution, 264

Decade of Women: A Ms. History of the Seventies in Words and Pictures, 144

Decades of Discontent: The Women's Movement, 1920–1946, 83

Deceptive Distinctions: Sex, Gender, and the Social Order, 787

Declarations of Independence: Women and Political Power in Nineteenth Century American Fiction, 873

Deeds Not Words: The Lives of Suffragette Teachers, 408

Development of Chicana Feminist Discourse, 1970–1980, 708

Development of Feminist Consciousness Among Asian-American Women, 701

Dialectic of Sex: The Case for Feminist Revolution, 560

Diary of a Conference on Sexuality, 849

Dictionary of American Women's History, 1192

Dictionary of Feminist Theory, 1193

Difference Within: Feminism and Critical Theory, 901

Differences and Identities: Feminism and the Albuquerque Lesbian Community, 283

Different Face: The Life of Mary Wollstonecraft, 442

Directory of Financial Aid for Minorities, 1993–1995, 1051

Directory of Financial Aids for Women 1993–1995, 1050

Discarded Legacy: Politics and Poetics in the Life of Frances E. W. Harper, 1825–1911, 374

Dissenting Feminist Academy: A History
   of the Barriers to Feminist
   Scholarship, 330
Diversity and Commonality: Theory and
   Politics, 621
Documentation: DuBois' Crisis and
   Woman's Suffrage, 53
Dogmatism and Locus of Control in
   Young Women Who Support,
   Oppose or Voice No Opinion on the
   Equal Rights Amendment, 201
Doing Comparable Worth: Gender, Class,
   and Pay Equity, 920
Doing Feminist Research, 613
Don't Bet On The Prince: Contemporary
   Feminist Fairy Tales in North America
   and England, 919
Double Jeopardy: To be Black and
   Female, 745
Dreamers and Dealers: An Intimate
   Appraisal of the Women's Movement,
   123
Dreaming the Dark: Magic, Sex and
   Politics, 987
Dreams and Dilemmas: Collected
   Writings, 585
Dyke Ideas: Process, Politics, Daily Life,
   304
Dynamics of Cooptation in a Feminist
   Health Clinic, 239
Dynamics of Race and Gender: Some
   Feminist Interventions, 691
Dynamics of Sex and Gender: A
   Sociological Perspective, 659

Early American Women: A Documentary
   History, 1600–1900, 1160
Echo In My Soul, 341
Economic Emergence of Women, 921
Economics of Sex Differentials, 832
Educating for Peace: A Feminist
   Perspective, 249
Education for Equality: Women's Rights
   Periodicals and Women's Higher
   Education, 1849–1920, 1171
Eleanor Flexner's Century of Struggle:
   Women's History and the Women's
   Movement, 80
Eleanor Marx in Chicago, 1886:

Revolutionary Feminism and the
   Haymarket Centenary, 582
Eleanor Roosevelt: Volume One
   1884–1933, 379
Electronic Discussion Groups on
   Women, 1181
Elizabeth Cady Stanton: As Revealed in Her
   Letters, Diary and Reminiscences, 437
Elizabeth Cady Stanton, Susan B.
   Anthony: Correspondence, Writings,
   Speeches, 1145
Ella Baker and the Origins of
   "Participatory Democracy", 424
Emancipation of Angelina Grimké, 415
Emancipation of Women, 575
Emma Goldman, 436
Encyclopedia of Feminism, 1218
Encyclopedia of the American Left,
   1168
Endless Crusade: Women Social
   Scientists and Progressive Reform, 393
Equal Access to Credit: Lenders'
   Attitudes Toward an Applicant's Sex
   and Marital Status, 966
Equal Rights Amendment: A
   Bibliographic Study, 1004
Equal Rights Amendment Activists in
   North Carolina, 176
Equal Rights Amendment Campaigns in
   California and Utah, 200
Equal Rights Amendment: The Politics
   and Process of Ratification of the 27th
   Amendment to the U.S. Constitution,
   204
Equal Rights Coverage in Magazines,
   Summer 1976, 182
Equality and the Rights of Women, 954
Equity Between the Sexes: The Pension
   Problem, 938
Equity Issues and Black-White
   Differences in Women's ERA Support,
   197
Erin's Daughters in America: Irish
   Immigrant Women in the Nineteenth
   Century, 67
Essays in Feminism, 485
Essays on La Mujer, 730
Essentially Speaking: Feminism, Nature
   and Difference, 480
Establishing Shelters for Battered

Women: Local Manifestations of a Social Movement, 244

Ethics and Human Reproduction: A Feminist Analysis, 221

Everyday World as Problematic: A Feminist Sociology, 665

Everyone Was Brave: The Rise and Fall of Feminism in America, 28

Experiencing Race, Class, and Gender in the United States, 1248

Exploring Identity and Gender: The Narrative Study of Lives, 609

Faces of Feminism: A Study of Feminism as a Social Movement, 622

Families We Choose: Lesbians, Gays, Kinship, 305

Family Interpreted: Feminist Theory in Clinical Practice, 899

Family Planning and Population Control: The Challenges of a Successful Movement, 1

Family Violence Research: Aid or Obstacle to the Battered Women's Movement, 229

Female Eunuch, The, 486

Female Experience: An American Documentary, 1153

Female Experience in Eighteenth and Nineteenth Century America: A Guide to the History of American Women, Volume I, 1178

Female Liberation: History and Current Politics, 1293

Female Revolt: Women's Movements in World and Historical Perspective, 631

Female Sexual Slavery, 850

Female Suffrage in New Jersey, 1790–1807, 43

Female World, The, 624

Female World from a Global Perspective, 779

Female-Friendly Science: Applying Women's Studies Methods and Theories to Attract Students, 907

Feminine Face of God: The Unfolding of the Sacred in Women, 973

Feminine Mystique, The, 476

Feminine Sentences: Essays on Women and Culture, 539

Femininity in Dissent, 306

Feminism and Black Activism in Contemporary America: An Ideological Assessment, 666

Feminism and Disability, 129

Feminism and Equality, 1280

Feminism and Foucault: Reflections of Resistance, 1249

Feminism and Materialism: Women and Modes of Production, 574

Feminism and Political Radicalism, 474

Feminism and Political Theory, 1295

Feminism and Politics: A Comparative Perspective, 930

Feminism and Psychoanalytic Theory, 455

Feminism and Science, 917

Feminism and Sexual Equality, 468

Feminism and Socialism, 568

Feminism and Sociology: An Unfortunate Case of Nonreciprocity, 668

Feminism and Suffrage: The Emergence of an Independent Woman's Movement in America, 1848–1869, 40

Feminism and the New Right: Conflict Over the American Family, 960

Feminism and the New Women in Public Office, 944

Feminism and the Women's Movement: Dynamics of Change in Social Movement Ideology and Activism, 159

Feminism and Women's Issues: An Annotated Bibliography and Research Guide, 1033

Feminism, Femininity, and the Television Series: A Content Analysis, 799

Feminism for the Health of It, 490

Feminism in Action: Building Institutions and Community Through Women's Studies, 326

Feminism in America: A History, 29

Feminism in the '80s: Facing Down the Right, 450

Feminism in the Labor Movement: Women and the United Auto Workers, 1935–1975, 818

Feminism or Unionism? The New York Women's Trade Union League and the Labor Movement, 815

Feminism Unmodified: Discourses on Life and Law, 576

Feminism Versus Minority Group Identity: Not for Black Women Only, 688

Feminism vs. Socialism: What Are Our Priorities?, 561

Feminism Within the Science and Health Care Professions: Overcoming Resistance, 908

Feminist Analysis of the New Right, 972

Feminist and Fundamentalist Attitudes toward Pornography Control, 854

Feminist Approaches to Science, 874

Feminist Art Criticism: An Anthology, 905

Feminist Challenge, 628

Feminist Challenge: Mormons for ERA as an Internal Social Movement, 205

Feminist Chronicles, 1953–1993, 97

Feminist Consciousness and Black Women, 771

Feminist Criticism: Women as Contemporary Critics, 891

Feminist Dictionary, 1198

Feminist Ethic for Social Science Research, 650

Feminist Experiences: The Women's Movement in Four Cultures, 623

Feminist Fatale: Voices from the "Twentysomething" Generation, 141

Feminist Frameworks: Alternative Theoretical Accounts of the Relations Between Men and Women, 1267

Feminist Frontiers III: Rethinking Sex, Gender, and Society, 1282

Feminist Literary Criticism: Explorations in Theory, 880

Feminist Methods in Social Research, 611

Feminist Movement: A Bibliography, 1017

Feminist Movement: Its Impact on Women in the State Legislatures, 145

Feminist Papers: From Adams to de Beauvoir, 1289

Feminist Philosophies: Problems, Theories, and Applications, 1273

Feminist Politics and Human Nature, 567

Feminist Praxis: Research, Theory and Epistemology in Feminist Sociology, 617

Feminist Research Methods: Exemplary Readings in the Social Sciences, 610

Feminist Revolution, 584

Feminist Scholarship: Kindling in the Groves of Academe, 314

Feminist Social Theory Needs Time: Reflections on the Relation Between Feminist Thought, Social Theory and Time as an Important Parameter in Social Analysis, 446

Feminist Sociology: An Overview of Contemporary Theories, 632

Feminist Studies/Critical Studies, 679

Feminist Theorists: Three Centuries of Key Women Thinkers, 590

Feminist Theory: A Critique of Ideology, 1272

Feminist Theory: From Margin to Center, 758

Feminist Theory: The Intellectual Traditions of American Feminism, 551

Feminist Thought: A Comprehensive Introduction, 537

Feminist Thought and the Structure of Knowledge, 1257

Feminist Thought: Desire, Power and Academic Discourse, 457

Feminists and Non-feminists: Contrasting Profiles in Independence and Affiliation, 502

Feminists as Agents of Social Change: Lobbying for the Equal Rights Amendment, 179

Feminists, Pornography, & the Law: An Annotated Bibliography of Conflict, 1970–1986, 1026

Feminists Reading/Feminist Readings, 580

Feminists Theorize the Political, 1243

Feminization of Power, 923

First Feminists, The, 130

First Sex, The, 462

Flying, 355

Food for our Grandmothers: Writings by Arab-American & Arab-Canadian Feminists, 714

For and Against Feminism: A Personal Journey into Feminist Theory and History, 460

For Crying Out Loud: Women and Poverty in the United States, 830

For Men Against Sexism: A Book of Readings, 528

For the Record: The Making and Meaning of Feminist Knowledge, 530

Forms of Power: From Domination to Transformation, 594

Forty-Nine Percent Majority: The Male Sex Role, 786

Framing Feminism: Art and the Women's Movement, 904

Free Riding, Alternative Organization and Cultural Feminism: The Case of Seneca Women's Peace Camp, 267

Free Speech For Me—But Not For Thee: How the American Left and Right Relentlessly Censor Each Other, 857

Freedom Summer, 645

Freespace: A Presentation on the Small Group in Women's Liberation, 89

Friends and Sisters: Letters Between Lucy Stone and Antoinette Brown Blackwell, 1846–93, 1151

Friends or Foes: Gerontological and Feminist Theory, 151

From a Broken Web: Separatism, Sexism and Self, 895

From Abortion to Reproductive Freedom: Transforming a Movement, 211

From Accommodation to Liberation. A Social Movement Analysis of Lesbians in the Homophile Movement, 281

From Equal Suffrage to Equal Rights: Alice Paul and the National Woman's Party, 1910–1928, 416

From Feminism to Liberation, 542

From Housewife to Heretic, 405

From Margin to Mainstream: American Women and Politics Since 1960, 935

From Parlor to Prison: Five American Suffragists Talk About Their Lives, 350

Frontiers in Social Movement Theory, 649

Fundamental Feminism: Contesting the Core Concepts of Feminist Theory, 564

Future Feminist Movements, 132

Gathering Ground, 702

Gay American History: Lesbians & Gay Men in the U.S.A., 289

Gay and Lesbian Liberation Movement, The, 278

Gender and Higher Education in the Progressive Era, 8

Gender and the Academic Experience, 654

Gender and Trade Unions, 829

Gender as a Mediator of the Activist Experience: The Case of Freedom Summer, 798

Gender Consciousness at Work: Modification of the Male Breadwinner Norm Among Steelworkers and Their Spouses, 795

Gender, Ideology, and the Role of Women in the 1920s Klan Movement, 956

Gender in America: Social Control and Social Change, 793

Gender in Intimate Relationships: A Microstructural Approach, 1284

Gender Politics. From Consciousness to Mass Politics, 939

Gender Shock: Practicing Feminism on Two Continents, 112

Gender Trouble: Feminism and the Subversion of Identity, 674

Gender/Body/Knowledge: Feminist Reconstructions of Being and Knowing, 1268

Give Us Each Day: The Diary of Alice Dunbar-Nelson, 1149

Going Out of Our Minds: The Metaphysics of Liberation, 406

Going Too Far: The Personal Chronicle of a Feminist, 422

Gone to Another Meeting: The National Council of Jewish Women, 1893–1993, 727

Good Fight, The, 339

Grassroots Activists in the Mississippi Civil Rights Movement, 748

Greenham Common: Women at the Wire, 256

Grounding of Modern Feminism, The, 65

Group Called Women: Sisterhood and Symbolism in the Feminist Movement, 100

Growing Up Female in America: Ten Lives, 420

Guide to Nonsexist Language, 1206

Guide to Social Science Resources in Women's Studies, 1019

Guide to the Transcripts of the Black Women Oral History Project, 1188

Guide to the Women's History Resources in the Delaware Valley Area, 1220

Guide to Women's Publications, 1195

Guide to Women's Studies, 1184

Guilt and Shame in the Women's Movement, 117

Gwendolyn Brooks: Poetry and the Heroic Voice, 722

Gyn/Ecology: The Metaethics of Radical Feminism, 279

Habit of Surviving: Black Women's Strategies for Life, 435

Handbook of American Women's History, 1231

Harriet Taylor Mill: Enfranchisement of Women, 589

Harriet Tubman, 378

Has Poverty Been Feminized in Black America?, 452

Has the Feminist Movement Influenced Adolescent Sex Role Attitudes? A Reassessment After a Quarter Century, 794

Healing the Wounds: The Promise of Ecofeminism, 266

Heart of a Woman, 333

Hearts of Men: American Dreams and the Flight from Commitment, 465

Helen Hunt Jackson and Her Indian Reform Legacy, 419

Helping Ourselves to Power: A Handbook for Women on the Skills of Public Life, 951

Her Name was Sojourner Truth, 401

Heretics and Hellraisers: Women Contributors to the Masses, 1911–1917, 569

Heritage of Her Own, A, 20

Hers: Through Women's Eyes, 1278

Her-story Unsilenced—Black Female Activists in the Civil Rights Movement, 746

Hillbilly Women, 72

Him/Her/Self: Sex Roles in Modern America, 790

Hispanic Women Leaders in the United States, 696

Historic U.S. Court Cases, 1690–1990: An Encyclopedia, 1196

Historical Background, The, 27

Historical Perspectives: The Equal Rights Amendment Conflict in the 1920s, 183

History of Woman Suffrage, Volumes I–VI, The, 1158

History of Women in America, 68

Holding the Line: Women in the Great Arizona Mine Strike of 1983, 827

Home Front and Beyond: American Women in the 1940s, 821

Home Girls: A Black Feminist Anthology, 769

Honey-Mad Women: Emancipatory Strategies in Women's Writing, 918

How I Became Hettie Jones, 351

How to Find Out About Financial Aid, 1052

Hurry Up Please, It's Time, 822

Hypatia Reborn: Essays in Feminist Philosophy, 309

Ida Tarbell: Portrait of a Muckraker, 375

Ideas of the Woman Suffrage Movement, 1890–1920, 45

Identity Politics and Women: Cultural Reassertions and Feminism in International Perspective, 685

Identity Politics: Lesbian Feminism and the Limits of Community, 686

Identity Status in Politically Active Pro and Anti ERA, 203

Ideological Purity and Feminism: The U.S. Women's Movement from 1966 to 1975, 160

Ideology and Feminism: Why the Suffragettes were Wild Women, 36

If They Come In The Morning: Voices of Resistance, 750

I'm Running Away from Home But I'm Not Allowed to Cross the Street, 453

Images of Women in American Popular Culture, 1250

Imagine My Surprise: Women's Relationships in Historical Perspective, 615

Impact of Feminist Research in the Academy, 316

Improper Behavior: When and How Misconduct Can Be Healthy for Society, 493

Improving on Sociology: The Problems of Taking a Feminist Standpoint, 658

In a Different Voice: Psychological Theory and Women's Development, 482

In Defense of Traditional Values: The Anti-Feminist Movement, 958

In Her Own Right: The Life of Elizabeth Cady Stanton, 399

In Her Own Write: Women's History Resources in the Library and Archives of the Missouri Historical Society, 1065

In Labor: Women and Power in the Birthplace, 224

In Quest of African American Political Women, 726

In Search of a Constituency for the New Religious Right, 970

In Search of Sisterhood: Delta Sigma Theta and the Challenge of the Black Sorority Movement, 753

In the Company of Educated Women: A History of Women in Higher Education in America, 86

Individual Voices, Collective Visions: Fifty Years of Women in Sociology, 639

Inessential Woman: Problems in Exclusion in Feminist Thought, 690

Inside/Out: Lesbian Theories, Gay Theories, 285

Integrating Women's Studies into the Curriculum: A Guide and Bibliography, 1025

Integrative Feminism, 684

Integrative Feminisms: Building a Global Vision, 1960s to 1990s, 578

International Directory of Women's Biography, 1219

International Handbook of Women's Studies (WISH), 1167

Interpreting Women's Lives: Feminist Theory and Personal Narratives, 620

Interview with Sonia Johnson, 195

Intimate Warriors: Portraits of a Modern Marriage, 1899–1944: Selected Works by Neith Boyce and Hutchins Hapgood, 359

Into the Mainstream: How Feminism Has Changed Women's Writing, 888

Introduction to Library Research in Women's Studies, 616

Inviting Women's Rebellion: A Political Process Interpretation, 105

Is the Future Female? Troubled Thoughts on Contemporary Feminism, 526

Is This America? Fannie Lou Hamer and the Mississippi Freedom Democratic Party, 412

Issues in Feminism, 1292

Jack Went Up the Hill ... but Where was Jill?, 803

Jailed for Freedom, 441

Jane Addams and the Men of the Chicago School, 1892–1918, 385

Jeannette Rankin, First Lady in Congress: A Biography, 407

Jessie Bernard: The Making of a Feminist, 370

John Stuart Mill: On Liberty, 458

Journals of Charlotte Forten Grimké, 440

Journey Toward Freedom: The Story of Sojourner Truth, 372

Knowledge Explosion: Generations of Feminist Scholarship, 322

Labeling Women Deviant: Gender, Stigma, and Social Control, 622

Ladies Against Women: Mobilization Dilemmas of Anti-feminist Movements, 967

Ladies in Pink: Religion and Political Ideology in the Anti-ERA Movement, 957

Ladies of Seneca Falls: The Birth of the Woman's Rights Movement, 25

Lady and the Mill Girl: Changes in the Status of Women in the Age of Jackson, 74

Lady from Montana, 59

Language, Gender, and Professional Writing: Theoretical Approaches and Guidelines for Nonsexist Usage, 885

Language, Gender and Society, 914

Language of the Goddess, 978

Latina Politics, Latino Politics: Gender, Culture, and Political Participation in Boston, 710

Law and the Sexes: Explorations in Feminist Jurisprudence, 946

League of Women Voters in St. Louis: The First Forty Years, 1919–1959, 62

Learning About Women: Gender, Politics, and Power, 1245

Learning Our Way: Essays in Feminist Education, 311

Left Index, The, 1204

Legitimation, Consent, and Anti-feminism, 937

Lesbian and Gay Studies Reader, The, 270

Lesbian Connections: Simone de Beauvoir and Feminism, 298

Lesbian Ethics, 286

Lesbian Identity and Community: Recent Social Science Literature, 291

Lesbian Issue, The, 284

Lesbian Nation: The Feminist Solution, 288

Lesbian Origins, 277

Lesbian Philosophies and Cultures, 272

Lesbian Sources: A Bibliography of Periodical Articles 1970–1990, 999

Lesbianism: An Annotated Bibliography and Guide to the Literature, 1976-1991, 1012

Lesbianism and the Women's Movement, 294

Liberation Now! Writings from the Women's Liberation Movement, 1239

Liberty, A Better Husband: Single Women in America, The Generations of 1780–1840, 454

Library and Information Sources on Women: A Guide to Collections in the Greater New York Area, 1135

Lillian D. Wald: Progressive Activist, 1144

Living of Charlotte Perkins Gilman: An Autobiography, 349

Long Day: The Story of a New York Working Girl, 431

Long Road to Freedom: 'The Advocate' History of the Gay and Lesbian Movement, 303

Looking Back on the Last 20 Years...., 109

Loosening the Bonds: Mid-Atlantic Farm Women, 71

Love and Politics: Radical Feminist and Lesbian Theories, 552

Lucretia Mott, 381

Lucretia Mott: Her Complete Speeches and Sermons, 1146

Lucy Parsons: American Revolutionary, 367

Lucy Stone: Pioneer of Women's Rights, 373

Lucy Stone: Speaking Out for Equality, 409

Lugenia Burns Hope, Black Southern Reformer, 433

Machina Ex Dea: Feminist Perspectives on Technology, 521

Macro and Micro Process in the Emergence of Feminist Movements: Toward a Unitary Theory, 633

Made to Order: The Myth of Reproductive and Genetic Progress, 913

Making a Difference: Psychology and the Construction of Gender, 489

Making Connections: Women's Studies, Women's Movements, Women's Lives, 320

Making Face, Making Soul: Haciendo Caras, 694

Making History: An Oral History of the Struggle for Gay and Lesbian Civil Rights, 1945–1990, 293

Making It Work: The Prostitutes' Rights Movement in Perspective, 136

Man Cannot Speak For Her: A Critical Study of Early Feminist Rhetoric, 3

Mapping the Moral Domain, 483

Margaret Dreier Robins: Her Life, Letters, and Work, 388

Margaret Sanger and the Birth Control Movement: A Bibliography, 1911–1984, 1014

Margaret Sanger: Pioneer of the Future, 387

Maria W. Stewart: America's First Black Woman Political Writer, Essays and Speeches, 432

Marxism and the Oppression of Women: Toward a Unitary Theory, 592

Mary Heaton Vorse: The Life of an American Insurgent, 397

Mary McLeod Bethune: A Biography, 402

Mary Ritter Beard: A Sourcebook, 411

Mary Wollstonecraft: A Vindication of the Rights of Woman, 515

Masculine, Feminine or Human? An Overview of the Sociology of Gender Roles, 1244

Masculine/Feminine: Readings in Sexual Mythology and the Liberation of Women, 1290

Mass Media and the Women's Movement, 1900–1977, 877

Materialist Feminisms, 498

Measure of Our Success: A Letter to My Children and Yours, 390

Men and the Women's Movement, 784

Men in Feminism, 594

Men, Women, and Work: Class, Gender, and Protest in the New England Shoe Industry, 1780–1910, 809

Men's Studies Modified: The Impact of Feminism on the Academic Disciplines, 329

Mermaid and the Minotaur: Sexual Arrangements and Human Malaise, 463

Mind Has No Sex? Women in the Origins of Modern Science, The, 912

Mirror Dance: Identity in a Women's Community, 292

Modern Feminisms: Political, Literary, Cultural, 1266

Montgomery Bus Boycott and the Women Who Started It: The Memoir of Jo Ann Gibson Robinson, 348

Most Difficult Revolution: Women and Trade Unions, 812

Mothering: Essays in Feminist Theory, 916

Motherself: A Mythic Analysis of Motherhood, 983

Motherwit: An Alabama Midwife's Story, 413

Movements of Writing: Is there a Feminist Auto/Biography?, 618

Movers and Shakers: American Women Thinkers and Activists 1900–1970, 85

Moving Beyond Words, 532

Moving the Mountain: The Women's Movement in America Since 1960, 106

Moving the Mountain: Women Working for Social Change, 61

Multiple Jeopardy, Multiple Consciousness: The Context of a Black Feminist Ideology, 762

My American Story: Lesbian and Gay Life During the Reagan/Bush Years, 297

My Four Revolutions: An Autobiographical History of the ASA, 625

Myths of Gender: Biological Theories About Women and Men, 882

National Conference on Socialist Feminism, 554

National Congress of Mothers: The First Convention, 17

National Woman's Party and the Origins of the Equal Rights Amendment, 1920–1923, 188

National Women of Color Organizations: A Report to the Ford Foundation, 1186

Native American Women: A Biographical Dictionary, 1165

Native American Women: A Contextual Bibliography, 1001

Natural Allies: Women's Association in American History, 18

Need for the Equal Rights Amendment, The, 190

Needle, A Bobbin, A Strike: Women Needleworkers in America, 824

New Attack on Feminism, A, 881

New England Girlhood: Outlined from Memory, 352

New Feminism, The, 142

New Feminism in Twentieth Century America, The, 166

New Feminist Movement, The, 98

New Feminist Scholarship: A Guide to Bibliographies, 1226

New Feminist Scholarship: Some Precursors and Polemics, The, 642

New Frontier for Women: The Public Policy of the Kennedy Administration, 192

New Historical Synthesis: Women's Biography, The, 600

New Our Bodies Ourselves: A Book By and For Women, The, 243

New Social Movements: Challenging the Boundaries of Institutional Politics, 652

New Wave or Second Stage? Attitudes of College Women Toward Feminism, 800

New Woman: Feminism in Greenwich Village 1910-1920, 529

New Woman, New Earth: Sexist Ideologies and Human Liberation, 157

New Women: An Anthology of Women's Liberation, 1246

New Women's Movement: Feminism and Political Power in Europe and the USA, 634

No More Nice Girls: Countercultural Essays, 872

No Stone Unturned: The Life and Times of Maggie Kuhn, 410

No Turning Back: Two Nuns' Battle with the Vatican over Women's Right to Choose, 210

Nobody Speaks for Me: Self-Portraits of American Working-Class Women, 844

Nonsexist Research Methods: A Practical Guide, 601

Nonsexist Word Finder: A Dictionary of Gender-Free Usage, 1200

Notable American Women 1607–1950: A Biographical Dictionary, 1194

Notable American Women: The Modern Period, A Biographical Dictionary, 1194

Notable Black American Women, 1210

Notable Hispanic-American Women, 1213

Notes From the Third Year: Women's Liberation, 572

Notifying Husbands About an Abortion: An Empirical Look at Constitutional and Policy Dilemmas, 223

NOW Confronts Racism, 91

Nuclear Summer: The Clash of Communities and the Seneca Women's Peace Encampment, 259

Occult of True Black Womanhood: Critical Demeanor and Black Feminist Studies, 680

Odd Girls and Twilight Lovers: A History of Lesbian Life in Twentieth Century America, 282

Of Woman Born: Motherhood as Experience and Institution, 906

Olive Schreiner Reader: Writings on Women and South Africa, 778

Olympia Brown: The Battle for Equality, 380

On Account of Sex: The Politics of Women's Issues, 1945–1968, 934

On Becoming a Social Scientist: From Survey Research and Participant Observation to Experiential Analysis, 612

On Her Own: Growing Up in the Shadow of the American Dream, 527

On Lies, Secrets, and Silence: Selected Prose 1966-1978, 430

On the Problem of Men: Two Feminist Conferences, 1255

On Their Own: Widows and Widowhood in the American Southwest, 1848–1939, 731

On Women: New Political Directions for Women, 503

On Writing a Feminist Biography, 606

Once a Cigar Maker: Men, Women, and the Work Culture in American Cigar Factories, 813

Once and Future Goddess, The, 977

One Hand Tied Behind Us: The Rise of the Woman's Suffrage Movement, 47

One Woman's Passion for Peace and Freedom: The Life of Mildred Scott Olmsted, 368

One World Women's Movement, 697

Opposition Then and Now: Countering Feminism in the Twentieth Century, 968

Origins of Modern Feminism: Women in Britain, France and the United States, 1780–1860, 31

Origins of Protective Labor Legislation for Women, 1905-1925, 831

Origins of the Civil Rights Movement: Black Communities Organizing for Change, 765

Origins of the Equal Rights Movement: American Feminism Between the Wars, 177

Other Half: Roads to Women's Equality, 1252

Other Perspective in Gender and Culture: Rewriting Woman and the Symbolic, 1274

Our Right to Choose: Toward a New Ethic of Abortion, 213

Out of the Frying Pan: A Decade of Change in Women's Lives, 133

Out to Work: A History of Wage-Earning Women in the United States, 825

Outercourse: The Be-Dazzling Voyage, Containing Recollections from My Logbook of a Radical Feminist Philosopher (Being an Account of My Time/Space Travels and Ideas - Then, Again, Now, and How), 343

Outrageous Acts and Everyday Rebellions, 533

Outside the Magic Circle: The Autobiography of Virginia Foster Durr, 335

Outspoken Women: Speeches by American Women Reformers, 1635–1935, 1137

Papers for the First Twenty Years, 1118

Paradoxes of Gender, 796

Partner and I: Molly Dewson, Feminism, and New Deal Politics, 444

Passionate Politics, 451

Patriarchal Attitudes, 472

Peace and Bread in Time of War, 245

Peace as a Women's Issue: A History of the U.S. Movement for World Peace and Women's Rights, 247

Personal is Political, The, 565

Personal Politics: The Roots of Women's Liberation in the Civil Rights Movement and the New Left, 113

Personal View of the History of the Lesbian S/M Community and Movement in San Francisco, 853

Pioneer Work in Opening the Medical Profession to Women: Autobiographical Sketches, 336

Pitied But Not Entitled: Single Mothers and the History of Welfare, 484

Plain Brown Rapper, 275

Pleasure and Danger: Exploring Female Sexuality, 871

Plow Women Rather Than Reapers: An Intellectual History of Feminism in the United States, 163

Political Generations and the Contemporary Women's Movement, 162

Political Ideology of Pro and Anti-ERA Women, 184

Political Organization in the Feminist Movement, 119

Political Protest and Cultural Revolution: Nonviolent Direct Action in the 1970s and 1980s, 635

Political Science, Part II: International Politics, Comparative Politics and Feminist Radicals, 546

Political Structures and Social Movement Tactics: Feminist Policy Agendas in the United States in the 1990s, 150

Politics and Scholarship: Feminist Academic Journals and the Production of Knowledge, 324

Politics and Sexual Equality: The Comparative Position of Women in Western Democracies, 512

Politics of Difference, The, 676

Politics of Education: Essays from *Radical Teacher*, 514

Politics of Housework, The, 900

Politics of Jewish Invisibility, The, 695

Politics of Pornography: A Critique of Liberalism and Radical Feminism, 867

Politics of Reality: Essays in Feminist Theory, 562

Politics of Reproduction, The, 220

Politics of the Equal Rights Amendment, The, 180

Politics of the Gender Gap: The Social Construction of Political Influence, 945

Politics of the Heart: A Lesbian Parenting Anthology, 295

Politics of Women's Liberation: A Case Study of an Emerging Social Movement and Its Relation to the Policy Process, 120

Politics of Women's Spirituality: Essay on the Rise of Spiritual Power Within the Feminist Movement, 985

Poor People's Movements: Why They Succeed, How They Fail, 655

Pornography and Silence: Culture's Revenge Against Nature, 856

Pornography: Men Possessing Women, 855

Postmodern Legal Feminism, 479

Poverty in the American Dream: Women and Children First, 804

Power and Passion of M. Carey Thomas, The, 403

Power of the People: Active Nonviolence in the United States, 253

Powers of Desire: The Politics of Sexuality, 866

Powers that Might Be: The Unity of White and Black Feminists, 716

Practical Guide to the Women's Movement, A, 1205

Pregnancy, Contraception, and Family Planning Services in Industrialized Countries: A Study of the Alan Guttmacher Institute, 215

Prisons That Could Not Hold, Prison Notes 1964-Seneca 1984, 345

Problem of Authority in Radical Movement Groups: A Case Study of a Lesbian-Feminist Organization, 273

Problem of Being a Woman: A Survey of 1,700 Women in Consciousness-Raising Groups, 146

Problem of Gender for Women's Studies, The, 315

Problems of Women's Liberation, 519

Pro-Choice Movement: Organization and Activism in the Abortion Conflict, 169

Progress of Afro-American Women: A Selected Bibliography and Research Guide, 1027

Progressive Women in Conservative Times: Racial Justice, Peace, and Feminism, 1945 to the 1960s, 75

Proliferation of a Social Movement: Ideology and Individual Incentives in the Feminist Movement, 99

Properties of Gender Identity and their Implications for Gender Consciousness, 791

Prostitution Papers: A Quartet for Female Voice, 579

Protecting Soldiers and Mothers, 19

Psychology of Women: Ongoing Debates, 538

Psychopathology of Everyday Racism and Sexism, 707

Public Man, Private Woman: Women in Social and Political Thought, 469

Public Years of Sarah and Angelina Grimké, 1143

Published Diaries and Letters of American Women: An Annotated Bibliography, 1000

Pure Lust: Elemental Feminist Philosophy, 280

Pushed Back to Strength: A Black Woman's Journey Home, 360

Queer Theory: A Review of the Differences Special Issue and Wittig's "The Straight Mind", 681

Quest for Equality: The ERA vs. Other Means, 186

Questioning Eclectic Practice in Curriculum Changes: A Marxist Perspective, 318

Questions on the Woman Question, 593

Race, Class, and Gender: An Anthology, 1235

Race, Class, and Gender in the United States: An Integrated Study, 1291

Race, Class, and Gender: Prospects for an All-Inclusive Sisterhood, 704

Race, Revolution and Women, 783

Race-ing Justice, En-gendering Power: Essays on Anita Hill, Clarence

Thomas, and the Construction of Social Reality, 969

Racialized Boundaries: Race, Nation, Gender, Colour and Class and the Anti-racist Struggle, 776

Racism and Feminism: A Schism in the Sisterhood, 689

Racism and Feminism: Is Women's Liberation for Whites Only?, 773

Radical Feminism, 573

Radical Future of Liberal Feminism, 556

Radical Sociologists and the Movement: Experiences, Lessons and Legacies, 653

Radical Spirits: Spiritualism and Women's Rights in Nineteenth Century America, 975

Radical Voices: A Decade of Feminist Resistance from Women's Studies International Forum, 571

Radical Women's Press of the 1850s, 32

Radicalism of the Woman's Suffrage Movement: Notes Toward the Reconstruction of Nineteenth Century Feminism, 41

Radicals of the Worst Sort: Laboring Women in Lawrence, Massachusetts, 1860–1912, 810

Rape and Rape Related Issues: An Annotated Bibliography, 1006

Rape of the Wild: Man's Violence Against Animals and the Earth, 252

Reading About the New Left, 1005

Reading Black, Reading Feminist: A Critical Anthology, 887

Reassessment of First Wave Feminism, 661

Rebel in Paradise: A Biography of Emma Goldman, 389

Rebirth of Feminism, 131

Reclaim the Earth: Women Speak Out for Life on Earth, 250

Reconstructing the Academy: Women's Education and Women's Studies, 325

Recreating Motherhood: Ideology and Technology in a Patriarchal Society, 225

Reflections on Black American Women: The Images of the Eighties, 737

Reflections on Gender and Science, 896

Reform, Labor, and Feminism: Margaret Dreier Robins and the Women's Trade Union League, 840

Regulating the Lives of Women: Social Welfare Policy from Colonial Times to the Present, 807

Regulation of Sexuality: Experiences of Family Planning Workers, 214

Relating to Privilege: Seduction and Rejection in the Subordination of White Women and Women of Color, 492

Relations of Rescue: The Search for Female Moral Authority in the American West, 1874–1939, 13

Relationship Between Attitudes Toward Feminism and Levels of Dogmatism, 518

Religion and Radical Politics: An Alternative Christian Tradition in the United States, 66

Remembered Gate: Origins of American Feminism, 58

Report of the World Conference of the United Nations Decade for Women: Equality, Development and Peace, Copenhagen, 14-30 July 1980, 736

Reproduction of Mothering: Psychoanalysis and the Sociology of Gender, 456

Rethinking Feminist Organizations, 149

Rethinking Social Movement Theory, 636

Rethinking the Family: Some Feminist Questions, 915

Return of the Actor: Social Theory in Postmodern Society, 669

Review Symposium: Feminist in Politics, 175

Revolt Against Chivalry: Jessie Daniel Ames and the Women's Campaign Against Lynching, 400

Revolution in Words: Righting Women, 1868–1871, 1156

Reweaving the Web of Life: Feminism and Nonviolence, 260

Rhetoric of Struggle: Public Address by African-American Women, 1159

Righteous Discontent: The Women's Movement in the Black Baptist Church, 1880–1920, 756

Rights and Wrongs: Women's Struggle for Legal Equality, 947

Rights of Passage: The Past and Future of the ERA, 193

Rise and Fall of Feminist Organizations in the 1970s, 164

Rise of a Gay and Lesbian Movement, The, 271

Rise of Historical Sociology, The, 664

Rise of Public Woman: Woman's Power and Woman's Place in the United States, 1630–1970, 76

Rising Song of African-American Women, The, 725

Rocking the Cradle or Rocking the Boat: Women at the 1972 Democratic National Convention, 943

Rocking the Ship of State: Toward a Feminist Peace Politics, 257

Roe v. Wade: The Untold Story of the Landmark Supreme Court Decision that Made Abortion Legal, 209

Roles Women Play: Readings Toward Women's Liberation, 1256

Room of One's Own, A, 540

Root of Bitterness: Documents of the Social History of American Women, 22

Roots of American Feminist Thought, The, 1247

Rosie the Riveter Revisited: Women, the War, and Social Change, 69

Routes to Feminist Orientation Among Women Autoworkers, 487

Running as a Woman: Gender and Power in American Politics, 953

Ruth Weisberg: Paintings, Drawings, Prints, 1968-1988, 892

Sacred Queens and Women of Consequence: Rank, Gender, and Colonialism in the Hawaiian Islands, 718

Safety in Numbers: Resisting Men's Violence Against Women and Girls, 236

Sanctuary: A Journey, 263

Sappho Was a Right-On Woman: A Liberated View of Lesbianism, 269

Sarah Grimké: Letters on the Equality of the Sexes and Other Essays, 1138

Scholarly Writing and Publishing: Issues, Problems, and Solutions, 884

Science and Gender: A Critique of Biology and Its Theories on Women, 875

Science Question in Feminism, The, 889

Seattle Liberation Front, Women's Liberation, and a New Socialist Politics, 559

Second Sex, The, 548

Second Stage, The, 477

Second to None: A Documentary History of American Women, 1155

Secret to Be Buried: The Diary and Life of Emily Hawley Gillespie, 1858–1888, 353

Securing Our Sanity: Anger Management Among Abortion Escorts, 208

Seeing the Second Sex through the Second Wave, 470

Segregated Sisterhood: Racism and the Politics of American Feminism, 675

Seneca Falls Woman's Rights Convention: A Study of Social Networks, 33

Serious Look at Consciousness-Raising, A, 158

Seven Women: Portraits from the American Radical Tradition, 425

Sex and Power: The Sexual Bases of Radical Feminism, 165

Sex Equality, 1251

Sex, Family and the New Right: Anti-Feminism as a Political Force, 963

Sex, Gender, and the Politics of ERA: A State and the Nation, 198

Sex, Power and Pleasure, 870

Sex, Race, and the Law: Legislating for Equality, 933

Sexism and the War System, 517

Sexist Justice, 928

Sexual Democracy: Women, Oppression, and Revolution, 471

Sexual Liberals and the Attack on Feminism, 862

Sexual Politics, 505

Sexual Politics of the New Right: Understanding the 'Crisis of Liberalism' for the 1980s, 962

Sexual Science: The Victorian Construction of Womanhood, 864

Sexuality and the Law: An Encyclopedia of Major Legal Cases, 1199

Sexuality Debates, The, 11

Shaping New Vision: Gender and Values in American Culture, Volume II of the Harvard Women's Studies in Religion Series, 974

Ship that Sailed into the Living Room: Sex and Intimacy Reconsidered, 495

Shoulder to Shoulder: A Documentary, 48

Significance of the 19th Amendment: A New Look at Civil Rights, Social Welfare and Woman Suffrage Alignments in the Progressive Era, 49

Significant Sisters: The Grassroots of Active Feminism, 1839–1939, 394

Signs Reader: Women, Gender, and Scholarship, 1232

Simone de Beauvoir: A Feminist Mandarin, 391

Sister Outsider, 763

Sisterhood and Socialism: The Soviet Feminist Movement, 587

Sisterhood and Solidarity: Feminism and Labor in Modern Times, 808

Sisterhood and Solidarity: Workers' Education for Women, 1914–1984, 828

Sisterhood Denied: Race, Gender, and Class in a New South Community, 823

Sisterhood is Global: The International Women's Movement Anthology, 648

Sisterhood is Powerful: An Anthology of Writings from the Women's Liberation Movement, 1277

Sisterhood: The True Story of the Women Who Changed the World, 103

Sisters, Sexperts, Queers: Beyond the Lesbian Nation, 300

Situating Feminism: From Thought to Action, 557

Social Change, Movement Transformation, and Continuities in Feminist Movements: Some Implications of the Illinois Woman Suffrage Movement, 38

Social Justice for Women: The International Labor Organization and Women, 833

Social Movement Continuity: The Women's Movement in Abeyance, 87

Social Movement Spillover, 647

Social Movements: A Cognitive Approach, 637

Social Movements and Network Analysis: A Case Study of Nineteenth Century Women's Reform in New York State, 15

Social Movements and Political Power: Emerging Forms of Radicalism in the West, 626

Social Movements: Development, Participation, and Dynamics, 672

Social Movements: Ideologies, Interests, and Identities, 651

Social Movements of the Sixties and Seventies, 638

Social Movements: Special Area or Central Problem in Sociological Analysis?, 670

Social Reconstruction of the Feminine Character, 114

Social Work and Social Order: The Settlement Movement in Two Industrial Cities, 1889–1930, 4

Socialist Feminism, The First Decade, 1966–76, 577

Socialist-Feminist Unions: Past and Present, 95

Sojourner Truth: God's Faithful Pilgrim, 392

Some Reflections on the Feminist Scholarship in Sociology, 643

Some Thoughts on the Patriarchal State and the Defeat of the ERA, 185

Song in a Weary Throat: An American Pilgrimage, 357

Sound of One Hand Clapping: Women's Liberation and the Left, 172

Sound of Our Own Voices, Women's Study Clubs, 1869–1910, 12

Sources: An Annotated Bibliography of Women's Issues, 1013

Southern Lady: From Pedestal to Politics, 1830–1930, 84

Speaking for Ourselves, 740

Specifying: Black Women Writing the American Experience, 739

Spectacle of Women: Imagery of the Suffrage Campaign, 1907–1914, 51

Spinster and Her Enemies: Feminism and
    Sexuality, 1880–1930, 860
Spiral Dance: A Rebirth of the Ancient
    Religion of the Great Goddess, 988
Spiritual Warfare: The Politics of the
    Christian Right, 961
Stability and Innovation in the Women's
    Movement: A Comparison of Two
    Movement Organizations, 170
Stepping Stones to Women's Liberty:
    Feminist Ideas in the Woman's
    Suffrage Movement, 1900–1918, 42
Stirring It: Challenges for Feminism, 1261
Storm Center: The Supreme Court in
    American Politics, 948
Story of Alice Paul and the National
    Woman's Party, The, 44
Stranger in Her Native Land: Alice
    Fletcher and the American Indians,
    418
Stretching the Boundaries of Liberalism:
    Democratic Innovation in a Feminist
    Organization, 323
Strong Is What We Make Each Other:
    Unlearning Racism Within Women's
    Studies, 310
Structure of Belief Systems Among
    Contending ERA Activists, 202
Subject Collections: A Guide to Special
    Book Collections and Subject
    Emphasis as Reported by University,
    College, Public and Special Libraries
    and Museums in the United States
    and Canada, 1061
Subject Women, 513
Suffrage and Religious Principle:
    Speeches and Writings of Olympia
    Brown, 1147
Survival in the Doldrums: The American
    Women's Rights Movement, 1945 to
    the 1960s, 81
Susan B. Anthony: A Biography of a
    Singular Feminist, 371
Sweeping Statements: Writings From the
    Women's Liberation Movement,
    1981–1983, 1269
Sweet Freedom: The Struggle for
    Women's Liberation, 104
Sylvia Pankhurst: Pioneer of Working-
    Class Feminism, 52

Symbolic Crusade: Status Politics and the
    American Temperance Movement, 9
Systemic Factors Underlying Legislative
    Responses to Woman Suffrage and the
    Equal Rights Amendment, 627

Take Back the Light: A Feminist
    Reclamation of Spirituality and
    Religion, 984
Take Back the Night: Women on
    Pornography, 861
Taking Charge: Nursing, Suffrage, and
    Feminism in America, 1873–1920, 46
Taking Responsibility for Sexuality, 869
Talking Back: Thinking Feminist,
    Thinking Black, 759
Tapestries of Life: Women's Work,
    Women's Consciousness and the
    Meaning of Daily Life, 55
Taste of Power: A Black Woman's Story,
    376
Teaching Science and Health from a
    Feminist Perspective: A Practical
    Guide, 614
Terrible Siren: Victoria Woodhull, 366
Their Sisters Keepers: Women's Prison
    Reform in America, 1830–1930, 5
Theorizing Black Feminisms: The
    Visionary Pragmatism of Black
    Women, 761
Theorizing Masculinities, 781
Theorizing Patriarchy, 537
There's Always Been a Women's
    Movement this Century, 167
These Modern Women: Autobiographical
    Essays from the Twenties, 358
Things That Divide Us: Stories by
    Women, 677
Thinking About Women: Sociological
    Perspectives on Sex and Gender, 1236
Thinking Feminist, 1281
Thinking Fragments: Psychoanalysis,
    Feminism, and Postmodernism in the
    Contemporary West, 473
Thinking Like a Woman, 478
This Bridge Called My Back: Writings by
    Radical Women of Color, 723
This Little Light of Mine: The Life of
    Fannie Lou Hamer, 421

This River of Courage: Generations of Women's Resistance and Action, 261

This Working-Day World: A Social, Political and Cultural History of Women's Lives, 1914–1945, 1279

Thorstein Veblen: A New Perspective, 660

Through a Women's I: An Annotated Bibliography of American Women's Autobiographical Writings, 1946–1976, 991

Through the Flower: My Struggle as a Woman Artist, 338

Tish Sommers, Activist and the Founding of the Older Women's League, 404

To Seize the Moment—A Retrospective on the National Black Feminist Organization, 751

To Toil the Livelong Day: America's Women at Work, 1790–1980, 820

Together Black Women, 687

Tomorrow's Tomorrow: The Black Woman, 717

Toward a Black Feminist Criticism, 770

Toward a Female Liberation Movement, 137

Toward a Feminist Theory of the State, 501

Toward a Holistic Paradigm for Asian-American Women's Studies: A Synthesis of Feminist Scholarship and Women of Color's Feminist Politics, 700

Toward a New Psychology of Women, 523

Toward a Theoretical Model of Counter Movements and Constitutional Change: A Case Study of the ERA, 199

Toward an Anthropology of Women, 523

Toward the Second Decade: The Impact of the Women's Movement on American Institutions, 139

Towards an Anti-racist Feminism, 93

Traditional and Non-traditional Patterns of Female Activism in the United Farm Workers of America, 1962–1980, 842

Traffic in Women, The, 523

Trashing: The Dark Side of Sisterhood, 138

Tribe of Diana: A Jewish Women's Anthology, 715

True Pioneers of the Women's Movement, The, 766

Tuning In To The Movement: Feminist Periodicals, 1217

Turncoats and True Believers: The Dynamics of Political Belief and Disillusionment, 398

Twelve American Women, 365

Twenty Years at Hull House, 322

Two Outstanding Black Women in Social Welfare History: Mary Church Terrell and Ida B. Wells-Barnett, 428

Tyranny of Structurelessness, The, 121

Unbought and Unbossed, 340

Underside of History, Volume 2: A View of Women Through Time, 60

Uneasy Access: Privacy for Women in a Free Society, 447

Uneasy Virtue: The Politics of Prostitution and the American Reform Tradition, 859

Unequal Before the Law: A Legal History of U.S. Women, 964

Unequal Sisters: A Multicultural Reader in U.S. Women's History, 705

Unfinished Revolution: Changing Legal Status of U.S. Women, 491

Unhappy Marriage of Theory and Practice: An Analysis of a Battered Women's Shelter, 240

Unruly Practices: Power, Discourse, and Gender in Contemporary Social Theory, 886

Up Against the Wall, Mother· On Women's Liberation, 1233

Up From the Pedestal: Selected Writings in the History of American Feminism, 1150

Valiant Friend: The Life of Lucretia Mott, 369

View from Women's Studies, The, 321

Violence Against Women: A Bibliography, 1018

Violence Against Women: Some Considerations Regarding Its Causes and Its Elimination, 237

Visible Women: New Essays on American Activism, 1263

Visions of History, 362

Visual and Other Pleasures, 902

Visual Images of American Society: Gender and Race in Introductory Sociology Textbooks, 788

Voices from Women's Liberation, 1297

Voices of the New Feminism, 1299

Votes and More for Women: Suffrage and After in Connecticut, 50

WAC STATS: The Facts about Women, 1229

Waiting for Prime Time: The Women of Television News, 911

Walks of Usefulness: Reminiscences of Mrs. Margaret Prior, 10

War Against Women, The, 475

We Are Your Sisters: Black Women in the Nineteenth Century, 734

We Cannot Live Without Our Lives, 254

We Gotta Get Out of This Place: Notes Toward a Remapping of the Sixties, 464

We, the American Women: A Documentary History, 1154

We Were There: The Story of Working Women in America, 848

Weaving the Visions: New Patterns in Feminist Spirituality, 982

Web They Wove: Correspondence Among Nineteenth Century Women of Letters, 1157

Webster v. Reproductive Health Services: Reproductive Freedom Hanging By a Thread, 216

Webster's First New Intergalactic Wickedary of the English Language, 1179

Welfare Mothers Speak Out: We Ain't Gonna Shuffle Anymore, 838

What is Feminism?, 506

What Women Want: The Ideas of the Movement, 541

What Women Want: The Official Report to the President, the Congress, and the People of the United States, 92

What's in a Name? The Limits of Social Feminism or Expanding the Vocabulary of Women's History, 459

What's So Feminist About Women's Oral History?, 603

What's So New About New Social Movements?, 656

What's So Special About Women? Women's Oral History, 604

When and Where I Enter: The Impact of Black Women on Race and Sex in America, 754

When Married Women Have Abortions: Spousal Notification and Marital Interaction, 226

Whence the Goddesses: A Source Book, 976

Where Are the Organized Women Workers?, 826

Where is the Women's Political Caucus Going?, 135

Where the Meanings Are, 534

White Feminist Movement: The Chicana Perspective, 709

White House Press Conferences of Eleanor Roosevelt, 1139

Who Am I If I'm Not My Father's Daughter?, 516

Who Joins Women's Liberation?, 171

Who Likes Women's Liberation—And Why: The Case of the Unliberated Liberals, 805

Who Opposed the ERA? An Analysis of the Social Basis of Anti-feminism, 959

Who's Who of American Women, 1224

Why Big Business is Trying to Defeat the ERA, 194

Why ERA Failed: Politics, Women's Rights, and the Amending Process of the Constitution, 178

Why I Want a Wife, 535

Why We Lost the ERA, 196

Wildfire: Igniting the She/Volution, 496

Witch and the Goddess in the Stories of Isak Dinensen: A Feminist Reading, 986

Witches, Midwives and Nurses: A History of Women Healers, 234

Woman and Philosophy: Toward a Theory of Liberation, 1260

Woman and Temperance: The Quest for Power and Liberty, 1873–1900, 2

Woman, Church, and State: The Original Expose of Male Collaboration Against the Female Sex, 24

Woman Citizen: Social Feminism in the 1920s, 73

Woman, Culture and Society, 1288

Woman Doctor's Civil War: Esther Hill Hawks' Diary, 443

Woman from Spillertown: A Memoir of Agnes Burns Weike, 445

Woman Hating, 553

Woman Herself: A Women's Studies Interdisciplinary Perspective on Self-Identity, 522

Woman in a Man-Made World: A Socioeconomic Handbook, 1258

Woman of Valor: Margaret Sanger and the Birth Control Movement in America, 377

Woman Power: The Courage to Lead, the Strength to Follow, and the Sense to Know the Difference, 96

Woman Power: The Movement for Women's Liberation, 774

Woman Question in Classical Sociological Theory, 640

Woman Suffrage and Politics: The Inner Story of the Suffrage Movement, 39

Woman Who Lost Her Name: Selected Writings by American Jewish Women, 721

Womanhood in America: From Colonial Times to the Present, 82

Woman's Body, Woman's Right: A Social History of Birth Control in America, 7

Woman's Consciousness, Man's World, 586

Woman's Estate, 581

Woman's Fate: Raps from a Feminist Consciousness-Raising Group, 110

Woman's Nature: Rationalizations of Inequality, 797

Woman's Proper Place: A History of Changing Ideals and Practices, 1870 to the Present, 910

Woman's Worth: Sexual Economics and the World of Women, 499

Women: A Bibliography of Bibliographies, 992

Women: A Feminist Perspective, 1254

Women Activists: Challenging the Abuse of Power, 396

Women Against Censorship, 851

Women, AIDS and Activism, 228

Women Analyze Women in France, England, and the United States, 448

Women and American Socialism, 1870–1920, 545

Women and Disability, 94

Women and Economics, 563

Women and Equality: Changing Patterns in American Culture, 102

Women and Evil, 511

Women and Feminism in American History: A Guide to Information Sources, 1032

Women and Interest Group Politics: A Comparative Analysis of Federal Decision-Making, 931

Women and Madness, 878

Women and Male Violence: The Visions and Struggles of the Battered Women's Movement, 241

Women and Men Midwives: Medicine, Morality and Misogyny in Early America, 233

Women and Political Conflict: Portraits of Struggle in Times of Crisis, 79

Women and Politics in the Age of the Democratic Revolution, 54

Women and Power, 168

Women and Public Policies, 125

Women and Revolution: A Discussion of the Unhappy Marriage of Marxism and Feminism, 588

Women and Social Protest, 88

Women and Society: A Critical Review of the Literature with a Selected Annotated Bibliography, 1023

Women and the American Labor Movement, 817

Women and the American Left: A Guide to Sources, 993

Women and the Politics of Culture, 1301

Women and the Politics of Empowerment, 1242

Women and the Public Interest: An Essay on Policy and Protest, 780

Women and the Socialist Revolution, 595

Women and Urban Policy, 929

Women and Work of Benevolence: Morality, Politics, and Class in the Nineteenth Century United States, 6

Women, Art, and Power, 903

Women as Culture Carriers in the Civil Rights Movement, 767

Women as Revolutionary Agents of Change: The Hite Reports and Beyond, 858

Women at the Hague: The International Congress of Women and Its Results by Three Delegates to the Congress from the United States, 246

Women, Class and the Feminist Imagination: A Socialist-Feminist Reader, 566

Women, Culture and Politics, 461

Women, Feminism and the 1980 Elections, 950

Women for All Seasons: The Story of the Women's International League for Peace and Freedom, 255

Women Grow More Radical with Age, 591

Women, History, and Theory, 570

Women, Housing Access and Mortgage Credit, 924

Women in a Changing World, 1300

Women in Academe: Progress and Prospects, 313

Women in America: A Guide to Books, 1963–1975, 1003

Women in Class Struggle, 550

Women in Modern America: A Brief History, 56

Women in New Jersey History, 78

Women in Political Theory: From Ancient Misogyny to Contemporary Feminism, 926

Women in Sexist Society: Studies in Power and Powerlessness, 1259

Women in Sociology: A Bio-Bibliographical Sourcebook, 386

Women in the Campaign to Organize Garment Workers, 1880–1917, 835

Women in the Civil Rights Movement: Trailblazers and Torchbearers, 1941–1965, 749

Women in the Old and New Left: The Evolution of a Politics of Personal Life, 671

Women in the Sanctuary Movement, 981

Women in U.S. History: An Annotated Bibliography, 995

Women, Knowledge, and Reality: Explorations in Feminist Philosophy, 481

Women Leaders in Contemporary U.S. Politics, 940

Women of Academe: Outsiders in the Sacred Grove, 308

Women of Color and Southern Women: A Bibliography of Social Science Research, 1975 to 1988, 1031

Women of Color and the Multicultural Curriculum: Transforming the College Classroom, 706

Women of Color in the United States: A Guide to the Literature, 1021

Women of Color in U.S. Society, 742

Women of Color: Organizations & Projects: A National Directory, 1170

Women of Color: Perspectives on Feminism and Identity, 683

Women of Ideas (and What Men Have Done to Them) from Aphra Behn to Adrienne Rich, 531

Women of Science: Righting the Record, 894

Women of the Grange: Mutuality and Sisterhood in Rural America, 1866–1920, 720

Women of the New Right, 965

Women on the US-Mexico Border: Responses to Change, 729

Women Online: Research in Women's Studies Using Online Databases, 1162

Women Organizers: A Beginning Collection of References and Resources, 1215

Women, Power, and Policy, 1241

Women Public Speakers in the United States, 1800–1925: A Bio-Critical Sourcebook, 1142

Women, Race and Class, 678

Women Religious History Sources: A Guide to Repositories in the United States, 1216

Women, Resistance and Revolution: A History of Women and Revolution in the Modern World, 154

Women Respond to the Men's Movement: A Feminist Collection, 488

Women Scientists in America: Struggles and Strategies to 1940, 709

Women, Sex and the Law, 868

Women State Legislators and Support for the Equal Rights Amendment, 191

Women Strike for Peace: Traditional Motherhood and Radical Politics in the 1960s, 268

Women Teaching for a Change: Gender, Class and Power, 806

Women—Terms of Liberation, 153

Women, the Courts, and Equality, 927

Women, the Family, and Freedom: The Debate in Documents, 1140

Women, the Family and Politics, 890

Women: The Last Colony, 836

Women, The Longest Revolution: Essays on Feminism, Literature and Psychoanalysis, 5–07

Women, The State, and Development, 925

Women Together, 30

Women Under Attack: Victories, Backlash, and the Fight for Reproductive Freedom, 207

Women, Violence and Social Control: Essays in Social Theory, 235

Women, War, and Work: The Impact of World War I on Women Workers in the United States, 819

Women Who Do and Women Who Don't Join the Women's Movement, 155

Women Who Do and Women Who Don't Join the Women's Movement: Issues for Conflict and Collaboration, 156

Women with Disabilities: Essays in Psychology, Culture, and Politics, 116

Women, Work and Protest: A Century of U.S. Women's Labor History, 837

Women Workers and the Sweated Trades: The Origins of Minimum Wage Legislation, 839

Women's Annual, 1982–1983, 1262

Women's Consciousness, Women's Conscience: A Reader in Feminist Ethics, 1237

Women's Culture and Lesbian Feminist Activism: A Reconsideration of Cultural Feminism, 302

Women's Culture: The Women's Renaissance of the Seventies, 897

Women's Desk Reference, The, 1183

Women's Dictionary of Symbols and Sacred Objects, The, 1222

Women's Encampment for a Future of Peace and Justice: Images and Writings, 251

Women's History of the World, 77

Women's History Sources: A Guide to Archives and Manuscript Collections in the United States, 1190

Women's Information Directory: A Guide to Organizations, Agencies, Institutions, Programs, Publications, Services, and Other Resources Concerned with Women in the United States, 1166

Women's Issues: An Annotated Bibliography, 1006

Women's Leadership in Marginal Religions: Explorations Outside the Mainstream, 990

Women's Liberation, 1234

Women's Liberation and Its Impact on the Campus, 317

Women's Liberation and Revolution, 1024

Women's Liberation and the Church: The New Demand for Freedom in the Life of the Christian Church, 108

Women's Liberation: Blueprint for the Future, 1294

Women's Liberation: Humanizing Rather than Polarizing, 148

Women's Liberation Movement: Its Origins, Structure, Activities, and Ideas, 122

Women's Movement and Electoral Politics: Where Do We Go From Here? , 942

Women's Movement and the Rebirth of Feminism: Conflicts and Contradictions, 161

Women's Movement in the Seventies: An International English-Language Bibliography, 1010

Women's Movement in the United States: Theory and Practice, 558

Women's Movement in the Working-Class, The, 789

Women's Movement Media: A Source Guide, 1185

Women's Movement: Political, Socioeconomic, and Psychological Issues, 107

Women's Movement: What N.O.W.?, 143

Women's Movements and State Policy Reform Aimed at Domestic Violence Against Women: A Comparison of the Consequences of Movement Mobilization in the U.S. and India, 231

Women's Movements in America: Their Successes, Disappointments and Aspirations, 663

Women's Movements in the United States: Woman Suffrage, Equal Rights and Beyond, 629

Women's Movements of the United States and Western Europe: Consciousness, Political Opportunity, and Public Policy, 641

Women's Movements of the World, 1197

Women's Oppression Today: Problems in Marxist Feminist Analysis, 544

Women's Organizations and Leaders, 1975–1976, 1164

Women's Peace Union and the Outlawry of War, 1921–1942, 248

Women's Periodicals and Newspapers from the Eighteenth Century to 1981, 1180

Women's Place in American Politics: The Historical Perspective, 34

Women's Realities, Women's Choices: An Introduction to Women's Studies, 319

Women's Reality: An Emerging Female System in a White Male Society, 525

Women's Rights and Law: The Impact of the ERA on State Laws, 181

Women's Rights Movement in the United States 1848–1970: A Bibliography and Sourcebook, 1009

Women's Rights: The Struggle for Equality in the Nineteenth and Twentieth Centuries, 646

Women's Studies: A Checklist of Bibliographies, 1022

Women's Studies: A Guide to Information Sources, 1174

Women's Studies: A Guide to Reference Sources, 1201

Women's Studies: A Recommended Core Bibliography, 1029

Women's Studies: A Recommended Core Bibliography, 1980–1985, 1011

Women's Studies: Its Focus, Idea Power, and Promise, 327

Women's Studies: The Social Realities, 331

Women's Thesaurus: An Index of Language Used to Describe and Locate Information By and About Women, 1172

Women's Unions and the Search for a Political Identity, 127

Women's Ways of Knowing: The Development of Self, Voice, and Mind, 449

Women's Welfare: Women's Rights, 941

Women's Words: The Feminist Practice of Oral History, 605

Women's Work 1849–1940, 841

Women's Work, Women's Movement: Taking Stock, 846

Word of a Woman: Feminist Dispatches 1968–1992, 583

Words to the Wise: A Writer's Guide to Feminist and Lesbian Periodicals and Publishers, 1176

Working-Class Feminism: A Consideration of the Consequences of Employment, 816

Working-Class Women and Grass-Roots Politics, 834

Working It Out, 23 Women Writers, Artists, Scientists, and Scholars Talk About Their Lives and Work, 434

Workshop on Autobiography/Biography, 1163

Worst of Times: Illegal Abortion— Survivors, Practitioners, Coroners,

Cops, and Children of Women Who Died Talk About its Horrors, 219
Writing a Woman's Life, 607
Writing I, the Seeing Eye: Papers from Two Writing Feminist Biography Conferences, 619
Written by Herself: Autobiographies of American Women, An Anthology, 342

You Can't Kill the Spirit, 262
Young Rebecca: The Writings of Rebecca West, 1911–1917, 417
Yours in Struggle: Three Feminist Perspectives on Anti-Semitism and Racism, 673

Zami: A New Spelling of My Name, 354